Nort,

Just the mad ramblings of an ex Big 10 president...

All the best!

[signature]

A UNIVERSITY

FOR THE

21ST CENTURY

A UNIVERSITY

FOR THE

21ST CENTURY

JAMES J. DUDERSTADT

ANN ARBOR

THE UNIVERSITY OF MICHIGAN PRESS

*A CIP catalog record for this book is available
from the British Library.*

Library of Congress Cataloging-in-Publication Data

Duderstadt, James J., 1942–
    A university for the 21st century / James J. Duderstadt.
        p.   cm.
    Includes bibliographical references and index.
    ISBN 0-472-11091-8 (alk. paper)
    1. University of Michigan—History.   2. Educational leadership—
Michigan—Ann Arbor.   3. Educational change—Michigan—
Ann Arbor.   I. Title.
LD3280.D83   2000
378.774'35—dc21   99-086823

To Anne, Susan, and Kathy,
the first family of
the University of Michigan,
1988-1996

CONTENTS

PREFACE

Inauguration Day, October 4, 1988, dawned as one of those extraordinary Michigan fall days. The sky was a brilliant blue. The crimsons and golds of the fall colors provided the perfect backdrop for the colorful robes of the academic procession marching across the campus toward Hill Auditorium. The university carillon rang out with the traditional music for such academic ceremonies.

Perhaps it was just my imagination, but instead of academic pomp and circumstance, the refrain of Berlioz's "March to the Scaffold" kept running through my mind as I followed the academic procession to my inauguration that fall morning. Perhaps it was an enhanced awareness of just how challenging the modern university presidency had become, facing the challenges of leading one of the most complex institutions in modern society while buffeted by a bewildering array of complex economic, social, and political issues. Perhaps it was the lingering stress of the fourteen-month-long process leading to my selection as president. Or perhaps it was just a sensory overload because of all of the activities of inauguration week.

Earlier in the week our graduate school had celebrated its fiftieth year with a symposium on the university's impact on graduate and professional education. A day later I had given my first "State of the University" address at our annual faculty awards ceremony. The day after my inauguration, Michigan would face its traditional rival, Michigan State University, in a football battle that would lead eventually to a Big Ten Championship and a victory over USC in the Rose Bowl. And, in a most fitting display of irreverence—fitting, at least, for Michigan—a small group of activists staged a protest at the inauguration ceremony on an array of issues that have long since faded into the obscurity of their 1960s antecedents. One student in the platform group even joined in the festivities by displaying a large sign stating, "Duderstadt is illegal!" referring to the fact that the regents had refused to open the presidential selection process to the prying eyes of the media, thereby triggering suits under the state's Open Meetings Act.

There is a well-worn definition of the modern university president as someone who lives in a large house and begs for a living. And, to be sure, many presidents do live in large, stately houses on their campuses, while all presidents are expected to be actively involved in fund-raising.

There are other roles: In a sense, the president and spouse are the first family of the university community, in many ways serving as the mayor of a small city of thousands of students, faculty, and staff. This public leadership role is particularly important when the university is very large. For example, the University of Michigan has over fifty thousand students, thirty-five hundred faculty members, and twenty-five thousand staff scattered about its various campuses. The flagship UM-Ann Arbor campus itself has over thirty-seven thousand students and twenty thousand faculty and staff, compared to the city's population of one hundred thousand—except on football weekends, when Ann Arbor doubles in size. As the university's most visible leader, the president must continually grapple with the diverse array of political and social issues and interests of concern to the many stakeholders of higher education—students and parents, state and federal government, business and labor, the press and the public at large, and, of course, the faculty.

The president of a large university also has a significant role as its chief executive officer, responsible for the management of a diverse collection of activities, ranging from education to health care to public entertainment (e.g., intercollegiate athletics). Returning to the University of Michigan as an example, the institution has an annual operating budget of $3 billion; more than 26 million square feet of physical facilities; more than $3 billion of funds under active management; and people, programs, and facilities scattered about the globe. If we were a business—and, of course, a president would *never* suggest this, at least within earshot of the faculty—the University of Michigan would rank roughly 470th on the Fortune 500 list as a rather complex global conglomerate.

However, unlike the corporate CEO, who is responsible primarily for shareholder value, the university president as CEO is responsible for everything that happens in the university—at least, everything bad. The old expression "The buck stops here" is chiseled in the cornerstone of the university administration building. Anything that happens, whether it involves the president—or, indeed, whether it is even *known* by the president—from student misbehavior to financial misdeeds to town-gown relations—eventually ends up on the president's desk. Presidents even find themselves blamed for the misfortunes of athletics teams, as I learned in 1993 when a Michigan basketball player called an illegal time-out that iced the NCAA basketball championship for North Carolina. (My seats at the Final Four in the New Orleans Superdome were so far from courtside that even if I had yelled to the players to call a time-out, nobody could have possibly heard me. But as president, it was all my fault!)

Further, unlike most corporate CEOs, the president is expected to play an active role generating the resources needed by the university, whether by lobbying state and federal governments, seeking gifts and bequests from alumni and friends, or clever entrepreneurial efforts. There is an implicit expectation on most campuses that the president's job is to raise money for the provost and deans to spend, while the chief financial officer and administrative staff watch over their shoulders to make certain they all do it wisely.

The presidential family also plays a pastoral role. In a very real sense, my wife, Anne, and I were the "mom and pop" of the extended university family. Students looked to us for parental support, even as they emphasized their rejection of *in loco parentis* (actually, by digging holes in our front yard to "bury student rights" during a particularly imaginative demonstration). Faculty and staff members also sought nurturing and understanding care during difficult times for the university. To those both inside and outside, we were expected to be cheerleaders for the university, always upbeat and optimistic, even though we frequently shared the concerns and were subject to the same stresses as the rest of the campus community.

The president is expected to be the defender of the faith, both of the institution itself and the academic values so important to a university. I sometimes thought of this latter role as roughly akin to that of a tired, old sheriff in a frontier western town. Every day I would have to drag my bruised, wounded carcass out of bed, strap on my guns, and go out into the main street to face whatever gunslingers had ridden in to shoot up the town that day. Sometimes these were politicians; other times the media; still other times various special interest groups on campus; even occasionally other university leaders such as deans or regents. And, each time I went into battle to defend the university, I knew that one day I would run into someone faster on the draw than I was. In retrospect, it was amazing that I managed to perform this particular duty of the presidency for almost a decade with only a few scars to show for the effort.

It is this myriad of experiences that has stimulated this book, intended to present at least one perspective on the issues currently associated with higher education. Needless to say, the issues and perspectives discussed in this book are heavily influenced by the experience of my Michigan presidency. The University of Michigan has long been viewed as a flagship of higher education in America—particularly that component represented by the public research university. Most of the issues, problems, and challenges of higher education in America swirl about and throughout the institution. Yet, since Michigan is also one of the largest and most complex universities in the world, the scope and complexity of the institution sometimes can magnify issues to levels far beyond that experienced by most other institutions.

For example, resource issues at Michigan tend to be measured in hundreds of millions of dollars. A typical student demonstration can involve thousands of participants. Controversial issues involving the university—whether in athletics or research administration or faculty/student behavior—tend to appear in the national news media, not just the local papers. Private-sector partnerships, whether with industrial corporations, hospital systems, or athletic equipment manufacturers, tend to be approached as strategic alliances between organizations of comparable size, worldwide scope, and, unfortunately, legal complexities. And the political environment is both intense and unforgiving, whether at the national, state, local, or campus level.

Leading the University of Michigan is a challenge, even during the most quiescent periods. To lead Michigan during a period of great change is something altogether different—a bit like taking over the wheel of an out-of-control automobile as it careens toward the edge of a cliff. Leading change at a major university can be an extraordinary experience, all-consuming, frustrating at times, and yet also exhilarating. Clearly this experience has also shaped—and perhaps distorted—the perspectives offered in this book.

The great diversity among institutions makes it difficult to discuss with any precision the entire expanse of the higher education enterprise in America. Hence, rather than moving to the level of vague—and probably inaccurate—generalizations, this book will focus on a specific class of institution, the American research university. These are certainly the most visible institutions of higher education in our society. They are also the most complex. And, candidly, they are the type of university with which I have the most direct personal experience—as a student, parent, faculty member, and administrator. Fortunately, the very complexity and comprehensive nature of these institutions make it likely that some of the issues considered in this book will have relevance to other types of colleges and universities.

Even with this focus, one still faces a formidable challenge in grappling with the extraordinary complexity and diversity of the research university. While there is a vast literature of articles, monographs, and books that deal with various aspects of higher education, it is my intent to attempt a more comprehensive treatment, in which a very broad array of issues is considered and interrelated.

It is important to stress that this book is not intended to be a scholarly treatment of contemporary issues in higher education, designed for contemplation by colleagues in the academy. It is written to convey to a broader audience the personal impressions, viewpoints, afterthoughts—and even a bit of Monday-morning quarterbacking—gained from the decade-long experience of leading the University of Michigan. It has intentionally been written while the memories—and the scars—are still quite fresh.

Distorted and biased as they may be, it is my hope that these observations and experiences may prove useful to others. At the very least, they should provide amusement to those who wish to understand the perspective of higher education as seen by one who has served as leader—or, rather, principal servant—of one of America's leading universities.

ACKNOWLEDGMENTS

Although the author accepts fully the responsibility for the content of this book, particularly its weaknesses and flaws, it is also important to acknowledge the impact that many people of great wisdom and experience have had on this project. I have had the good fortune of learning the arcane trade of academic administration from some extraordinary leaders at Michigan including Harold Shapiro, Robben Fleming, Harlan Hatcher, Frank Rhodes, and Billy Frye.

Since stepping down from the Michigan presidency, I have also had the opportunity to benefit from an array of discussion groups, institutes, and workshops that influenced my views on issues in higher education. In this regard, it is important to recognize the impact of discussions with Robert Zemsky, Patricia Gumport, Marvin Peterson, Stanley Ikenberry, Nils Hasselmo, Peter Magrath, David Gardner, and John Seely Brown.

During the decade covered by this book, the University of Michigan was particularly fortunate to have a truly remarkable executive officer team, many of whom continued on to other significant leadership roles in higher education, all of whom had extensive experience with higher education, and all of whom deserve my profound gratitude:

Provost: Chuck Vest, Gil Whitaker, Bernie Machen
VP–Chief Financial Officer: Farris Womack
VP–Research: Linda Wilson, Bill Kelly, Homer Neal
VP–Student Affairs: Henry Johnson, Mary Ann Swain, Maureen Hartford
VP–University Affairs: Walt Harrison, Lisa Baker
VP–Development: Jon Cosovich, Tom Kinnear, Joe Roberson
Dean of the Graduate School: John D'Arms, Bob Weisbuch
Secretary of the University: Dick Kennedy, Harold Johnson, Roberta Palmer
Vice Provosts and Associate VPs: Bob Holbrook, Doug Van Houweling, George Zuidema, Chuck Moody, Lester Monts, Rhetaugh Dumas, Harold Jacobson, Tom Butts, Paul Spradlin,Bill Krumm, Norman Herbert, Chandler Mathews, Randy Harris, and Cynthia Wilbanks
Chancellors: Blenda Wilson, Clint Jones, Jim Renick, Charlie Nelms
Athletics Directors: Bo Schembechler, Jack Weidenbach, Joe Roberson
Assistants: Robin Jacoby, Shirley Clarkson, Connie Cook, Ejner Jensen
Secretary to the President: Nona Mustard

So too, during this period, Michigan was clearly a "deans' university," providing deans with unusual authority and opportunity, depending heavily upon their leadership, and attracting some truly remarkable academic leaders. These deans also deserve acknowledgment for their impact on this book.

It is also important to acknowledge the work of all of those who have worked with me over the years in drafting and editing the array of speeches, reports, policy documents, memoranda, and other materials that are so clearly linked with this book: Shirley Clarkson, Robin Jacoby, Connie Cook, Ejner Jensen, Aaron Schutz, Mary Jo Frank, Carole LaMantia, Liene Karels, Julie Steiff, Ann Curzon, and Elise Fraser.

Finally, it is essential to recognize the extraordinary impact that the other half of the presidential team, the first lady of the university, Anne Duderstadt, had during the decade of our service in leadership roles at Michigan. Only those who serve in a major university presidency understand the absolutely critical role played by the president's spouse. Indeed, such presidencies are team roles, and this book has benefited greatly from her wisdom and experience. She was not only a critical member of the university leadership team, but she was also probably the best appointment I made during my administration (although Anne sometimes views the first lady role as more akin to indentured servitude than professional employment)!

PART 1 A TIME OF CHANGE

CHAPTER 1   Introduction

The dogmas of the quiet past are inadequate to the stormy present. The occasion is piled high with difficulty, and we must rise to the occasion. As our case is new, so must we think anew.

—Abraham Lincoln, signing the July 2,1862, Morrill Act of Congress providing for the state land-grant colleges

A hot summer day in late August. Still air under the wide, timeless branches of the tree canopy shading the University of Michigan Diag. A moment of quiet, before Ann Arbor begins to fill once again with returning students and faculty for the fall term. The only premonition of impending change, the muffled thunder of an approaching summer storm.

Today, that storm of change is our reality. Our world is once again entering a period of dramatic social change, perhaps as profound as earlier periods such as the Renaissance and the Industrial Revolution—except, while those earlier transformations took centuries, today's often take only a few years. We live in an era of breathtaking and accelerating change. If education was once simpler, our world was simpler too.

Universities have long defended the thorough but slow academic decision-making process, which enables controlled change. "New" programs have been built up for two centuries over "old" ones in almost archaeological layers. But we can no longer afford the luxury of uncritical preservation. Obsolescence lies in store for those who cannot, in some manner, adapt to our new reality.

The most predictable feature of modern society is its unpredictability. We no longer believe that tomorrow will look much like today. Universities must find ways to sustain the most cherished aspects of their core values, while discovering new ways to respond vigorously to the opportunities of a rapidly evolving world.

This is the principal challenge to higher education as we enter a new century. This was also the major challenge to the University of Michigan during my presidency. We sought to integrate the practice of change into the day-to-day life of the institution, even as we held to the ancient values and traditions that give us direction in a shifting world. But, beyond simply adapting to a time of change, we sought to influence the nature of our changing world. Instead of simply following society, we tried to be leaders in the journey.

This book is intended to examine the nature of the challenges facing higher education and their implications for the future of the American university as we prepare to enter a new century. If there is a single theme that runs throughout the book, it is this theme of *change*. The profound nature and rapid pace of the changes occurring in our society will demand corresponding transformations in social institutions such as the university if they are to continue to serve future generations.

A Time of Concern

In an age of knowledge in which educated people and their ideas have become the wealth of nations, the university has never been more important, and the value of a college education never higher. The educational opportunities offered by the university, the knowledge it creates, and the services it provides are key to almost every priority of contemporary society, from personal prosperity and well-being to economic competitiveness to national security to protecting the environment to enriching our culture. There is a growing recognition that few public investments have higher economic payoff than those made in higher education. After two decades of erosion of federal support of student financial aid programs and campus-based research, a strong economy has allowed the federal government to begin to increase once again its investments in higher education. Similarly, strong tax revenues are allowing many of the states to restore funding cuts of the early 1990s.

Yet, despite this recent vote of confidence, there is great unease on our campuses. The media continue to view the academy with a frustrating mix of skepticism, ignorance, and occasional hostility that erodes public trust and confidence. The danger of external intervention in academic affairs in the name of accountability remains high. Throughout society we see a backlash against earlier social commitments such as affirmative action, long a key mechanism for diversifying our campuses and providing educational opportunity to those suffering discrimination in broader society. The faculty feels the stresses from all quarters: There is fear that research funding will decline again when the economy cools and entitlement programs grow. Faculty members are apprehensive about the future of long-standing academic practices such as tenure and academic freedom. They express a sense of loss of scholarly community with increasing specialization, together with a conflict between the demands of grantsmanship, a reward structure emphasizing research, and a love and sense of responsibility for teaching.

There are increasing concerns that the intensifying market forces characterizing a knowledge-driven economy may sweep over our colleges and universities, pushing aside their academic values and traditions and replacing their civic purpose with the demands of the marketplace.[1] Some doomsayers even suggest that the university, a social institution lasting a millennium, may soon disappear.[2]

While most believe that the university will remain an important, perhaps even essential social institution in our future, it is also clear that we are entering a period of profoundly important debate about the future of higher education. The singularly productive partnership, the social contract that universities have developed with our society, is not likely to continue on the same terms and conditions that we have relied upon for the past century.

We are all familiar with the recent criticism of universities coming from many ideological directions, within and outside our walls. For the most part, this criticism has been scattered and sporadic, but it is gaining force and direction. The values of the academy are being challenged, from scholarly ethics to academic freedom to tenure. Our commitment to teaching is being questioned, as is our ability to teach well. Faculty tenure is under serious attack. The quality and relevance of scholarly research is coming under closer scrutiny. Political forces are encroaching on the governance of our institutions. Tuition hikes are being protested. And the list of concerns continues.

Universities across the country have worked hard to address many of these issues. Undergraduate education has again become a priority and today is greatly improved. We have increased the availability of student financial aid. University hiring at all levels is more open, rigorous, and fair. We have succeeded in raising billions of dollars in private support to compensate for the losses of public funding. We have invested in state-of-the-art information technology to support teaching, research, and service, as well as to improve overall productivity. Costs have been cut and administrations streamlined to free dollars for our core missions of teaching and learning. The physical plant on most campuses has been renewed. We are communicating more effectively with key sectors of the public to build support and understanding for higher education.

Universities have ventured further and set goals for more far-reaching change to meet the challenge of the twenty-first century. We show significant progress in increasing the representation of people of color among students, faculty, and staff. Women are advancing in the academy. Our campuses are internationalizing at every level. Our technological infrastructure is revolutionizing the way we preserve, discover, transmit, and transfer knowledge. Researchers are able to take on ever larger and more fundamental issues: global change, the human genome, and the origin of the universe.

We will need this foundation of strength and stability in the years ahead as academia faces more fundamental questioning. Politicians, pundits, and the public increasingly challenge us at the same time that technology increasingly drives us. No question is out of bounds: What is our purpose? What are we to teach, and how are we to teach it? Who teaches under what terms? Who measures quality, and who decides what measures to apply? Who pays for education and research? Who benefits? Who governs and how? What and how much public service is part of our mission? What are appropriate alliances, partnerships, and sponsorships?

Some of the most significant short-term pressure for change in universities is driven by a converging political agenda at every level with multiple, not always compatible goals: to limit educational costs, even at the expense of quality; to make education ever more widely available; to draw back from the national commitment to research support, at least in the forms and amounts we have depended on since World War II; and to accelerate institutional transformation through application of information technology.

Running counter to these goals are a few troublesome trends already affecting our universities. Public funding for higher education has been declining in a climate where education is seen increasingly as a personal economic benefit rather than as a public good in and of itself. Long-standing policies such as affirmative action that represented earlier commitments to equity and social justice are now being challenged both by governing bodies and in the courts. The allocation of research funding is increasingly driven by those who mobilize the most voters, politicians, or celebrities, thus distorting the research and graduate teaching agenda. Our curriculum is deformed by the competitiveness and vocational demands of students whose debt load impels them toward excessive careerism, even as other voices call for a return to an idealized "classical" curriculum based on the great works of Western civilization.

Of particular concern is the intrusion of political forces in nearly every aspect of university governance and mission. State and federal government seek to regulate admissions decisions and financial aid. There are egregious examples of political or judicial intrusion in the research process itself, for example, star chamber hearings before government bodies investigating scholarly research integrity or the expenditure of research funds. We are only beginning to feel the crippling effects of open-meetings requirements on the conduct of business and on hiring. We are over regulated, and the costs of accountability are excessive both in dollars and in administrative burden. Governance of public institutions is too often in the hands of people selected for partisan political reasons rather than for their understanding and support of higher education. These trends, symptomatic of the erosion of public confidence in universities, parallel the loss of trust in our institutions across the board.

Not that we in universities are blameless. We too often have been reactive rather than proactive in responding to demands from students, faculty, government, politicians, patrons, ideologues, and demagogues who distort or undermine our fundamental values and purposes. Academic structures are too rigid to accommodate the realities of our rapidly expanding and interconnected base of knowledge and practice. Higher education as a whole has been divided and competitive at times when we need to speak with a single unequivocal voice. Our entrenched interests block the path to innovation and creativity. Perhaps most dismaying, we have yet to come forth with a convincing case for ourselves, a vision for our future, and an effective strategy for achieving it.

The university remains one of the most extraordinary and enduring social institutions of our civilization. For a thousand years, it has not only served as a custodian and conveyor of knowledge, wisdom, and values, but it has transformed the very society it serves, even as social forces have transformed it in turn. Yet, during most periods, change in the university has proceeded in slow, linear, incremental steps—improving, expanding, contracting, and reforming without altering our fundamental institutional mission, approach, or structure. The old saying that progress in a university occurs one grave at a time is sometimes not far off the mark. Today, however, we do not have the luxury of continuing at this leisurely pace, nor can we confine the scope of changes under way. We are witnessing a significant paradigm shift in the very nature of the higher education enterprise, both in America and worldwide, which will demand substantial rethinking and reworking on the part of our institutions.

This impending revolution in the structure and function of higher education stems from the worldwide shift to a knowledge-based society. Educated people and the knowledge they produce will increasingly become the source of wealth for nations. Knowledge itself is expanding exponentially with no slowing in sight. Today's society demands citizens who remain active learners throughout their lives, and hence it requires educational institutions capable of meeting their learning needs whenever and wherever they may occur. In a very real sense, higher education is both driving and being driven by technological, social, and economic forces at work throughout the world.

These forces challenge each one of us in higher education to re-envision what we do and how we do it. We will need to question everything. We must become more fault-tolerant, more encouraging of experimentation with seemingly radical solutions. If we do not lead in reinventing our mission and our institutions, we risk seeing the role of universities marginalized and our values compromised as the forces of change (and the multitude of competitors they generate) overtake us.

American higher education has a responsibility to help show the way to change, not to react to and follow it. Our voice must be loud, clear, and unified in the public forum. At the same time, we must engage in vigorous debate and experimentation within academia, put aside our narrow self-interest, and accept without fear the challenges posed by this extraordinary time in our history.

The Continuity of Change

As we approach a new century, we can take great pride in the accomplishments of our universities. Working together, Americans have built the finest system of higher education in the world. But we have built universities for the twentieth century, and that century has come to an end. The universities that we have built, the paradigms in which we have so excelled, may no longer be relevant to a twenty-first century world.

As our society changes, so too must institutions such as the university, as they have so often in the past. Change has always characterized the university, even as it has sought to preserve and propagate the intellectual achievements, the cultures, and the values of our civilization. The university has endured as an important social institution for a millennium, perhaps because it has evolved in profound ways to serve a modernizing world. Higher education in America has likewise been characterized by change, embracing the concept of a secular liberal education, then weaving scholarship into its educational mission, and broadening its activities to provide public service and research to respond to societal needs.

The ways we teach today seem so obvious and natural, it seems incredible that at one time the seminar, the teaching laboratory, and even the lecture were controversial innovations.[3] Before the university, in America's early colleges, students memorized or translated the central works of the distant past, learning ancient languages, rhetoric, and simple mathematics by rote. Professors emphasized accuracy, not comprehension. Conservative and conformist, early colleges had little interest either in expanding knowledge or in inciting critical thinking. Lessons were infused with a deeply religious vision of the world and of the duties of citizenship. The colleges saw themselves as bulwarks against change, training the pastors and lawyers of the next generation.

But change arrived regardless, driven by the needs of an evolving society. The burgeoning Industrial Revolution and the new middle class it created challenged the dominance of the old "elite" families and the traditional notion of "culture." By the middle of the nineteenth century, the consensus around the "classical" approach to higher education had begun to fray. College enrollments remained flat as the population of the country soared and the prestige of graduates declined.

As our nation shifted from an agricultural to an industrial economy, from a rural to an urban population, the needs of students and society also shifted radically. The institutions that survived were the ones that responded to these new needs. In the post–World War II era, higher education again faced a period of radical change as vast numbers of returning GIs filled our universities, and a college education became a common aspiration for all levels of our society. Today, we face yet another era of change as we shift from a national to a global economy and as the driving force of economic wealth increasingly becomes the production of knowledge instead of the production of things. The speed of change, for the first time, has become the defining theme of our age. At the same time, we have begun to awaken from an often cruel fantasy of homogeneity to face the real challenges that diversity in all its many facets brings to us. Over the past two centuries, the university has remained vibrant and relevant to our society only by adapting and changing radically.

What explains the power of this durable and pervasive social institution? Lord Eric Ashby pointed out that whatever their flaws, "universities are broadly accepted as the best means for social investment in human resources."[4] Society believes in and supports the fundamental university missions of teaching and research. It entrusts to these institutions its children and its future. Our universities exist to be repositories, transmitters, and creators of human heritage. They serve as guardians and creators of that knowledge.

This mission is the glue that binds our universities to society and accounts for our successful adaptation throughout the centuries, across so many disparate societies. It is relatively easy to carry out our task in societies and times that are homogeneous and static, where there exists a high degree of consensus and only gradual change. It is quite another to carry out our mission today in our increasingly pluralistic society and interdependent world, a world characterized by revolutionary transformations in knowledge and in the very nature of our role.

Most colleges and universities are attempting to respond to the challenges and opportunities presented by a changing world. They are evolving to serve a new age. But most are evolving within the traditional paradigms, according to the time-honored processes of considered reflection and consensus that have long characterized the academy. The changes that have occurred in the university, while important, have been largely reactive rather than strategic. For the most part, our institutions still have not grappled with the extraordinary implications of an age of knowledge, a culture of learning, which will likely be our future.

While most of our colleges and universities are changing to adapt to a changing world, they are not yet transforming themselves into educational institutions suitable for our future. The glacial pace of academic change simply may not be sufficiently responsive to allow the university to control its own destiny. There is a risk that the tidal wave of societal forces could sweep over the academy, both transforming higher education in unforeseen and unacceptable ways while creating new institutional forms to challenge both our experience and our concept of the university.

There should be little doubt that higher education will flourish in the decades ahead. In a knowledge-intensive society, the need for advanced education will become ever more pressing, both for individuals and for society more broadly. It is also likely that the university as we know it today—or rather, the current constellation of diverse institutions comprising the higher education enterprise—will evolve in exciting and probably unforeseen ways.

As we look to the profound changes ahead of us, as we explore possible visions for the future, it is important to keep in mind that throughout their history, universities have evolved as integral parts of their societies to meet the challenges of their surrounding environments. This disposition to change is a basic characteristic and strength of university life, the result of our constant generation of new knowledge through scholarship that, in turn, changes the education we provide and influences the societies that surround us.

This propensity of universities to change is nicely balanced by vital continuities, especially those arising from our fundamental scholarly commitments and values and from our roots in a democratic society. While the emphasis, structure, or organization of university activity may change over time to respond to new challenges, it is these scholarly principles, values, and traditions that animate the academic enterprise and give it continuity and meaning. Specifically, an integral part of the life of the university has always been to evaluate the world around us in order to adjust our teaching, research, and service missions to serve the changing needs of our constituents while preserving basic values and commitments. Today we must once again try to anticipate the future direction of our society in order to prepare students for the world they will inherit.

To be sure, we must always bear in mind those deeper purposes of the university that remain unchanged and undiminished in importance. Our institutions must remain places of learning where human potential is transformed and shaped, the wisdom of our culture is passed from one generation to the next, and the new knowledge that creates our future is produced. So too, we should understand that to most of our faculty, the academy is a calling rather than a profession, requiring a love of and dedication to scholarship and teaching.

Yet, if we are to sustain these deeper purposes of the university, its time-tested values and traditions, we need to understand better the nature of the world in which the university now finds itself, as well as the changing nature of its activities. To insist upon sustaining a vision for the university from some distant past—or, more likely, an idyllic dream than never really existed—puts our institutions, not to mention our society, at considerable risk.

Change will not only be the challenge to the American university; it will be the watchword for the years ahead. With change will come unprecedented opportunities for those universities with the vision, the wisdom, and the courage to lead in the century ahead.

CHAPTER 2 # The Challenge of Change

The trouble with our times is that the future is not what it used to be.
—Paul Valery, The Art of Poetry [1]

One of the long-standing traditions in higher education is a university president's welcoming address each fall to the new entering class of students. This provides a rare opportunity to offer a few words of advice before students develop the college survival tactics of tuning out the deluge of boring, extraneous, or confusing information that confronts them during their college days.

With this rare opportunity of student attentiveness in mind, I would generally begin my comments with the simple observation that our entering students would be spending most of their lives in the twenty-first century. They would face the challenge of preparing for a time very different from the twentieth century society that shaped the lives of those on the faculty, those who would serve as their educators. Furthermore, many of the features of the social institution responsible for their education, the university, could be traced back to far earlier times, decades or even centuries earlier.

Each time I raised this theme at a new student convocation, I became increasingly uneasy. It was clear that the forces driving change in our society were far stronger than most realized. Perhaps a more fundamental issue was whether the university, as we know it in the last years of the twentieth century, was prepared to educate the citizens, to serve the society, of a future that will almost certainly be radically different than anything we have known or even imagined.

This concern should, in fact, be neither alarming nor surprising. It has been one of the most important themes throughout the long history of the university. As one of civilization's most enduring institutions, the university has been extraordinary in its capacity to change and adapt to serve a changing society. Far from being immutable, the university has changed considerably over time and continues to do so today. Across our nation, the remarkable diversity of institutions of higher education, ranging from small liberal arts colleges to gigantic university systems, from storefront proprietary colleges to global "cyberspace" universities, demonstrates the evolution of the species.

The situation of higher education today seems comparable in significance to two other periods of great change in the nature of the university in America: the period in the late nineteenth century when the major public universities first appeared, and the years following World War II, when the research university evolved to serve the needs of postwar America.[2] A century ago, the Industrial Revolution was transforming our nation from an agrarian society into the industrial giant that would dominate the twentieth century. The original colonial colleges, based on the elitist educational principles of Oxbridge, were joined by the land-grant state universities, committed to broad educational access and service to society. In the decades following this period, higher education saw a massive growth in enrollments at the undergraduate, graduate, and professional level, as a college education became available to ever-broader elements of our society.

A similar period of rapid change in higher education occurred after World War II. The educational needs of the returning veterans, the role of the universities in conducting the research critical to national defense, and the booming postwar economy led to an explosion in both the size and number of major universities. The direct involvement of the federal government in the support of student financial aid, campus-based research, and professional schools such as medicine and engineering led to the evolution of the contemporary university as we know it today.

We now face challenges and opportunities similar to those of these two earlier periods of transformation. Many people point to negative factors, such as the rapidly growing costs of quality education and research during a period of limited resources, the erosion of public trust and confidence in higher education, and the deterioration in the partnership between the research university and the federal government. But far more important will be the challenges presented by fundamental changes in our society: the degree to which knowledge itself is becoming a key driving force in determining economic prosperity, national security, and social well-being; the growing interdependence of nations; the changing demography of America as we become an ever more diverse society; the search for new national priorities in a post–Cold War world; and the need to develop sustainable futures as humankind increasingly pushes against the limits of our planet. The sweeping nature and rapid pace of changes in the world we serve will demand similar changes in the university.

A Time of Challenge and Change

We are living in the most remarkable of times. Just consider, for a moment, some of the changes that have occurred in our world within the past decade: The Cold War has ended, and Communism has been rejected around the world, swept away by the winds of freedom and democracy. A new global order is evolving. We are now manipulating the human gene directly to cure disease, and we may soon be doing it to create new life forms and possibly even influence the evolution of the human species. Computing power—speed, memory, communication rates—continues to increase by a factor of one-hundredfold each decade, with worldwide networks connecting hundreds of millions of people, enabling them to communicate with ease and sophistication, any place on the planet or even beyond.

Yet the changes in recent years are only the tip of the iceberg. There has been a worldwide explosion of ethnic tensions, even as the nation-state has become less relevant to the world economy and security. Many of our traditional social structures have deteriorated, from our cities to our neighborhoods to the family itself. The explosion of new communication and transportation technologies has given us both new mobility and new markets, linking us both domestically and internationally in ways we never dreamed possible. Yet it has also increasingly threatened long-standing social institutions such as businesses, governments, and perhaps universities with obsolescence and even irrelevance.

Some believe that we are going through a period of change in our civilization as momentous as any in our earlier history. In contrast to earlier social transformations that evolved over centuries, the changes characterizing our times occur on time scales of decades or less.

This time of great change, of shifting paradigms, provides the context in which we must consider the evolving nature of the American university. We must take great care not simply to extrapolate the past, but rather to examine the full range of possibilities for the future. To this end, let us first discuss in more detail the forces driving change in our world, our society, and in our social institutions. While there are many ways to classify these forces, let us consider first broader societal forces of change and then focus on those of particular importance in driving change in higher education.

Themes of Change

The Age of Knowledge

Looking back over history, one can identify certain periods of profound change in the nature, the fabric, of our civilization such as the Renaissance, the Age of Discovery, and the Industrial Revolution. There are many who contend that our society is once again undergoing such a fundamental shift in perspective and structure.

The signs are all around us. We are evolving rapidly into a postindustrial, knowledge-based society, just as a century ago an agrarian America evolved into an industrial nation.[3] Today industrial production is steadily shifting from material- and labor-intensive products and processes to knowledge-intensive products and services. A radically new system for creating wealth has evolved that depends upon the creation and application of new knowledge.

We are in a transition period where intellectual capital, brainpower, is replacing financial and physical capital as the key to our strength, prosperity, and well being.

In a very real sense, we are entering a new age, an *age of knowledge*, in which the key strategic resource necessary for prosperity has become knowledge itself, that is, educated people and their ideas.[4] As our society becomes ever more knowledge-intensive, it becomes ever more dependent upon those social institutions that create knowledge, that educate people, and that provide them with knowledge and learning resources throughout their lives.[5]

Our rapid evolution into a knowledge-based society has been driven in part by the emergence of powerful new information technologies such as computers, digital communications networks, multimedia, and virtual reality. Modern electronic technologies have increased vastly our capacity to know and to do things and to communicate and collaborate with others. They allow us to transmit information quickly and widely, linking distant places and diverse areas of endeavor in productive new ways. This technology allows us to form and sustain communities for work, play, and learning in ways unimaginable just a decade ago. Of course, our nation has been through other periods of dramatic change driven by technology, for example, the impact of the steam engine, telephone, automobile, and railroad in the late nineteenth century, which created our urban industrialized society.[6] But never before have we experienced a technology that has evolved so rapidly, increasing in power by a hundredfold every decade, obliterating the constraints of space and time, and reshaping the way we communicate, think, and learn.

Unlike natural resources such iron and oil that have driven earlier economic transformations, knowledge is inexhaustible. The more it is used, the more it multiplies and expands. But knowledge is not available to all. It can be absorbed and applied only by the educated mind. Hence, schools in general and universities in particular will play increasingly important roles as our society enters this new age. The increasingly sophisticated labor market of a knowledge-driven economy is driving new needs for advanced education and training. Even today roughly two-thirds of America's high school graduates will pursue some form of college education, and this will likely increase as a college degree becomes the entry credential to the high-performance workplace in the years ahead. There is an increasingly strong correlation between the level of one's education and personal prosperity and quality of life.

But the age of knowledge holds an even deeper significance for higher education. In a sense, knowledge is the medium of the university. Through the activities of discovery, shaping, achieving, transmitting, and applying knowledge, the university serves society in myriad ways: educating the young, preserving our cultural heritage, providing the basic research so essential to our security and well-being, training our professionals and certifying their competence, challenging our society and stimulating social change. Yet in a world in which knowledge and educated people have become the key to prosperity and security, there has been an increasing tendency for society to view the university as an engine for economic growth through the genera-tion and application of new knowledge. From a broader perspective, just as the loss of faith in government intervention has shifted political attention away from the distribution of wealth to its production, there has been a shift of emphasis within the university away from simply distributing and analyzing knowledge, for example, "teaching" and "scholarship," to creating knowledge, to activities such as "innova-tion" and "creativity."

Demographic Change: The New Majorities

When Americans hear references to the demographic changes occurring in our na-tion, we probably first think of the aging of our population.[7] It is true that the baby boomers have moved into middle age and soon will be approaching retirement, with worrisome consequences for our current entitlement programs such as Social Secu-rity and Medicare. After a brief decline in the number of young adults during the 1980s and 1990s, we once again are seeing a growth in the number of college-age students, an echo of the baby boom generation. Yet this growth in the number of young people is far exceeded by the growth in the number of senior citizens. In this country, there will soon be more people over the age of sixty-five than there are teenagers, and this situation is certain to continue for the remainder of our lives. Furthermore, the growth rate in both our population and our workforce is declining to the lowest level in our nation's history. Since fertility and mortality rates are below their long-term averages, it has become clear that the United States will not be a nation of youth again in our lifetimes. As our society ages, it has become more con-servative, with national priorities increasingly focusing on the concerns of the el-derly rather than the needs of the young.

There is a certain irony here. While America and much of Europe are aging, the rest of the world is becoming ever younger. Today, half of the world's population is under the age of twenty, with over two billion teenagers on planet Earth, most living in Asia, Africa, and Latin America. Just as the forty million teenagers born in America during the postwar decade determined our culture, drove our consumption patterns during the 1950s, dominated our politics during the 1960s, and contributed our presi-dent in the 1990s, so too will teenagers around the globe have a profound impact on world culture.

Add to this youth-dominated world the capacity for cheap, global communica-tion, and you can imagine the scenario.[8] Within a decade, hundreds of millions of young people will be linked together by the ubiquitous information technology rap-idly appearing throughout the world. A glance at early forms of popular culture aris-ing from such "wired communities" of young people—MTV or *Wired* magazine—provides ample evidence that their future is certainly *not* our present. While these

networked teenagers will not homogenize world culture, they will certainly incorporate and mix cultures from around the world to spawn new societies. And their demand for education will be staggering.[9]

An equally profound demographic phenomenon is the increasing diversity of
American society with respect to race, ethnicity, and nationality. Women, minorities, and immigrants now account for roughly 85 percent of the growth in the labor
force, currently representing 60 percent of all of our nation's workers. Those groups
we refer to today as minorities—African, Hispanic, Asian, and Native Americans—
have already become the majority population in states such as California, Arizona,
and Texas. By the late twenty-first century, the United States could become a nation
of minorities, without a majority ethic group. Women, who have already become the
predominant gender in our nation and our educational institutions, are rapidly
assuming leadership roles in both the public and private sector.

The full participation of currently underrepresented minorities and women is
crucial to our commitment to equity and social justice, as well as to the future strength
and prosperity of America. Our nation cannot afford to waste the human talent, the
cultural and social richness, represented by those currently underrepresented in our
society. If we do not create a nation that mobilizes the talents of all our citizens, we
are destined for a diminished role in the global community and increased social turbu-
lence. Most tragically, we will have failed to fulfill the promise of democracy upon
which this nation was founded. Yet the challenge of increasing diversity is compli-
cated by social and economic factors. Far from evolving toward one America, our
society continues to be hindered by segregation and nonassimilation of minority
cultures.

So what are the implications of these demographic changes for higher education? Throughout its history, higher education in America has always responded to
the needs of a changing population. As America expanded to the frontier and then
evolved into an industrial society, our universities expanded enrollments, developed
professional schools, and rapidly transformed themselves to stress applied fields such
as engineering, agriculture, and medicine favored by the federal land-grant acts. Higher
education expanded both scope and mission again after World War II to absorb returning veterans and the baby boom generation in the 1950s and 1960s. With the
help of federal programs such as the Higher Education Act of 1965, our colleges and
universities have reached out to increase the participation of those racial, ethnic, and
cultural groups not adequately represented among our students, faculty, and staff.
We have tried to build supportive environments that accept, embrace, and sustain
diversity as essential to the quality of our missions of teaching, research, and service.

Today our college-age population is growing once again, with a 30 percent growth
projected in the number of traditional college students by the year 2015.[10] Some

regions of the nation will face a particular challenge with growing populations and changing demographics, such as California's Tidal Wave II of almost a million college-age students over the next decade or the Texas challenge of a college population dominated by heretofore underrepresented minorities.

The changing character and needs of the American population are driving a major redefinition of the concept of a college student and hence the character of our institutions. Only 17 percent of students enrolled in college today are in the eighteen to twenty-two-year-old group we generally think of as traditional college students. No longer are the students on our campuses drawn primarily from the ranks of middle and upper-class high school graduates. Colleges and universities are increasingly challenged to build educational programs for a student population diverse in essentially every human characteristic: age, gender, race, socioeconomic background, and so on.

Today's college student is more typically a working adult with a family, commuting to campus or enrolling through cyberspace, who seeks the education and skills necessary for his or her career. When it is recognized that the magnitude of this need for adult education at the college level may be significantly larger than our current population of young students as the learning needs of the high-performance workplace become ever more demanding, the challenge to traditional, residential colleges and universities becomes apparent. With these new adult students come new expectations, as they demand a higher degree of quality and relevance in their education. We are beginning to see pressures for a shift from faculty-centered to learner-centered institutions. Furthermore, there are also calls for a shift from "just in case" education, where we have traditionally expected students to complete degree programs at the undergraduate or professional level long before they actually need the knowledge, to "just in time" education, where learning is provided, frequently through nondegree programs, when careers require it, to "just for you" education, highly customized to meet the needs of the student.

However, events of the past several years suggest that the road to serving an increasingly diverse population may also become even more difficult. Even as universities come to understand the educational benefits of a diverse student population and faculty, they are increasingly constrained in the mechanisms they may use to achieve this. Throughout society we see a backlash against earlier social commitments and programs. Both the courts and legislative bodies are now challenging long-accepted programs such as affirmative action and equal opportunity. The polarization of our society by race, class, and nationality has become ever more intense, ironically even as our nation and the world have become more linked together in a political, economic, and cultural sense by modern communications and transportation technologies.

The growing pluralism of our society is one of our greatest challenges as a nation. It is also among our most important opportunities, because it gives us an extraordinary vitality and energy as a people. As both a reflection and leader of society at large, the university has a unique responsibility to develop effective models of multicultural, pluralistic communities for our nation. We must strive to achieve new levels of understanding, tolerance, and mutual fulfillment for peoples of diverse racial and cultural backgrounds both on our campuses and beyond. But it has also become increasingly clear that we must do so within a new political context that will require new policies and practices.

The Globalization of America

Whether through travel and communication, through the arts and culture, or through the internationalization of commerce, capital, and labor, the United States is becoming increasingly linked with the global community. The world and our place in it have changed. A truly domestic United States economy has ceased to exist. It is no longer relevant to speak of the health of regional economies or the competitiveness of American industry, because we are no longer self-sufficient or self-sustaining. Our economy and many of our companies are truly international, spanning the globe and intensely interdependent with other nations and other peoples.[11] Worldwide communication networks have created an international marketplace, not only for conventional products, but also for knowledge professionals, research, and educational services.

Trends toward internationalization affect our nation beyond commerce and national security. The United States has become the destination of choice of the world's immigrants, with over one million new immigrants arriving in this nation every year. With falling fertility rates among U.S. citizens, immigration has become an important determinant of the variability in our population. As we have been throughout our history, we continue to be nourished and revitalized by wave after wave of immigrants coming to our shores with unbounded energy, hope, and faith in the American dream. Today, America is evolving into a "world nation" with not simply economic and political ties, but also ethnic ties to all parts of the globe.

From this perspective, it becomes clear that understanding cultures other than our own has become necessary, not only for personal enrichment and good citizenship, but for our very survival as a nation. Among the contemporary university's many priorities, one of the highest must be the development and maintenance of programs that reflect a greater international perspective. Certainly we have a long way to go in this country to master what we need to know to participate fully as members of our global village. American knowledge of other languages and cultures is abysmally inadequate. Too many of our graduates have never been exposed to a foreign language or visited a foreign country. Many have not had a chance to feel the texture of life in another era or another culture through literature and poetry or film. By every measure we fall short educationally of the knowledge and skills it will take to do business, to work cooperatively on common problems, or to advance our common ideals for humanity.

Ironically, the contemporary American university is a truly international institution. It not only reflects a strong international character among its students, faculty, and academic programs, but it also stands at the center of a world system of learning and scholarship. Yet, despite the intellectual richness of our campuses, we still suffer from the inherited insularity and ethnocentrism of a country that for much of its history has been protected from the rest of the world and self-sufficient in its economy—perhaps even self-absorbed. To respond, we must reexamine the way in which we foster, manage, and promote the international dimension of our educational mission. If our institutions are to serve America in its role as a member of the global community, we must think and act more imaginatively, more aggressively, and more strategically to strengthen our role as truly international centers of learning. The international component of our teaching and scholarship should pervade the curriculum of the liberal and the professional schools. Above all, we must enable our students to appreciate the unique contributions to human culture that come to us from other traditions—to communicate, to work, to live, and to thrive in multicultural settings whether in this country or anywhere on the face of globe.

The Post–Cold War World

For almost half a century, the driving force behind many of the major public investments in our national infrastructure has been the concern for national security in the era of the Cold War. The evolution of the research university, the national laboratories, the interstate highway system, our telecommunications systems and airports, and the space program were stimulated by concerns about the arms race and competition with the Communist bloc. Many of the technologies that we take for granted, from semiconductors to jet aircraft, from computers to composite materials, were originally spin-offs of the defense industry.

In the wake of the extraordinary events of the last decade, the disintegration of the Soviet Union and Eastern Europe, the reunification of Germany, and the major steps toward peace in the Middle East, the driving force of national security has weakened—at least from superpower confrontation if not from terrorism and regional ethnic conflict—and, along with it, much of the motivation for major public investment. Peace has not freed up new resources in the post–Cold War world for investment in key areas such as education and research; instead the nation is drifting in search of new driving imperatives. While there are numerous societal concerns, such as economic competitiveness, national health care, crime, and K–12 education, none of these has yet assumed an urgency sufficient to set new priorities for public investment.

Much of the existing intellectual infrastructure, which developed to underpin national defense, is now at risk. The national laboratories are facing massive downsizing and are searching for new missions out of necessity. Intensely competitive markets coupled with the quarter-by-quarter pressure on bottom-line results by institutional investors have forced corporate America to refocus industrial research activities from long-term research to short-term product development.

Equally serious are signs that the nation may no longer be willing or able to invest in research performed by universities, at least at the same fiscal level or with the same support for curiosity-driven basic research. Congress has made it clear that it will seek new levels of accountability from those engaged in federally sponsored research, just as it will from other areas of government through requirements such as the Government Performance Results Act.[12] The federal government has yet to develop a successor to the government-university research partnership that served so well during the Cold War years.[13] Hence, it is likely that many of society's most important research institutions, including the research university, will stand at some risk until a new social agenda is developed for post–Cold War America.

Spaceship Earth

There is mounting evidence that the growing population and invasive activities of humankind are now altering the fragile balance of our planet. The concerns are both multiplying in number and intensifying in severity: the destruction of forests, wetlands, and other natural habitats by human activities leading to the extinction of millions of biological species and the loss of biodiversity; the buildup of greenhouse gases such as carbon dioxide and their possible impact on global climates; the pollution of our air, water, and land.

With the world population now at 6 billion, we are already consuming 40 percent of the world's photosynthetic energy production.[14] Current estimates place a stable world population at 8 to 10 billion by the late twenty-first century, assuming fertility rates continue to fall over the next several decades. Yet even at this reduced rate of population growth, we could eventually consume all of the planet's resources, unless we take action. Because of this overload of the world's resources, even today, over 1.2 billion of the world's population live below the subsistence level, and 500 million live below the minimum caloric-intake level necessary for life.

It could well be that coming to grips with the impact of our species on our planet, learning to live in a sustainable fashion on Spaceship Earth, will become the greatest challenge of all to our generation. This will be particularly difficult for a society that has difficulty in looking more than a generation ahead, encumbered by a political process that generally functions on an election-by-election basis, as the current debate over global change makes all too apparent. Universities must take the lead in developing the knowledge and educating the world's citizens to allow us to live upon our planet while protecting it.

Challenge and Change in Higher Education

Higher education has been and will continue to be greatly affected by the changes in our society and our world. In an increasingly knowledge-driven society, more and more people seek education as the hope for a better future, the key to good jobs and careers, to meaningful and fulfilling lives. The knowledge created on our campuses addresses many of the most urgent needs of society, for example, health care, national security, economic competitiveness, and environmental protection. The complexity of our world, the impact of technology, the insecurity of employment, and the uncertainty of our times have led all sectors of our society to identify education in general and higher education in particular as key to the future.

Yet, in the midst of this growing importance—indeed, perhaps because of it—higher education has become the focus of increasing concerns and criticism.[15] Many see the contemporary university as big, self-centered, and even greedy as it gouges parents with high tuition and the government with inappropriate charges for research. Some characterize our students as spoiled and badly behaved, our faculties as irresponsible and lazy ("the new leisure class"). Our campuses are portrayed as citadels of intolerance, plagued by a long list of "isms": racism, sexism, elitism, and extremism. Some have even charged us with an erosion of our fundamental academic values, using as examples the faculty's lack of concern for undergraduate education, numerous well-publicized cases of scientific fraud or misconduct, and incidents of political correctness.

We could try to answer our critics with logic or a righteous dismissal of any who would question our purposes and privileges. There is much that is refutable in the recent spate of books and articles from the right and the left that questions our performance and even rejects the very foundation of our mission. It would be a mistake, however, simply to dismiss the criticisms of higher education. They represent the genuine concerns of the American public—albeit characterized by a great misunderstanding of what we are and what we do—and they unfortunately contain a good deal of truth about us. They also suggest a significant mismatch between what the public wants from us and what we are currently providing.

Another harbinger of change can be found in the stresses felt by the faculty, particularly in research universities. Forums held on university campuses across the nation reveal a growing gulf between those characteristics faculty value (e.g., an emphasis on basic research, a highly disciplinary focus, and strong, long-term support for individual investigators) and the terms dictated by federal and industrial sponsors (e.g., more applied investigations of a highly interdisciplinary nature involving large research teams).[16] Most faculty members recognize the importance of the efforts by their institutions to cut costs, raise revenues, and capitalize on new technology. But they also believe these activities create burdens on faculty members that distract them from their core academic activities of teaching and scholarship. While today's stresses on the academy have many symptoms, they have fundamentally one major cause: change, in our world and our institutions, change occurring far more rapidly than we in the academy find comfortable.

There is also a growing gap between today's generation of students and the faculty responsible for teaching them. Today's students come from very different backgrounds than their teachers; they have different intellectual objectives, and they think and learn in different ways. They are far more diverse in every human characteristic—race, gender, nationality, economic background—than the rather homogeneous faculty that teaches them. This mismatch between instructor and student is an important factor in the new tensions surrounding teaching, particularly at the undergraduate level.

At the administrative level, the challenge of change manifests itself in the extraordinary turnover in university leadership in recent times.[17] During the past several years, the leadership of almost every major university in the nation has changed, from Harvard, Yale, Columbia, Penn, Brown, and Cornell to Stanford, Caltech, and MIT; from the Universities of California (and many of its campuses), North Carolina, and Texas to most of the Big Ten. The average tenure of public university presidents has dropped to less than five years—far too brief to provide the stability in leadership necessary for achieving effective change. While some of these changes in university leadership are the result of natural processes such as retirement, many others reflect the serious challenges and stresses faced by universities, which all too frequently destabilize their leadership. The politics characterizing college campuses—whether arising from students, the faculty, or governing boards—coupled with the external pressures exerted by state and federal governments, alumni, the media, and the public at large, all make the university presidency a very hazardous profession these days. At a time when universities require strong, decisive, courageous, and visionary leadership, the eroding tenure and deteriorating attractiveness of the modern university presidency pose a significant threat to the future of our institutions.[18]

But these phenomena—public concerns, stresses on the faculty, and the turnover in university leadership—are only symptoms of the profound challenges faced by the American university in the 1990s, several of which merit further discussion:

- The cost, price, and value of a college education
- The rising costs of academic excellence and the limits on resources
- The changing relationship with diverse constituencies
- The changing social contract
- The challenge of intellectual change
- The increasing relevance of the university

The Cost, Price, and Value of a College Education

Perhaps no other issue in higher education has become so controversial as its cost. Students, parents, politicians, the press, and the public at large all have expressed strong concerns about the price of a college education, usually measured in terms of the tuition, room, and board prices charged to undergraduate students.[19] There is a widespread belief that a college education is being priced out of the reach of many— if not most—Americans. Some cannot help but wonder whether a college education is worth the investment.

There is a paradox here, however. Despite the rising costs of a college education, the rate at which young people are enrolling in college continues to rise. And there is substantial evidence to suggest that in an increasingly knowledge-intensive society, the value of a college education—at least as measured by the difference in earning capacity afforded by a college degree—is continuing to increase.[20]

In discussing this issue, it is important to distinguish among the *costs* experienced by the university in the conduct of educational programs, the *prices* charged to students enrolled in these programs, and the *value* to the student of this education. This distinction highlights three important points or trends. We have already noted the first of these trends: the increasing value of advanced education in a world in which one's knowledge is key in determining personal prosperity and well being.

The second trend is the rapidly increasing cost of education in fields in which the knowledge content is exploding exponentially. While the costs of traditional programs such as literature and history are relatively stable, those associated with high-demand, technology-intensive fields such as science, engineering, and medicine understandably increase at far more rapid rates.

The third trend involves the price of a college education. Since the tuition charged to students in all institutions, public or private, is generally far less than the actual cost of the education they receive, pricing in higher education is strongly dependent on subsidies from other stakeholders. During the decades following World War II, there was a rapid expansion in both state and federal support of higher education, which allowed relatively low tuition levels. As such public support weakened in the 1980s, both public and private universities were forced to increase prices so that students and families would bear more of the true costs. Although universities increased their efforts to seek private gifts to compensate for eroding public support, they also faced the additional burden of providing sufficient financial aid to enable low and middle-income students to continue to have access to their institutions. This dramatic shift in who pays for a college education, from public tax dollars to individual tuition payments, was one of the most important forces driving change in the 1990s, and it is likely to continue in the years ahead.

Despite a brief decline in the number of high school graduates during the 1980s and early 1990s, college enrollments have continued to rise, driven by the educational needs of adult students in the workplace. Financial aid programs and a prosperous economy largely mitigated the impact of rising tuition levels. Today enrollments of traditional students are increasing once again from the echo of the baby boom generation, and when combined with an even more rapid growth in the number of nontraditional students, higher education continues to be in high demand. Yet public support and hence public subsidy of the costs of higher education remain relatively flat. Therefore tuition levels continue to increase somewhat faster than the inflation rate at both public and private institutions, and concerns about the affordability of higher education continue to be high on the public agenda.

The Rising Costs of Excellence and the Limits on Resources

Higher education has faced the challenge of making a transition from the growth era of the 1950s and 1960s, characterized by increasing populations, public and private support, and prestige, to the no-growth era of the 1980s and 1990s. Today we face a future in which the costs of excellence in education and scholarship will almost certainly increase faster than the resources available to most institutions.[21] Of course, there have probably never been enough resources to meet the needs of enterprising faculty, students, and administrators.[22] But higher education is in the midst of a period of budgetary straits in which the resources available from traditional sources in future years will likely be inadequate to support the desired level and quality of activities sought by most institutions.

This statement may appear to be at odds with recent experience. After all, in the late 1990s, the economy appears prosperous and the federal government has balanced the federal budget, apparently accompanied by a major increase in support for student financial aid and campus-based research. The states also seem relatively prosperous, and appropriations for public colleges and universities are on the rise.

Yet, from a broader perspective, higher education in America continues to face significant challenges from structural flaws in national and state budget policies that have yet to adapt to the realities of today's global, knowledge-driven economy.[23] At the federal level, funding for higher education has been stagnant or declining since the late 1970s. While tax revenues as a share of personal income have increased over this period, the impact of federal entitlement programs such as Social Security, Medicare and Medicaid, and the national debt have consumed an ever-larger share of the federal budget, now accounting for about 67 percent of federal expenditures.

Cuts in federally supported financial aid during the 1980s shattered the dream of equal educational access for many students. Universities have had to scramble to make up the difference, in part through increasing tuition for those who can afford the costs of education. The federal government also has taken steps to shift more of the costs of federally sponsored research to the universities through limits on reimbursement for overhead costs and through requirements for higher university cost sharing on federal grants. This has forced many universities to reallocate resources away from education and service in order to subsidize federal research projects.

While higher education was a priority in the budget-balancing agreement of 1997 and the Higher Education Act of 1998, the primary beneficiaries of these federal actions are likely to be not colleges and universities but rather middle-class students and families. More specifically, the roughly $40 billion of federal tax benefits included in the budget agreement will flow directly to students and parents through tax credits and deductions aimed at mitigating the cost of a college education. In the end, these dollars are likely to be channeled into alternative forms of consumption, rather than into increasing educational opportunity or enhancing the quality of our institutions.

Furthermore, while the federal budget deficit has been erased by stronger-than-expected economic growth, this was accomplished by using the surplus in Social Security payments to finance other operations. As the baby boomers approach retirement in the next two decades, entitlement obligations will place enormous pressure on the discretionary component of the federal budget used to fund financial aid and research programs.

The states are also in more serious trouble than may be apparent. State appropriations for higher education dropped throughout the 1980s and early 1990s. While there has been some modest recovery in state support of higher education in recent years, the burden of other funding priorities such as health care, social services, K–12 education, and corrections will continue to squeeze the funds available for public colleges and universities.[24] Because of the legal obligations for funding federal mandates such as Medicaid and other state services such as corrections and K–12 education, all too frequently higher education finds itself fighting for the scraps remaining in the state budget after most of the funding has been distributed.

As for the public support of higher education that remains, there is concern that much of this investment has been deployed to achieve continued expansion of our system of higher education rather than improved quality. Because of strong local interests, there has been a tendency to proliferate institutions of higher education, particularly those claiming research as a mission. Community colleges have become almost as common as high schools in many parts of the country. The aspirations of community colleges to become four-year institutions, of four-year institutions to start graduate programs, of state colleges to become research universities, has led to an overbuilt system of higher education in many parts of the nation. The obligations created by what one of my colleagues refers to as the "Harvardization of higher education," a culture of unrealistic expectations in which each institution aspires to the overly ambitious objective of becoming another Harvard, has effectively reduced the share of the public resources pool available to any given institution.

Yet American higher education continues to face a growing demand for its services: increased enrollments; new forms of education; research to address critical national priorities; and public service at the local, state, and national level. These educational services are becoming ever more expensive, both because of the degree to which costs are driven by the growth in knowledge itself and by the difficulty colleges and universities have had in achieving productivity gains. Furthermore, many universities are facing the bleak prospect of limited resources with seriously deteriorating infrastructures. Failure to build and maintain facilities in the past has resulted in the inadequate quality of facilities that constrains quality research and teaching at many institutions. While there was substantial investment in the 1960s, this declined appreciably in the 1970s and 1980s. And equipment has been continually underfunded for several decades.

Even if we were to restore national resolve in investing in the future, our resource base will simply not expand as rapidly as the desires, the opportunities, or the needs of higher education. It may be difficult to inspire this kind of resolve in the face of other major societal needs, such as health care, primary and secondary education, reducing crime, and rebuilding our national infrastructure. Society will continue to ask harder questions about whether the social product of higher education is commensurate with the resources invested in it.

What are the alternatives facing higher education? Traditionally, private institutions have relied heavily upon tuition and fees as a source of needed income. But the tuition at these institutions is rapidly approaching levels that only the wealthy can afford. The tuition charged by public universities, while still only a small fraction of that at private institutions, is seriously constrained by political considerations. As a consequence, tuition increases are unlikely to play a significant role in meeting the increasing costs of quality in the years ahead.

Some institutions have the opportunity to attract new resources through private giving. The number and magnitude of recent university fund-raising campaigns provide strong evidence that this is viewed as an important component of the resource portfolio for universities. However, it is also the case that these opportunities may be limited for many institutions, which could well find themselves spending as much on the fund-raising effort as they manage to attract in new resources.

For some universities, highly targeted federal support has been an option. Some have even used professional lobbying firms to push special facilities or program support through the congressional appropriation process. Although efforts have been made to constrain such pork-barrel efforts, their apparent success has encouraged more and more institutions to climb on the bandwagon.

Universities engage in a host of other activities with resource implications. For example, technology-transfer activities such as patent development and business start-ups have provided revenue streams for some research universities. Others engage in health-care delivery, extension services, and continuing education. But again it is unlikely that these auxiliary activities can bear much of the cost of quality education, particularly given the strong evidence that government may act to constrain—or at least tax—such activities.

The limits on resources will inevitably force most institutions to shift from a focus on the revenue side to the expenditure side of the ledger. Cost containment has already become a priority at all institutions, along with strategies borrowed from the corporate world such as total quality management and continuous improvement. As a part of this effort, institutions have accepted the necessity of reducing the number of activities they sponsor in order to better focus their resources—to sustain quality at the expense of breadth and capacity.

Despite early efforts at cost containment, higher education has yet to take the bold steps to constrain cost increases that have been required in other sectors of our society such as business and industry. This lag is due in part to the manner in which our colleges and universities are organized, managed, and governed. But, even if our universities were to acquire both the capacity and the determination to restructure costs radically, it is debatable whether actions used to contain cost and enhance productivity in business can have the same impact in education. The current paradigm of higher education may be simply too people and knowledge-intensive.

Some institutions may be able to shield themselves from these cost pressures by relying on their established reputations and relative prosperity to continue to attract and retain the best students and faculty and to attract the massive resources necessary to sustain quality programs. While this may allow them to protect their traditional missions, quality, and character, it could also isolate them from the critical restructuring efforts that will likely occur in the broader higher education enterprise, as new learning paradigms evolve to serve a radically different future. One might well ask whether it is in the best long-term interests of the leading universities—or of the higher education enterprise more generally—for a few institutions to skim the cream off the top of the resources pool simply to maintain their traditional roles. Such a strategy could lead to the decoupling and increasing irrelevance of such universities to the rest of higher education in America and throughout the world, thereby calling into question their leadership roles.

But there is a broader issue here, as emphasized in the 1997 report by the Commission on National Investment in Higher Education.[25] While some individual institutions may be able to cope with the current environment of limited resources, the implications for the higher education enterprise and for our nation are far more serious. At a time when the level of education needed by our society is increasing, the opportunity to attend college will likely be denied to millions of Americans unless a coordinated effort can be made to control costs while increasing public support. Given current funding projections, it will be difficult even to maintain the present enrollment levels, much less respond to the growing educational needs of the future. It is estimated that the level of underfunding of the higher education enterprise will grow to almost $40 billion by the year 2015 without concerted action. There is no way that tuition income alone can compensate for this funding gap—to rely entirely on this revenue source would drive the cost of higher education beyond the capacity of millions who need it. A unified effort to enhance productivity and restore public support will be needed, and even this may not be adequate if higher education insists on retaining its current paradigms for teaching and service.

It seems increasingly clear that the basic system we use for financing higher education, controlling its costs, and determining its prices is in need of major overhaul if not total replacement. The long-standing premise that one generation will pay for the education of the next either through tax support or tuition payments seems to be eroding. The faculty-centered character of the contemporary university seems unable to control escalating costs. It is time to step back and consider new approaches if we are to respond to the nation's growing needs for quality higher education.

The Changing Rules of the Game

Throughout much of its history, the American university has been seen as an important social institution, created by, supported by, and accountable to society at large.[26] The key social principle sustaining the university was the perception of education as a *public good*—that is, the university was established to benefit all of society. Like other institutions such as parks and police, it was felt that individual choice alone would not sustain an institution serving the broad range of society's education needs. Hence public policy dictated that the university merited broad support by all of society, rather than just by the individuals benefiting from its particular educational programs.[27]

From the earliest days of the nation, the benefits of the American university were expressed in terms of its public, democratic role. Through the writings of Jefferson and early legislation such as the Federal Ordinance of 1785, education was seen as important to the nation's democratic well being. Government policies and social priorities were clearly conveyed through a series of important actions such as the Land-Grant (Morrill) Acts, the GI Bill, the Higher Education Acts, and federal financial aid programs such as the Pell Grants. The intent was to promote equal liberty to differing individuals and groups and to enable citizens to understand their responsibility as citizens of a free society. During this period higher education expanded from its traditional role of educating the elite for leadership roles to providing mass education, perhaps best captured by the belief of the Truman Commission in 1952 that every high school graduate should have the opportunity for a college education. Today, we have evolved still further toward universal education, where our institutions have been asked to address the educational needs of our citizens throughout their lives with affordable, high-quality learning opportunities.

Yet, today, even as the needs of our society for postsecondary education intensify, we also find an erosion in the perception of education as a public good deserving of strong societal support.[28] There has been a clear trend in recent decades to shift the costs of public higher education from general tax revenues to the tuition charged to students and their parents. More specifically, in the 1970s there was a conscious policy to shift higher education toward high-tuition, high-financial-aid models, even in public higher education. The 1980s saw yet another shift, this time from grants to loans as the foundation of financial aid programs. Then in the 1990s, there was still another shift, this time from federal support of financial aid programs to tax benefits for the middle class through the 1997 budget-balancing agreement.[29] Over this three-decade period concerns about affordability have replaced access as the driving force in federal higher education policy. Federal programs have shifted from investment in the higher education enterprise (appropriations to institutions or students) to investment in the marketplace for higher education services (tax benefits to students and parents).

In a sense we have set aside the consensus that has governed the public support of higher education for the past century—that since broader society benefits, it should also pay a substantial portion of the costs of higher education.[30] Whether a deliberate or involuntary response to the tightening constraints and changing priorities for public funds, the new message is that education has become a private good that should be paid for by the individuals who benefit most directly, the students. At the same time, this has shifted the perspective of higher education from that of a social institution, shaped by the values and priorities of broader society, to, in effect, an industry, increasingly responsive to the marketplace of individual students and clients.

A similar social contract evolved to support and sustain the role of universities in creating new knowledge. In the years following World War II a partnership evolved between the federal government and the research universities based on the belief that the nation's health, economy, and military security required the continual development and deployment of new scientific knowledge. It was considered to be in the national interest that the federal government provide support for campus-based research to ensure basic scientific progress and the production of trained personnel.

However, once again, the rules seem to have changed. With the end of the Cold War, the driving force of national security has ebbed as a primary motivation for major public investment in basic research. Today the nation is drifting in search of new driving imperatives. In an environment in which balancing the federal budget has become a dominant priority, discretionary domestic spending and, hence, federal research support could well fall victim to unconstrained but politically more popular entitlement programs. In addition, the basic character of the government-university research partnership is changing as the government shifts from being a partner with the university—a patron of basic research—to becoming a procurer of research, just as it is for other goods and services. This has undermined the sense of trust and confidence that has characterized this important relationship for the past half-century.

The Changing Relationships with Diverse Constituencies

Another dilemma confronting higher education may be best illustrated by the old parable of the blind men each feeling different parts of an elephant and arguing over just what kind of an object they are touching. The modern university is complex and multidimensional. People on and off our campuses perceive the university in vastly different ways, depending on their vantage point, their needs, and their expectations. Students and parents want high-quality but low-cost education. Business and industry seek high-quality products: graduates, research, and services. Patients of university hospitals seek high-quality and compassionate care. Federal, state, and local governments have complex and varied demands that both sustain and constrain us. And the public itself sometimes seems to have a love-hate relationship with higher education. They take pride in our quality and revel in our athletic accomplishments, but they also harbor deep suspicions about our costs, our integrity, and even our intellectual aspirations and commitments.

One of the great challenges to the contemporary university arises from a serious mismatch between public perception and institutional reality. To most of society—including parents, politicians, and the press—the nature of the university is best captured by the phrase "sending the kids to college." While it is true that residential undergraduate education of traditional students is still an important part of higher education, in reality it comprises only a modest fraction of our activities. Much of the attention, resources, and faculty of the university is devoted to graduate and professional education, continuing education, research, and service to society (particularly health care).

Higher education faces greater pressures than ever to establish its relevance to its various stakeholders in our society. Our colleges are drawn into new and more extensive relationships with each passing day. Yet at the same time they are expected to act as independent and responsible critics of society. The tension between these roles and responsibilities is sometimes difficult to resolve.

The university as we know it today has been shaped by public policies that focused on American higher education as critical to the nation's future in meeting needs such as national security, health care, and social mobility. Beyond the classic triad of teaching, research, and service, society has assigned to the university an array of other roles. Through the academic medical center, universities have become one of the nation's leading providers of quality health care. Campus-based research underpins the technology necessary for national security. Through efforts to provide the opportunity for a college education to all of society, the university enables social mobility. And through intercollegiate athletics, we entertain armchair America.

As society develops a different set of needs, universities must evolve if they are to continue to earn public support. They must re-establish their relevance to this new social agenda or run the risk of being marginalized and replaced by other social institutions. Clearly, responsive and responsible change will be necessary. Today, our nation is turning to the university for assistance in addressing new priorities such as revitalizing K–12 education, improving race relations, rebuilding our cities and other infrastructure, and securing economic competitiveness. Yet most people—and most components of state and federal government—can picture the university "elephant" only in terms of the part they can feel, for example, research procurement, student financial aid, and economic development. Few seem to see, understand, or appreciate the entirety of the university. Few understand or care that shifting state or federal priorities, policies, or support aimed at one objective or area will inevitably have an impact on other roles of the university.

The contemporary university is accountable to many constituencies: to its students, faculty, staff, and alumni; to the public and elected leaders in government; to business and labor; to industry and foundations; and to the full range of other private institutions in our society. The diversity—indeed, incompatibility—of the values, needs, and expectations of the various constituencies served by higher education poses a major challenge. The future of our colleges and universities will be determined, in many cases, by their success in harmonizing the many demands and values of these diverse groups, even as they respond in an effective fashion to their own institutional needs and concerns.

In many ways, the increasing complexity and diversity of the modern university and its many missions reflect the character of American and global society. To be sure, such intellectual and social diversity on our college campuses leads to fragmentation and a lack of unity in purpose on the part of students, faculty, and staff. However, the ideal of a "community of scholars," united by a sense of common values and purpose, has, in reality, never existed in American higher education. Our universities have been energized and enlivened by the rich diversity of people and ideas interacting with one another, just as has American society more generally. While this diversity and complexity can pose great challenges, particularly when attempting to build consensus within the university about directions or needed changes, or when relating to a broad array of external constituencies, these characteristics also represent one of the great strengths of higher education in America.

Intellectual Challenges

To some degree, many of the challenges faced by today's university—the ever-increasing demands of society for its services, the imbalance between available resources and imperative responsibilities and attractive opportunities, the complexity of the relationships with ever more diverse constituencies—flow from the university's role as a source of new knowledge. With the doubling time of human knowledge in many fields now only a few years, universities—particularly research universities—are ever pressed to keep at the cutting edge.

This explosion in knowledge, driven in part by the federal funding of faculty research, has reshaped the intellectual organization of the university, fragmenting knowledge into disciplines and subspecialties. It has triggered a major debate over the balance between the disciplines and interdisciplinary teaching and scholarship. It is certainly true that the academic disciplines tend to dominate the modern university—whether in the areas of curriculum, administration, or resource flow. Students, scholars, and administrators all are compelled by the discipline-dominated, professional culture of the modern university to turn inward to their chosen fields.

Today the knowledge of the world is available almost anywhere, anytime, to anyone through modern computer and communications networks and through digital libraries. Perhaps due to such access to vast amounts of knowledge, we have also entered a period of great intellectual change and ferment. New ideas and concepts are exploding forth at ever-increasing rates. We have ceased to accept that there is any coherent or unique form of wisdom that serves as the basis for new knowledge. We have simply seen too many instances in which a new concept has radically changed our traditional views of a field.

The way in which we acquire, understand, and apply new knowledge is changing rapidly. With the explosion in multimedia technology and the MTV generation of students, we may be witnessing the passage of human society from a writing and reading culture to one that is based on oral and visual communication—in an ironic sense, returning to the traditions of the classical past.

The focusing and specialization of scholarship that began at the end of the nine-teenth century and intensified after World War II was one of the great advancements in the history of higher education, allowing scholars to gain expertise and engage in coherent debate amid a growing cacophony of voices. Today, however, as the pace of change increases, it has become more and more evident that we need to make basic alterations in the intellectual organization of the university. One of the greatest challenges for universities will be learning to encourage more people to participate in the high-risk, unpredictable, but ultimately very stimulating confrontations of stag-nant paradigms. We must jar as many people as possible out of their comfortable ruts of conventional wisdom, fostering experiments, recruiting restive faculty, turning people loose to "cause trouble," and simply making conventionality more trouble than unconventionality.

While the remarkable growth in new knowledge characterizing our times pre-sents the university with many challenges, it also brings the excitement of new op-portunities. To address these, it has become increasingly clear that those within the academy will need to learn to tolerate more ambiguity, to take more risks. This may mean we will be less comfortable in our scholarly neighborhoods; we may have to relax the relatively stable professional selves that we have preserved for so long. Yet most will find working together much more fulfilling than working apart. Ultimately this will release incredible creativity.

The Increasing Relevance of the University

Throughout much of American history, universities were protected enclaves, respected well enough, but mostly unnoticed and allowed to carry on unchallenged and gener-ally unfettered. What a contrast to today when the university finds itself defined as a key economic, political, social, and cultural institution. Beyond the traditional mis-sions of teaching, research, and service, the university is now expected to provide the intellectual capacity necessary to build and sustain the strength and prosperity of our society. Through its research, the university produces the new knowledge so neces-sary to the well being of society. It trains the teachers and scholars, the leaders, the managers, and the decision-makers necessary to apply this knowledge. And it pro-vides the key to knowledge transfer, through its graduates, through traditional schol-arly mechanisms such as publications, through public service, and through compa-nies spun off from its research activities.

This is an important point. While once universities were valued primarily for their production of human capital, educated citizens and professionals, today we increasingly seek knowledge capital from them, which may include educated people of course, but which also includes basic and applied research, professional expertise, and economic impact.

It is not surprising that as the university has become a key player in our society, it has also become the focus of much concern. We are victims of our own success. We have entered an era in which educated people and the ideas they produce have become the wealth of nations, and universities are clearly among the prime producers of that wealth. This central role means that more people today have a stake in higher education and more people want to harness it to their own ends. We have become both more visible and more vulnerable as institutions. We attract more constituents and support, but we also attract more opponents.

Thus we should not be surprised by our critics or by their assaults on the academy. Society has an increasingly vital stake in what we do and how we do it. Given the divisions in society at large, the tensions between tradition and change, liberty and justice, social pluralism and unity, nationalism and internationalism, it is no wonder that we find ourselves the battleground for many competing values and interests, both old and new. The more important question is whether we can survive this new attention with our missions, our freedoms, and our values intact.

Ironically, the university was far better understood and accepted when it played a far less relevant role in our society. As long as we remained in the familiar "Mr. Chips" role, providing a safe haven where families could send the kids to college, we were understood, accepted, and supported by society. In some sense, many of our critics may be asking us to return to our earlier and far narrower role, rather than continuing to provide the vast array of services of a modern corporation. They may be asking for a return to an earlier social contract, suggesting that the academy narrow its missions and its relevance, accepting a more modest role as a condition for respect and understanding.

However, we cannot go back. Our knowledge-intensive world has become far too dependent upon the modern university. Indeed, if we were to return to the past, society would simply have to invent new social institutions to play our more expanded roles.

The Constancy of Change

The evolution of the university is shaped by dynamic social forces of a democratic, economic, and technological nature. The profound nature of these forces today seems comparable in significance to other periods of great change in the nature of the university in America. During each of these periods, the American university was transformed in response to changing societal needs. New kinds of educational institutions appeared, for example, the state university, the research university, and the community college. Higher education demonstrated a remarkable ability to adapt to the needs of the society that the enterprise was created to serve.

Yet, when one speculates about the extraordinary nature of the changes that might occur over the decades ahead, it becomes increasingly apparent that there may be no useful precedent upon which we can draw. We face a future in which permanence and stability become less important than flexibility and creativity, in which one of the few certainties will be the presence of continual change.

The triad mission of the university as we know it today—teaching, research, and service—was shaped by the needs of an America of the past. Our nation today is changing at an ever-accelerating pace. Our present concept of the university was developed largely to serve a homogeneous, domestic, industrial society. It seems natural to assume that this institution too must evolve rapidly if it is to serve the highly pluralistic, knowledge-intensive world-nation that will be America of the twenty-first century.

Of course, many in recent years have suggested that the traditional paradigm of the American university must evolve to respond to the challenges that will confront our society in the years ahead. But will a gradual evolution of our traditional paradigm be sufficient? Or will the changes ahead force a more dramatic, indeed revolutionary, shift in the paradigm of the contemporary university?

It is clear that much of the impetus for change is coming from external forces over which the university has little control. Yet the most significant challenges facing higher education today may lie not in the tangible external issues such as resources or public perception, but rather in the need to understand better and gain broader consensus about the central goals and beliefs that guide decisions made about the university. The intellectual renewal of the role, mission, values, and goals of the university may be the key challenge before us. And to respond to this challenge, it may well be that the process of renewal itself, the debate over these qualities of the modern university, is far more important than the ability to converge on a particular solution.

As with other institutions in our society, those universities that will thrive will be those that not only can respond to this future of change, but that also have the capacity to relish, stimulate, and manage change. The capacity for intellectual change and renewal has become increasingly important to us as individuals, and to our institutions. As the pace of discovery of new knowledge accelerates, we are entering a period in which the capacity to nourish and manage change will be one of the most important abilities of all.

CHAPTER 3

Reacting to a Changing World

The art of progress is to preserve order amid change and to preserve change amid order.
—Alfred North Whitehead

How have American universities responded thus far to this time of challenge, opportunity, and change? Not surprisingly, their responses have been as numerous and varied as the great diversity of colleges and universities across our nation. Institutions have reevaluated their priorities, developed new ways to generate resources and control costs, and reached out to their many constituencies. Many have attempted to restructure, reengineer, and reinvent their administrative processes. Some have even begun to address the issue of change in their core academic activities.

Yet, while most colleges and universities have grappled with change at the pragmatic level, few have contemplated the more fundamental transformations in mission and character that may be required by our changing world. Most institutions continue to approach change by reacting to the necessities and opportunities of the moment rather than adopting a more strategic approach to their future.

This response (or lack thereof) is not surprising, since to many, the changes of our times represent just another turn of the wheel. The fortunes of higher education in America seem to ebb and flow from generation to generation. The principal themes of America's colleges and universities during the latter half of the twentieth century have been those of diversification and growth. Although the nation's population has only doubled since 1930, enrollment in higher education has increased tenfold, evidence of the ever-increasing importance of a college education. Strong public investments allowed our system of higher education to expand rapidly to keep pace with expanding populations and growing aspirations. The research university became the cornerstone of our national effort to sustain American leadership in science and technology, thereby underpinning both our economic prosperity and military security. The triad mission of our colleges, in teaching, research, and service, acquired a degree of prestige and public support unprecedented in our history.

Today, higher education faces a much different world and a much different future. To be sure, the demand for the services of higher education, our teaching, research, and service, continues to grow. Yet, so do the costs of educational activities continue to increase, driven in part by the people- and the knowledge-intensive nature of higher education and by the difficulty of achieving productivity gains. And, unfortunately, these increasing demands and costs are in an environment in which public support of higher education at both the state and federal level is relatively stagnant. As the share of college costs financed by both state and federal governments has fallen, the share borne by families has inevitably increased. And as families have been asked to pay a higher percentage of the costs of education for their offspring, the outcry about the "excessive" cost of a college education has reached a crescendo.

Cost is only one among many concerns that have been raised about the American university. Like so many other institutions in our society, we find ourselves roundly criticized from all quarters—indeed, even from within by many of our own faculty, students, and staff—for flaws large and small, fundamental and trivial, real and imagined. Little wonder that at times the academy feels under siege: criticized by parents and students for the uncontrolled escalation of tuition; attacked by state legislators and governors for insufficient attention to state needs; investigated by the Department of Justice for price fixing of tuition and financial aid; criticized by Washington and indeed our own faculties for rising research overhead costs; investigated by Congress for misconduct in research; assailed by legislators for the tenure system; attacked by the left and the right for the quality and nature of undergraduate education; and generally blasted by the media in essentially any and all of our activities, from teaching to health care to intercollegiate athletics.

Among this array of criticisms, there is one that stands out in particular: the growing frustration of society with the hesitancy or reluctance of the university to face up to the challenge of change. A rapidly evolving world has demanded profound and permanent change in most, if not all, social institutions. Corporations have undergone restructuring and reengineering. Governments and other public bodies are being overhauled, streamlined, and made more responsive. Individuals are increasingly facing a future of impermanence in their employment, in their homes, and even in their families. The nation-state itself has become less relevant and permanent in an ever more interconnected world.

Unlike many other institutions, at least according to our critics, the university has responded to the needs of a changing society largely by defending the status quo. To be sure, change has always occurred in higher education on glacial time scales—not surprising since the typical career of a tenured faculty member spans three or more decades. But at a time when our society, our nation, and the world itself are changing rapidly, the university still tends to frame its contemporary roles largely within traditional paradigms. It resists major changes in curricula or pedagogy. Students continue to be evaluated and credentialed relative to "seat time" rather than learning outcomes. The technology that is revolutionizing our world has largely bypassed the classroom, which continues to function largely as it has for decades, if not centuries. Tenure is seen not as a protection for academic freedom but rather as a perquisite that shields the faculty from accountability and change. And higher education tends to respond to resource constraints by raising funds from other sources rather than prioritizing programs or increasing productivity.

We can always respond to our critics by noting that, while our universities do have many shortcomings, they are nevertheless world-class. The American university is the envy of the world, both as measured by the multitude of foreign students seeking education in our institutions and by the effort of other nations to imitate the American approach to higher education. But this argument may no longer suffice should the university become more detached from a changing world or should other social institutions compete more effectively for our roles.

Beyond stubbornness and tradition-bound practices such as tenure, consensus decision making, and disciplinary rigidity, there are other profound forces that inhibit change in higher education. The extraordinary complexity of the university, its many missions, and its array of constituencies make rapid change difficult. Furthermore, the very diversity in the nature of the institutions comprising the higher education enterprise in America leads to great diversity in the responses to changes at the microscopic level of individual institutions and may mask changes in the enterprise at a macroscopic level. So too the responsive capacity of universities has been undermined by the fluctuating rules of the game for public financing of higher education. The very nature of the modern university, structured as a loosely linked collection of highly entrepreneurial faculty members, makes change far more reactive than strategic. Furthermore, our style of shared governance is more attuned to preventing than facilitating change. These are important issues that deserve more detailed consideration.

The Changing Role of the University

What is a university? There are perhaps as many different definitions as there are individuals who have attended, served, or been served by these marvelous and enduring institutions. To some, the university is "a place of light, of liberty, and of learning"[1] or "a place of instruction where universal knowledge is professed."[2] The university has played a critical role in the evolution of Western civilization by stressing broad-minded empiricism over dogma and orthodoxy and conveying the fundamental values that undergird individual freedom and constitutional democracy.[3]

To others, perhaps more skeptical of such lofty definitions, the university is a far more utilitarian entity, defined by the many roles it plays in contemporary society: to provide an education for our citizens; to produce the scholars, professionals, and leaders needed by our society; to preserve and transfer our cultural heritage from one generation to the next; to perform the research necessary to generate new knowledge critical to the progress of our nation; and to provide service to society across a number of fronts that draw on the unique expertise of our institutions.[4]

Colleges and universities have long been considered essential to our nation's well being, anchoring the values of a democratic society and producing the educated citizens capable of governing a nation.[5] America's system of higher education extended far beyond the education of the elite in its efforts to provide an education to a significant fraction of our population. A diverse array of institutions evolved to serve the many and varied needs and aspirations of our society.

To many students and families, this educational role has been best symbolized by the university's power in granting degrees. Most view the formal educational program as a ticket to lifetime rewards and security rather than as a road to the lofty goals of a liberal education. In a recent survey, while 75 percent of college students considered financial success to be a very important goal of their education, only 40 percent saw it as an opportunity to develop a meaningful philosophy of life, a reversal of student motivations in the 1960s.[6]

Beyond formal education in the traditional academic disciplines and professional fields, the university has been expected to play a far broader role in the maturation of students. Few young college students arrive on campus with the emotional and intellectual maturity to learn—or even to live—on their own in our complex society. Colleges provide not only the structured learning and discipline necessary for advanced education, but also a secure environment, a place where the young can spend their first years away from their families, both learning and exploring without concern for the risks posed by "the real world." An undergraduate education is designed to be a time of challenge and curiosity, discovery, and intellectual development. The campus experience we tend to associate with undergraduate education does a remarkable job in preparing the student for later life, and clearly it does so through a complex social experience extending far beyond the classroom and the curriculum.

The second traditional role of our colleges and universities has been scholarship: the discovery, integration, evaluation, and preservation of knowledge in all forms. While the academy would contend that knowledge is important in its own right and that no further justification is required for this role, it is also the case that such scholarship and research have been essential to the university's related missions of instruction and service. The public willingly supports this activity in anticipation of eventual application and benefit to key priorities such as national defense, health care, and economic prosperity. So too it looks to the university as a social institution committed to preserving our culture and heritage for future generations.

The third traditional mission of the university has been to provide service to society. American higher education has long been concerned with furnishing special expertise to address the needs and problems of society. For example, a unique type of institution, the land-grant university, was created in part to respond to the needs of agriculture and industry. The commitments of our universities to the development of professional schools in fields such as medicine, nursing, dentistry, law, and engineering are adequate testimony to the importance of this role. In today's increasingly knowledge-driven society, the service role of the university has become increasingly important.

Finally, higher education in the United States has been expected to provide leadership for society more generally. There has been a conviction that the university could serve both as a laboratory and a model where the major problems of our society could be addressed. In this way, the students and faculty of the university have been challenged to become an intellectual community in which the human mind could be brought to bear on the largest and most enduring questions that confront us.

While all of these traditional roles remain important, there has been a restructuring in the priorities given to the various roles of our colleges and universities. The traditional reasons for strong public support of higher education are shifting rapidly. For example, while instruction of the young will continue to be an important priority for most institutions in the years ahead, it is also the case that adult education will become a more central activity of many institutions. We can no longer justify public support of higher education simply to provide needed services. It is true that the great land-grant universities have demonstrated the importance of public investment to support America's agricultural base. But long ago we made the transition from an agrarian to an industrial society; today we are evolving yet again from an industrial to a knowledge-driven society. And there is little evidence that many of the services traditionally provided by universities such as health care cannot be delivered just as effectively by the private sector.

To many there is a new and equally compelling reason for support of higher education in general and the comprehensive research university in particular. Knowledge has now become an engine of economic growth, key both to the prosperity and security of a nation and to the welfare of its citizens. If, in an age of knowledge, educated people and their ideas have become the most important resources of modern society, then universities must be valued and supported as the source of this intellectual capital.[7] This role shifts somewhat the perspective of a university from that of a social institution primarily focused on the development of human resources to one centered about the discovery, processing, transmission, and application of knowledge itself. This strategic role of the university in a knowledge-driven society explains why most nations are moving rapidly to build or strengthen their systems of higher education.

Yet here we face a challenge, since universities are not simply knowledge factories. We must not narrow our perspective by valuing these remarkable social institutions merely for the earning capacity of their graduates or the wealth they contribute to our society. The university is a complex institution, evolving over centuries to serve our civilization in myriad ways and based upon ancient and time-honored values. It serves as a custodian not simply of the knowledge, but also the values, traditions, and culture of our society. It not only educates and discovers, but it also challenges the existing order and drives change. It remains essential to produce the educated citizens necessary for a democratic society. It affirms the fundamental values, principles, and integrity of learning and reason. It not only honors the past, serves the present, and creates the future, but it does so with the aim of transforming knowledge into wisdom.

The Higher Education Ecosystem

Higher education in the United States is distinguished by a number of factors.[8] One of the most obvious is the remarkable diversity of higher education institutions, ranging from small liberal arts colleges to gigantic multicampus university systems. American colleges and universities are intensely competitive, seeking to attract the most outstanding students and faculty, along with resources from the public and private sector. Our educational institutions are unusually responsive to the needs of society, spawning missions and programs to position themselves better for their societal role.

In America, our colleges and universities, both public and private, are relatively free from government control, at least compared to institutions in other nations. Many nations have approached mass education by creating a uniform educational system constrained by the lowest common denominator of quality. In the United States, we have allowed a diverse system of colleges and universities to flourish in response to the complex and heterogeneous nature of American society. From small colleges to big universities, from religious to secular institutions, from single-sex to coeducational colleges, from vocational schools to liberal arts colleges, from land-grant to urban to national research universities, there is a rich diversity both in the nature and the mission of America's roughly 3,600 post-secondary institutions.

The Taxonomy of Higher Education

The taxonomy of institutions of higher education has long been determined by a classification scheme of the Carnegie Foundation for the Advancement of Teaching:[9]

- Research Universities I and II: These institutions offer a full range of baccalaureate programs, are committed to graduate education through the doctorate, and give a high priority to research. Both RU I's and RU II's award 50 or more doctoral degrees; RU I's receive annually $40 million or more in federal support of research; RU II's receive between $15.5 million and $40 million.

- Doctoral Universities I and II: These institutions offer a full range of baccalaureate programs and are committed to graduate education through the doctorate. DU I's award 40 or more doctoral degrees in five or more disciplines; DU II's award at least 10 doctoral degrees in three or more disciplines.

- Master's (Comprehensive) Universities and Colleges I and II: These institutions offer a full range of baccalaureate programs and are committed to graduate education through the master's degree. CU I's award 40 or more master's degrees in three or more disciplines; CU II's award 20 or more master's degrees in one or more disciplines.

- Baccalaureate (Liberal Arts) Colleges: These institutions are primarily undergraduate colleges with major emphasis on baccalaureate degree programs. They award 40 percent of their degrees in liberal arts fields.

- Baccalaureate Colleges II: These institutions are primarily undergraduate colleges with major emphasis on baccalaureate degree programs. They award less than 40 percent of their degrees in liberal arts fields.

- Associate of Arts Colleges: These institutions offer associate of arts certificate or degree programs, and with few exceptions, offer no baccalaureate degrees.

- Specialized Institutions: These institutions offer degrees ranging from the bachelor's to the doctorate. They include theological seminaries and other religious institutions, medical schools and medical centers, and separate health professional schools, and schools of engineering and technology.

The current breakdown of institutions within this classification scheme is:

Doctorate Granting Institutions	236
—Research Universities I	88
—Research Universities II	37
—Doctoral Universities I	51
—Doctoral Universities II	60

Master's Colleges and Universities	529
—Comprehensive Universities I	435
—Comprehensive Universities II	94
Baccalaureate Colleges	637
—Liberal Arts Colleges	166
—Baccalaureate Colleges II	471
Associate of Arts Colleges	1,471
Specialized Institutions	693
Tribal Colleges and Universities	29
Total	3,595

The growth in the higher education enterprise over the last several decades has been exceptional. From an enrollment of 3 million students and a $7 billion expenditure in 1960, higher education in the United States today enrolls over 15 million students and spends over $180 billion per year.[10] The majority of this growth has been due to public colleges and universities, which today enroll over 80 percent of all college students.

The diversity of our society leads not only to great diversity in the character of institutions, but also to remarkable diversity in how institutions respond to a changing society. For example, community colleges and regional four-year public universities tend to be closely tied to the needs of their local communities. They are the most market-sensitive institutions in higher education, and they tend to respond very rapidly to changing needs. When the population of traditional high school graduates declined in the 1980s, community colleges moved rapidly into adult education, with a particular emphasis on providing the training programs important to regional economic development. Many four-year regional universities have developed specialized programs to meet key regional needs such as for health-care practitioners and engineering technologists.

Liberal arts colleges tend to respond to change in somewhat different ways. Their core academic mission of providing a faculty-intensive, residential form of liberal education remains valued and largely intact. However, they too have had to adapt rapidly both to changing demographics and financial constraints. In recent years many of these colleges have provided leadership in constraining costs and even reducing tuition levels.

The research university, because of the complexity of its multiple missions, its size, and its array of constituencies, tends to be most challenged by change. While some components of these institutions have undergone dramatic change in recent years, notably those professional schools tightly coupled to society such as medicine and business administration, other parts of the research university continue to function much as they have for decades. They have been largely insulated from a changing society both by the intellectual character of their activities (e.g., the humanities) or by their academic culture (e.g., tenure and academic freedom). But here too change *will* eventually occur, although perhaps with more difficulty and disruption.

The Public University

Many regard the public university as among the most significant social institutions of twentieth-century America. Beyond the traditional university missions of creating and transmitting knowledge to students, the public university is also viewed as a primary mechanism for distributing knowledge to society. These institutions reflect some of society's most cherished goals: opportunity through education, progress through research, and cultural enrichment. They are bound closely to society, responsible to and shaped by the communities that founded them.

The great state universities have served as models of the true public university, responsible and responsive to the needs of the people who founded and supported them, even as they sought to achieve quality comparable to that of the most distinguished private institutions. They have provided a model of how higher education serves society through the triad mission of teaching, research, and public service. These institutions grew up with our nation. They have responded to the changing needs and aspirations of its people as America expanded to the frontier, as it evolved through the Industrial Revolution, as our population surged following the war years, and most recently as America has sought to strengthen and diversify its economic base.[11]

Perhaps, before we get too far ahead of ourselves, it is useful to define what we mean by a "public" university. The public frequently thinks of these institutions as large undergraduate teaching factories, supported primarily by tax dollars. Public universities are also expected to provide an array of services such as health care, agricultural extension, and industrial development. Yet, attempting to distinguish between public and private universities based upon funding sources, size and mission, or responsibilities to society can be misleading.

For example, all colleges and universities receive some degree of public funding from local, state, or federal taxes. Public universities are unique in the support they receive from state appropriations. This direct state support subsidizes their very low tuition levels relative to private institutions, as well as supporting some of their more applied missions such as agricultural extension. But private universities also seek and receive substantial public support. For example, the leading private research universities receive significant federal support in the form of research grants and contracts. Their students also are eligible for financial aid from both federal and state governments, which, in part, allow private universities to sustain their relatively high tuition levels. And, perhaps most significant of all, private universities benefit very significantly from the favorable tax treatment of private gifts and endowment. For example, gifts to private universities are deductible as charitable contributions. The appreciation of endowment assets and income from them is also tax-exempt.

Like private universities, many public universities today draw the majority of their support from nonstate sources such as student tuition and fee income, research grants and contracts, private gifts, and income from auxiliary activities such as health care or intercollegiate athletics. Most public universities are now heavily involved in private fund-raising, with several having launched successful billion-dollar fund-raising campaigns rivaling those of leading private universities. Both public and private universities alike are increasingly dependent upon the revenue generated through auxiliary activities such as health care and continuing education. And most research universities, public and private, are actively exploring the income potential of technology transfer activities, ranging from licensing and royalty income to equity interest in spin-off companies. In summary, public and private universities are becoming remarkably similar in the way that they are financed. In fact, there are many private institutions that receive far greater public subsidies—particularly when tax exemptions on gifts or endowment appreciation are included—than some public universities!

Yet another contrast between public and private universities, at least in the popular view, would be size. The image of education in large public universities is one of thousands of students wandering in and out of large lecture courses in a largely random fashion, taught by foreign teaching assistants. Campus images are of football stadiums, fraternity and sorority parties, or student protests. We think of undergraduate students in these institutions as identified only by their ID numbers until the time of their graduation, when they are asked to stand and be recognized along with thousands of their fellow graduates. Here again, one must temper this image by recognizing that most public colleges and universities are relatively small, no larger than a few thousand students in enrollment. Furthermore, many private universities are comparable in size to large public universities and face the same challenges of mass education.

One might also consider the degree of public responsibility and accountability as a way to distinguish between public and private institutions. Yet, here too, there is more similarity than difference, since both types of institutions have accepted significant social obligations through public service and by serving broad and diverse constituencies. Since both are supported by society, both are obligated to be responsive to the needs of society and to be publicly accountable for the use of tax funds. Because of societal support, the services provided by universities should be available to all who are qualified, without regard to race, religion, socioeconomic status, or other academically irrelevant criteria. In summary, public support requires public accountability, responsibility for service to all without discrimination, and dedication to the public interest. In fact, all of America's colleges and universities, whether public or private, are public assets and influenced by public policy.

Probably the most important distinction between public and private institutions involves their governance. Public universities are creatures of the state, clearly owned and governed by the public. They are held accountable to myriad state regulation and laws. This is reflected in the rules and regulations governing their operations, such as sunshine laws (e.g., freedom of information and open-meeting acts). It is also manifested in layer after layer of state structures and bodies that coordinate and fund higher education, ranging from legislative committees to coordinating boards to statewide higher education systems. In fact, since public and private universities are increasingly similar in size, mission, and financing and most sharply distinguished by their ties to government, it has become common to refer to private universities as "independent" universities.

The governing boards of private universities are generally self-perpetuating in nature, and their members or trustees are charged with always acting in the best interest of the institution they serve. In contrast, the governing boards of public universities are generally political in nature, frequently selected through partisan political mechanisms, for example, gubernatorial appointment or popular election. Rather than serving as trustees for the institution they are viewed as representing the public's (i.e., taxpayer's) interest. This contrast between the "trustee" philosophy of the governing boards of private universities and the "watchdog" stance assumed by public governing boards is one of the most significant differences and greatest challenges faced by public higher education today.

Furthermore, public universities tend to have far broader missions and to serve more diverse constituencies. Their instructional activities range from the most sophisticated advanced education to the most practical training and enrichment programs. Their research activities range from fundamental investigations to highly applied knowledge services such as agricultural extension and economic development. As the needs of society evolve in complexity, the public university mission similarly broadens. This multipurpose and comprehensive character poses difficulties, particularly during periods of constrained resources. However, most public universities are reluctant to focus their missions because of the risk of cutting their bonds to large segments of the society that support them.

One could well conclude that the most important theme of American higher education in the twentieth century was the development of the public university. With an expanding population, a prosperous economy, and compelling needs such as national security and industrial competitiveness, the public was willing to make massive investments in higher education. While elite private universities were important in setting the standards and character of higher education in America, it was the public university that provided the capacity and diversity to meet our nation's vast needs for postsecondary education.

During the past century, the public university has become the dominant form of higher education in America.[12] Although only one-quarter of the 2,215 four-year colleges in the United States are public, these enroll almost 5.8 million students or two-thirds of all college students in four-year institutions. When the additional 5.3 million students enrolled in public two-year colleges is taken into account, some 11.1 million students attend public colleges and universities, over 80 percent of the total.

Public universities conduct the majority of the nation's academic research, with eight public universities ranking nationally among the top ten institutions in research expenditures. Public universities produce most of our doctors, lawyers, engineers, teachers, and other professionals. They provide critical services such as agricultural and industrial technology, health care, and economy development throughout society. They enable social mobility, providing generations of students with the stepping stones to more rewarding careers and more meaningful lives. The elite private universities such as Harvard and Stanford tend to dominate the attention of the national media. But the backbone of higher education in America today is provided by our public colleges and universities, institutions like Michigan and Ohio State, Cal State and Florida A&M, Maricopa Community College and Lake Superior State.

The Research University

At the top of the evolutionary ladder in the higher education ecosystem—at least in terms of prosperity and prestige—is the research university. Technically these are institutions that offer "the full range of baccalaureate programs, are committed to graduate education through the doctorate, and give high priority to research." The Carnegie classification scheme assigns eighty-eight universities to status as Research I institutions (graduating at least fifty doctorates per year and spending over $40 million on research) and thirty-seven as Research II institutions ($25 million per year). In reality, there is another pecking order more widely accepted in higher education: membership in the Association of American Universities, which is comprised primarily of the sixty most prestigious research universities (e.g., Harvard, Yale, Princeton, Stanford, MIT, UC-Berkeley, Michigan, Wisconsin, and Virginia).

Although the criteria used to classify an institution as a research university or elect it for membership in AAU involves factors such as the amount of research, number of graduate degrees, and reputation of the faculty as scholars, these institutions also have very significant involvement in undergraduate education and public service. Although the nation's 125 research universities represent in number only 3 percent of the thirty-six hundred institutions of higher education, they produce three-quarters of the Ph.D.s who will comprise the faculties of America's 3,600 institutions of higher education. They also produce 35 percent of the baccalaureate degrees and 56 percent of the B.S. degrees in science and engineering. They provide the bulk of this nation's professionals—its doctors, lawyers, business executives, and engineers. To an overwhelming degree America's research universities have furnished the cultural, intellectual, economic, and political leadership of the nation.

This is an important point. Although the very name "research university" suggests to some that these institutions waste the time of their faculty and the taxpayers' dollars on frivolous research at the expense of teaching undergraduates, in reality, these institutions have evolved because of a very conscious and strategic public policy. Largely as a result of the role of the university in supporting the Allied effort during World War II, a social contract evolved that led to a partnership between the federal government and the American university aimed at the support and conduct of basic research on the campus. The federal government decided to support university faculty investigators to engage in research of their own choosing in the hope that significant benefits would flow back to American society in the forms of military security, public health, and economic prosperity.

The American research university has had great impact on our nation. The knowledge produced on our campuses has been absolutely critical to our national security, our public health, and our economic strength. These institutions have produced the scientists, engineers, and other professionals so important to our society, while providing much of the leadership for our nation. Perhaps as much as any other contemporary institution, the research university has determined both the shape and the character of our knowledge-driven society and economy.

Certainly, as a primary source of basic research and the next generation of scholars and professionals, the research university will remain an asset of great value. At a time when both industry and government are shifting more toward applied research and development, the research university has become ever more important as an intellectual force in our society. Today the research faculty members in these institutions have become both the leaders and the arbiters of science and scholarship for the world. This group not only leads in knowledge production and distribution, but they have become the gatekeepers and standard-bearers, leading a complex knowledge system that both drives and sustains world education and learning.

Furthermore, as highly educated scholars and professionals are increasingly sought as leaders in a knowledge-driven world, these institutions should continue to play a critical role.

The Entrepreneurial University

The nature of the contemporary university and the forces that drive its evolution are complex and frequently misunderstood. The public still thinks of us in very traditional ways, with images of students sitting in large classrooms listening to faculty members lecture on subjects such as literature or history. The faculty thinks of Oxbridge, themselves as dons and their students as serious scholars. The federal government sees the university as just another R&D contractor or health provider—a supplicant for the public purse. And armchair America sees the university on Saturday afternoon as yet another quasi-professional athletic franchise. Needless to say, the reality is far more complex.

Several years ago, in a planning exercise at Michigan, we attempted to list the various activities of the university. It was our foolish hope that we might be able to red-pencil a few items of secondary importance and focus our limited resources more effectively on core activities. Our brainstorming sessions led to the network of activities, beginning with a chart of the classic triad of higher education, teaching, research, and service branching off into a dozens of related missions.

The resulting branching charts went on for page after page. Teaching branched into undergraduate, graduate, professional and continuing education, then each of these branched into additional subsets of activities. In fact, we eventually ended up with over twenty pages of missions, roles, and activities. After hours of heated debate, we were able to cross only two items off the list. (These were later reinstated by faculty defenders who had been absent from the red-lining session.)

This branching network of multiple missions presents a different image of the modern research university than that commonly perceived by students, faculty, or society: that of a very complex, international conglomerate of highly diverse businesses. To illustrate, imagine how one might characterize the business lines of the "University of Michigan, Inc." With an annual budget of $3 billion and an additional $3 billion of investment assets under active management, the U of M, Inc., would rank roughly 470th on the Fortune 500 list. The university educates roughly fifty thousand students on its several campuses at any given moment—an educational business amounting to about $1 billion per year. The university is also a major federal R&D laboratory, conducting over $500 million a year of sponsored research, supported primarily by federal contracts and grants. The University of Michigan operates a massive health-care company. University-owned hospitals and clinics currently treat almost a million patients a year, with a total medical center income of $1.2 billion. It has a managed-care corporation with over one hundred thousand "managed lives." In 1994, we formed a nonprofit corporation, the Michigan Health Corporation, with the aim of making equity investments in joint ventures to build a statewide integrated health-care system of roughly 1.5 million subscribers—the patient population we believe necessary to keep afloat our tertiary hospitals that we own.

The university is already too big and complex to buy insurance, so we have our own captive insurance company, Veritas, incorporated in New Hampshire. We have become actively involved in providing a wide array of knowledge services, from degree programs offered in Hong Kong, Seoul, and Paris, to cyberspace-based products such as the Michigan Virtual Automotive College. And, of course, the university is involved in public entertainment, the Michigan Wolverines, characterized by roughly $250 million of commercial activities a year. Fortunately for the University, the operations budget of the Michigan Athletic Department is only about $50 million per year. But, when we include licensing and marketing—including even the "block M," which we have copyrighted—our college sports activities become a far larger enterprise. It is big-time show business.

This corporate organization would compare in both scale and complexity with many major global corporations. And it is not unique to the University of Michigan. Most of the major research universities in America are characterized by very similar organizational structures, indicative of their multiple missions and diverse array of constituencies. In fact, the university today has become one of the most complex institutions in modern society—far more complex, for example, than most corporations or governments. We are comprised of many activities, some nonprofit, some publicly regulated, and some operating in intensely competitive marketplaces. We teach students; we conduct research for various clients; we provide health care; we engage in economic development; we stimulate social change; and we provide mass entertainment (athletics). In systems terminology, the modern university is a "loosely coupled, adaptive system," with a growing complexity, as its various components respond to changes in its environment.[13]

The modern university has become a highly adaptable knowledge conglomerate because of the interests and efforts of our faculty. We have provided our faculty with the freedom, the encouragement, and the incentives to move toward their personal goals in highly flexible ways. We might view the university of today as a loose federation of faculty entrepreneurs, who drive the evolution of the university to fulfill their individual goals.[14] We have developed a transactional culture, in which everything is up for negotiation. The university administration manages the modern university as a federation. It sets some general ground rules and regulations, acts as an arbiter, raises money for the enterprise, and tries—with limited success—to keep activities roughly coordinated.

Furthermore, the growing pressures on faculty, not only to generate the resources necessary to support their activities, but also to manage the boundary between the academy and the external world, are immense.[15] Imagine the plight of the young faculty member in medicine: responsible for teaching medical students and residents; providing sufficient clinical revenue to support not only his or her salary but as well the overhead of the medical center; securing sufficient research grants to support laboratories, graduate students, and postdoctoral fellows; exploring opportunities for technology transfer and business start-ups; and building the scholarly momentum and reputation to achieve tenure. Imagine as well the conflict that inevitably arises among responsibilities to students, patients, scholarship, and professional colleagues. Not an easy life!

As a result, the entrepreneurial university has developed an array of structures to enable it to better interact with society and pursue attractive opportunities. It has formed multidisciplinary research centers and institutes within the institution that allow it to seek project-focused research funding. It has created administrative units that develop expertise in contracting, licensing, and technology transfer. It has also spawned an array of external organizations such as foundations, nonprofit corporations, and for-profit subsidiaries to handle major activities ranging from health-care delivery to fund-raising to intercollegiate athletics.

The entrepreneurial university has been remarkably adaptive and resilient throughout the twentieth century, but it still faces some major challenges as it moves into the next century. Many contend that we have diluted our core business of learning, particularly undergraduate education, with a host of entrepreneurial activities. We have become so complex that few, whether on or beyond our campuses, understand what we have become. We have great difficulty in allowing obsolete activities to disappear. We now face serious constraints on resources that no longer allow us to be all things to all people. We also have become sufficiently encumbered with processes, policies, procedures, and past practices so that our best and most creative people no longer determine the direction of our institution.

If we are to respond to future challenges and opportunities, the modern university must engage in a more strategic process of change. While the natural evolution of a learning organization[16] may still be the best model for adapting to a changing environment, it must be guided by a commitment to preserve our fundamental values and mission. We must find ways to allow our most creative people to drive the future of our institutions rather than simply reacting to the opportunities and challenges of the moment. Our challenge is to tap the great source of creativity and energy associated with our faculty's entrepreneurial activity in a way that preserves our core missions, character, and values.

Balancing the Roles and Managing the Relationships

The relationship between the university and the society it serves both determines and is determined by the characteristics of the American university. Our universities have always been granted unusual autonomy from external influence, particularly from government. Despite this autonomy, American universities are unusually responsive to society. The very independence and competitive nature of universities cause them to pay close attention to social needs. As Eric Ashby put it, "The great American contribution to higher education has been to dismantle the walls around the campus."[17]

The modern university interacts with a diverse array of constituencies that depend on the university in one way or another, just as our educational institutions depend upon each of them: students, faculty, staff, and alumni; the public and their elected leaders in government; business and labor; industry and foundations; and the full range of other public and private institutions in our society. The management of the complex roles and relationships between the university and these many constituencies is one of the most important challenges facing higher education, particularly when these relationships are rapidly changing. How does one achieve an optimum balance between teaching and research? Between service and serving as an independent critic of society? Between the liberal arts and the professions? Between core missions such as education and peripheral activities such as health care and intercollegiate athletics? The tensions among these various roles often arise from incompatibility in the needs, values, and expectations of the various stakeholders served by higher education.

If ever there were ivy-covered walls surrounding our universities, protecting us against the intrusions of politics or the economy, these walls have long since tumbled down. The environment beyond our campuses is very different today than it was even a decade ago. Today we are neither isolated nor protected. We are very much engaged and exposed in the world. If you doubt it, you have only to read the headlines. Hardly a day passes without some news story on higher education; state budget cuts; court tests of affirmative-action policies; or some legislative committee out to regulate, legislate, or fact-find in areas that were once privileged academic territory. And, in today's world of more sharply defined expectations and special interests, we are evaluated and supported increasingly based on how we answer the question of "What have you done for me lately?"

To understand better the challenges faced by higher education during a period of change, it is useful to consider the perspective of the university from the vantage of each of its many stakeholders:

The Campus Constituencies: Students, Faculty, Staff, and Governing Boards

The contemporary university is much like a city, comprised of a sometimes bewildering array of neighborhoods and communities. To the faculty, it has almost a Balkan structure, divided up into highly specialized academic units, frequently with little interaction even with disciplinary neighbors, much less with the rest of the campus. To the student body, the university is an exciting, confusing, and sometimes frustrating complexity of challenges and opportunities, rules and regulations, drawing them together only in cosmic events such as fall football games or campus protests. To the staff, the University has a more subtle character, with the parts woven together by policies, procedures, and practices evolving over decades, all too frequently invisible to, or ignored by, the students and faculty.

In some ways, the modern university is so complex, so multifaceted, that it seems that the closer one is to it, the more intimately one is involved with its activities, the harder it is to understand its entirety. It is easy not to see the forest for the trees. Clark Kerr, the former president of the University of California, once portrayed the community of the multiversity as connected only by a common concern for parking.[18] But perhaps it is better characterized as a tropical rain forest, with an extraordinarily complex and evolving ecosystem, highly diverse, highly interdependent, and yet rarely visible, even to its inhabitants.

On most campuses, there is a chronic shortage of information—and hence understanding—about how the university really works. Little wonder that the faculty frequently feels powerless, buffeted about by forces only dimly understood, and thwarted by bureaucracy at every turn.[19] So, too, students sometimes feel that they are only tourists, traveling through the many adventures—or hurdles—of their university education, entering as raw material and being stamped and molded into graduates during their brief experience on campus. Staff members, too, sometimes view themselves as only a small cog in a gigantic machine, working long and hard for an institution that sometimes does not even appear to recognize or appreciate their existence or loyalty.

Yet the people of the university, its faculty, students, and staff, are its greatest asset. The character, role, and interaction of these important communities are key in defining the nature of the university.

The Students. Although educators generally like to articulate the purpose of an undergraduate education in lofty terms such as educating future citizens or preparing students for a meaningful life, to most of our society and to many students and their parents, a college education has a more utilitarian function. A college degree is seen by many first and foremost as a key to a good job, and to personal prosperity and security, rather than preparation for a meaningful and fulfilling life or for responsible citizenship in a democratic society. This more limited perspective has led in turn to a more demanding, consumerist approach toward higher education.

Students, parents, and the public at large are rightfully concerned with access to high-quality higher education. Students want colleges and universities to focus on their particular degree programs, whether at the associate, baccalaureate, or professional/graduate level. They want to be taught by top-flight faculty. They expect strong counseling, placement, and other student services. They seek degree programs that will provide them with the skills necessary for immediate employability. And they want all of this at a low cost.

The Faculty. Probably the most important internal constituency of a university is its faculty, since the quality and achievements of this group, more than any other factor, determine the quality of the institution. While the faculty plays the key role in the academic policy of most universities, its ability to become directly involved in the detailed management of the institution has long since disappeared as issues have become more complex and the time-scale of the decision process has shortened.

From the perspective of the academy, any great university should be "run by the faculty for the faculty" (an objective that would be contested by students or elements of broader society, of course). No matter how large and complex, institutions seek ways to involve faculty in the key policy decisions affecting the institution. As one might expect from the diversity present in American higher education, different institutions approach this challenge in very different ways. Some have moved to highly decentralized organizational structures where individual academic units have great responsibility and authority over their programs and resources. Others have utilized a highly democratic form of faculty governance in which key academic administrators, such as chair or deans are, in effect, elected by the governing faculty of the unit. Most distinguished universities tend to choose their senior administrative officers from faculty ranks, thereby seeking leaders with both an understanding of the academic process and a credibility with the faculty.

However it is done, the involvement of faculty in the governance of the modern university in a meaningful and effective fashion is both an important goal and a major challenge. Broad faculty participation through traditional governance bodies is all too often frustrated by inadequate information, the rapid pace of the decisions required by contemporary issues, and the imbalance between responsibility and authority for most university leadership positions.

The Staff. Although frequently invisible to faculty and students, the operation of the university requires a large, professional, and dedicated staff. From accountants to receptionists, investment officers to janitors, computer programmers to nurses, the contemporary university would rapidly grind to a halt without the efforts of thousands of staff members who perform critical services in support of its academic mission.

While many faculty members view their appointments at a particular institution as simply another step up the academic ladder, many staff members spend their entire career at the same university. As a result, they frequently exhibit not only a greater institutional loyalty than faculty members or students, but they also sustain the continuity, the corporate memory, and the momentum of the university. Ironically, they also sometimes develop a far broader view of the university, its array of activities, and even its history than do the relative short-timers among the faculty and the students. Needless to say, their understanding and support is essential in university efforts to respond to change.

Governing Boards. American higher education is unique in its use of lay boards to govern its institutions. In the case of private institutions, governing boards are typically elected by alumni of the institution or self-perpetuated by the board itself. In public institutions, board members are generally either appointed by governors or elected in public elections, usually with highly political overtones.

While the primary responsibility of such lay boards is at the policy level, they also frequently find themselves drawn into detailed management decisions. Boards are expected first and foremost to act as trustees, responsible for the welfare of their institution. But, in many public institutions, politically selected board members tend to view themselves more as governors or legislators rather than trustees, responsible to particular political constituencies rather than simply to the welfare of their institution. Instead of buffering the university from various political forces, they sometimes bring their politics into the boardroom and focus it on the activities of the institution.[20]

Federal Government

Compared with higher education in other nations, American higher education has been relatively free from government interference. Yet, while we have never had a national ministry of education, the impact of the federal government on higher education in America has been profound. The federal land-grant acts of the nineteenth century created the great public universities. The GI Bill broadened educational opportunity and expanded the number and size of educational institutions. Federal funding for campus-based research in support of national security and health care shaped the contemporary research university. Federal programs for key professional programs such as medicine, public health, and engineering have shaped our curriculum. Federal financial aid programs involving grants, loans, and work-study have provided the opportunity for a college education to millions of students from lower- and middle-class families. And federal tax policies have not only provided colleges and universities with tax-exempt status, but they have also provided strong incentives for private giving.

Clearly federal higher education policies and programs have had great impact on higher education in America. But in the process, the university has become particularly dependent upon its relationship with the federal government. Many universities receive hundreds of millions of dollars every year for research, financial aid, or specific academic programs, funding that has become critical to their survival. Faculty cultures have evolved that stress grantsmanship in salary and promotion decisions. Universities have become sophisticated in lobbying for federal funds and policies.[21]

Not surprisingly, with federal legislation and support has come federal intrusion. Universities have been forced to build large administrative bureaucracies to manage their interaction with those in Washington. From occupational safety to control of hazardous substances to health-care regulations to accounting requirements to campus crime reporting, federal regulations reach into every part of the university with a cost burden that increases every year, now estimated to contribute more than 10 percent of the costs of university operations. Furthermore, universities tend to be whipsawed by the unpredictable changes in Washington's policies with regard to regulation, taxation, and funding, shifting with the political winds each election cycle.

For example, in today's more conservative federal approach to government, tax and budget committees tend to have more influence than authorization or appropriations committees. In an era in which budget constraints on discretionary spending drive the federal agenda, the objective today has become to spend as little as possible. Although campus-based research continues to be an important part of the federal agenda for key priorities such as health care and economic competitiveness, for most of higher education the dominant federal concern has become affordability.

State Government

As with many other federal initiatives, it has been left to the states and the private sector to provide the majority of the resources necessary to support and sustain the contemporary university, even though higher education has been so clearly shaped and influenced by federal policies and priorities. This creates a certain tension when the university is caught between conflicting state priorities and federal policies. (Here, an example would be the conflict between the state freedom of information laws and federal right to privacy laws.) Furthermore, in sharp contrast to Washington, which is at least geographically distant even if occasionally meddlesome and ponderous, elected public officials in state government are right in the university's backyard. And, unfortunately, while higher education is a major priority and source of pride to most legislators, it can also provide a tempting opportunity for political gain.

The relationship between public universities and state government is a particularly complex one, and it varies significantly from state to state. Some universities are structurally organized as components of state government, subject to the same hiring and business practices as other state agencies. Others possess a certain autonomy from state government through constitutional or legislative provision. All are influenced by the power of the public purse—by the strings attached to appropriations from state tax revenues.

The most frequent cause of tension between the university and the state has to do with the multiple missions of the contemporary university. This diversity of missions corresponds to a complex array of constituencies and engenders a particularly complex set of political considerations. As universities strive to serve broader segments of society, they occasionally encounter the political wars over affirmative action and racial preference currently raging across America. In their efforts to stimulate economic development, they run afoul of private-sector concerns about unfair competition from tax-exempt university activities, whether these are local commercial enterprises or equity interest in high-tech spin-offs. Those institutions with selective admissions policies frequently face pressure from elected public officials responding on behalf of constituents who are disappointed when their children are denied admission.

One of the most difficult issues in many states involves achieving an appropriate division of missions among state colleges and universities. Although most states have flagship state universities, they also have many other public colleges and universities that aspire to the full array of missions of the public research university. Community colleges seek to become four-year institutions, undergraduate colleges seek to add graduate degree programs, and comprehensive universities seek to become research universities. Since all colleges and universities generally have regional political representation, if not statewide influence, they can frequently build strong political support for their ambitions to expand missions. Even in those states that are driven by "master plans" such as California, there is evidence of politically driven mission creep, leading to unnecessary growth of institutions and wasteful overlap of programs.

Another cause of intrusion is simply the desire within the state bureaucracy to exercise power. State administrative agencies attempt to include higher education under their jurisdiction, even when issues of autonomy are involved. Sometimes universities are successful in making the case that their special requirements and history justify independence in many areas such as hiring and contracting. But there is also a sense on the part of many—particularly elected public officials—that state government should have some role in managing the affairs of publicly funded institutions if they are to be responsive to the public interest.

We should not underestimate the growing frustration on the part of many state leaders about what they perceive as higher education's lack of accountability and its unwillingness to consider the changes characterizing other parts of society. In recent years there has been a trend toward expanding the role of state governments in shaping the course of higher education, thereby lessening the institutional autonomy of universities. In many states, public universities are caught in a tight web of state government rules, regulations, and bureaucracy. Statewide systems and coordinating bodies exercise greater power than ever over public institutions. Of particular note is the increasing use of performance-based funding, in which appropriations are linked to institutional performance on a range of outcomes—e.g., graduation rates, post-graduate placement, and faculty productivity. Roughly half of the states have already instituted some type of performance-based funding, and another quarter anticipate using it within the next five years. Ironically enough, this trend toward increasing state control of higher education is in sharp contrast to the pattern of deregulation in other enterprises such as health care and telecommunications.

Even if state government can be persuaded to back away from excessive regulation of higher education, there will always be the political temptation for individual government officials to become involved. A legislator can always demonstrate that he or she is working hard by landing a new building or a budget increase for the local college or university—whether they need it or even want it. The more powerful the legislator, the stronger the opportunity for pork-barrel politics. Even those legislators without a home college can get into the act, simply by using higher education as a convenient scapegoat. By decrying the costs of education or student behavior on campus, they can unleash a torrent of concerns that not only gains attention but also represents votes. Even the very efforts of many of our public universities to achieve excellence lay them open to charges of "elitism."

Town-Gown Relationships

The relationship between a university and its surrounding community is usually a complex one, particularly in cities dominated by major universities such as Madison, Berkeley, Cambridge, Chapel Hill, and Ann Arbor. Although the town and the gown are linked together with intertwined destinies, there is nevertheless always a tension between the two. On the plus side is the fact that the university provides the community with an extraordinary quality of life. It stimulates strong primary and secondary schools, provides rich cultural opportunities, and generates an exciting and cosmopolitan community. The income generated by the university insulates these communities from the economic roller coaster faced by most other cities. Without such universities, these cities would be like any other small city in America; with them they become exciting, cosmopolitan, richly diverse, and wonderful places to live and work.

But there are also drawbacks. The presence of such large, nonprofit institutions takes a great amount of property off the tax rolls. The impact of these universities, whether it is through parking, crowds, or student behavior, can create inevitable tensions between town and gown. Members of the city community who are not directly associated with the university are sometimes viewed as outsiders in the life of both the university and the city.

It is clear that the most important thing a university can do to help its surrounding community is to continue doing what it does best: It can attract exciting, talented people as students, faculty, and staff. It can work closely with the community to stimulate economic growth, for example, by attracting new companies or spinning off technology to the private sector. It can serve as the cultural center through its extraordinary array of activities in the performing arts, the visual arts, and intercollegiate athletics. Many universities provide their communities with world-class health care. Universities can play a vital role in strengthening K–12 education.

Beyond these traditional activities, there are other things the university can do. Our institutions should be open to the consideration of a broad array of possible joint ventures. The university, working hand in hand with the community, might be of assistance in going after federal or state financing for projects of major importance to the city, such as development of the downtown area, mixed use of facilities, or transportation systems. The university might well consider participation in a variety of other types of activities. It should at least consider possible participation in commercial ventures adjacent to the campus area (*on* the tax rolls, of course).

Perhaps of greater importance, the university could assist the city in the development of a strategic vision of the future. Universities have the resources, both on their campuses and through their reputations, to attract to their communities leaders in areas such as urban planning, public financing, and business development. It is important to sustain a broad range of strategic efforts designed to improve relationships with the local community. Of course, there will always be issues on which town and gown disagree. But universities should strive to be good citizens and to work with their communities to improve the future quality of life for everyone. After all, divorce is not an option.

The Public

The public's perception of higher education is ever changing. Public opinion surveys reveal that at the most general level the public strongly supports high-quality education in our colleges and universities.[22] Surveys of leaders in the public and private sector believe that the United States continues to have the strongest higher education system in the world, a fact they believe of vital importance to our nation's future.[23] They believe it essential that higher education remain accessible to every qualified and motivated student; they also remain convinced that the vast majority of our population can still get a college education if they want it. But, when we probe public attitudes more deeply, we find many concerns, about cost, improper student behavior (alcohol, drugs, political activism), and intercollegiate athletics. There is a growing concern that too many students entering our universities are not sufficiently prepared academically to benefit from a college education.

Perhaps more significantly, there has been an erosion in the priority that the public places on higher education relative to other social needs. This is particularly true on the part of our elected officials, who generally rank health care, welfare, K–12 education, and even prison systems higher on the funding priority list than higher education. This parallels a growing spirit of cynicism toward higher education and its efforts to achieve excellence.

Universities are clearly accountable to many constituents. People want to know what we are doing, where we are going. We have an obligation to be forthcoming. But here we face several major challenges. First, we have to be honest in admitting that communication with the public, especially via the press, doesn't always come easily to academics. We are not always comfortable when we try to reach a broader audience. We speak a highly specialized and more exacting language among ourselves, and it can be difficult to explain ourselves to others. But we need to communicate to the public to explain our mission, to convey the findings of our research, to share our learning.

Second, as noted earlier, the public's perception of the nature and role of the modern university is inconsistent with reality. Sure, we remain a place where one sends the kids off to college. Public concerns such as cost, student behavior, athletics, and political correctness are real and of concern to us just as they are to the public. But the missions and the issues characterizing the contemporary university are far more complex than the media tends to portray them.

Another set of surveys[24] revealed an interesting paradox. In a series of interviews it was found that those without a college education and only a vague understanding of the nature of the university were generally very positive about higher education. In contrast, a series of interviews with leaders of business, journalism, and government—people who knew a great deal about higher education—revealed more cynical attitudes toward the contemporary university. Few people knew what the term research university or academic medical meant, terms academics take for granted.

This leads to the third challenge. The torrent of criticism now deluging higher education is coming from just the people who used to defend us in the past—business leaders, public officials, and the press. But today these groups have become some of our most strident critics. With our former advocates now either sitting on the sidelines or leading the cheers against us, we are having great difficulty in getting the word out that, despite all of its shortcomings, higher education remains one of America's few truly world class enterprises.

This is not to say we should shy away from criticism; we certainly deserve it from time to time. Furthermore, we have an obligation for accountability. After all, it is the public, through tax dollars or exemptions, tuition payments or private gifts, that sustains the university. But much of the public criticism now inundating us is both uninformed and simplistic. While well intentioned, the press, public leaders, and even business leaders propose simplistic remedies to our problems. If only professors would do more teaching. We should focus on our "core competencies," and "restructure our operations," just as the business world. We should accelerate "throughput," meaning students should be rushed through our programs more rapidly. Ah, if only life were so simple.

One of the curses of the American public is our willingness to embrace the simplest possible solutions to the most complex of problems. Higher education is certainly an example. People seem eager to believe that our system of higher education—still the envy of the world—is wasteful, inefficient, and ineffective, and that its leaders are intent only on protecting their perquisites and privileges.

Public university presidents recognize there is a very simple formula for popularity with the public:

1. Freeze tuition and faculty salaries.
2. Support populist agendas such as sunshine laws.
3. Limit the enrollment of out-of-state students.
4. Sustain the status quo at all costs.
5. Win at football.

But most university leaders also recognize this as a Faustian bargain, since it would put their institutions at great risk with respect to the academic program quality, diversity, and their capacity to serve society.

The Press

In earlier times, the relationship between the university and the press was one of mutual trust and respect. Given the many values common to both the profession of journalism and the academy, journalists, faculty, and academic leaders related well to one another. The press understood the importance of the university, accepted its need for some degree of autonomy similar to its own First Amendment freedoms, and frequently worked to build public understanding and support for higher education.

In today's world, where all societal institutions have come under attack by the media, universities prove to be no exception. Part of this is no doubt due to an increasingly adversarial approach taken by journalists toward all of society, embracing a certain distrust of everything and everyone as a necessary component of investigative journalism. Partly to blame is the arrogance of many members of the academy, university leaders among them, in assuming that the university is somehow less accountable to society than other social institutions. And it is in part due to the increasingly market-driven nature of contemporary journalism as it merges with, or is acquired by, the entertainment industry and trades off journalistic values and integrity for market share and quarterly earnings statements.

Rare indeed is the newspaper that assigns high priority to covering higher education. Even in college towns, the local papers assign far more resources to covering athletics than academics. While it is certainly true that the academy does not understand how the press operates, it is equally true that the press is remarkably ignorant of the major issues facing higher education.

In recent years, however, the press has gone beyond accusation and investigation; they now use their formidable powers to manipulate and control institutions. Relying on weapons such as sunshine laws and First Amendment protections, the press has brought strong pressure to bear on universities in an effort to control who, what, and how they teach. In sharp contrast to earlier times in which they helped to protect academic institutions from inappropriate intrusion by governments or private groups, today the press actually intensifies and focuses political pressures on the university.

The issue of sunshine laws is a particular concern for public institutions. Although laws requiring open meetings and freedom of information were created to ensure the accountability of government, they have been extended and broadened through court decisions to apply to all public institutions. Ironically the only public organizations typically exempted are those very legislative bodies responsible for the drafting of the laws and those judicial bodies that have extended them. Today public universities increasingly find these sunshine laws seriously constraining their operations. They prevent governing boards from discussing sensitive policy matters. They allow the press to go on fishing expeditions through all manner of university documents. They have also been used to hamstring the searches for senior leadership such as university presidents.

Politics

Most of America's colleges and universities have more than once suffered the consequences of ill-thought-out efforts by politicians to influence everything from what subjects can be taught, to who is fit to teach, and who should be allowed to study. As universities have grown in importance and influence, more political groups are tempted to use them to achieve some purpose in broader society. Too often, such interference is a shortsighted effort to exploit public fears and passions of the moment for immediate political gain. The long-term costs to citizens are high because politically motivated intrusions into academic policy lead, in the long run, to educational mediocrity.

A good example is provided by the efforts in many states to dismantle affirmative-action programs in admissions, hiring, and financial aid decisions in public colleges and universities. This intensifying political pressure to narrow the criteria used in the admissions process to high school grades or standardized test scores could not only undermine the American university's historic role of serving all members of the society, but as well the diversity of educational experiences it is able to provide the future citizens of an increasingly diverse nation. And, if politics are allowed to influence admissions policies, will they also influence faculty hiring, the curriculum, and academic research as well?

To some degree, the changing political environment of the university reflects a more fundamental shift from issue-oriented to image-dominated politics at all levels, federal, state, and local. Public opinion drives political contributions, and vice-versa, and these determine successful candidates and eventually legislation. Policy is largely an aftermath exercise, since the agenda is really set by polling and political contributions. Issues, strategy, and "the vision thing" are largely left on the sidelines. And since higher education has never been particularly influential either in determining public opinion or in making campaign contributions, the university is left with only the option of reacting as best it can to the agenda set by others.

A Growing Tension

Higher education today faces greater pressure than ever to establish its relevance to its various constituencies in our society. For example, the increasing pace in the development and application of new knowledge, from laboratory to industry to marketplace, requires new types of partnerships between universities and industry. So too does the direct support of university activities by institutions in both the public and private sector. Our colleges are drawn into new and more extensive relationships with each passing day. Yet, at the same time, they are expected to act as an independent and responsible critic of society. Some contend that the university's consent to play an active, participatory role in society has saturated it with the backlog of society's problems, thereby jeopardizing its role as an island of intellectual freedom where all views are investigated without constraint.

The diversity—indeed, incompatibility—of the values, needs, and expectations of the various constituencies served by higher education poses one of its most serious challenges. The future of our colleges and universities will be determined in many cases by their success in linking together the many concerns and values of these diverse groups, even as the relationships with these constituencies continue to change.

The Environment for Change

All colleges and universities, public and private alike, face today the challenge of change as they struggle to adapt and to serve a changing world. An array of cultural, operational, governance, and political factors can inhibit change.

Cultural Issues

In business, management approaches change in a highly strategic fashion, launching a comprehensive process of planning and transformation. In political circles, sometimes a strong leader with a big idea can captivate the electorate, building a movement for change. The creative anarchy that characterizes the contemporary university poses quite a different challenge. Most big ideas from top administrators are treated with either disdain (this too shall pass . . .) or ridicule. The same usually occurs for formal strategic planning efforts, unless, of course, they are attached to clearly perceived and immediately implementable budget consequences or faculty rewards. As Don Kennedy, former president of Stanford, noted, "The academic culture nurtures a set of policies and practices that favor the present state of affairs over any possible future. It is a portrait of conservatism, perhaps even of senescence."[25]

This same resistance to change characterizes the response of the academy to external forces. For example, the higher education establishment has usually opposed new federal programs, including the GI Bill (the veterans will overrun our campuses), the Pell Grant program (it will open our gates to poor, unqualified students), and the direct lending program (we will be unable to handle all the paperwork). Yet in each case, higher education eventually changed its stance, adapted to, and even embraced the new programs.

Change occurs in the university through a more tenuous, sometimes tedious, process. Ideas are first floated as trial balloons, all the better if they can be perceived to have originated at the grassroots level. After what often seems like years of endless debate, challenging basic assumptions and hypotheses, decisions are made and the first small steps are taken. For change to affect the highly entrepreneurial culture of the faculty, it must address the core issues of incentives and rewards. Change does not happen because of presidential proclamations or committee reports, but instead it occurs at the grassroots level of faculty, students, and staff. Rarely is major change motivated by excitement, opportunity, and hope; it more frequently is in response to some perceived crisis. As one of my colleagues put it, if you believe change is needed, and you do not have a convenient big bad wolf at the front door, then you had better invent one.

Of course, the efforts to achieve change following the time-honored traditions of collegiality and consensus can sometimes be self-defeating, since the process can lead all too frequently right back to the status quo. As one of my exasperated presidential colleagues once noted, the university faculty may be the last constituency on Earth that believes the status quo is still an option. To some degree, this strong resistance to change is both understandable and appropriate. After all, the university is one of the longest enduring social institutions of our civilization in part because its ancient traditions and values have been protected and sustained.

Operational Issues

All of higher education faces a certain dilemma related to the fact that it is far easier for a university to take on new missions and activities in response to societal demand than to shed missions as they become inappropriate or threaten the core teaching mission of the institution. This is a particularly difficult matter for public universities because of intense public and political pressures that require the institution to continue to accumulate missions, each with an associated risk, without a corresponding capacity to refine and focus activities to avoid risk.

An example illustrates this. University presidents sometimes joke that the academic programs at the core of the university are a rather fragile enterprise, delicately balanced between two great and usually opposing forces on the modern university campus: the Department of Athletics and the University Medical Center. The high public visibility of intercollegiate athletics can sometimes distort the perception of the university and threaten its academic integrity. Furthermore, the financial challenges faced by health-care delivery, education, and research can threaten the financial integrity of a university, particularly if it happens to own a hospital system. Despite their differences in mission, financing, and intellectual content, intercollegiate athletics and academic health centers actually have some commonalities. Both reflect the evolution of the modern university to serve societal needs, that is, through public entertainment and health care. Both involve values and principles quite different from those governing academic programs, and both have been buffeted by an unprecedented degree and pace of change. And both can pose rather considerable threats to the university. Yet few universities have been able to take the actions necessary to reduce the risk associated with these enterprises, for example, by downsizing them, spinning them off, or building firewalls to better isolate their risks from the rest of the institution.

Much of the difficulty universities have in continuing to accumulate activities with consequent risk can be traced directly to governing boards. In fact, the two examples above, intercollegiate athletics and medical centers, probably cause the majority of the political problems with most governing boards. After all, all board members occasionally seek health care from doctors in the university medical center, who have been known to lobby hard on their agendas. Rare, indeed, is the university board member who is not drawn like a moth to the flame of intercollegiate athletics, by the public spectacle and the perks.

There are many other examples of risk accumulation—equity interest in spin-off companies, real estate ventures, economic development—all exposing the university to considerable risk, and all subject to strong political forces.

Governance Issues

Many university presidents—particularly those associated with public universities—believe that the greatest barrier to change in their institutions lies in the manner in which their institutions are governed, both from within and from without. Universities have a style of governance that is more adept at protecting the past than preparing for the future. The complex web of governance, from lay boards to complex relationships with state and federal governments to "shared governance" between the administration and the faculty, is awkward at best and certainly not conducive to decisive action.

The 1996 report of the National Commission on the Academic Presidency[26] reinforced these concerns when it concluded that the governance structure at most colleges and universities is inadequate. "At a time when higher education should be alert and nimble, it is slow and cautious instead, hindered by traditions and mechanisms of governing that do not allow the responsiveness and decisiveness the times require." The Commission went on to note its belief that university presidents were currently unable to lead their institutions effectively, since they were forced to operate from "one of the most anemic power bases of any of the major institutions in American society."

This view was also voiced in a study[27] performed by the RAND Corporation, which noted, "The main reason why institutions have not taken more effective action (to increase productivity) is their outmoded governance structure—i.e., the decision-making units, policies, and practices that control resource allocation have remained largely unchanged since the structure's establishment in the 19th century. Designed for an era of growth, the current structure is cumbersome and even dysfunctional in an environment of scarce resources."

Political Issues

Many universities find that the most formidable forces controlling their destiny are political in nature—from governments, governing boards, public opinion, or perhaps even their own faculty. Unfortunately, these bodies are not only usually highly reactive in nature, but they frequently either constrain the institution or drive it away from strategic objectives that would better serve society as a whole.

Private universities are generally more nimble, both because of their smaller size and the more limited number of constituencies that have to be consulted—and convinced—before change can occur. Whether driven by market pressures, resource constraints, or intellectual opportunity, private universities usually need to convince only trustees, campus communities (faculty, students, and staff) and perhaps alumni before moving ahead with a change agenda. Of course, this can be a formidable task, but it is a far cry from the broader political challenges facing public universities.

The public university must always function in an intensely political environment. Public university governing boards are generally political in nature, frequently viewing their primary responsibilities as being to various political constituencies rather than confined to the university itself. Changes that might threaten these constituencies are frequently resisted, even if they might enable the institution to serve broader society better. The public university also must operate within a complex array of government regulations and relationships at the local, state, and federal level, most of which tend to be highly reactive and supportive of the status quo. Furthermore, the press itself is generally far more intrusive in the affairs of public universities, viewing itself as the guardian of the public interest and using powerful tools such as sunshine laws to hold public universities accountable.

As a result, actions that would be straightforward for private universities, such as enrollment adjustments, tuition increases, program reductions or elimination, or campus modifications, can be formidable for public institutions. For example, the actions taken by many public universities to adjust to eroding state support through tuition increases or program restructuring have triggered major political upheavals that threaten to constrain further efforts to balance activities with resources.[28] Sometimes the reactive nature of the political forces swirling about and within the institution is not apparent until an action is taken. Many a public university administration has been undermined by an about-face by their governing board, when political pressures force board members to switch from support to opposition on a controversial issue.

Little wonder that administrators sometimes conclude that the only way to get anything accomplished within the political environment of the public university is by heeding the old adage, "It is simpler to ask forgiveness than to seek permission." Yet even this hazardous approach may not be effective for the long term. It could well be that many public universities will simply not be able to respond adequately during periods of great change in our society.

The Inevitability of Change

Yet, despite these challenges, throughout history American higher education has responded to meet the perceived needs—and opportunities—of American society. In the nineteenth century, our universities developed professional schools, then rapidly transformed themselves to stress the applied fields favored by the federal land-grant acts, such as engineering, agriculture, and medicine. In the post–World War II years, they reshaped themselves again, growing to serve the expanding educational aspirations of a growing society and developing an extraordinary capability in basic research and graduate education in response to federal initiatives.

Today, universities are evolving rapidly, responding once again to their perception of the needs of society. The knowledge-intensive nature of our society, the age of knowledge, is creating a knowledge-driven economy in which the activities of the university—creating, integrating, preserving, transmitting, and applying knowledge—have become more valuable than ever. New forms of organizations are evolving to conduct these activities, competing ever more intensely with the university in the global marketplace. In effect we are seeing the emergence of an international knowledge and learning industry that will challenge the traditional university. Some of the most prestigious and selective private universities may not feel pressure to change and may successfully resist these new competitive forces. However, most colleges and universities will find themselves in an increasingly competitive market for many of their traditional educational services. They will have to demonstrate anew that they are the best qualified to define the substance, standards, and process of higher education.

As we prepare for the second millennium of universities, let us remember that while the world will likely continue to need the traditional contributions universities are capable of providing, they will need far more than this from us in the future. And if we are not willing to meet these new needs, other institutions will almost surely evolve to do so.

There will, undoubtedly, be those among us who will resist change, arguing in favor of the status quo, the traditional mission and values of the university, and against any actions that might transform our institutions into what they believe would be inappropriate forms. What they do not see is that during a period of great change, it is usually far more dangerous to stand still than to risk innovation. To insist on the status quo could well run the risk of being bypassed by others, leaving our institutions to deteriorate in an impoverished, educational backwater that characterizes many universities in other parts of the world.

The choice before us seems clear. We can accept the challenge—and the risk—of transforming our institutions into new forms more appropriate to the age of knowledge. Or we can accept the near certainty of stagnation and decline as the capacity of our traditional universities to serve our changing world erodes.

The years ahead could represent one of the most exciting periods in the history of higher education, if we are willing to respond positively and creatively to the challenges, opportunities, and responsibilities before us. We must demonstrate that we are willing to take the actions necessary to serve a changing society, thereby earning the renewed commitment of all of our many stakeholders: students, parents, state and federal governments, business, and the general public.

PART 2 SIGNS OF CHANGE

CHAPTER 4

Education

Colleges have their indispensable office, to teach elements. But they can only serve us when they aim not to drill but to create; when they gather from far every ray of various genius to their hospitable halls, and by the concentrated fires, set the hearts of their youth on flame.

—Ralph Waldo Emerson, Phi Beta Kappa Lecture, Harvard University (1838) [1]

The most important mission of the university in America has been education. In a general sense, the university plays a role in providing each new generation of students with the opportunity to better understand themselves, to discover and understand the important traditions and values of our past, and to develop the capacity to cope with the complexity and change characterizing the world of their future. In this way the university has a civic purpose, to provide students with the knowledge and understanding to be good citizens and lead meaningful lives.

Beyond formal education in the traditional academic disciplines and professional fields, the university has been expected to play a broader role in the maturation of young students. The college campus provides a structured, secure environment where students can spend their first years away from home, both learning and preparing for life in a complex society. Yet, while two-thirds of high school graduates attend college, most do so not as residents but as commuters or correspondents (increasingly via the Internet). Only one-sixth of today's college students are enrolled in undergraduate programs on residential campuses.

We generally think of the education mission of the university as focused on undergraduate education. Yet the evolution of the educational mission of the American university during the past century has seen an increasing level of activity focused on graduate and professional education, and extension and continuing education. In fact, a quick glance at the balance sheet for any major university reveals that the majority of its resources—its faculty, its facilities, and its expenditures—are directed at the education, training, research, and professional services associated with graduate and professional degree programs. Hence, if we are to consider the array of complex issues facing the university as it performs its educational mission, we must do so within the broader context of these multiple educational roles.

Undergraduate Education

Perhaps because college has such a formative impact on our lives, coinciding with our intellectual and emotional maturation, we tend to view contemporary undergraduate education through the rose-colored glasses of our own experiences. The traditional image depicts college students as young adults, roughly between eighteen and twenty-two years of age, enrolled either in academic degree programs such as history or science or in professional programs such as engineering and business. They learn by going to classes, listening to lectures by professors, studying in libraries, writing papers, and taking examinations. They live in either campus-based residence halls or fraternities and sororities, participate actively in social and athletic activities, and are preparing themselves for good jobs while searching for mates.

Little wonder then that the range of concerns about undergraduate education can be disturbing. Have faculty really abandoned the classroom for their personal research agendas, subjecting students to unprepared teaching assistants, many of whom can barely speak English? Are students on our campuses out of control, overindulging in alcohol, drugs, and political activism? Are our young undergraduates subjected to indoctrination in the latest fads of political correctness and intolerance? And, perhaps of most concern, has a quality college education become so expensive that it is now priced out of reach of all but the privileged few—unless one is fortunate enough to be subsidized by a government-sponsored financial aid program?

Separating Myth from Reality

The Nature of Contemporary Undergraduate Education. As with many issues in higher education these days, there is far more myth than reality in both the traditional images of and the concerns about an undergraduate education. Less than 20 percent of today's college students fit the stereotype of eighteen- to twenty-two-year-olds living on campus and attending college full-time. Most college students are adults—in fact, one-quarter are over the age of thirty. They are not attending college to get away from home or grow up. Rather they see a college degree as the key to a decent job in a knowledge-driven society.

Because living in university-provided housing or Greek houses can be expensive, not to mention disruptive for family life and employment, the majority of undergraduates these days prefer to live in their own homes and commute to campus for their education. A great many students attend local community colleges for the first two years to save hard-earned dollars for upper-class studies at a four-year college or university. In fact, roughly 40 percent of today's college students cannot afford either the time or the funds to attend college full time and instead accumulate the education and the college credits necessary for a degree on a part-time basis. Needless to say, most of today's undergraduates take longer than four years to complete their degree; five years or more is typical.

Most of these students see a college education as critical to their future quality of life, the key to a good job, financial security, and well being. Most have definite career objectives, majoring in professional or pre-professional programs such as engineering, business, pre-med, or pre-law. While they may have strong academic abilities and enjoy learning, both financial and family responsibilities motivate a far more utilitarian approach to their education. Since the residential college experience is not as central to their lives, they seek a different kind of relationship with the university, much as they would other service providers such as banks or filling stations. They approach their education as consumers, seeking convenience, quality, relevance, and low cost.

Curriculum Wars. Perhaps also stemming from our nostalgia for our own college years is the belief that the quality of undergraduate education has deteriorated significantly in recent years. It has become fashionable to criticize the quality of the undergraduate experience provided by American colleges and universities. Some proclaim that the classical curriculum, once aimed at providing students with the knowledge of the great tradition of philosophy and literature necessary to become aware of the order of nature and one's place in it, has been replaced by a "democracy of disciplines" that offers no university-wide agreement about what a student should study.[2] Others are more strident, complaining that higher education has not only abandoned its commitment to undergraduate education, but its commitment to academic values as well.[3] The faculty is viewed as both underproductive and overpaid, and the curriculum is portrayed as barren of intellectual content or moral relevance. Critics propose a return to the golden years of undergraduate education decades ago when students were serious, faculties were dedicated, and a liberal arts education reigned supreme.

Yet, throughout the history of American higher education, the actual experience of students and faculty has been dramatically different from the grand designs of educators. In the early colonial colleges, undergraduate education was essentially professional training for the clergy or government service. It involved a kind of intellectual indoctrination, passing on yesterday's wisdom to tomorrow's leaders using a rhetorical tradition of rote learning. This only began to change with the emergence of the public university—particularly the land-grant university—which provided a broader spectrum of professional training and a new level of access to higher education. Throughout much of the early twentieth century, most undergraduates did not take the academic curriculum or their educational experience seriously.[4] Most learned far more from extracurricular activities than from their classes. A college education was not viewed as a serious intellectual affair.

The undergraduate experience became more rigorous following World War II, in part due to the impact of the returning veterans, adult students who took their college education far more seriously. The GI Bill reflected a qualitatively new attitude toward the benefits of higher education. In addition, as the population of baby boomers began to swell, there was an increased competition for admission to elite institutions, thereby focusing more public attention on academic quality. The growth of the research university also served to enhance the quality of the undergraduate experience through the increased scholarly requirements on faculty and the synergy of teaching with research.

Today the quality of undergraduate education in America's colleges and universities is arguably better than ever—and considerably better than that available for the general population in any other nation. Yet, while vastly improved over previous eras, undergraduate education has not improved as quickly or responded as successfully to society's needs as have faculty efforts in research. The changing needs of our society and expectations of our students demand an even greater effort to improve it.

To be sure, the philosophical battles continue within the academy over the content of the undergraduate curriculum. Some prefer the great books approach. As Bloom puts it, "Philosophy and liberal studies, in general, require the most careful attention to great books. This is because these are expressions of teachers such as we are not likely to encounter in person, because in them we find the arguments for what we take for granted without reflection, and because they are the sources of forgotten alternatives."[5] Others argue for a more inquiry-based approach, stressing an acquaintance with the principal ways by which the human mind apprehends the world—that is, methods of understanding and inquiring about literature, art, moral philosophy, history, economy, and society, as well as natural sciences. Still others prefer a cafeteria approach, achieving breadth by requiring students to take a certain number of courses in each of several diverse categories such as the social sciences, natural sciences, humanities, and arts, assuming that different disciplines have separate and valuable ways of apprehending the world and that requiring students to sample a wide variety will suffice to broaden their minds.

Yet, such curriculum wars may be largely beside the point. When alumni are asked what they really value in their college education, they almost never mention the curriculum or the subject matter of their courses, which fades rapidly after finals and graduation. Instead they remember the groups they joined, the teachers and students they met, the friendships they made. These memories of learning communities may be far closer to the real value of a college education than the arcane debates over the undergraduate curriculum. College for young undergraduates is as much a place to learn how to live as it is to live to learn.

The Purpose of an Undergraduate Education. What should be the aim of undergraduate education? Should we aim toward the lofty goals stated in the quote from Emerson at the beginning of this chapter? Or perhaps as Derek Bok, former President of Harvard, put it, the most important product of an undergraduate education in a changing, fragmented society may be "a critical mind, free of dogma but nourished by humane values."[6] To achieve this, we need a spirit of liberal learning, one that strives not just to impart the facts but to encourage and support our students in developing a philosophy of life.

A concept still quite relevant to undergraduate education but usually misunderstood is that of a liberal education. Today educators and others use the term to refer to everything from an education based on the great books to a broad but superficial survey of all of the liberal arts. Harold Shapiro defines a liberal education as "The need to better understand ourselves and our times, to discover and understand the great traditions and deeds of those who came before us, the need to free our minds and our hearts from unexamined commitments, in order to consider new possibilities that might enhance both our own lives and build our sympathetic understanding of others quite different from us; the need to prepare all thoughtful citizens for an independent and responsible life of choice that appreciates the connectedness of things and peoples."[7]

Although such a liberal education might be regarded as preparation for more specialized or professional studies—and, in fact, in Europe the role for providing such general education is assigned to secondary schools—it is actually available or sought by only a small fraction of college students, those who are fortunate enough to experience the intense intellectual environment of elite colleges and universities, where the shaping of mind and character dominates the educational philosophy. The college experience of most students tends to rely on mass-education methods, in which the transmission of knowledge and preparation for professional careers take precedence over the shaping of character.

To most students and parents, the purpose of a college education is to earn the college degree necessary for a good job, for personal economic security and well-being. Many of today's students approach their college education with very definite career goals in mind. They enroll with plans to become doctors or engineers or lawyers or teachers. While many will change their minds during their undergraduate years, almost all will emerge with quite specific career goals still uppermost in mind.

Employers reinforce this utilitarian approach. The recruiters companies send to campus are looking for very definite skills. Perhaps they seek something highly specific such as a particular undergraduate major or Internet navigation skills. Or perhaps they seek some evidence that the student can communicate well and work comfortably in a diverse environment. Students are extremely sensitive to these signals from the employment marketplace, and the experience other students have with job interviews and placements can have a very significant impact on their own educational plans. In sharp contrast, however, surveys of business leaders suggest that they seek something quite different than practical knowledge or utilitarian skills from college graduates.[8] They seek graduates who exhibit strong communication skills, a capacity for and commitment to lifetime learning, a tolerance for diversity, and an ability to adapt to change–characteristics more associated with a liberal education than a professional program of study.

In a sense, the university is caught between the contradictory forces of responding to more pragmatic goals of students and employers while providing the liberal education that equips a student with the broader skills important for good citizenship and a meaningful life. Furthermore, in a world of ever-changing needs, one objective of an undergraduate education certainly must be to prepare a student for a lifetime of learning. The old saying that the purpose of a college education is not to prepare a student for their first job but rather their last job still has a ring of truth.

To be sure, the notion of a liberal education for the twenty-first century will be different than that characterizing our times. There has already been a radical change in undergraduate majors over the past several decades. For example, today only 13 percent of undergraduates major in the humanities, 7 percent in the sciences, and 15 percent in the social sciences. Perhaps this is a reflection of the belief that students view today's post-modernized and deconstructed humanities programs as largely irrelevant to their lives; the sciences are far more relevant, but also far too difficult for those increasingly ill-prepared by their K–12 education; and the social sciences are seen as somewhat relevant and suitably soft.[9] Most of today's undergraduates prefer instead more professional and marketable majors such as business, accounting, and engineering. And the cafeteria curriculum favored by most universities provides them with the opportunity to cascade through a jumble of courses during their undergraduate studies without structure, rigor, or liberal purpose.

Where do we find Newman's classic vision of a college education that "includes the great outlines of knowledge, the principles on which it rests, the scale of its parts, its light and its shades, its great points and its little, so that it produces an inward endowment, a habit of mind of which the attributes are freedom, equitableness, calmness, moderation and wisdom?"[10] Certainly not in the undergraduate curriculum as taught and experienced on most campuses.

As difficult as it is to define and as challenging as it is to achieve, perhaps the elusive goal of liberal learning remains the best approach to prepare students for a lifetime of learning and a world of change. After all, a college education should prepare one for life, and a career is only one of life's experiences.

Teaching and Research. Next to the college curriculum, no aspect of university education has provoked more concerns than the balance between faculty research and teaching. It is widely believed by many that universities slight their students when they emphasize research in making faculty appointments and refuse to promote professors who are not productive scholars or research grant entrepreneurs, even though they may be highly successful classroom teachers.

And certainly there is an element of truth in these criticisms,[11] particularly in the American research university. The importance of academic research to national priorities has shifted somewhat the balance among the various activities of the faculty. The professionalization of the faculty and the dominance of the disciplines in determining faculty rewards have contributed to this shift, not to mention the pressures on the faculty to attract research grants. So too has the highly competitive faculty marketplace of the past two decades, which has increased the scholarly standards for appointment, tenure, and advancement. This climate helps to tip the scales away from teaching, especially the degree to which quantitative measures of research productivity or grantsmanship have replaced more balanced judgments of the quality of research and professional work. So too, the fragmentation of disciplines driven in part by increasing specialization of scholarship has undermined the coherence of the undergraduate curriculum. There appears to be a growing gap between what faculty members like to teach and what undergraduate students need to learn. [12]

As we consider the criticisms of the impact of research on education, it is important that we bear in mind several caveats. First, if undergraduate education suffers from research, we would expect to find the most negative impact in our nation's research universities. However, by most measures such as performance on standardized tests or career success, the "value-added" to undergraduate education provided by research universities appears to be at least comparable to—and in many cases, significantly better than—that provided by other types of institutions where research is not a high priority. Furthermore, the marketplace as reflected in the decisions of students, parents, and employers continues to suggest that research universities remain the institutions of top choice.

The second caveat follows from the observation that critics suggest that *all* universities do far too much research. In reality, however, most colleges and universities do little research. As we noted earlier, higher education is comprised of thirty-six hundred institutions, ranging from two-year and four-year colleges to comprehensive universities to research universities. Only a small number of these, certainly less than one hundred and arguably less than fifty, stress large-scale research, graduate education, and advanced professional training as the cornerstones of their many missions.

The relationship of research to teaching quality is far from obvious. Studies to examine the impact of federally funded research on undergraduate education were unable to find any quantitative evidence to support the supposition that, in general, strong emphasis on research by an institution hinders the quality of undergraduate education.[13] While it was certainly true that some universities strongly emphasize research achievement in promotion and tenure decisions, this philosophy has apparently not degraded the quality of their baccalaureate graduates compared to undergraduate colleges where teaching skills weigh more heavily in tenure decisions. To be sure, this study did not rule out the possibility that there were some institutions at which the emphasis on research had degraded the quality of undergraduate education, only that such a phenomenon was not strong and pervasive across higher education.

Perhaps part of the problem arises from the tendency to portray this as an issue of "research versus teaching." Certainly that is how the public and many within the academy have come to see the relationship. There are many who say that for faculty members to do one well, they have to slight the other. This is a simplistic and mistaken view. Teaching and scholarship are integrally related and mutually reinforcing, and their blending is key to the success of the American system of higher education. Student course evaluations suggest that more often than not, our best scholars are also our best teachers.

Hence the issue is not teaching versus research, but rather what is the proper balance between the two. After all, both activities are simply different manifestations of *learning*. And the most effective learning environments encourage both student and teacher to become involved in both forms of learning, in teaching and research.

Are Our Universities Ignoring Undergraduate Education? For some time now there has been a resurgence of efforts to reexamine and improve undergraduate education in our colleges and universities. One might explain this by saying that curriculum reform is cyclic, and the pendulum is now swinging back after the deconstruction of undergraduate curriculum stemming from student unrest in the 1960s. Clearly market forces are also at work. Perhaps universities are responding to criticism suggesting inadequate attention to the undergraduate experience. It could also be that the increasing costs of a college education and its value in a knowledge-intensive society have stimulated more attention from parents and public officials. Demographic shifts have also been a factor, first as our nation dipped through the downside of the postwar baby boom, and now as some regions of our nation face substantial growth in the population of college-age students. So too there is a growing awareness that the increasing needs of adult learners may require a significant change in the traditional paradigm for undergraduate education.

In another light the focus on undergraduate education could be part of a long-needed rebalancing of the priorities of our institutions. For several decades following World War II, most of our large universities focused their attention on building strong programs in the professions—developing high-quality schools of law, medicine, business, engineering, agriculture, and so forth. Perhaps this was due to a sense of public responsibility. Or perhaps it was due to the demand for these programs from both students and employers or the availability of funding for such efforts. Yet, the cornerstone of any distinguished academic institution is its undergraduate college. One could well make the case that undergraduate education and those intellectual disciplines that derive from these programs form the academic heart, the intellectual core of our institutions, and over a period of time will determine both the distinction of the university as well as the strength of its other endeavors in the professions, in research, and in service.

At many colleges and universities, steps have been taken to improve undergraduate education.[14] Faculty incentive and reward structures, including the evaluation for tenure, are being reshaped to place more emphasis on teaching. Faculties are working to make the undergraduate curriculum more coherent in the face of the fragmentation and specialization that now characterize the academic disciplines. Investments are being made to improve the quality of the learning environment—classroom, libraries, and laboratories—as well as to provide better counseling and guidance. More systematic attention is being given to important learning experiences outside of the classroom, such as undergraduate research, community service, and residential living-learning communities.

While this attention to undergraduate education is admirable, it is primarily aimed at improving the undergraduate experience within the traditional educational paradigms. Most efforts focus on improving teaching and learning within the context of the traditional degree program. Although a variety of learning activities are considered, including research, community service, and residential learning, the primary focus is on improving the classroom experience as the dominant pedagogical tool of undergraduate education. Unlike earlier times such as the 1960s, there are relatively few efforts to explore radically different forms of undergraduate education

It is impossible to say, therefore, that what is happening on our campuses today represents a revolution in undergraduate education. Many argue that we do not need a revolution, because, by and large, our universities are already doing a very good job at educating undergraduate students. Rather they suggest that what we need instead is a renewal of our commitments to quality in undergraduate education, stimulated by our sense of responsibility to our students and society and by our aspirations for excellence.

There are others, however, who believe that the present effort to improve undergraduate education through the existing model, while certainly well intentioned, cannot respond adequately to the changing needs and nature of our students nor our changing world. The true challenge before us may be to create a new paradigm of undergraduate education for a new century.

Shifts in the Undergraduate Paradigm

Despite the great diversity in colleges and universities, in learning environments, and in curricular content, most of us have a very specific notion of an undergraduate degree program. Stated in the most simplistic terms, this consists primarily of four years of study, divided into thirty semester hours a year, five courses per semester. These courses are selected to meet either the requirements of a particular area of concentration or major (e.g., psychology or physics or philosophy) or from more general survey courses designed to broaden one's education. Most of these courses are taught in a lecture format, augmented by occasional seminars, discussion sections, and laboratories.

This classroom form of pedagogy dominates learning at the undergraduate level. The teaching function occurs through a professor teaching a class of students, which in turn responds by reading assigned texts, writing papers, solving problems or performing experiments, and taking examinations. To be sure, the student might also take advantage of faculty office hours for a more intimate relationship, but this is rather rare for most students.

Yet the classroom paradigm is a rather recent form of pedagogy in the millennium-long history of the university. A more common form of learning through the centuries was via a one-on-one relationship, an apprenticeship. Both the neophyte scholar and craftsman learned by working as apprentices to a master. While this type of one-on-one learning still occurs today in skilled professions such as medicine and in advanced education programs such as the Ph.D. dissertation, it is simply too labor-intensive for most undergraduate education.

Furthermore, the university professorship is almost unique among the professions in providing little or no training in the fundamental activity of the profession, teaching. In fact, most graduate programs tend to assume that students learn how to teach simply by attending college rather than through formal training in pedagogical methods. Few faculty members have any awareness of the rapidly expanding knowledge about learning from psychology and cognitive science. Almost no one in the academy has mastered or used this knowledge base. One of my colleagues observed that if doctors used science the way that college teachers do, they would still be trying to heal with leeches.

The Digital Generation. The classroom paradigm is being challenged today, not so much by the faculty, who have by and large optimized their teaching effort and their time commitments to a lecture format, but by our students. Today's students are different from earlier generations. They are citizens of the digital age. They have spent their early lives surrounded by robust, visual, interactive media—not the passive broadcast media, radio and television, of our youth, but rather Nintendo, home computers, the Internet, MUDs and MOOs, and virtual reality. They learn by experimentation and participation, not by listening or reading passively. They take no one's word for anything. Rather they embrace interactivity, the right to shape and participate in their learning. They are comfortable with the uncertainty that characterizes their change-driven world.

For a time, such students may tolerate the linear, sequential lecture paradigm of the traditional college curriculum. They still read what we assign, write the required term papers, and pass our exams. But this is decidedly not the way they learn. They learn in a highly nonlinear fashion, by skipping from beginning to end and then back again, and by building peer groups of learners, by developing sophisticated learning networks. In a very real sense, they build their own learning environments that enable interactive, collaborative learning, whether we recognize and accommodate this or not.

However, their tolerance for the traditional classroom and four-year curriculum model may not last long. Students will increasingly demand new learning paradigms more suited to their learning styles and more appropriate to prepare them for a life-time of learning and change. There are already signs that the entire classroom experi-ence—that is, the transmission of knowledge content associated with courses—may soon be packaged through electronic media as a commodity and distributed to mass markets, much like today's textbooks. What will happen the first time a student walks into the dean's office and states: "I have just passed all of your exams after taking the Microsoft Virtual Physics course, developed by three Nobel laureates, rather than suffering through your dismal classes taught by foreign graduate teaching assistants. I now want you to give me academic credits toward my degree!"

Learning in the Age of Knowledge. The new interactive resources provided by emerging information technology represent the wave of the future for our society. As our knowledge base expands, isolated individuals will increasingly lose their ability to know everything they need to grapple with complex challenges. We must equip our faculty and students with the ability to exploit these new technologies. We must learn the difficult art of communicating across disciplinary and cultural differences in the pursuit of common goals, discovering which collaborative tools serve us best for our different purposes.

The reality of our new students, diverse and often technically savvy, requires new educational approaches. Encouragingly, our growing base of technology has begun to create the possibility of new, more flexible roles for both students and faculty, within and beyond the classroom. Richard Lanham calls the social, techno-logical, and theoretical challenges that these changes create an "extraordinary conver-gence," catalyzing fundamental shifts in higher education, allowing more interactive learning, and giving students the ability to interrogate or even create knowledge instead of simply absorbing it.[15]

The new knowledge media may fundamentally change what it means to be a professor and a student at our universities. Faculty may soon become more like coaches or consultants than didactic teachers, designing learning experiences and providing skills instead of imparting specific content. Even our introductory courses may take on a form now reserved for only the most advanced seminar classes, thereby allowing more personal interaction. Not only do these new technologies create educational opportunities, they also represent the literacy of our future. The medium of intellectual communication is in the process of evolving from the journal article to more comprehensive multi-media and even interactive documents. These shifts portend vast changes in the ways information is manipulated and interaction is structured in our society. Universities cannot call themselves successful unless they provide students with the fundamental skills they will require as they enter the world of the twenty-first century.

In these new learning paradigms, the word *student* becomes largely obsolete, because it describes the passive role of absorbing content selected and conveyed by teachers. Instead we should probably begin to refer to the clients of the twenty-first-century university as active *learners*, since they will increasingly demand responsibility for their own learning experiences and outcomes.

The intellectual structure of the learning process will become increasingly non-linear, allowing far more student control over the learning experience. The hyperlearning model proposed by Perelman[16] may be more typical of the learning paradigms of the future than today's classroom-based curriculum in which students move along together lockstep. In Perelman's model, learning consists of a number of learning modules or stations. Students employ the modules of their choice until a certain level of competency is achieved rather than competing with other students for a grade.

In a similar sense, the concept of a *teacher* as one who develops and presents knowledge to largely passive students may become obsolete. Today, faculty members who have become experts in certain subfields are expected to identify the key knowledge content for a course based on their area of interest, to organize this into a course, and then to present the material, generally in a lecture format, in this course. Frequently others, including graduate teaching assistants and professional staff, are assigned the role of working directly with students, helping them to learn, and providing them with guidance and counseling. In a future increasingly dominated by sophisticated educational commodities and hyperlearning experiences, the role of the faculty member will shift. In these new paradigms the role of the faculty member becomes that of nurturing and guiding active learning, not of identifying and presenting content. That is, they will be expected to inspire, motivate, manage, and coach students.

More specifically, faculty members of the twenty-first-century university will find it necessary to set aside their roles as teachers and instead become designers of learning experiences, processes, and environments. In the process, tomorrow's faculty members may have to discard the present style of solitary learning experiences, in which students tend to learn primarily on their own through reading, writing, and problem solving. Instead, they may be asked to develop collective learning experiences in which students work together and learn together, with the faculty member becoming more of a consultant or a coach than a teacher.

Learning Communities. Such learning communities seem better aligned with how learning really occurs in a university. The classroom paradigm is usually dominated by one-way information flow from the faculty member to the student. But learning is not simply information transfer. It involves a complex array of social interactions in which the student interacts not only with the faculty member, but with other students, the environment, and possibly objects as well, for example, books! The role of the university and the faculty is to facilitate the formation of learning communities, both through formal academic programs and through social, extracurricular, and cultural activities that contribute to learning in the university. When students and faculty join such communities, they share the ideas, values, and practices that lead to learning.

As Brown and Duguid suggest, we might even identify the value-added of the university as that of creating learning communities and then introducing students into these communities.[17] Undergraduates are introduced to communities associated with academic disciplines and professions. Graduate students and professional students are involved in more specialized communities of experience and expertise.

In true learning communities the distinction between teachers and students blurs. Both groups become active learners, working together to benefit each other. While this duality is commonplace at the level of graduate education, where graduate students frequently learn more about a specialized subject than their faculty advisors, it is far less common in undergraduate education. Yet, we have long known that some of the most significant learning occurs when one also serves as a teacher. Advanced undergraduates should be encouraged to assume such teaching roles, not only to other undergraduates, but even on occasion to faculty members themselves.

Teaching, Research, and Service. Today we see an important shift in education from a focus on teaching knowledge and skills to a focus on active student learning. Increasingly, learning occurs not simply through study and contemplation but through the active discovery and application of knowledge. There is a certain irony here. The contemporary university provides one of the most remarkable learning environments in our society—an extraordinary array of diverse people with diverse ideas supported by an exceptionally rich array of intellectual and cultural resources. Yet we tend to focus most of our efforts to improve undergraduate education on traditional academic programs, on the classroom and the curriculum. In the process, we may have overlooked the most important learning experiences in the university.

Think about it from another perspective. When asked to identify the missions of the university, faculty and administrators generally respond with the time-tested triad:

teaching, research, and service. Undergraduate education, however, is usually thought of only from the perspective of the first of these missions, teaching. Clearly, we should broaden our concept of the undergraduate experience to include student involvement in other aspects of university life.

For example, in most research universities there is an ever-widening gap between the research activities of the faculty and the undergraduate curriculum. Although research universities possess a rich array of intellectual resources, through their scholars, laboratories, and libraries, little of this is made available to undergraduates. We should challenge the American research university to develop new models of undergraduate education that take advantage of the extraordinary intellectual assets of these institutions. Perhaps every undergraduate should have the opportunity—or perhaps even be required—to participate in original research or creative work under the direct supervision of an experienced faculty member. The few students who have been fortunate enough to benefit from such a research experience usually point to it as one of the most important aspects of their undergraduate education; unfortunately most receive their education only through the more standard curriculum. Interestingly enough, many faculty members who have supervised undergraduate research projects also find it to be an exhilarating role, because undergraduate students are frequently more questioning and enthusiastic than graduate students!

There is ample evidence to suggest that student learning also benefits significantly from participating in community or professional service. Such activities provide students with experience in working with others and applying knowledge learned in formal academic programs to community needs. Many students arrive on campus with little conception of broader community values, and the experience of doing something for others can be invaluable.

Knowledge is created, sustained, and transformed in "communities of practice."[18] While there are numerous opportunities for volunteer community service at all universities, a more structured approach would better align these experiences with the goals of an undergraduate education. Such community or professional service might even be considered as a requirement for an undergraduate degree.

The undergraduate experience should be reconsidered from a far broader perspective, encompassing the multiple missions of the university. All too frequently each of the missions of the university is associated with a different component; a liberal education and teaching with the undergraduate program, research with the graduate school, and practical service with professional schools. In reality, all components of the university should be involved in all of its missions—particularly undergraduate education.

Lifelong Learning. Perhaps part of our difficulty in reconceptualizing the undergraduate experience is that we still tend to think of the baccalaureate degree as a well-defined learning experience that prepares a student for life. But today learning has become a lifelong activity. Today's students will need to continue to learn, through both formal and informal methods, throughout their lives.

Of course, a college education was never intended to provide all of the knowledge needed for a lifetime. But in years past, most of the additional knowledge necessary for a career could be acquired informally, through on the job learning or self-study. Today, however, both the rapid growth of knowledge and the multiple career transitions facing graduates demand a more strategic approach to lifetime learning. We need to rethink educational goals from this lifetime perspective. We should view undergraduate education as just one step—an important step to be sure—down the road of a lifetime of learning. This would allow us to better match learning content and experiences with both the intellectual maturation and the needs of the learner.

For example, primary and secondary education should focus on the development of fundamental skills in areas such as language and quantitative reasoning. Undergraduate education would prepare the student for lifelong learning, while providing the skills and competence to succeed in the workplace. The early years of one's career might be the time for experimentation, for risk taking, since it is frequently then that the most creativity occurs. Later in life, there may be more of an interest in and acceptance of the need for a liberal education, to enrich one's later years.

In a world driven by knowledge, learning can no longer be regarded as a once-is-enough or on-again/off-again experience. People will need to engage in continual learning in order to keep their knowledge base and skills up to date. Given this need, the relationship between a student/graduate and the university may similarly evolve into a lifetime membership in a learning community. Just as we have suggested that the word *student* is no longer appropriate to describe an active learner, perhaps the distinction between student and *alumnus* is no longer relevant.

The relationship between a university and its graduates that is more appropriate for our future is conveyed by the term *lifelong member of a learning community*. Enrollment should be viewed less as participation in a particular degree program and instead as a lifetime contract with the university, in which the university agrees to provide whatever learning resources are required by its learners or members throughout their lives, whatever, whenever, and wherever their educational needs. Clearly, the rapid evolution of distance learning technology will increasingly facilitate this. We also see increasing interest on the part of alumni in remaining connected to their university and to learning opportunities throughout their lives.

The Future of Undergraduate Education

So what is the future of undergraduate education? Clearly the classroom will not disappear. Nor will the residential campus experience of undergraduate education for young adults be overwhelmed by virtual universities or "edutainment." These traditional forms of pedagogy will remain valuable opportunities for learning for many in our population at certain formative times of their lives.[19]

These traditional models will coexist with new learning paradigms, providing a broader spectrum of learning opportunities in the years ahead. The transitions from student to learner, from teacher to designer/coach/consultant, and from alumnus to lifelong member of a learning community seem likely. And with these transitions and new options will come both an increasing ability and responsibility to select, design, and control the learning environment on the part of learners.

There will be strong pressures on universities to shift away from being faculty-centered institutions in which faculty determine what to teach, whom to teach, how to teach, and where and when to teach. Instead universities will likely evolve into learner-centered institutions, in which learners have far more options and control over what, how, when, where, and with whom they learn. This should not be surprising. In our increasingly democratic, market-driven world, the concerns of individuals/customers/clients have become the focus of most successful organizations.

The university will remain a place where future leaders are shaped and educated. The broader intellectual development of the young, preparing them not simply for careers but for meaningful lives as contributing citizens, will remain a fundamental purpose of undergraduate education.

Graduate Education

Graduate school is a term loosely used to identify those graduate programs in a university leading to the advanced degrees of master of the arts (M.A.) or sciences (M.S.) and the doctor of philosophy (Ph.D.). In some universities these programs are conducted and administered by a well-defined school of graduate studies; in others they are dispersed among the academic departments themselves. Many professional schools offer other advanced degrees such as the master of business administration (M.B.A.) and public health (M.P.H.) or the doctor of education (Ed.D.) and engineering (D.Eng.). The M.S. and Ph.D. degrees are usually distinguished from these other graduate professional degrees by more fundamental studies in the academic disciplines (as contrasted with professional training) and, in the case of the Ph.D., the requirement of performing original research leading to a Ph.D. dissertation.

Typically, the first two years of graduate study, sometimes associated with the M.A. or M.S. degree, are primarily comprised of formal courses, in either lecture or seminar format. Students intending to continue on to the Ph.D. are usually required to pass a comprehensive examination over the core material in their field, a so-called preliminary or candidacy examination. If they succeed in meeting course and examination requirements and are admitted to candidacy in a Ph.D. program, their remaining work consists of independent research under the supervision of a faculty member, their dissertation advisor. Note that during this period, graduate education becomes almost an apprenticeship, with a single faculty member providing most of the guidance for the dissertation research, not to mention control over the content and duration of the graduate student's remaining educational activities.

After the research is completed and the dissertation is written, it is then defended by the candidate before a faculty dissertation committee, the final hurdle before completing the Ph.D. The time required from initial entry to the program to final completion of the Ph.D. varies significantly from field to field, ranging from four to six years in the natural sciences and engineering to as much as ten years or more in the humanities.

Most students find graduate school one of the most intellectually stimulating and satisfying experiences of their education. Although the subjects they study may be esoteric, the mentoring relationship between student and faculty is more akin to the very practical approaches used in professional schools such as medicine. Under the tutorage of an experienced faculty member, graduate students are expected to develop the intellectual maturity to determine their own course of study, to set their own pace. They experience a very rapid sense of personal responsibility and control that sets graduate education apart from their undergraduate studies. The freedom to delve into a subject as deeply as one wishes can be both satisfying and rewarding— as well as unlikely to occur again in one's later career.

Our current paradigm of graduate education is based on an important yet fragile relationship between the graduate student and the faculty member that evolves from mentorship into collegiality. In the latter stages of their studies, many graduate students acquire knowledge in a narrow area that exceeds that of their faculty supervisor. At this point, the learning relationship changes from the master-apprentice nature of undergraduate education to the peer-to-peer relationship that characterizes collaborators and colleagues. Many faculty members will acknowledge that some of their closest friends were their graduate students. This is natural, since the bonds between the faculty and graduate students are strong in almost every discipline. Faculty members and their graduate students work together and learn together.

Graduate education introduces students to diverse roles in the academy, as students, teachers, scholars, and faculty colleagues. Graduate education can be a particularly enjoyable experience, since students can develop a true love of scholarship, drawing upon the reputation of their institution and their faculty mentors, without being subject to the other pressures of the academy such as grantsmanship or the achievement of tenure.

However, life as a graduate student is not without stresses, foremost among them being the concern about future employment. Like many of my faculty colleagues, my own graduate education occurred during the mid-1960s. While the post-Sputnik emphasis on science had attracted many of us into graduate studies, the Vietnam War and the end of the Apollo program brought a significant downturn in the job prospects for Ph.D.s. While the rumors of Ph.D.s driving taxicabs were a bit exaggerated, it nevertheless was a time of concern to new graduates.

It was a time much like today, when questions are being raised about the needs of our society for Ph.D.s and whether our doctorate programs are responsive both to the needs of graduate students and of society.

Growing Concerns

It is not surprising that during these times of challenge and change in higher education, the nature and quality of graduate education have also come under scrutiny. Traditionally the faculties and their universities prefer to focus concerns on the adequacy and nature of financial support for graduate education. Graduate students are more concerned with the job market for graduates and the time to obtain a degree. The federal government has expressed concerns about the number of advanced degrees relative to market needs and the high percentage of foreign graduate students.

But there are deeper and more troubling issues. The current highly specialized form of graduate education may no longer respond to the needs both of our students and our society. The attrition in many graduate programs has risen to unacceptable levels, with more than 50% of those who enroll in PhD programs failing to graduate (compared to attrition rates in law and medicine of less than 5%). Tragedies such as graduate student suicides and emotional instability suggest that the relationship between student and advisor may need to be reexamined. The increasing trend toward unionization of graduate student assistants on many of our larger university campuses suggests we may need to reconsider their broader role in supporting our university teaching and research.

The View of the Academy. Recent studies both by the national academies and government agencies confirm a strong consensus that graduate education in America represents the world's leading effort for producing the next generation of researchers. By conducting graduate education in the same institutions where a large portion of the nation's basic research is done, our research universities have created a research and training system that is one of the nation's great strengths—and the envy of the rest of the world.

Most faculty members strongly believe that graduate education is essential to the research enterprise. It is through the process of graduate students working closely with the faculty in collaborative research partnerships that we educate and train the next generation of teachers in how to create new knowledge. Some even suggest that the most important role of the federal government in graduate education is its support through research assistantships for graduate students, since this provides the most direct link between education and research.[20]

But there seems to be a growing sense that it may be time to rethink the way we are preparing a generation of students whose career paths may look very different than did the career paths of their mentors. Related, but not identical, is concern for the employment dilemma facing graduate students and the need to revise graduate education in accordance with the current and future job market.

Supply and Demand. The American system of graduate education evolved when the demand for research was either stable or rising. The national security demands of the Cold War and domestic priorities such as health care and the environment stimulated federal support of the academic research infrastructure, which drove similar commitments to graduate education. The annual production of Ph.D.s by American universities increased by a factor of four from the 1960s to the 1990s.

This situation is now changing. The end of the Cold War, the rapid growth of international competition in technology-based industries, and various constraints on research spending have altered the market for Ph.D.s. The three traditional areas of employment for Ph.D.s—universities, industry, and government—are all experiencing very significant changes which are likely to alter considerably their needs for individuals with research training. There is a growing concern that we need to reexamine the nature, capacity, and support of graduate education in America.[21]

Is there an oversupply of Ph.D.s? While unemployment rates for recent Ph.D.s have remained very low, there do seem to be far more graduates seeking faculty appointments than there are available positions. There are also some worrisome indicators of weakness in the marketplace, such as the substantially longer delays in the initial placement of new graduates. These signs suggest that the current oversupply of Ph.D.s—at least for the available university faculty positions—will continue and may well worsen in the near term should federal support of campus research decline.

There are already signs that in some fields the production of Ph.D.s far exceeds the availability of academic or research jobs. For example, the rapid growth in federal research funding in the life sciences over the past decade has driven a 42 percent increase in the annual production of Ph.D.s, now estimated to be almost 2.5 times the number that can be accommodated by the academic market.[22] As a result, an increasing number of doctorates find themselves in temporary positions such as postdoctoral appointments or part-time faculty or research positions. More specifically, only about 60 percent of Ph.D.s in the life sciences have permanent positions six years after graduation. The average life scientist is likely to be thirty-five to forty years old before obtaining his or her first permanent job.

What about the impact of foreign graduate students on the market? The quality of America's graduate programs has long served as a strong magnet for attracting outstanding international students. In fact, over the past decade, most of the growth in the graduate student population in American universities has been a result of the growth in the number of foreign nationals enrolled in these programs. The enrollment of domestic students has remained relatively flat or even declined in some cases.

Because of the advanced, highly specialized nature of American graduate training, many of these foreign students have been unable to find employment that takes advantage of their newly learned skills in their home countries. As a result, a significant fraction of U.S.-educated foreign nationals attempts to enter the American job market. While the domestic employment of these students represents an extraordinary human resource for this country—and a significant brain drain from their home countries—they do intensify considerably the competition for the limited job market for faculty and research positions. So too, the disintegration of the Soviet Union and Eastern bloc has triggered a mass exodus of talented scientists and engineers to the West. These have flooded the marketplace in many areas such as physics and mathematics.

Furthermore, the downsizing of the national defense effort, coupled with a reorientation of industrial research laboratories away from basic research toward product research, has reduced employment opportunities in the federal and industrial sector. It has released to the marketplace scientists and engineers formerly employed in these areas.

The Needs of the Broader Higher Education Enterprise. There has also been concern expressed about the relationship between the current model of graduate education in America's research universities and the broader needs of higher education. In his final letter to the membership of the American Council of Education, its past president Robert Atwell suggested that doctoral education, rather than the crown jewel of American higher education, may be at the root of many of our problems.[23] He suggested that the mismatch between doctoral education and the needs of the higher education marketplace is great. Too many faculty members in our research universities are out of touch with the mainstream of higher education—not to mention societal changes and fiscal realities. They go on trying to clone themselves in the persons of their graduate students to assist in their research. As a result, many new Ph.D.s who find jobs in nonresearch colleges become frustrated and often exert pressure on these institutions to become research universities—which implies, of course, offering Ph.D.s. Atwell contends that the research/graduate university paradigm has created a pecking order in American higher education that is out of touch with the needs of the nation and the academic marketplace.

Disciplinary Specialization and Cloning. Ph.D. students are expected to focus on a very narrow slice of disciplinary investigation in their studies and their dissertation. Although graduate students are expected to explore thoroughly and deeply a narrow intellectual area in their dissertation research, the hope is that in this process, they will acquire a powerful methodology for formulating and solving broader problems. In this sense, the purpose of doctoral education is to learn how to learn at a very sophisticated level. In a paradoxical sense, through such specialized inquiry, Ph.D. students acquire training that is well suited to broader investigation. Ironically, it is this specialist experience of the Ph.D. that provides training for a later role as an advanced generalist. Unfortunately, few Ph.D. students recognize this feature of graduate education, perhaps because few faculty members acknowledge or value it.

Many new Ph.D.s have far too narrow a set of personal and career expectations. They think that their graduate training has prepared them to solve certain highly technical and specialized problems. Of course, what they actually know that is of lasting value is how to formulate questions and partially answer them starting from powerful and fundamental points of view. Most do not understand that this is what gives them any edge they may have over young people of their own age who are already out in the workplace without Ph.D.s but with a several-year head start in experience.

Yet today's research problems are becoming increasingly complex, and their solution requires interdisciplinary teamwork. The training of new Ph.D.s currently is often too narrow intellectually, too campus centered, and certainly too long. The acceptance of overspecialization can result in a lack of both perspective and self-confidence. New Ph.D.s often believe themselves ill prepared to venture outside their specialty. This is due in part to the lack of serious requirements for breadth in the typical graduate curriculum. It is also due to the fact that there is little or no encouragement and a lot of implicit discouragement for one who wants to depart from the straight and narrow.

A Feudal System. The success of the United States basic research endeavor has relied to a large extent on individual effort, as reflected in the investigator-initiated grant process. This emphasis on individuals is strongly reflected in the promotion and tenure system at research universities. It is also reflected in our approach to graduate education. Ph.D. training is best described as an apprenticeship. Graduate students are expected to attach themselves early and tightly to individual professors. In fact, since many are supported by research grants, they are required to work on problems relevant to their faculty advisor's research grant with little opportunity to broaden their studies or their interests. In most universities, the faculty supervisor of a graduate dissertation becomes the primary determinant of the intellectual content, the duration, and the financing of the remaining education of the Ph.D. student, until the dissertation is written and the final dissertation defense is completed. In the best of circumstances, this final phase of graduate study can be very rewarding, since under the supervision of a skilled dissertation advisor, the graduate student learns the intricacies not only of basic research but also the trade of a faculty member. But this is also the point at which many of the problems arise.

Many faculty members have little experience in supervising graduate students, and abuses sometimes occur. In some cases, faculty members are simply not adequately concerned about or attentive to a student's progress. In other cases they may even wish to prolong a student's studies so that he or she can continue to contribute to a key research project of the faculty member. There are also great differences in the nature of the relationship between graduate student and dissertation advisor among the disciplines. For example, in science and engineering, graduate students generally work side by side in the laboratory with faculty advisors, interacting with them almost on a daily basis. By way of contrast, in the humanities, it is not uncommon for a graduate student to meet with a dissertation advisor only a few times a year, sometimes receiving very little guidance.

While the vast majority of faculty members regard the supervision of graduate students as both a significant privilege and sacred responsibility, there are inevitably cases of exploitation. Some faculty members adopt almost a feudal attitude, in which graduate students are regarded first and foremost as serfs to work on their research projects rather than as students seeking an education and a degree. As a result, some graduate students are seriously abused, required to perform menial tasks unrelated to their education, spending unnecessary years to get their degree, and tolerating the most excessive examples of faculty irresponsibility.

It is not surprising that students rarely complain about such abuses, since in most graduate programs, the faculty supervisor has ultimate control over the graduate student's ability to complete the degree and find employment. Universities have been extremely reluctant to interfere with this relationship between student and faculty supervisor, even when there is strong suspicion or possible evidence that significant mistreatment has occurred. Clearly there is a need to change the current model for graduate education, even if this encounters serious faculty resistance to keep the status quo.

Unionization. The increasing trend toward unionization of graduate student assistants on the campuses of American universities is driven primarily by economic issues and power relationships. But it may also stem in part from the abuse of graduate students that all too frequently occurs in our feudal culture of graduate education in which a single faculty member has complete authority over the academic progress, the career, and even the quality of life of a graduate student. Today sixteen of our largest university campuses have graduate student teaching assistant unions, including the Universities of Wisconsin, Michigan, and California, with more likely to follow in the years ahead.

Such efforts may not be in the best interests of students, however. Most faculty members are intensely loyal to their graduate students, guiding their research and professional development, and frequently securing grant funding to support their tuition payments, their living expenses, and their research activities. The faculty works hard to obtain funding for graduate education and pushes hard to make this a high priority for support by the university. Unfortunately, unionization brings both new players and a new adversarial culture into what should be a mutually beneficial and supportive relationship between the faculty and the graduate students. The union leadership negotiates the status of the graduate students directly with the university administration within the framework of collective bargaining. Ironically, both faculty and graduate students give up one of the most cherished values of the university, academic freedom, since everything can end up on the table during such negotiations—not just compensation and benefits, but also academic matters such as course structure, class size, and the selection of graduate students for teaching assignments. The confrontational nature of labor-management bargaining is orthogonal to the collegial, learning-centered relationship that should exist between graduate students and the faculty.

While unionization may be the wrong approach to addressing either the issues of graduate student welfare or faculty responsibility, it is important that we understand that this movement in part reflects the need for real changes in the nature of graduate education. The faculties of our graduate schools have a responsibility to face the shortcomings of our current graduate education paradigm, which all too frequently tolerates serious graduate student abuse at the hands of insensitive or irresponsible faculty supervisors. They need to understand and address the growing chasm between the education of graduate students and the contemporary university's increasing dependence on their labor as teaching and research assistants. To fail to recognize and address these shortcomings of the current feudal system of graduate education will damage it just as surely as imposing on it the alien culture of collective bargaining.

Postdoctoral Education. Of course, graduate education does not end with the Ph.D. In many fields, an appointment as a postdoctoral fellow in a university research laboratory has become not only commonplace but effectively a requirement for a later academic position. To be sure, there are strong intellectual reasons for postdoctoral appointments in some fields. Perhaps this level of advanced training and specialization simply cannot be achieved within a conventional Ph.D. program. Or an individual may need the experience of working with a senior scientist to learn not only advanced research techniques but also the ropes of grantsmanship. Postdoctoral appointments also allow young scholars to accumulate the publication record necessary for a more permanent appointment.

There are other reasons for the rapid increase in postdoctoral appointments seen in many fields over the past two decades—from 16,829 in 1975 to 35,379 in 1995.

We have already noted that in some fields such as the life sciences there is a current glut of Ph.D. production. As a result, although postdocs are supposed to be temporary, they have become a holding pattern for many young Ph.D.s who are unable to find permanent jobs in research or who need more time to assemble the kind of publishing record that such jobs now require. Many scholars spend five or more years in postdocs, frequently moving from one appointment to the next, in their unsuccessful search to find a more permanent appointment. This leads to what one scientist has called "the Laguardia effect, in which many recent graduates are circling in postdoctoral positions, burning up very important and useful intellectual fuel, and waiting for their turn to land in a permanent academic or research position."[24]

More significant, perhaps, is the role postdoctoral fellows play in the research enterprise. Unlike graduate students, postdocs have the sophistication to be highly productive in the laboratory or in a research group of senior scientists. They are highly motivated and work extremely hard, since they realize that their performance as a postdoc may be critical in attaining the faculty references necessary for further employment. And they are cheap, typically working at only a small fraction (20 to 30 percent) of the salary of a faculty member or research scientist. In fact, since most postdocs are not assessed tuition for their advanced training, in many institutions postdoctoral appointments are less expensive to support than graduate students.

Hence, it is not surprising that in many fields, the postdoctoral student has become the backbone of the research enterprise. In fact, one might even cynically regard postdocs as the migrant workers of the research industry, since they are sometimes forced to shift from project to project, postdoc to postdoc appointment, even institution to institution, before they find a permanent position. And, as with graduate students, they are all too frequently at the mercy of their faculty supervisor, with little university oversight or protection.

Most institutions make little effort to control the number or quality of postdocs, since these are identified, recruited, and supported through the efforts of individual faculty. (In fact, in recent surveys, some institutions did not even know the number of postdocs on their campuses.)[25] There are few institutional policies governing postdocs, such as compensation or benefit policies or time limits on appointments. Few institutions have job placement services for postdocs, aside from the efforts of their faculty supervisors. The lack of institutional oversight of postdocs, coupled with the evolution of postdoc education in a number of disciplines into a virtual requirement for a tenure-track faculty appointment, has created an unacceptable degree of variability and instability in this aspect of the academic enterprise.

The Fundamental Questions

The key issues swirling about graduate education can be summarized in a series of questions. First, what is the purpose of graduate education? Is it to produce the future researchers needed by our nation? Clearly, the current system of graduate education does this quite well. What about the role of graduate education in producing the future faculty needed by higher education? Some suggest that the current graduate education paradigm of the research university does not serve the majority of colleges and universities, which place far more emphasis on teaching than research. And what about the production of the next generation of scientists, engineers, and other disciplinary specialists? Should graduate education provide, in part, the educational background needed for other key professions in areas such as medicine, business, and law? There is a sense that an increasing number of students with advanced training in science and engineering are moving into other professional careers such as medicine, law, and business. Should our graduate programs be responsive to this?

Beyond the production of human resources, what role should graduate studies play in providing the labor necessary to sustain the research and teaching mission of the university through graduate research or teaching assistantships? Unfortunately, the size of many graduate programs in science and engineering seems to be determined less by national need or employability for Ph.D.s than by the graduate assistant needs of local research projects or instructional programs.

The majority of Ph.D. programs have traditionally seen their role as training the next generation of academicians, that is, self-replication. The process of graduate education is highly effective in preparing students whose careers will focus on academic research. But more than half of new Ph.D.s will find work in nonacademic, nonresearch settings, and our graduate programs should prepare them for these broadened roles. Most academic positions will be in colleges and universities that do not stress research.

How appropriate is the current graduate education paradigm for the broader range of careers available to graduates? The current system, stressing specialization and depth of investigation, is frequently accused of cloning the current cadre of research faculty. In particular, the specialized training provided their graduate students leaves them ill prepared for the broader teaching responsibilities of colleges primarily focused on undergraduate education.

What is the best way to fund graduate education? The research assistantship is clearly the preference from the faculty perspective, since it provides the principal investigator maximum control over graduate students. Yet, one might well argue that the fundamental purpose of graduate research assistantships should not be to provide cheap labor for research projects but to support graduate education.

The graduate fellowship has been the traditional alternative to research assistantships, although there have also been concerns about this form of graduate student support. These include whether graduate fellows are too disconnected from the research interests of faculty and whether the portable nature of these fellowships tends to benefit the most prestigious institutions (not to mention those with warm climates).

An interesting alternative is provided by the graduate traineeship. Here the principal distinction between *traineeships* and *fellowships* is that traineeship grants are made to university programs and departments for a specified purpose or program and then assigned to graduate students by the institutions. While traineeships have not been a major device for graduate student support in science and the humanities, they have been an important form of graduate student support in other areas, such as the health sciences, since they can allow a more carefully designed graduate experience.

Finally, what is the relationship of graduate education in research universities to the rest of the higher education enterprise? There is a sense among some that the research university—where most graduate education is conducted—is becoming increasingly detached from the rapidly changing higher education enterprise both in this country and abroad. In the past these universities have provided not only most of the faculty but most of the pedagogical models and curriculum content for higher education in America. Today, the relevance of the research university paradigm to the learning needs of our society is being seriously questioned.

An Agenda for Action

To address these challenges, we need to consider possible actions at various levels: the graduate department or program, the university, and the national level of the higher education enterprise.

The Department Level. Actions at the department or program level are likely to be most effective in responding to the challenges to graduate education. Although the issues of graduate program size and Ph.D. production are important, these are not generally issues addressed at the department level. Nor are the basic policies and regulations governing graduate education determined at this level. Rather, it is the culture of graduate education, determined primarily by the relationships between graduate students and the faculty, that is most directly influenced at this level.

It is at the department level that one needs to examine seriously the feudal system of graduate education that has evolved over the years. In particular, departments—and department chairs—must accept far greater responsibility for protecting the interests of graduate students in their relationships with faculty members in their roles as dissertation chairs, research project directors, or instructional supervisors. Such relationships are rarely reviewed unless formal grievances are filed. This benign neglect must be replaced by a culture in which department faculties as a whole accept more responsibility for the welfare of graduate students. A student's progress should be the responsibility of the entire department or program and not under the control of a single faculty advisor. The quality and character of faculty supervision of graduate students should be assessed on a regular basis. In those rare cases where abuse occurs, either because of faculty inexperience or temperament, there should be no hesitation in withdrawing the privileges of graduate supervision. New faculty members and graduate students should be educated concerning their rights and responsibilities in graduate education.

Departments should review carefully the degree to which the size of their graduate programs is determined by faculty capacity and employment opportunities, rather than by the need for graduate teaching and research assistants to meet instructional and research needs. Departments should be challenged to develop alternatives to graduate student assistants to meet these needs, such as the use of adjunct faculty to assist in teaching or permanent research scientists to meet the needs of research projects. The primary objective of graduate education should be the education of students. The value of activities such as work as research assistants or teaching assistants should be judged according to the extent that they contribute to a student's education.

Departments should be far more involved in providing both information about career opportunities and placement assistance to graduate students. While many professors already participate in efforts to place their Ph.D. graduates, there should be a broader acceptance of responsibility for placing graduates. Indeed, this might be one way to stress the importance of aligning Ph.D. training with society's needs. Graduate students should certainly receive more up-to-date and accurate information about career opportunities. This should not only be provided directly by the graduate program or department, but academic units should consider assigning a faculty member as an ombudsman for graduate placement. Perhaps each faculty member who accepts the responsibility of the chair of a dissertation committee should also be asked to accept personal responsibility for the placement of the Ph.D. student!

Most important—and most difficult—of all is to get the faculty to change both the values and expectations they pass along to their graduate students. The current system tends to replicate itself by producing graduates trained for increasingly narrow—and increasingly limited—academic and research roles, largely ignoring the broader interests of our best students, the increasing diversity of today's generation of students, and the complex and rapidly broadening roles in our society played by those with advanced degrees. The opportunities of the twenty-first century will be far different than that for which today's faculty members prepared during their own graduate studies. It will require far greater breadth in scholarship, a deeper commitment to teaching and service, and far greater adaptability.

The University Level. At the university level, there is clearly a need to encourage a broadening of Ph.D. requirements. While we must retain the paradigm of research training, the acknowledged strength of the current system, we must also implement changes if our academic institutions and their graduates are to make their optimal contribution to society. We need to develop doctoral programs that emphasize disciplines at the borders between fields, as well as programs that include interaction among scholars within different disciplines. Careful attention must be given to striking the right balance between training individuals capable of spanning fields and those with deep understanding of a highly specialized field. In a sense, we might well redefine the Ph.D. as the graduate analog of a liberal education, shifting it away from the cloning of the academy, and instead designing it to prepare an individual for a lifetime of learning.

It also seems clear that a greater number of job opportunities will be available to Ph.D.s who have experience and connections beyond the campus. To produce more versatile graduates, programs should provide options that allow students to gain a wider variety of skills. They should be discouraged from overspecializing. To this end, it is important that students be given a far more realistic perspective on the hiring market. In particular, they should have a better understanding of the kinds of experiences and training that nonresearch institutions seek in their new faculty.

Universities should develop integrative, practice-oriented degree programs in some fields in order to better respond to the needs of society, perhaps by redefining the master's degree or by instituting an alternative form of the doctorate. There has been strong national interest in making available internship experiences to graduate students.[26] Internship programs that provide students with experience in industry, government, or different types of academic institutions could prove useful in broadening graduate education. Teaching internships might also achieve this goal. Doctoral students interested in academic careers could spend a period on the campus of a different type of educational institution—perhaps a liberal arts college or a community college.

Yet another challenge at the university level is reducing the time to degree. The time required for the Ph.D. has steadily increased for the past several decades, in some cases doubling to over ten years. Universities, their graduate programs, and their faculties must accept the responsibility for reducing the time to degree. There have even been suggestions of a radically different approach, based on programs that establish a fixed time to degree. For examine, one might imagine all students beginning with a one-to-two year M.S. program that might also serve as a terminal degree for those interested in other professional careers such as law, business, or medicine. The Ph.D. itself would require two additional years of study including a dissertation (or a total of four years, including the M.S. degree) and suffice for most advanced positions in the public or private sector. Finally, for those students interested in careers in either the academy or basic research, further study beyond the Ph.D. would be achieved through postdoctoral studies. These studies would provide the highly specialized training needed to move to the cutting edge of research.[27]

Such dramatic changes would likely be highly controversial within the academy and would undoubtedly meet with the objection that there will always be considerable variation among programs and individuals in the time required to master a field and produce original research. Of course, one might also make the same argument about professional education in complex areas such as medicine, which long ago accepted fixed-period educational models. Instead of debating the issue, several graduate programs actually should develop and implement Ph.D. programs with fixed terms for study and then let the graduate student and employer market decide which is more appropriate and attractive.

The National Level. It has become increasingly clear that the forces within the university driving the production of Ph.D.s are decoupled from the marketplace. More specifically, there is little relationship between the supply of Ph.D.s and the demand for them. There are few internal or external incentives for graduate programs to reduce Ph.D. production. In most universities, the size of the Ph.D. programs and the consequent production of doctorates are driven primarily by the need for university teaching and research assistants. In science in particular, Ph.D. production is driven primarily by the level of research funding and not the needs of our society.

Rapidly reducing the size of graduate programs in those areas experiencing an oversupply of doctorates could prove disruptive to the research enterprise, but there are already calls for restraint in further growth of graduate education in some fields such as the life sciences. This will be difficult, since as long as federal funds for research continue to flow to departments, there will be pressure to expand Ph.D. production. Nevertheless, universities and federal agencies should work together to achieve a better balance between the size of graduate programs and the availability of employment opportunities.

There does not appear to be a compelling case for draconian limitations on foreign student enrollments in our graduate programs. Foreign Ph.D. graduates who remain in this country make significant contributions to the national interest. Furthermore, there is already some indication that the rapidly evolving economies in those nations sending the largest numbers of students to American universities are beginning to create major growth in job opportunities. As a consequence many foreign national doctorates, both new and experienced, are beginning to return to their home countries.

The way that we support graduate education has been of particular concern. The current research-driven paradigm tends to view graduate education as either a by-product activity, driven by the level of research funding, or as a source of cheap labor for research projects. Graduate students supported through research assistantships are forced to work on problems necessary for their advisor's research project but all too frequently unrelated to their dissertation topic. There are no incentives to reduce time to degree, particularly if the graduate student is making valuable contributions to the research project. Nor is there generally an opportunity for students to elect other courses or experiences to widen their horizons.

There is a need for a better balance among research assistantships, teaching assistantships, fellowships, and traineeships in the support of graduate education. To foster versatility, there should be broadening of the mechanisms for the federal support of graduate students. The shift from portable fellowships and traineeships to research assistantship as the predominant method of graduate student support in the early 1970s created a situation in which training is driven primarily by the needs of sponsored research projects. Perhaps a more balanced effort, utilizing training grants, fellowships, and research assistantships, would allow more flexibility in graduate education. The National Institutes of Health have long used well-designed training-grant programs to stress the development and support of graduate education in key areas. This paradigm should probably be used more frequently in other areas of graduate study.

The federal government can have a major impact on concerns such as time to degree by imbedding appropriate incentives in the peer review process indexed to the average time-to-degree experience of the academic program submitting the proposal. There needs to be a recognition that the support of graduate education should be the responsibility of all federal agencies that utilize research and employ individuals with advanced degrees.

The Need for a New National Policy

The research university has been extraordinarily successful in meeting the needs of our society for research and well-trained scholars and researchers during the past half-century. Yet today many of those needs have changed, and the role of the research university and the character of its activities in graduate education are being questioned.

Since federal policies played a key role in stimulating the evolution of the American research university in the decades following World War II, it is reasonable to expect there is an appropriate role for government in addressing some of the concerns about graduate education. There seems little doubt that the prosperity, security, and social well-being of our nation will continue to require an adequate supply of graduates with advanced degrees. It is therefore alarming to note that the United States has not had a definitive, coherent policy for human resource development related to graduate education for decades—since the massive efforts represented by the GI Bill in the 1940s and the National Defense Education Act in 1960s. Instead, the nation has drifted on autopilot, with its human resource development largely determined as a by-product of federal research-and-development programs rather than through a strategic consideration of national needs.

It seems imperative that the nation develop both a vision and a closely aligned federal policy concerning graduate education capable of responding to the contemporary and future needs of the nation.[28] This policy should be closely coordinated with parallel policies concerning research and technology development and deployment. It should be executed through federal programs that are sustained for a period sufficient to yield the necessary changes in the academic culture and to broaden the roles that those with graduate training will play in our knowledge-driven society. This policy should also respond to the changing nature of national needs and to the increasing diversity of the American people.

While there is a general consensus that the quality of graduate education in America has been second to none, there are signs of strain that will likely intensify. It is time that the faculty, our universities, and our national leadership to step up to the challenge and responsibility of developing a new set of policies, guidelines, and practices appropriate both for graduate education and for serving the changing needs of society in a new century.

Professional Education

One of the most important missions for the American university involves providing the advanced education necessary to prepare students for professional careers. The early colonial colleges stressed preparation primarily for the clergy or government service. Over the years, our universities have introduced an ever-increasing number of professional education programs to serve an increasingly complex society. Familiar professions such as medicine, law, and engineering now coexist with emerging professional areas such as knowledge management or health systems administration.

Although undergraduate education in the liberal arts remains the core mission of most universities, their commitment to professional education is considerable.[29] In fact, because of the very large size of many professional schools (notably engineering, business, law, and medicine) many universities devote a significant fraction, and in many cases the majority, of their faculty and financial resources to education in the professions.

The Place of Professional Education in the University

The Copernican view of the solar system of the university would place the liberal arts college and its core academic disciplines as the sun, the four inner planets as the most powerful professional schools—medicine, engineering, law, and business—and then a series of elliptical orbits for the remaining professional schools, depending upon their quality and priority within a particular institution. (Actually, some universities have evolved almost into a binary star system in which the medical center has assumed a size and financial importance almost comparable to that of the rest of the university. Some of my liberal arts colleagues suggest that a more appropriate astronomical metaphor would be that of the university as a star orbiting about a large black hole . . .)

Despite their central role, both undergraduate education and graduate education in the academic disciplines have strong professional characteristics in the modern university. This is true for those undergraduate degree programs intended to prepare students for professional careers, such as engineering, nursing, teaching, or business. It is also the case for "preprofessional" undergraduate majors designed to prepare students for professional programs at the graduate level such as premed or prelaw. Even traditional disciplinary majors are based on sequences of courses designed to prepare students for further graduate study in the field, that is, for possible careers as academicians or scholars. In this sense the contemporary university is strongly engaged in professional education and training. In reality, this is nothing new, since even the medieval university was based on the learned professions of theology, law, and medicine.

But there are some important differences. Because most professional education requires an ongoing relationship with the world of professional practice, professional schools tend to be closely coupled to the needs of society. Professional practice and service are usually expected components of the activities of both students and faculty. Further, since professional schools are so tightly coupled to practice, these schools tend to respond much more rapidly to changes in society. Good examples are provided by the dramatic changes that have occurred in medical and business schools in recent years.

The relationship between students and faculty is also somewhat different in most professional schools. Most professional school faculties take their responsibilities in preparing the next generation of professional practitioners very seriously. This provides these schools with a coherent intellectual focus, but beyond that, an espirit de corps that pulls students and faculty into tightly knit professional communities. This stands in sharp contrast to the loosely coupled enterprise characterizing the academic disciplines of an undergraduate college. As a result, surveys usually indicate that students enrolled in professional schools tend to be not only more highly motivated but more satisfied with their educational experience.

However, there are drawbacks to professional education as well. For example, the pressure on faculty to balance professional practice with teaching and scholarship can create unusual stress, particularly during the pretenure probation period. This is particularly pronounced in the health professions such as medicine, where there are intense pressures for faculty in clinical specialties to generate financial resources through their clinical activity.

So too the rapid growth of knowledge required for professional practice has overloaded the curricula of many professional schools. This has been particularly serious in undergraduate professional degree programs such as engineering, since the tendency is to include more and more specialized material at the expense of the liberal arts component of an undergraduate education. The knowledge overload has led to major restructuring of the curricula in many professional schools, notably medicine and business administration.

While many undergraduates continue directly on to graduate or professional schools, an interesting trend has developed in recent years at major research universities such as the University of Michigan. We now find that roughly one-third of our senior class applies for admission to law school. And the majority of these students will be admitted and will attend law schools across the nation. However many of these students never intend to enter practice as lawyers; instead they see a law degree as a ticket to careers in business and government. They understand that the baccalaureate degree, particularly in the liberal arts, is not sufficient to provide them with challenging careers, so they choose law to provide the further ticket to success.

Of course, law is not alone in attracting liberal arts graduates. Roughly 20 percent of our graduates will attend medical school. And another 20 percent will eventually attend business school, although usually after they have gained the experience in the workplace that is required by most programs.

This trend toward professional schools stands in contrast to the experience of the 1960s, in which graduate education in the academic disciplines was more popular. But today, graduate school is seen as narrowing rather than broadening one's opportunities. Further, the well-defined, time-limited curriculum of professional education is far more appealing than the long, uncertain period of study required for a graduate degree such as the doctorate.

However, this trend also raises an interesting question: If professional programs such as law and business have become, in effect, a graduate "liberal education" for students with far broader career interests, then perhaps the faculty of those professional schools need to rethink the nature of their educational programs. After all, the education of a public or corporate leader might benefit from a somewhat different educational experience than that designed to provide the skills for litigation. They might also require a somewhat different value system as well, where truth is not always negotiable and the bottom line is not always the dominant objective.

The Role of Professional School Faculty in the University

Most faculties in professional schools would acknowledge the important and central role played by undergraduate education and the liberal arts. Yet, particularly within public universities, professional schools have long-standing traditions and reputations comparable to those of liberal arts disciplines. Although there is always some academic bigotry, many faculty of professional schools work in fields closely aligned with the traditional academic disciplines and move across disciplinary boundaries with ease. Professional schools share a deep commitment to quality education and scholarship.

Most faculties in professional schools have the same strong, rigorous traditions of scholarship and teaching as faculty in the academic disciplines. Many faculty members in professional schools have educational backgrounds and degrees essentially indistinguishable from those of their liberal arts colleagues. Indeed, many are far more "liberally educated" than their highly specialized liberal arts colleagues. It has always seemed a bit odd—and ironic—that faculty members in the liberal arts sometimes look down on their professional school colleagues, treating them almost as second-class citizens within the university. In reality, these professional school faculty members are frequently among the most valued teachers, scholars, and citizens of the university.

It is also important to recognize that many professional school faculty members are quite interested in undergraduate education. Their unique experience as professional practitioners, coupled with their own scholarly training and interests, enables them to make important contributions to both undergraduate teaching and research.

The Future of Professional Education

Today's college graduates will face a future in which perpetual education will become a lifetime necessity since they are likely to change jobs, even careers, many times during their lives. To prepare for such a future, students need to acquire the ability and the desire to continue to learn, to become comfortable with change and diversity, and to appreciate both the values and wisdom of the past while creating and adapting to the new ideas and forms of the future. These objectives are, of course, those that one generally associates with a liberal education.

Unfortunately many students are rapidly channeled into specialized studies and training even as undergraduates because they choose to major in those professional programs conducted at the undergraduate level, for example, engineering, education, nursing, business administration, art, and music. And though many such undergraduate professional programs attempt to broaden the educational experience of their students through distribution requirements in the liberal arts, it is also the case that the rapidly expanding knowledge base of these professions adds more and more material to the professional training component of the curriculum.

Our graduate and professional schools are skillful in producing specialists of various kinds. While it is true that our knowledge-intensive world will need highly focused specialists, our ability to access specialized knowledge on worldwide knowledge networks, perhaps with the assistance of intelligent software agents, will likely allow breadth of education to become more valuable than depth in many professions. The age of knowledge will need broadly educated problem solvers who move easily across professional disciplines. Clearly, this will place a premium on a liberal education as preparation for further professional study.

One approach would be to simply shift all professional education and training to the graduate level, so that students would first be required to complete a liberal arts degree before entering a professional school. But such an approach faces obstacles. First, it would place a very substantial additional financial burden on the student. Second, such a shift would probably not be accompanied by a significant increase in the value of the professional degree as seen by employers, at least as measured by starting salaries.

The current approach to professional education requires the student to acquire a portfolio of knowledge that, it is hoped, will be useful later in professional practice. Certainly some level of basic training is necessary in order to be able to practice in highly skilled professions such as medicine or engineering. But what about business administration? Most entry-level positions in business will require few of the skills learned during an M.B.A. degree program and instead are frequently provided through on-the-job training programs. To be sure, the more formal knowledge and skills provided by a university education may well be valuable later in one's career, but perhaps it would be more efficient, both from the student's and the employer's perspective, to wait until certain skills are needed before acquiring the necessary education.

In a world of continual change, we should no longer assume that a professional education can provide sufficient knowledge to suffice for a substantial portion of a career. Perhaps we should rely more heavily on "just in time" education, practical knowledge provided in modules and perhaps even through distance learning paradigms to practitioners when and where they need it.

Such just-in-time education is becoming increasingly common in many professions. For example, many business schools now find their faculty more heavily involved in nondegree continuing education programs such as executive education than in traditional B.B.A. or M.B.A. programs. They find that learning in such programs is more efficient—the students are more mature and highly motivated. Furthermore, since both the students and their employers know more accurately the value of the program, they are far more willing to pay tuition levels that reflect the true cost.

One of the most significant implications of the age of knowledge is the need to continue to learn throughout one's life. Without such perpetual learning, many graduates will be swept aside by the rapid changes occurring in our world. This need for lifelong learning poses great challenges to higher education, since it is becoming increasingly clear that our old paradigms of campus-based degree programs will not serve this emerging need. Although many institutions have created separate educational divisions to serve adult learners—for example, extension, continuing education, lifelong learning—these have been viewed traditionally as lower priority activities.

Even today we see that the forces of change in our world will demand a perpetual commitment to learning, along with a merging of various educational levels and objectives—from broad general education to professional education to specialized training. In a very real sense, learning, working, and living will become increasingly woven together, inseparable in character and content. In this culture of learning, degrees as we currently understand and value them—particularly as tickets to opportunity—could well be replaced by more instantaneous measures of knowledge and skills. Instead the educational activities of the university would need to be more distributed over the careers and lifetimes of their students.

Renewing the University's Commitment to Education

The university faces the challenge of resolving several paradoxes related to its educational mission. Its primary mission should be developing human potential. Yet all too often it focuses on selecting rather than developing talent, designing its admissions policies and even its curriculum as a gauntlet to weed out and filter rather than develop the capacity of students to enroll in certain programs. Most universities are committed to creative scholarship and public service, yet few institutions have integrated these activities into undergraduate education.

Furthermore, the academy tends to reject scholarship or technology that might improve learning, particularly if this threatens familiar pedagogical paradigms. For all of the emphasis on research, universities have been reluctant to investigate their own educational activities with the rigor they focus on their research interests. And while they have played leading roles in developing the information technology that is now transforming our society, they have been slow to apply this to their own educational efforts. When finally challenged to address undergraduate education, the faculty tends to do so through arcane debates over curricular minutia rather than addressing the total student experience that provides the lasting value of a college education.

To be sure, the faculty must recapture control of the undergraduate curriculum, wresting it away from the Balkanized tyranny of individual departments, and instead basing it on what students need to learn rather than what faculty members prefer to teach. While the liberal arts in general and the humanities in particular will be important contributors to such an effort, they have no monopoly on wisdom in the contemporary universities. Many of the purposes of an undergraduate education—critical thinking, communication skills, judgment, and tolerance—can also be achieved through professional courses.

Yet the value of a college education extends far beyond the curriculum. It involves a complex set of experiences in a learning community, among students, faculty, and staff, supported by the rich array of intellectual resources and opportunities provided by the university. It depends upon personal relationships, some formal through academic programs, many informal through extracurricular or community experiences. And at the heart of the experiences and relationships offered by the university is a deep commitment to learning, a recognition that inquiry, discovery, and creativity should be the foundations for a university education at all levels, and that all members of the university community, whether students, faculty, or staff, are learners.

CHAPTER 5

Research and Scholarship

The solution of virtually all the problems with which government is concerned: health, education, environment, energy, urban development, international relationships, space, economic competitiveness, and defense and national security, all depend on creating new knowledge—and hence upon the health of America's research universities.
—Erich Bloch, Director, National Science Foundation, 1986

One generally thinks of the research role of the university as a more recent characteristic of higher education in the twentieth century. However, the blending of scholarship with teaching occurred first in European universities, and it was introduced into American higher education in the mid-nineteenth century. As the nineteenth century advanced, knowledge began to expand at a staggering rate, driven by new scientific methods and responding to the demands of the Industrial Revolution. Scholars returning to America from Europe brought a new vision of research and academic freedom to higher education. Throughout this era, as researchers became more specialized, departments were created in a great burst of energy to form the basic intellectual topography of the university that is familiar to us today.

The university, through on-campus scholarship and off-campus extension activities, was key to the agricultural development of the United States and then our transition to an industrial society. World War II provided the incentive for even greater activity as the universities became important partners in the war effort, achieving scientific breakthroughs in areas such as atomic energy, radar, and computers. During this period our universities learned valuable lessons in how to develop and transfer knowledge to society and how to work as full partners with government and industry to address critical national needs. In the postwar years, a new social contract evolved that led to a partnership between the federal government and the American university aimed at the support and conduct of basic research. This led to a new institutional form, the American research university.

The seminal report, *Science, the Endless Frontier,* produced by a World War II study group chaired by Vannevar Bush, stressed the importance of this partnership: "Since health, well-being, and security are proper concerns of government, scientific progress is, and must be, of vital interest to government."[1] At the heart of this partnership was the practice of federal support of competitive, peer-reviewed grants, and a framework for contractual relationships between universities and government sponsors. In this way the federal government supported university faculty investigators to engage in research of their own choosing in the hope that significant benefits would accrue to American society in the forms of military security, public health, and economic prosperity.

The resulting partnership between the federal government and the nation's universities had an extraordinary impact. Federally supported academic research programs on the campuses greatly strengthened the scientific prestige and performance of American research universities. The basic research produced on our campuses has had great impact on society.[2] The academic research enterprise also played a critical role in the conduct of more applied, mission-focused research in a host of areas including health care, agriculture, national defense, and economic development. It made America the world's leading source of fundamental scientific knowledge. It produced the well-trained scientists, engineers, and other professionals capable of applying this new knowledge. And it laid the technological foundations of entirely new industries such as electronics and biotechnology.

The American university continued to evolve and change throughout the postwar decades. Although the formation of new academic disciplines and professional schools slowed, the tendency toward specialization increased. Departments became more splintered, made up, in some cases, of loose confederations of faculty in rarefied subfields who had more in common with peers in their disciplines at other universities than with campus colleagues. Generous funding for the sciences also widened the gulf between the social sciences, the natural sciences, and the humanities.

The specialization within the academic disciplines, driven by the explosion in knowledge that occurred over the past century, was one of the most important trends in higher education. It allowed scholars and students alike to probe deeply into particular subjects, creating focused academic communities capable of coherent communication and debate. Today, however, as the speed of change increases, it has become more evident that we need to make basic alterations in the discipline-focused culture and structure of the university. New funding policies have made this even more imperative, as agencies move increasingly toward supporting more multidisciplinary teams of scholars. We have entered another period of rapid intellectual change in higher education.

All of these factors—changing national priorities, shifting intellectual currents, and the evolving character of the university itself—suggest that a primary mission of higher education in America, research and scholarship, is likely to change as well.

The Government-University Research Partnership

The basic structure of the academic research enterprise of the past half-century was set out in the Bush report some fifty years ago. The central theme of the document was that the nation's health, economy, and military security required continual deployment of new scientific knowledge and that the federal government was obligated to ensure basic scientific progress and the production of trained personnel in the national interest. It insisted that federal patronage was essential for the advancement of knowledge. It stressed a corollary principle: that the government had to preserve "freedom of inquiry," to recognize that scientific progress results from the "free play of free intellects, working on subjects of their own choice, in the manner dictated by their curiosity for explanation of the unknown."[3]

Since the federal government recognized that it did not have the capacity to manage effectively either the research universities or their research activities, the relationship became essentially a *partnership*, in which the government provided relatively unrestricted grants to support part of the research on campus, with the hope that "wonderful things would happen." And, indeed they did, as evidenced by the quality and impact of academic research.

Federal support was channeled through an array of federal agencies: basic research agencies such as the National Science Foundation and the National Institutes of Health; mission agencies such as the Department of Defense, the Department of Energy, the National Aeronautics and Space Administration, and the Department of Agriculture; and an assortment of other federal units such as the Departments of Commerce, Transportation, and Labor. In most cases, the mechanism used to support research was the merit-reviewed research grant, where faculty members submitted unsolicited proposals detailing the research they were interested in conducting. The funding agency then asked various experts, including peers of the investigators, to review the proposal and evaluate its quality and importance. Based on this review and available funding, the agency then decided whether to fund the work or decline the proposal. If the decision were to fund, a grant would be provided to the host institution for the support of the work, typically for a one- to several-year period.

Although grants arising from unsolicited proposals were the most common form of support, some funding agencies did approach select institutions with requests-for-proposals to conduct research directed toward specific needs. For example, NASA might seek a particular type of scientific instrument for a space mission, or the Department of Defense might need a better understanding of radar reflection from unusual aircraft wing geometries. Such procured research was usually provided through research contracts between the agency and the host institution rather than through relatively unrestricted grants.

The most common form of research support was through research grants to individual faculty—so-called single-investigator research grants. The grants would support a portion of the faculty member's salary; the wages paid to student research assistants and research staff; equipment and facilities; and incidental expenses such as travel, publications, and such. In addition, the grants would provide support for those institutional costs associated with the research that were difficult to identify on a project-by-project basis, termed indirect costs or overhead, at rates established through negotiation between the host institution and the federal government.

Although funding was also provided through research grants and contracts to larger groups of investigators, particularly through various research centers and laboratories supported by federal agencies, most funding was channeled directly to a single investigator or a small team of investigators. Hence, a culture rapidly developed on university campuses in which faculty were expected to become independent "research entrepreneurs," capable of attracting the federal support necessary to support and sustain their research activities. In many areas like the physical sciences, the capacity to attract substantial research funding became an even more important criterion for faculty promotion and tenure than publication. Some institutions even adopted a freewheeling entrepreneurial spirit, best captured in the words of one university president who boasted, "Faculty at our university can do anything they wish—provided they can attract the money to support what they want to do!"

Of course, there were many drawbacks to the research university culture. Faculty soon learned that the best way to attract funding for their research was to become as specialized as possible, since this narrowed the group of those likely to review their proposals to the few peers in the field. Universities encouraged faculty to seek more sponsored research support for a portion of their academic salary, thereby freeing up funds to hire more faculty members. As a result, many universities soon walked far out on the limb of dependence on sponsored research to support their faculty. In many fields, the pressures on faculty to generate research funding became extreme. And, understandably, many faculty soon became more loyal to their discipline—and their funding agency—than to their university.

Challenges to the Research Partnership

Although the Carnegie classification identifies 125 institutions as research universities, in reality there are fewer than 60 universities among the 3,600 institutions of higher education in America that would be truly identified as research/graduate-intensive. These institutions are the envy of both the nation and the world. A few years ago, a *New York Times* editorial referred to our nation's research universities as the "jewel in the crown" of our national economy. It went on to assert that university research "is the best investment taxpayers can ever make in America's future."[4]

In fact, in our increasingly knowledge-intensive society, the rate of return from investment in research is rising. While the average rate of return on capital investment in the United States today is roughly 10 percent to 14 percent, the private rate of return of R&D investment is estimated to be 25 percent to 30 percent. The social rate of return—the rate that accrues to society more generally—is estimated to be as high as 50 percent to 60 percent, roughly four times the rate for other types of investment.[5] In a recent survey, when asked to identify the one federal policy that could most increase the long-term economic growth rate, economists put further investment in education and research at the top of the list.

The importance of publicly financed scientific research on economic prosperity was made even more evident in a recent study of American industrial patents. It found that 73 percent of the primary research papers cited in these patents were based on research financed by government and nonprofit agencies. Such publicly financed science, the study concluded, has turned into a "fundamental pillar" of industrial advance and pays handsome dividends to society.[6]

If the good news is that our research universities are the strongest in the world—at a time when the benefits from R&D investment have never been higher—the bad news is there is a frightening sense of crisis at many of our nation's most distinguished campuses.[7] The signs of stress are everywhere.

The recent deluge of attacks on the academy has revealed a skepticism—indeed, hostility—on the part of the media and government toward higher education in general and the research university in particular. This has eroded public trust and confidence. The breakdown of mutual trust has led to increasingly adversarial relationships between universities and government as manifested in recent skirmishes over matters such as indirect cost reimbursement, scientific misconduct, and pressures to restrict the flow of technical information. In fact, some members of Congress have even ridiculed university research from time to time, e.g., the Golden Fleece award.

Forces from both outside and within the universities, like the rapidly escalating costs of research and public calls for greater attention to undergraduate teaching, are pushing toward a rebalancing of missions away from research and toward teaching and public service. The morale of academic researchers has deteriorated significantly over the past decade, due in part to the pressures and the time-consuming nature of the need to obtain and manage sponsored research funding and to the disintegration of a scholarly community within the university. As Charles Vest, president of M.I.T., put it, today the research university is overextended, underfocused, overstressed, and underfunded.[8]

What is going on here? To some degree, we may be seeing evidence of the increasing estrangement of the American public—and their elected representatives—from science itself. The gap grows even wider between the omnipresence of science in modern society and the scientific and technological literacy of the body politic. We also may be experiencing the same forces of populism that rise from time to time to challenge many other aspects of our society—a widespread distrust of expertise, excellence, and privilege. Unfortunately, many scientists, universities, and university administrators have made themselves easy targets for accusations of arrogance and elitism.

But something else may be happening that is illustrated by an interesting paradox. An analysis of research funding during the 1980s reveals that real R&D support increased at rates comparable to the 1960s, at roughly 6 percent per year. Yet the attitudes of the scientists themselves indicate a belief that there is serious underfunding. In 1976, 63 percent of those surveyed thought funding was adequate; in 1990, only 11 percent believed this.[9] In an effort to understand this discrepancy, the National Academy of Sciences and the National Science Foundation conducted during the mid-1990s a series of town hall meetings of faculty investigators at all levels, from beginning to experienced, on dozens of university campuses across the nation.[10] These discussions identified several important areas of concern.

The Erosion of Public Support

Faculty are concerned that the growing imbalance between revenues and expenditures in both state and federal government threatens to undermine investment in priorities such as higher education as governments struggle to meet short-term demands at the expense of long-term needs. These financial stresses are particularly threatening to the research university.

Federal outlays for R&D declined throughout most of the 1990s. The strength of the American economy in the late 1990s has allowed some reinvestment in federally sponsored basic research, particularly in the life sciences with major increases in the budget of the National Institutes of Health. However most federal research programs, particularly those conducted by mission agencies such as the Department of Defense and the National Aeronautics and Space Administration, have still not recovered to the level of the 1980s. Furthermore, there remains concern that discretionary domestic spending, research and education programs, and federal support of the research university are at some risk over the longer term as long as entitlement programs remain unchecked, particularly as the baby boom generation approaches retirement.

Cost Shifting

Another dilemma arises here. The constituencies served by universities seek to minimize the resources they provide while maximizing the services they receive. Each party wants more out of the university than it is willing to put in and seeks to leverage other contributors. Few of these constituencies seem to be able to perceive the university and its diverse missions. Most state and federal agencies picture the university only in terms of the part they perceive and interact with, e.g., research procurement or student financial aid.. This is particularly true in Washington, where each element of the federal government attempts to optimize the procurement of the particular products or services they seek from our universities. There seems to be little recognition that shifting federal priorities, policies, or support aimed at one objective will inevitably have an impact on other roles of our institutions.

Two examples illustrate the point: First, efforts to reduce the costs of federally sponsored research by imposing limits on indirect cost reimbursement rates are an example of cost shifting. While complex to calculate, indirect costs are nevertheless *real* costs associated with the conduct of federally sponsored research and must be paid by someone. Indeed, many of these costs are driven directly by the federal government through layer after layer of regulation, accounting, audits, and policy shifts. To put it in the starkest of terms, most universities have only one recourse in responding to federal efforts to pay less than the full costs of the research they procure: increasing student tuition and fees. If the federal government decides it wants to reduce federal research expenditures by several hundred million dollars by capping indirect costs, in reality it is asking students and parents to pick up this much of the tab for federal research projects, since this is the only alternative funding source for most universities.

The same can be said for cost-sharing requirements on federal grants. While there is a certain simplistic rationale behind such requirements—after all, cost sharing can be viewed as a kind of earnest money demonstrating the sincerity of the institution seeking the grant—they can have serious negative implications, since they usually result in the diversion of discretionary funds away from educational programs and into federally sponsored projects.

The Changing Role of the Faculty

While the benefit of the government-university research partnership to our society has been extraordinary, there has been a downside for the academy. The faculty reward system has evolved far beyond "publish or perish"; instead, grantsmanship, the ability of faculty members to attract sponsors for their research projects, has become a key factor in promotion and salary decisions. Pressures for success and for national recognition imposed on individual faculty members have led over time to major changes in the culture and governance of research universities. The system fosters fierce competition, imposes intractable work schedules, and contributes to a loss of shared purpose and collegiality. It drives research investigators to shift their commitments away from their institutions and their teaching and education responsibilities.

Some faculty members express their concern that the research university has become in effect "a holding company for research entrepreneurs." Many professors exhibit experience little identification with or loyalty to the institution, but instead view their research as part of a free market economy. We seem to have lost the institution-building philosophy of past federal research programs. There is particular concern that junior faculty are thrown far too early into the dog-eat-dog world of sponsored research grants. Further, it is all too easy for mature scientists to lose funding and fall permanently out of this competitive sponsored research marketplace. More generally the faculty believes they are deprived of the opportunity to do what they do best—thinking, dreaming, talking, teaching, and writing—by the daily pressures that force them to hustle contract research, manage research projects, and deal with government and university bureaucrats, all of which takes them out of not only the classroom but the laboratory as well.

Intellectual Forces

The curiosity-driven search for new knowledge and the publication of results in scholarly journals has become a one-dimensional criterion for academic performance and prestige. It emphasizes primarily publication activity and grantsmanship and all too frequently works against the synergy that should exist between research and education. Beyond that, the scientific method itself favors a reductionist process that depends upon greater and greater specialization to discover new knowledge.

While the social contract underlying the government-university research partnership was based on the premise of practical benefits to society, it was also based on a linear model in which basic research successively led to innovation, development, production, and societal benefit. In reality, however, the process of innovation and application is far less straightforward, involving a fusion of activities and ideas. There is less of a distinction between basic and applied research, since commercial application frequently enables basic research. In fact, benefit to society involves the integration of knowledge across many disciplines, just the type of activity that is falling through the cracks in the university reward system.

The Real Issue: Shifting Paradigms

The stresses on the academy in general and the research university in particular are driven once again by change. We are in the midst of several simultaneous paradigm shifts: in the character of the government-university research partnership, in the character of the university itself, and in the nature of scholarship itself.

A Shift in National Priorities

As we have noted in earlier chapters, the concerns about national security that stimulated the growth of the American research university have dissipated with the end of the Cold War. Many of the major investments in our national infrastructure including the research university were driven by the concern for national security in the era of the Cold War. Part of our challenge today is to understand and articulate the new national priorities that would motivate a continued investment in research. While our concerns are many—economic competitiveness, national health care, crime, K–12 education—it is not obvious how these can be addressed by our existing research infrastructure.

There is also great confusion about the appropriate balance between basic and applied research, or perhaps better stated, between curiosity-driven research stimulated by the interests of investigators and strategic research aimed at addressing national priorities. The nonlinear, interactive character of technology transfer from the research laboratory into application has also muddled the distinction between basic and applied, research and development, and university and industry.

Finally, there are growing concerns about the way that the federal government sets priorities and funds programs in these areas. The American research enterprise triad–research universities, national laboratories, and industrial research laboratories–is generally approached through the institutional structure of Congress where most committees and, therefore, budget decisions, are organized around specific mission-oriented agencies (e.g., defense, energy, health, and environment). While it certainly makes sense to attempt to redirect the entire American research enterprise to focus on new strategic objectives, to do so within a single committee or budget category could lead to a damaging distortion of our research capacity.

A Change from Partnership to Procurement

In recent years, the basic principles of the extraordinarily productive research partnership between the federal government and the research university have begun to unravel. Today this relationship is rapidly changing from a partnership to a procurement process. The government is increasingly shifting from being a partner with the university—a patron of basic research—to becoming a procurer of research, just as it procures other goods and services. In a similar fashion, the university is shifting to the status of a contractor, regarded no differently from other government contractors in the private sector. In a sense, today a grant has become viewed as a contract, subject to all of the regulation, oversight, and accountability of other federal contracts. This view has unleashed on the research university an army of government staff, accountants, and lawyers all claiming to want to make certain that the university meets every detail of its agreements with the government.

To be sure, we must all be concerned about the proper expenditure of public funds. But we also must be concerned about restoring the mutual trust and confidence of a partnership and move away from the adversarial contractor/procurer relationship that we find today. Surely, the most ominous warning sign for academic research is the erosion, even breakdown, in the extraordinarily productive fifty-year partnership uniting government and universities. Scientists and universities are questioning whether they can depend on the stable and solid relationship they had come to trust and that has paid such enormous dividends in initiative, innovation, and creativity. It is alarming that the partnership that has been in large measure responsible for our national prosperity and security should be threatened at the very moment when it has become most critical for our future.

A Shift in Attitudes toward Teaching and Research

In recent years, public attitudes toward the priorities of a university have shifted away from research and toward undergraduate education. The public acceptance that universities were expected to create as well as transmit knowledge, a consensus that supported strong investment in the scientific, technological, and scholarly preeminence of this nation, has begun to erode. There is a new devaluing of research for its overshadowing of undergraduate education. Society is beginning to question whether it should continue to pay for the faculty's preoccupation with esoteric research. Why should it tolerate the desire of individual faculty members to discover and apply knowledge to transform so many four-year institutions into self-declared "research universities" at public expense? The concept of professors as teacher-scholars has narrowed to the idea that most university faculty should be confined primarily to the role of teachers.

For decades, the conventional wisdom has been that research and teaching were mutually reinforcing and should be conducted together, at the same institutions by the same people.[11] For example, in 1996, the National Science Board recommended in a major policy statement that

> The integration of research and education is in the national interest and should be a national objective. To advance this goal, federal science and engineering policies should strengthen efforts to promote the integration of research and education at all levels and should support innovative experiments in this area. Confidence that academic research enriches the educational process at U.S. colleges and universities underpins public support for science and engineering. Federal science and engineering policies should promote public awareness of model higher education institutions and programs that have demonstrated leadership in strengthening the synergy between research and education.[12]

Higher education has long attempted to weave together research and education, particularly in making the case for public support of the research mission of the university. In reality, however, these two missions have usually been treated separately at the federal level. The Department of Education focuses its higher education efforts almost entirely on the financial aid programs designed to enhance access to education. Research agencies such as the National Science Foundation and the National Institutes of Health, along with various mission agencies such as the Department of Defense and the National Aeronautics and Space Administration, focus most of their attention on the support of research, much of it related to specific agency programs and national objectives. (A notable exception here is science education, which has long been a responsibility of the National Science Foundation.)

In reality, the research and education missions merge only on the campus itself. Doubts have been raised about the impact of the research university culture on education. Today the public and its elected leaders are asking many questions about the role of research within the university. Peter Drucker speaks for far too many public leaders when he states, "I consider the American research university of the last forty years to be a failure. The great educational needs of tomorrow are not on the research side but on the learning side."[13]

Why should the public pay for the faculty's preoccupation with research, particularly when this may come at the expense of their participation in classroom teaching? Why should certain universities receive substantial funding for expensive research facilities when many others struggle just to maintain adequate teaching space?

The Deification of the Disciplines

Academic disciplines continue to dominate the modern university, developing curriculum, marshaling resources, administering programs, and doling out rewards. It is understandable why faculty members tend to focus their loyalty on their disciplines instead of their home institutions. The formation of virtual communities of scholars using rapidly evolving information technology has accelerated this trend. Some fear we are losing the cohesiveness of a broad community of scholars. As we have built stronger and stronger disciplinary programs, we have also created powerful centrifugal forces that threaten to tear our university community apart.

To some degree this is a reflection of the dominance of a reductionist approach to teaching and scholarship over the past several decades. Perhaps buoyed by the startling success of twentieth century sciences such as physics and chemistry, there was an implicit assumption that even the most complex phenomena were governed by quite simple principles. Chemistry can be understood in terms of atomic physics, which in turn, is described by mathematical principles. Biological organisms can be reduced to the biochemistry of molecules. Feynman once suggested that the observation of nature through the scientific method is a bit like observing a complex game and trying to guess the simple rules.[14] Of course, in reality, scientific research is quite messy and frequently illogical, making many mistakes, following many blind leads. However, when we finally present or teach what we have learned, we generally try to make it all look very simple—and, we hope, very elegant as well.

The success of the reductionist approach to both scholarship and teaching has been one of the driving forces behind the increasing specialization in the academy. But it produces graduates with an exceptionally narrow view of the world. Even in science itself there has been a growing skepticism of the utility of such reductionism in many areas, along with an increasing respect for those with the capacity to integrate various disciplinary knowledge. Many today believe that the most important intellectual problems of our time will not be addressed through disciplinary specialization but rather through approaches capable of integrating many different areas of knowledge.

The Challenge of Interdisciplinary Scholarship

Concerns about the fragmentary nature of knowledge are not new. Calls for more fluidity in intellectual inquiry arose as soon as the disciplines began to form at the end of the nineteenth century, and some scholars cite evidence of "interdisciplinary" agendas in the work of Hegel, Kant, and even as far back as Plato and Aristotle. So why has today's effort to break down the barriers between the disciplines taken on special importance? In part, the new emphasis comes with the shifting nature of knowledge production. Never before has the speed of change itself become the central issue of intellectual life. Disciplinary configurations are changing so rapidly that departments have difficulty coping with new ways of seeing. Biology has evolved from the macroscopic to the microscopic, becoming more dependent upon fields such as physics and chemistry. Physics and astronomy have become more dependent upon engineering fields such as electronics and computers in acquiring and interpreting data. Literary criticism depends more heavily on fields such as anthropology and history.

At the same time, we can no longer ignore the importance of the knowledge we produce for the wider society. We began to realize the social impact of knowledge in the 1950s, but today information is replacing material objects as a primary economic and social force. We have made the transition from atoms to bits, from material goods to knowledge. In our increasingly complex, interdependent world, narrow answers will not succeed. The interdisciplinary momentum is not a fad, but a fundamental and long-term restructuring of the nature of scholarly activity.

Many major funding agencies have begun to shift away from the traditional disciplinary focus, fueling a rapid increase in the amount of federal support going to multidisciplinary teams of investigators instead of isolated researchers restricted to a single discipline. This is especially true in the natural and social sciences, but a nascent movement in this direction is also visible in the humanities. English departments, for example, have become fundamentally concerned with issues that affect our culture, examining, among other issues, how power and ideologies structure the way we see the world.[15] The complexities of internationalism challenge daily our attempts to define what we mean by the words *culture* and *world*, as national and cultural boundaries become more permeable and untidy.

Clearly, these small shifts are encouraging but not nearly enough. Far more is needed. Yet, our goal should not be to force scholars to conform to the new mantra of interdisciplinarity. Not all interdisciplinary endeavors are good; neither are all disciplinary efforts bad. High-quality interdisciplinary work will look different in different disciplines and even for different individuals in the same discipline. Despite the pressures, a few faculty stress simply doing interesting things—their research or teaching—instead of allowing themselves to be pigeon-holed into a discipline. These all-too-rare scholars often develop an intellectual span that not only carries them across disciplinary boundaries with ease, but also allows them to collaborate with colleagues from quite different fields. They are the potential seeds for a new and vibrant intellectual community—human connections between the isolated bulwarks of different departments.

For some pursuits, scholars may need to shift from the current "small think" to "big think." They may be able to overcome their lack of specialized knowledge, especially in areas like engineering and the sciences, when intelligent software agents roam far and wide, instantly and effortlessly extracting necessary details from networks containing the knowledge of the world. For some exceptional scholars, the solution may be appointments to university-wide positions. We will need to learn to value a diversity of approaches and develop a more flexible vision of faculty career paths. There should be places for eclecticism, places for extremely specialized research, and places for colleagues to learn from each other. We will need to learn to work both in isolation and in communities.

Cultural Constraints

Over time, we have seen a faculty performance evaluation system develop that strongly rewards specialization. We have developed a corporate style of faculty reward that uses very crude measures of faculty achievement, generally based on quantity of papers published or grants received rather than quality of scholarship, not to mention teaching. Furthermore, faculty promotion and tenure committees place great weight on the ability of faculty members to work independently. A faculty member soon learns that the best way to conform to this system, i.e., to produce more, is to specialize even further.

In a very real sense, we may have been forcing our faculty into narrow disciplinary roles because of our failure to develop more sophisticated measures of faculty performance and achievement. This is perhaps most evident in the way that we search for and hire new faculty by first defining highly specialized, discipline-based areas.

Until we start hiring people rather than filling positions, we are doomed to continue down this ever-narrowing path.

To be sure, there is a certain degree of clan instinct at work here. Most of us feel more comfortable belonging to a group, a tribe, a discipline. We often even define ourselves and one another by our disciplines rather than our own activities. "I'm a physicist. You're an historian." In a sense, we need our disciplinary cultures. This identification often leads us to resist interdisciplinary scholarship and teaching. In fact, our research proposal review panels and curriculum committees often look down on broader efforts as simply hodgepodge collections of watered-down material.

Yet there are a few among us who step back from the crowd and simply stress doing things—their research or teaching—rather than allowing themselves to be confined in a single discipline. It is a great challenge to the university to encourage such "doers" rather than just "belongers"—and to portray and protect their work so that it will be better accepted and tolerated by the disciplinary clans.

The sponsored research culture itself has reinforced this disciplinary rigidity in the past. For years, universities have been dominated by the single-investigator model of sponsored research, in which each individual faculty member is expected to secure whatever resources are necessary for research and graduate training in his or her narrow area. This pattern has diverted faculty from broad institutional goals and directed them toward personal and specialized career tracks.

Finally, it is also clear that there is a definite hierarchy of academic prestige—or, perhaps better stated, an intellectual pecking order—within the university. In a sense, the more abstract and detached a discipline from "the real world," the higher its prestige. In this ranking, perhaps mathematics or philosophy would be at the pinnacle, with the natural sciences and humanities next, followed by the social sciences and the arts. The professional schools fall much lower down the hierarchy, with law, medicine, and engineering followed by the health professions, social work, and education at the bottom. Of course, academic arrogance knows no bounds. As Lord Rutherford once stated, "All science is either physics or stamp collecting."

Clearly, within this culture of academic snobbery, the distinction of basic versus applied research becomes significant. In reality, however, the progression of basic knowledge from the library or the laboratory to societal application is far from linear, and the distinction between basic and applied research is largely in the eye of the beholder.[16] Furthermore, although scholarly reflective work has a certain elegant and refined appearance, at least when compared to the complex, confused, and occasionally messy way that innovative creativity is conducted, the intellectual content and importance of the latter is increasingly significant in a world in which the creation of what has never existed before becomes more valued than the analysis of what currently or has existed in the past. We must set aside our academic bigotry and recognize and value the intellectual achievements of those who think great thoughts, those who create important new things, and those who are simply great teachers, practitioners, or leaders. The contemporary university and our broader society depend on them all.

Some Ideas for Stimulating Intellectual Change

To be sure, the intellectual character of the university is dynamic. Achieving the appropriate balance between the disciplines and interdisciplinary teaching and scholarship, between basic and applied research, between analysis and creativity, is just one of the many intellectual challenges before the modern university. Yet, these are not new. The birth of, competition among, and disappearance of scholarly areas have always been a critical part of the university's history.

We must find ways to adapt the disciplines to a new reality that is intolerant of stasis and inflexibility. Departments are beginning to realize that if they do not learn to bend, they will surely break. The creation of a sustained dialogue is as important to most interdisciplinary work as it has been to the disciplines. Departments set standards, evaluate faculty, monitor quality, and provide the university as a whole with a sense of its overall mission. The goal should not be to eliminate these coherent dialogues but to open them up, encourage new foci, wider communities, and perhaps entirely new paradigms. In fact, many argue that departments may be the most promising organizational unit to guide the process of transformation. It is clear, however, that the university of the future will be far less specialized and far more interconnected through a web of structures, some real and some virtual, that provide both horizontal and vertical integration among the disciplines.

We already have a strong foundation of interdisciplinary work upon which to build in many of our universities. For example, the multiple offices that professors have in some universities are something of a standing joke (as well as a financial challenge). It is not unusual to see a calendar on a professor's door listing a different location almost every day of the week. Furthermore, there is already a considerable flow of resources across rather than through the disciplines in most universities. More specifically, the resources for education flow down along disciplinary lines; that is, to the schools and colleges, the departments and programs. The resources for scholarship flow across disciplines, since external funding agencies rarely respect disciplinary lines and tend to favor interdisciplinary research efforts. Furthermore, new proposals tend to win out over those that aim to sustain or strengthen ongoing programs. While this can be dangerously faddish at times, it also represents an ability to look forward and a growing capacity for phasing out efforts that have outlived their productivity.

Yet, while there is a balance in resource flow along and across the disciplines, other forms of power and authority are captured by and reinforce the disciplines.

The disciplinary departments control new faculty appointments, tenure and promotion decisions, salaries, and the allocation of discretionary resources. Despite these promising strengths, there are still examples of worn-out programs across the campus that manage to limp along, draining resources from more vital areas. And although some resources do flow across the disciplines, most other forms of power and authority here, as elsewhere, reside in narrow specialties.

Perhaps the most straightforward strategy would be to facilitate the creation within the university of alternative intellectual structures that are nondisciplinary in nature. These new units could then compete with conventional disciplines within a free-market system for funding, faculty, students, and perhaps even degree programs. Through this competition, the alternative intellectual structures could stimulate change in the disciplines—essentially a process of natural selection and evolution.

A caveat here: While encouraging the easy formation of such interdisciplinary efforts is important, so too is the recognition that they should be easy to discard when they have outlived their usefulness. We need to adopt different operational rules for different activities. For example, in the disciplines, in which tenure rests, the premise is usually that the discipline will be continued unless there is good reason for discontinuing it. Perhaps interdisciplinary activities should operate under sunset provisions, or at least the premise that they will disappear unless they can continually demonstrate their quality and importance.

Another possibility would be to use the challenge of building a more coherent undergraduate experience as an opportunity to draw faculty together. It has long been recognized that disciplinary specialization can fragment the undergraduate curriculum. Perhaps we could challenge faculty to come together to redesign the undergraduate experience, basing it on courses and other learning experiences involving teams of faculty. Rather than simply carving up the curriculum into small pieces for each faculty member, we could ask each member of the faculty team to master all of the components of the undergraduate education they are providing. After all, this is what we ask our undergraduates to do, isn't it? It could be an interesting opportunity for faculty members not only to work together across disciplinary boundaries, but also to broaden their own intellectual span.

The Need for a New Social Contract

As in our earlier chapters, the changing nature of research and scholarship once again suggests that the status quo is no longer an option for the American research university. As we enter the new century, there is an increasing sense that the social contract represented by the government-university research partnership simply may no longer be viable.[17] The number and interests of the different stakeholders in the university have expanded and diversified, drifting apart without adequate means to communicate and reach agreement on priorities. Political pressures to downsize federal agencies, balance the federal budget, and reduce domestic discretionary spending may reduce significantly the funding available for university-based research. Government officials are concerned about the rapidly rising costs of operating research facilities and the reluctance of scientists and their institutions to acknowledge that choices must be made to live with limited resources and set priorities.

While the research partnership has had great impact in making the American research university the world leader in both the quality of scholarship and the production of scholars, it has also had its downside. Pressures on individual faculty for success and recognition have led to major changes in the culture and governance of universities. The peer-reviewed grant system has fostered fierce competitiveness, imposed intractable work schedules, and contributed to a loss of collegiality and community. It has shifted faculty loyalties from the campus to their disciplinary communities. Publication and grantsmanship have become a one-dimensional criterion for academic performance and prestige, to the neglect of other important faculty activities such as teaching and service.

There has been a similar negative impact on the higher education enterprise, as faculties pressure more and more institutions to adopt the culture and value system of research universities. To put it bluntly, there are many more institutions that claim a research mission, that declare themselves "research universities," and that make research success a criterion for tenure, than our nation can afford. With hundreds of institutions seeking or claiming this distinction, the public is understandably confused. The immediate result is a further eroding of willingness to support or tolerate the research role of our most distinguished universities.

Furthermore, the government-university partnership has not adequately taken into account other key stakeholders in the scientific enterprise. Academic researchers often seem to place the support for the specialized pursuit of their self-initiated projects well above the importance of addressing the social and economic challenges of our nation. Others, however, including some in Congress, are beginning to view the persuasiveness of the research methods and its cost to taxpayers as a prerogative that faculty claim for themselves—almost an entitlement—regardless of the particular mission of the host institution or the importance of the research undertaking. They question whether the faculty is upholding its end of the social contract represented by the research partnership, since even curiosity-driven research is expected to benefit society over the long term.

Interestingly enough, other elements of the national research enterprise have faced similar challenges in recent years. Industrial research laboratories have had, and continue, to engage in a thorough reexamination of their past effectiveness and their present relevance to corporate goals. Federal research laboratories have had to reconsider and refocus their missions, particularly in the wake of the end of the Cold War. The academic sector is just beginning this agonizing but inevitable reappraisal.[18]

Something else may also be happening, however. We may be seeing a shift in public attitudes toward higher education that will place less stress on values such as "excellence" and "elitism" and more emphasis on the provision of cost-competitive, high-quality services—from "prestige-driven" to "market-driven" philosophies. For the past half-century, the Bush paradigm of the government-university research partnership has been built upon the concept of relatively unconstrained patronage: The government provided faculty members with the resources to do the research they felt was important in the hopes that this research would benefit society in the future. Since the quality of the faculty, the programs, and the institution was felt to be the best determinant of long-term impact, academic excellence and prestige were valued.

Today society seems reluctant to make such long-term investments, preferring instead to seek short-term services from universities. While quality is important, even more so is cost, since the marketplace seeks low-cost, quality services rather than prestige. The public is asking increasingly, "If a Ford will do, then why buy a Cadillac?" It could be that the culture of excellence, which has driven both the evolution of and competition among research universities for over half a century, will no longer be accepted and sustained by the American public.

Rather than moving ahead to a new paradigm, we may find ourselves returning to the paradigm that dominated the early half of the twentieth century—the land-grant university model. Recall that a century and a half ago, America was facing a period of similar change, as we left behind an agrarian, frontier society for the industrial age. At that time, a social contract was developed between the federal government, the states, and public colleges and universities designed to assist our young nation in making this transition. This social contract was best manifested in the series of land-grant Acts and contained the following commitments: First, the federal government provided federal lands as the resources to fund higher education. Next, the states agreed to create public universities designed to serve both regional and national interests. As the final element, these public or "land-grant" universities accepted new responsibility to broaden educational opportunities for the working class while launching new programs in applied areas such as agriculture, engineering, and medicine aimed at serving an industrial society.

Today our society is undergoing a similarly profound transition, this time from an industrial society to a knowledge-based society. Hence it may be time for a new

social contract aimed at providing the knowledge and the educated citizens necessary for prosperity, security, and social well-being in this new age. Perhaps it is time
for a new federal act, similar to the land-grant acts of the nineteenth century, that
will help the higher education enterprise address the needs of the twenty-first century.

Other national priorities such as health care, the environment, global change,
and economic competitiveness might be part of an expanded national service mission for universities,[19] forming the basis for a new social contract. Institutions and
academic researchers would then commit to research and professional service associated with such national priorities. To attract the leadership and the long-term public
support needed for a valid national public service mission, academics would be called
upon to set new priorities, collaborate across campus boundaries, and build upon
their diverse capabilities.

Of course, a twenty-first century land-grant act is not a new concept. Some have
recommended an industrial analog to the agricultural experiment stations of the land-
grant universities. Others have suggested that in our information-driven economy,
perhaps telecommunications bandwidth is the asset that could be assigned to universities much as federal lands were a century ago. Unfortunately, an industrial extension service may be of marginal utility in a knowledge-driven society. Furthermore,
Congress has already given away most of the bandwidth to traditional broadcasting
and telecommunications companies.

Frank Rhodes, former president of Cornell University, has taken a somewhat
different approach by observing that the land-grant paradigm of the nineteenth and
twentieth centuries was focused on developing the vast natural resources of our nation.[20] The agricultural and engineering experiment stations and the cooperative extension programs were enormously successful. Today, however, we have come to realize
that our most important national resource for the future will be our people.

A land-grant university for the next century might be designed to develop our
most important resource, our human resources, as its top priority, along with the
infrastructure necessary to sustain a knowledge-driven society. The field stations and
cooperative extension programs could be directed to the needs and the development
of the people in the region. While traditional professional fields would continue to
have major educational and service roles and responsibilities, new interdisciplinary
fields should be developed to provide the necessary knowledge and associated prob-
lem-solving services in the land-grant tradition.[21]

In an era of relative prosperity in which education plays such a pivotal role, it
may be possible to build the case for new federal commitments. But certain features
seem increasingly apparent. New investments are unlikely to be made within the old
paradigms. For example, while the federal government-research university partner-

ship based on merit-based, peer-reviewed grants has been remarkably successful, this remains a system in which only a small number of elite institutions participate and tend to benefit. The theme of a twenty-first century land-grant act would be to broaden the base, to build and distribute widely the capacity to contribute both new knowledge and educated knowledge workers to our society, not simply to channel more resources into established institutions.

Second, although both Congress and the White House seem increasingly confident in the strength of our economy, they are unlikely to abandon entirely the budget balancing constraints that many believe contributed to today's prosperity. Hence, major new investments via additional appropriations seem unlikely. However, there is another model, provided, in fact, by the 1997 Budget Balancing Agreement, in which tax policy was used as an alternative mechanism to invest in education.

An example illustrates one possible approach. Suppose the federal government were to provide a permanent R&D tax credit to industry for those research and development activities undertaken jointly with public universities in special research parks. The states would commit to matching the federal contributions, perhaps by developing the research parks and assisting their public universities in building the capacity to partner with industry. The participating universities would not only agree to work with industry on projects of interest, but would restructure their intellectual property ownership policies to facilitate such partnerships. Participating universities would go beyond this to build the capacity to provide more universal educational opportunities, perhaps through network-based learning or virtual universities. Universities would also agree to form alliances, both with other universities as well as with other parts of the education enterprise such as K–12 education and workplace training programs.

This is but one example. There are many others. But the point seems clear. At the dawn of the age of knowledge, it may be time for a new social contract, linking together federal and state investment with higher education and business to serve national and regional needs, much in the spirit of the land grant acts of the nineteenth century.

Preserving a National Resource

American universities have always responded to the needs and opportunities of American society. In the nineteenth century they responded to the federal land-grant acts with the establishment of professional schools and the development of applied knowledge in essential areas. In the post–World War II years, they responded again by developing a thriving capability in basic research and advanced training in response to the federal initiatives embodied in the Bush report, *Science, the Endless Frontier*.

This is not at all surprising, considering the individualistic, entrepreneurial nature of the faculty and the loosely coupled, dynamic organizational structure of universities. We can argue that these institutions have taken on far too many missions as a result, but we cannot deny that they do respond to the opportunities and challenges presented by society. Today, universities are evolving rapidly, responding once again to their faculties' perception of the marketplace.

But there is a danger here. While they may not like it, the faculty is remarkably sensitive to the criticisms voiced about the academy: too much emphasis on research over teaching, too many Ph.D.s and not enough jobs, the need for a shift toward more applied activities. And they are responding, quite rapidly, to adapt to this brave, new world. Just survey any group of junior faculty members.

There are already signs of concern. The key drivers of prosperity in a knowledge-driven economy are factors which contribute to innovation such as federal R&D expenditures, the production of R&D personnel, the share of our GDP spent on secondary and tertiary education, steps taken to protect intellectual property, and international openness.[22] All of these increased in the 1980s, which some believe lay the foundation for our remarkable national prosperity during the 1990s. Yet the indicators for each of these areas point downward during the 1990s, which raises serious concerns about the continued growth of our innovation- and technology-driven economy in the decade ahead.

The world and the structure of academic research have changed greatly since Vannevar Bush wrote his report. However, the major principles he advanced merit reaffirmation. Now more than ever before, the national interest calls for an investment in human and intellectual capital. As Bush so clearly put it, the government-university partnership is not simply about the procurement of research results. It is also about nurturing and maintaining the human strengths of a great technological nation and sowing the seeds that will ultimately bear fruit in new products and processes to fuel our economy and improve our quality of life.

We need to sound the wake-up call to America sufficiently loudly and clearly that our faculties can hear the reverberations, before the American research university has evolved into some new paradigm, perhaps responding to other societal needs, but no longer with the capacity to respond to our intellectual needs. While it may indeed be time to develop a new social contract that rebalances the priorities given to education and research, we must not lose the capacity of our nation's research universities to produce the new knowledge necessary to respond to national needs.

The research partnership between the university and the federal government continues to be a relationship of great value to our nation and the world. The American public, its government, and its universities should not surrender the long-term advantage of this research partnership because of a short-term loss of direction or confidence. At a time when many of society's other institutions do not seem to be working well, the research university is a true success story. We must get that message across to the American public. We must re-articulate and revitalize the remarkably successful partnership that has existed between our government, our society, and our research universities over the past half-century.

CHAPTER 6   Service to Society

Perhaps in no other particular is the contrast between the old college and the new university more marked than in the close relation of the university, and especially the university in the West, to the public and to the schools. It is not easy for us to realize how great an extent the college of 50 years ago was isolated from the public. By the great mass of common people it was regarded as the home of useless and harmless recluses, of the mysteries of whose life they knew nothing and for whose pursuits they cared nothing. But we all know how conspicuous most of the universities have been in recent years. They have abandoned their monastic seclusion. They have sought to make their aims and their life known to the public and to interest all classes of men in their welfare. Public and private generosity thus rival each other in the hearty support of the universities which have had the wisdom to dedicate themselves with all their resources to public service.

—James Burrill Angell, President,
The University of Michigan (1874)[1]

Service to society and civic responsibility may be the most unique themes of higher education in America.[2] The bonds between the university and society are particularly strong in this country. Historically our institutions have been responsible to and shaped by the communities that founded them.

Our colleges and universities, their curricula, their research and professional programs, their outreach activities, have all evolved to serve a civic purpose.[3] These social institutions are a primary societal mechanism for the creation, preservation, and dissemination of knowledge through their instructional and research activities. But our universities are also expected to distribute and apply this knowledge to serve society. And one of the most important mechanisms for this broader civic role is the mission of public service.

Public service, the transfer and application of the knowledge of the university to serve specific needs of society, has long been an important mission of the American university. From the earliest days of higher education, lead by educators such as Ezra Cornell and Charles Van Hise, and implemented through federal and state programs such as the Morrill Land-Grant Act and the Wisconsin Idea, universities were expected to respond to the particular needs of society.[4]

As we have noted earlier, there is an evolving social contract between the university and the society it serves. The public supports the university, contributes to its financing, accepts its scholarly and professional judgment, and grants it a unique degree of institutional autonomy and scholarly freedom. But in return, the university has an obligation for impartial scholarship, high professional integrity, a commitment to the development of the human resources represented by its students, and a sensitivity toward the need for its services in society at large. For all its independence and autonomy, the university has a social responsibility and a public obligation. Public service is just such a major institutional obligation, and universities must be prepared to provide the means and incentives to pursue this role.

Public service is the extension of the research, teaching, and professional expertise of the faculty. The support of universities, both public and private, through general taxation implies particular service responsibilities, and the commitments that such institutions are willing to assume for society cannot remain implicit. The public has the right to ask how public universities are responding to its needs, and these institutions have an obligation to provide a clear answer.

Today's universities are more heavily involved than ever in public service activities, ranging from economic development to health-care delivery to public entertainment (e.g., intercollegiate athletics). Yet, in a world of intense economic competition, technological change, and social complexity, demands that they do even more to serve the public continually besiege universities. This growing demand for our services may be one of our greatest contemporary challenges. Increasingly, the public's willingness to support higher education tends to be determined not by the value placed on its traditional missions of teaching and scholarship, but, rather, by the perception of direct and immediate benefit through its public service activities.

The Nature of Public Service

The term public service in higher education usually triggers images of outreach and extension, of regional systems such as the Cooperative Extension Service, massive medical centers, lifelong learning programs, community economic development, and a host of other activities specifically designed to respond to public needs. Many universities have developed major organizations staffed with professionals to conduct these activities, sometimes with only peripheral ties to academic programs.

While public service might best be defined in its broadest sense as those activities, including teaching and research, that benefit the public at large, it is more often defined more narrowly. Public service, in this restricted sense, consists of those activities that are aimed at serving the needs of society as dictated by an agenda set by the public and its representatives, rather than the institution itself. Public service in this context is primarily a *responsive* activity, designed to react to societal needs, rather than a proactive effort that is aligned with the primary academic objectives of the university.

Another common restricted definition construes public service as work that draws upon one's professional expertise—an outgrowth of one's academic discipline. This includes applied research for an external client, consultation and technical services, clinical work or performance, or instruction within continuing education programs. In this sense, public or "professional" service is an applied version of teaching or scholarship.

While there continue to be complaints that higher education is unresponsive to the needs of society, quite the opposite is true, since the competitiveness of American universities causes them to pay close attention to their constituencies. This intense desire to respond has led many institutions to reallocate limited resources away from their primary responsibilities of teaching and research in an effort to generate more direct public awareness and support. By attempting to respond to unrealistic public aspirations and expectations, to be all things to all people, higher education has whetted an insatiable public appetite for a host of service activities of only marginal relevance to its academic mission. A quick glance around any community with a local university provides numerous examples of this, from extension offices for continuing education to medical clinics to incubation centers for high-tech business formation to athletic camps for K–12 students.

Yet such responsiveness to the needs—indeed, even the whims—of society by higher education may in the long run be counterproductive. Not only has it fueled an inaccurate public perception of the primary mission of a university and an unrealistic expectation of its role in public service, but it has also stimulated an increasingly narrow public attitude toward the support of higher education. Powerful forces of parochialism compel institutions to spread themselves ever more thinly as they scramble to justify themselves to their elected public officials. Faculty and administrators alike feel under intense pressure to demonstrate their commitment to public service, even when they recognize that this will frequently come at the expense of their primary academic missions.

Many faculty members are concerned that much of university public service is simply not linked closely enough to its academic mission. But this may be in part a matter of definition, for it is clear that a very wide range of university activities do benefit both the campus and the public alike. For example, universities benefit the public directly through their libraries and museums (preservation of knowledge), their theaters and concerts (provision of cultural experiences), intercollegiate athletics (entertainment for the masses), their custodianship of the young, and a host of direct services including hospitals, testing laboratories, publishing companies, hotels and restaurants, and so on. While not an "extension service" in the traditional sense, these activities certainly provide important services to the public.

The basic functions of the university continue to be core academic activities. Other major activities of the university gain legitimacy only to the degree that they are linked with education and scholarship. In this sense, public service that is based on teaching and research is not a *function* but one of a number of *principles* that animate and guide the basic work of a university.

However, we should consider broadening the traditional definitions of the teaching and research mission of the university such that they take on more of a service character. The teaching function must be able to respond effectively to the major changes now occurring in society. The graying of America, the increasing fraction of our population comprised of underrepresented minorities, the need for lifelong learning in the face of rapid technological change, all of these factors demand an expansion—indeed, an extension—of the traditional teaching function of the university. Similarly, while basic research will continue to be the cornerstone of the university's quest for knowledge, there will continue to be a growing need for applied research to respond to the very real needs of society. As the time between fundamental discovery and application continues to shrink in many fields, the distinction between basic and applied research rapidly loses its relevance. It is essential that these research activities be integrated with the teaching mission of the institution.

There is little doubt that the need for and the pressure upon universities to serve the public interest more directly will intensify. The possibilities are endless: economic development and job creation; health-care; environmental quality; the special needs of the elderly, youth, and the family; peace and international security; rural and urban decay; and the cultural arts. There is also little doubt that if higher education is to sustain both public confidence and support, it must demonstrate its capacity to be ever more socially useful and relevant to a society under stress.

As we enter the age of knowledge, the traditional articulation of the mission of the university as a triad of teaching, research, and service may be too narrow. We need to consider more contemporary forms of our fundamental mission of creating, preserving, integrating, transferring, and applying knowledge.[5]

An Example of Public Service: The Academic Medical Center

Education in the health professions—medicine, dentistry, nursing, pharmacy, and public health—has been an important mission of comprehensive universities in America. Many universities own and operate hospitals to support their teaching and research efforts in the health sciences; others have developed affiliations with community hospitals to serve as sites for clinical training.

Beyond this teaching and research role, the American university has long played a major role in the delivery of health care. Teaching hospitals have evolved into complex health care centers and systems, offering a broad range of services. The changing nature of health care delivery and costs stimulated both major growth and concentration of health care services in these centers to the point where many have become comparable in size to their host university.

Perhaps no other area of public service of the modern university has experienced such powerful forces of change—and required so much of the time and attention of university leaders—as health care. The academic medical center is both the largest and most complex component of the contemporary university, engaging in education, research, and clinical care, all on a scale that dwarfs most other university programs. The profound changes in the ways in which medical education is provided, medical research is conducted, and health care is delivered and financed poses great challenges both to these centers and to their host universities.

The medical curriculum has already undergone profound change with the explosion in technology-intensive medicine and the shift from macroscopic biological sciences, such as anatomy and physiology, to microbiology and molecular medicine. The rapid growth of the scientific knowledge base associated with medical practice has overloaded the traditional lecture format. Many medical schools have moved to more integrated programs in which medical students are involved at an early stage with clinical practice, developing the investigative tools to seek the necessary knowledge as they need it.[6] The research enterprise also has become far more expensive and competitive, with the need for complex laboratories and highly trained technical staff.

Today, we find that most academic medical centers are under great stress because of the changing nature of the marketplace for health care. The rapid growth of managed care organizations—that is, payment not for clinical services but rather on a fixed basis for maintaining the health of each individual—capitation—has dramatically changed the nature of health care financing. The marketplace has become intensively competitive because of both an excess of hospital capacity and the entry of for-profit organizations. Because their teaching function, tertiary clinical mission, and their service to indigent patients add as much as 25 percent to their cost structure over local community hospitals, many academic medical centers face serious financial challenges today that threaten their very survival. The marketplace will not subsidize expensive research, teaching, or clinical innovations.

In simple terms, what is really occurring is a shift in the risk associated with providing health care.[7] In the past, the "fee for services" payment system placed most of the risk on third-party payers, such as the federal government or insurers. Physicians and patients focused on the quality of health care rather than the costs, since others picked up the tab. Managed care shifts the risk from third-party payers to health-care providers. Managed care organizations negotiate a fixed cost per person, regardless of the costs of their medical treatments. The burden is placed on health-care providers to manage the costs of maintaining the health of the "managed lives" in the contract. In most academic medical centers, this risk has been borne initially by the hospitals.

It is increasingly clear that for teaching hospitals to survive, they must have freedom to control their costs—to operate like a business—with attention given to the bottom line, even if this conflicts on occasion with their teaching and research mission. In particular, most teaching hospitals are taking a far more aggressive stance toward negotiating physician services from their associated medical schools. In reality, they are seeking to shift the risk associated with health-care costs once again, this time to the clinical faculty and the medical school. And the implications, for both medical schools and their host universities, are serious indeed.

For decades, medical schools have been viewed as among the most prosperous academic units on their campuses. Medical school faculties earn salaries considerably larger than those of other schools—in the case of clinical specialties such as surgery or radiology, several times larger, in fact. Medical school facilities are both extensive and expensive. And medical school faculty includes some of the most aggressive entrepreneurs on the campus, with extensive outside interests, for example, consulting or spin-off companies.

Medical schools have become, however, rather fragile enterprises financially. Although our nation's medical schools had expenditures in 1995 of more than $30 billion, only about 10 percent to 20 percent of their revenues came from secure sources such as tuition, endowment earnings and gifts, or state support.[8] Another 20 percent of their support came from sponsored research grants and contracts. The remainder, about 50 percent of medical schools' aggregate revenues, came from clinical activities, either payment for the clinical services provided by their faculty or direct payments from teaching hospitals.[9] It is this clinical income that is at most risk as the health-care industry is restructured.

The changes driven by the marketplace have been wrenching. It has been clear for some time that there is an imbalance between the needs of our society for physicians and the production of new health care practitioners by our medical schools and teaching hospitals. In most specialties, there is an oversupply of physicians, which is likely to become worse as an increasingly competitive marketplace drives down costs, closes hospital beds, and focuses health-care increasingly on the prevention, rather than treatment, of disease. Although the rate of 17,000 new M.D.s a year graduated by our medical schools is in rough balance with total physician needs, the more significant number is the 25,000 new residents produced each year by our medical centers. The difference between the two is due to foreign-educated physicians being educated in medical specialties, although sometimes these are U.S. citizens who receive their training from foreign medical schools.

There is also a significant mismatch between the focus of most medical centers in producing specialists and the primary-care physicians needed by our society. In managed care, primary-care physicians become revenue producers, since they are the entry points to the health-care delivery system. In contrast, specialist care is a cost function, since more expensive medical procedures must be paid for out of the limited capitation payments available to the provider.

Perhaps the most serious challenges to medical schools will inevitably involve a restructuring and likely downsizing. The size and focus of most medical schools today have been determined primarily by the needs for physician services of their associated hospitals, operated in a fee-for-service mode. Furthermore, many medical schools today not only have a disciplinary focus toward specialization, with less than 10 to 20 percent of faculty in primary-care areas, but they are also overstaffed relative to their teaching needs by several fold. As hospitals negotiate more aggressively for physician services, perhaps even turning to physician groups not associated with the university, these very large clinical faculty cadres will pose great risk both to medical schools and their host universities. Since the downsizing of academic units is very difficult, many universities will find the restructuring of their medical schools one of their most formidable challenges in the years ahead.

For many universities, the academic medical center has now become comparable in size and complexity to the university itself. The stresses and challenges it faces threaten the university as well. As one of my colleagues put it, organizations are loath to change until they see the wolf at the door—and become convinced that it is big enough to eat them! If so, they need only look at their academic medical centers, since these are indeed large enough to devour their host institutions. Currently over 20 percent of academic medical centers are losing money, with this fraction estimated to double over the next several years as the full impact of the Balanced Budget Act of 1997 on Medicare payments takes effect.

Like many other service roles assumed over the years, it could well be that the delivery of health-care has reached the stage where it is time to distance it from the university. Some universities have reached the conclusion that it is time to spin off their hospitals, creating independent health-care systems, merging them with other health-care providers, or even selling them to for-profit organizations. The academic management culture and the glacial speed of the academic decision process makes it increasingly difficult for a university to manage a viable health-care system in the intensely competitive world of modern health care. To attempt to do so puts the university at financial risk and distracts the attention of its leadership from the core missions of teaching and scholarship.

To be sure, such devolution of teaching hospitals from universities reduces the influence of medical schools over the academic medical center and, not surprisingly, is generally resisted by medical faculty. But the management demands and financial risks attendant to health-care delivery on a sufficient scale for financial viability seem increasingly incompatible with the mission and culture of the university. Yet, here again, public universities may be at a significant disadvantage. Public pressures may prevent them from spinning off their ownership and/or management of massive health-care enterprises, even though these put the university at very considerable financial risk.

Another Example (Even More Extreme): Intercollegiate Athletics

An even more extreme example of a "service" activity of the contemporary university that increasingly threatens its core missions is intercollegiate athletics. Long ago college sports programs such as football and basketball evolved far beyond the role of simply providing extracurricular experiences for undergraduates or community experiences for students, faculty, and alumni. Today big-time intercollegiate athletics in most large universities have clearly become, in effect, yet another area of public service with the primary mission of entertaining the American public. To be sure, many would go further to characterize big-time college sports as commercial businesses conducted by the university rather than service activities. But since few intercollegiate athletics generate a profit and instead require a very substantial subsidy, it also seems appropriate to regard them as a university service aimed at public entertainment.

However, whether a commercial business or a public service, it is also clear that the conduct of big-time college sports by universities has raised serious questions both within and beyond the academy: the quasi-professional nature of college sports and their apparent inconsistency with academic priorities; the degree to which college sports are taking advantage of student-athletes, as evidenced by low graduation rates and the awarding of meaningless degrees; the perceived pressure to win at all costs, which leads to cheating and scandals; and images of misbehavior, such as players taunting one another or coaches engaging in tirades against officials or college athletes getting into trouble with crime or drugs.

Yet college sports have become a major source of public entertainment in America. Coaches have become media celebrities, with multimillion-dollar contracts that rival those in professional sports. Although student-athletes labor in relative poverty, they frequently are treated as celebrities who are set apart from the campus community. Dollars from television have warped institutional priorities, dictating the scheduling of sporting events and the length of seasons, and the realignment or dismantling of athletic conferences. And the media has created a feeding frenzy in which sports columnists have imitated gossip columnists in their efforts to pander to public curiosity. All of these factors have transformed intercollegiate athletics from its original status as an extracurricular activity into a form of show business. The traditional organizations that should be resisting this, such as the NCAA or the athletic conferences, have become too unwieldy and cumbersome to be effective. And they too have been co-opted by the lure of additional dollars. In this regard, we should bear in mind that most of the problems in intercollegiate athletics arise in college football and basketball—ironically, the two sports that were originally spawned on our campuses. While the many other varsity sports conducted by our universities face challenges, they pale in comparison with the two highly visible "revenue" sports that have been taken over by those who pander to armchair America.

Like other service activities that have long since evolved apart from the university, the key flaw in intercollegiate athletics as we conduct it today is its isolation from our educational mission and our academic values. In a sense, we have allowed the alien culture of the entertainment industry to invade our institutions and infect a highly visible portion of our activities, intercollegiate athletics. It is this culture that not only drives but sometimes even sanctions the disregard for educational values by those involved in college sports—coaches, players, and fans—as well as those who derive their livelihood from its entertainment value—the media, the press, and others who profit from college sports. The university is not only unable to control this culture; it is all too frequently co-opted and distorted by it.

Many within higher education are aware of the tenuous connection of big-time college sports to the educational mission of the university. Many recognize the serious damage that has been caused to higher education not simply by its occasional scandal and corruption, but its very culture of commercialism and hypocrisy. Many have tried over the years to reform intercollegiate athletics, or at least limit their growth and negative impact on higher education.

But the insatiable appetite of the American public for the entertainment provided by college sports, whetted by the self-serving, promotional role of the sports media, has thwarted attempts at reform and de-emphasis. The pervasive influence and commercial opportunity afforded by modern media, from television to the Internet, has driven the expansion and evolution of college sports into a national entertainment industry. And university leaders, presidents and trustees alike, have largely acquiesced, preferring to join in the commercial arms race of big-time sports rather than risk the wrath of the press or the public by attempting true reform.

Yet, today, higher education is entering an era of extraordinary change. Even the very survival of the university as a social institution is being called into question because of its increasing difficulty in meeting the needs of a knowledge-driven society. This time of great change, of shifting paradigms, provides a context and a rationale for once again examining the proper role and character of all university activities, including intercollegiate athletics.

We are obliged to ask the difficult question of whether it makes sense for the twenty-first century university to conduct commercial activities at the current level of big-time college football and basketball. Is there any logical reason for an academic institution, with the fundamental mission of teaching and scholarship, to mount and sustain a professional and commercial enterprise simply to satisfy the public desire for entertainment and the commercial goals of the marketplace? Why should the university squander its resources, distract its leadership, and erode its most fundamental values and integrity with these commercial activities, particularly at a time when it will face so many other challenges in responding to the changing educational needs of our society?

The answers are obvious. We have no business being in the entertainment business. We must either reform and restructure intercollegiate athletics on terms congruent with the educational purpose of our institutions, or spin big-time football and basketball off as independent, professional, and commercial enterprises no longer related to higher education.

The most straightforward approach would be to restructure and retain intercollegiate athletics on our terms. We need to decouple college sports from the entertainment industry and reconnect it with the educational mission of our institutions. Here, the key to the control of intercollegiate athletics and to proper alignment with the academic values and priorities of the institution will be the effort of universities to resist the pressures to transform college sports into an entertainment industry. The academy simply must recapture control of college sports from those who promote them for their own financial gain: the media, the entertainment industry, and even the coaches and athletic directors themselves.

Clearly this will not be easy, as a century of ill-fated efforts to de-emphasize and reform college sports so clearly indicates. Those who benefit most from big-time college sports as an entertainment industry, the coaches and athletic directors, the sport media and the networks, the sports apparel industry and the advertisers, all will vigorously defend the status quo. So too will those millions of fans and boosters who see the American university only as a source of entertainment on Saturday afternoons in the fall resist change. But the forces of change in our society are powerful, and they are reshaping all of our institutions—our corporations, our governments, our universities, even our nation-states. This unique period of change for higher education may provide an unusual opportunity to reform college sports, to reconnect it with our mission as educators.

If we are unable to do this, we must then insist that society respect our roles as educational institutions and allow us to spin off big-time college sports to more appropriate venues. Minor league baseball and hockey franchises have long provided opportunities for young, aspiring athletes to develop their skills while entertaining the public. There is no reason why similar leagues could not be created in football and basketball, allowing those athletes and coaches interested in participating in professional athletics to do so, and allowing our campuses to reintroduce de-emphasized versions of these sports back into our existing portfolios of intercollegiate sports programs. Certainly there would be some cost associated with spinning off these programs, particularly in the sense that the revenue from big-time football and basketball would no longer be available to subsidize our other varsity programs. But these costs are a small price to pay to refocus our attention on our core mission of education and restore our integrity as academic institutions.

As we enter a new century of intercollegiate athletics in America, it is essential for universities to establish their own priorities, objectives, and principles for college sports. Higher education must then commit itself to holding fast to these objectives in the face of the enormous pressure exerted by the media and the public-at-large. In the end, college athletics must reflect the fundamental academic values of the university. There is no other acceptable alternative if we are to retain our academic values and integrity while serving the true educational needs of our society.

A Third Example (Somewhat More Benign): Economic Development

Research universities have become important players in regional economic development. The key ingredients in technology-based economic development are technological innovation, technical manpower, and entrepreneurs. Research universities produce all three. Through their on-campus research, they generate the creativity and ideas necessary for innovation. Through their faculty efforts, they attract the necessary "risk capital" through massive federal R&D support. Through their education programs they produce the scientists, engineers, and entrepreneurs to implement new knowledge. And they are also the key to knowledge transfer, both through traditional mechanisms, such as graduates and publications, as well as through more direct contributions such as faculty/staff entrepreneurs, the formation of start-up companies, strategic partnerships, and so on.

The Bayh-Dole Act of 1980 clearly reflected the federal interest in the transfer of technology from the campuses into the marketplace and permitted universities and small businesses to retain title to inventions developed with federal R&D funds. Furthermore, there is ample evidence to support the impact of research universities on technology-driven economic development.[10] We need only look at MIT's impact on the Boston area, Stanford's and UC-Berkeley's impact on Northern California, Caltech's impact on Southern California, and the Research Triangle activity stimulated by the University of North Carolina, North Carolina State University, and Duke University.

In examining such experiences, one can identify several key stages to technology transfer:

1. To attract the key people;
2. To create the knowledge;
3. To facilitate the transfer of knowledge;
4. To create a sufficiently entrepreneurial culture both on and off campus;
5. To form or attract new companies; and
6. To help these companies grow and flourish.

The new knowledge necessary to stimulate economic activity flows directly from the research performed by universities. Estimates suggest that over 50 percent of the new job growth in America can be traced to new knowledge coming out of our research laboratories.[11] Through research grants and contracts, the federal government, augmented by industry, foundations, and internal university support, supplies the resources for the development of new knowledge. Here it is important to keep in mind that such support continues to be provided primarily through a competitive process based upon merit review. The quality of the faculty and students determines the quality of the proposals and hence the success in attracting external support for research. There is strong evidence that the most highly ranked universities attract the most research support, generate the most new knowledge, and thus stimulate the most regional economic development. Excellence determines impact.

Research universities—particularly public research universities—have a major obligation to make every effort to transfer intellectual properties resulting from their academic activities into the private sector where they will benefit society more broadly, in a manner consistent with their academic missions, of course. Such technology transfer will occur most rapidly when those who create the new knowledge—faculty and staff—have maximum incentive, opportunity, and support to transfer it to the private sector. A research university's ability to recruit and retain outstanding faculty and staff will be increasingly influenced by the environment it provides to allow, encourage, and facilitate such knowledge-transfer activities. There is strong evidence suggesting that in many cases the best "academics" and "entrepreneurs" are one and the same!

Further there is considerable evidence that interaction with the broader society is a critical factor in stimulating creative research in some areas. Knowledge transfer activities can have a positive impact on the quality of basic research since they create pressures to work in exciting, high risk, interdisciplinary areas to achieve the quantum leaps in knowledge not normally available in the industrial setting. In this sense, it is wrong to equate commercial value with applied research. Frequently the real barriers to application are due to a shortage of basic knowledge, only gained through fundamental research.

Although there are some notable exceptions, it seems unlikely that most universities will reap substantial income through direct control of intellectual property through mechanisms such as patent licenses and equity interest in spin-off companies, at least in the near term. Institutions could gain substantial indirect benefits from aggressive technology transfer efforts through increased public support and private gifts. The strong support of Stanford by William Hewlett and David Packard is but one example.

Universities must take care to avoid a paternalistic attitude toward their faculty and staff. In their perhaps well-intentioned efforts to protect them from the harsh, cruel world of private enterprise, the university may constrain and frustrate those already experienced in such activities. It would also prevent the development of a learning process among others (albeit sometimes by the school of hard knocks), while removing the incentive for widespread faculty involvement in technology transfer activities. It is best to begin with the premise that faculty and staff in universities are mature, responsible individuals who will behave properly in balancing the university's interests and their own responsibilities for teaching and research against their interests in intellectual property development and technology transfer. The key to avoiding conflict of interest is public disclosure.

In summary, knowledge transfer from the campus to the market will only succeed if we recognize that it is highly people-dependent. It is essential to stimulate and encourage the individual researcher-inventor to participate in these activities and to remove the constraints to provide maximum incentive and opportunity for this process to occur.

An important element in technology transfer is the formation of strategic alliances between university researchers and industry and government. Such university-industry alliances should be viewed as symbiotic associations between two unlike organisms for the benefit of each. Of course, both industry and university have a "service to society" component. But their fundamental goals are quite different: industry seeks to make a profit, while universities seek to create and maintain knowledge and impart it to students. In a university-industry partnership, it is important that each partner focus on what it does best.

While such partnerships have existed for many years, they have tended to rely on traditional relationships, such as the hiring of graduates, the use of faculty consultants, or the sponsorship of research. Today, we face new challenges. The time required for technology transfer from university to industry must be reduced dramatically to meet the needs of existing companies and to spawn new industries. Yet academic institutions are ill equipped to respond to the highly focused immediate needs of industry without considerable disruption of on-campus responsibilities. We need to improve mechanisms for achieving direct industrial support of academe through financial assistance, equipment donations, and visiting staff. It is clear that both industry and academia need stronger, more sophisticated, and sustained relationships with each other in order to respond to the needs and capabilities of each type of organization.

The Need for a New Paradigm for Serving Society

As we have noted, the relationship between the university and American society has evolved over the years and continues to do so today. The land-grant acts established a model through which universities distributed and applied existing knowledge to serve an emerging industrial nation. The federal government-university research partnership shifted the emphasis to the generation of new knowledge through campus-based research. Today, as the role of the federal government as a major agent in addressing social concerns has shifted to the states and the communities, the university will be expected to assume new roles. For example, the increasing pace in the development and application of knowledge requires forming new relationships with both private industry and government agencies. So, too, does the direct support of university activities by institutions in both the public and private sector. Our colleges are drawn into new and more extensive relationships with each passing day.

This is understandable because American universities have vast resources capable of contributing to public needs. They are civic institutions with a long history of contributing to the nation through their educational, research, and service activities. Yet, despite this past history and contemporary need, few universities are strategically situated for public service. Few university leaders and even fewer faculty members would place public service toward the top of the university's priorities. As Derek Bok put it, "Most universities continue to do their least impressive work on the very subjects where society's need for greater knowledge and better education is most acute."[12]

To be sure, the public service role can, if not carefully managed, undermine the stability of our educational institutions. Part of the challenge here is not only knowing what are appropriate public service activities to conduct, but also knowing when it is time to cease or spin off a particular service activity, and then to accomplish this task without alienating important constituencies of the university. There are times when a particular service activity has simply outlived its usefulness. At other times, a service activity might be more effectively and appropriately performed by other social institutions, perhaps in the private sector. And there are some occasions when the service activity becomes so large and complex that it begins to distort the fundamental academic character of the university.

For example, the early growth of the Internet was managed by a consortium of universities through federally sponsored projects such as NSFnet. But in the 1990s it became apparent that the rapid evolution of the Internet and its increasingly commercial character required that it be spun off to private contractors. Today there are many signs that the changing nature of health-care delivery and financing may require the spin-off of major academic medical centers and health-care systems. And some would contend that intercollegiate athletics—at least the commercially dominated sports of football and basketball that serve as a source of public entertainment—so threaten the academic integrity of the university that it is time that they be spun off before they damage our institutions.

Education and scholarship are the primary functions of a university, its primary contributions to society, and hence the most significant roles of the faculty. When universities become overly distracted by other activities, they not only compromise this core mission but they also erode their priorities within our society. Yet, public service must be a major institutional obligation of the American university. The public supports the university, contributes to its finance and grants it an unusual degree of institutional autonomy and freedom, in part because of the expectation that the university will contribute not just graduates and scholarship, but the broader efforts of its faculty, staff, and students in addressing social needs and concerns. It is of some concern that the role of public service in higher education has not received greater attention in recent years, since this was an original mandate for many of our institutions.

Our institutions need a continually refreshed vision of their role that responds to the ever-changing needs of the society we serve. As we evolve along with broader society, the linkages between us become more varied, complex, and interrelated. Within this context of change, it is clear that public service must continue to be an important responsibility of the American university.

CHAPTER 7   # The Academy

We call on our colleagues in universities to recognize their unique responsibilities to and opportunities in their communities, regions, and the larger global society by affirming that teaching is a moral vocation, scholarship is a public trust, and public service is a major institutional obligation.
—The Glion Declaration:
The University at the Millennium (1998)

Many university presidents these days move from campus to campus, rising up through the administrative ranks until they arrive at the helm of a college or university. My experience was somewhat different, since I had spent my entire career as a faculty member at a single institution, the University of Michigan, prior to becoming its president. As a result, I regarded myself first and foremost as a member of the Michigan faculty. The presidency was just another assignment, much like chairing a committee, that took me temporarily away from the classroom and the laboratory.

It is this perspective, gained from years of toiling in the vineyards of teaching and scholarship, that shapes my own views of the challenges facing the university faculty probably more than my sentence to years of hard labor as a university administrator. In truth, being a college professor, a member of the academy, is far more of a calling than a profession. After all, our core activities are—or at least should be— learning, teaching, and discovering. Few other endeavors offer such freedom of expression and activity. Few other environments can compete with the concentration of stimulating and dedicated people that populate our university campuses. And few other professions offer such a rich and satisfying array of opportunities to serve.

Yet there is also a sense of unease in the academy today. To be sure, the past several decades have been a golden age for most faculty members. Their institutions have been expanding; support for their teaching and scholarship has continued to grow; their salaries have increased somewhat more rapidly than inflation; and their prestige remains intact, at least relative to most other professions. However, conversations within the academy reveal signs of stress, a worry that all may not be well, and that a time of change may be approaching, in both their institutions and their profession.

The American Professorate

The public—and, in fact, many faculty members—tend to think of the faculty as a homogenous group, all engaged in similar activities of teaching and research, and all experiencing similar stresses of publish or perish, tenure or out. Yet there is as much diversity among faculty and their roles as across any other aspect of American society. The range of faculty activities cover a wide spectrum: teaching at the undergraduate, graduate, professional, postdoctoral, and continuing education levels; basic and applied research; scholarly modalities ranging from solitary individuals to teams of hundreds of peers; disciplinary versus interdisciplinary teaching and research; and public service in myriad forms.[1]

There are indeed many faculty members of the "Mr. Chips" stereotype: dedicated classroom teachers, committed to the intellectual development of their students, and limiting their scholarship to an occasional research paper. But contrast this with a professor of internal medicine, with long hours devoted to patient treatment and care, engaged in ongoing efforts to attract the research funding to support a laboratory and students, teaching in a one-on-one mode medical students and residents, and perhaps trying to start a spin-off company to market a new piece of medical technology. Or the professor of violin, working one day with master classes of students and performing the next on the concert stage. Or the engineering professor, teaching large classes of undergraduates, managing a state-of-the-art research laboratory staffed by research assistants and graduate students, serving on high-level government advisory committees, and working to develop patents into marketable products. All are valued members of the university faculty, but their activities, their perspectives, their needs, and their concerns are remarkably different.

So, too, the role and activities of a faculty member change considerably over the course of a career. Most faculty members concentrate early in their careers on building scholarly momentum and reputation and developing teaching skills. Once the early hurdles of tenure and promotion have been achieved, professors become more involved in service both within and external to the university. Some become involved in deeper games where they use their intellectual power to shape their field of scholarship. Others assume important roles as advisors or consultants to government or industry. Still others become campus politicians, representing their colleagues in faculty governance. Still others take on administrative roles as chairs, deans, or perhaps even university presidents. Yet, despite this extraordinary diversity of faculty across fields and careers, there is a tendency both in perception and in policy to regard all faculty the same, as if all were assistant professors in history or economics.

Perhaps the greatest source of variation in the academy is due to the great diversity in the nature of colleges and universities. Today there are roughly 700,000 faculty in the United States, with 28 percent in research universities, 26 percent at comprehensive institutions, 20 percent at two-year colleges, 8 percent at liberal arts colleges, and the remainder in specialized institutions such as proprietary schools. Of these, about two-thirds hold full-time positions, with the majority of these tenured. The majority of faculty work in two-year or four-year public colleges and universities where teaching is the primary role. Although research and service are technically part of their portfolio, their heavy classroom loads and limited intellectual resources (laboratories, libraries, and graduate students) make scholarship difficult. Furthermore, the faculties at most institutions are unionized, and hence their relationship with their administration and trustees tends more toward that of a negotiated labor-management contract than shared governance.

In sharp contrast, faculty members in research universities do enjoy the opportunity to participate in teaching, research, service, and administrative activities on a far more balanced basis. Although there is great diversity in faculty roles throughout the contemporary research university, determined by academic discipline, career level, and administrative assignments, all faculty members are both encouraged and expected to maintain some level of activity in scholarship or creative work and to teach at the graduate and professional level. Yet, with this freedom and opportunity to undertake broader roles than simply classroom teaching comes an additional responsibility: research university faculty members are expected to generate a significant fraction of the resources necessary to support their activities. That is, most faculty members at research universities are expected to be entrepreneurs as well as teachers and scholars.

The Faculty and the University

The principal academic resource of a university is its faculty. The quality and commitment of the faculty determine the excellence of the academic programs of a university, the quality of its student body, the excellence of its teaching and scholarship, its capacity to serve broader society through public service, and the resources it is able to attract from public and private sources.

Hiring, Retention, and the Marketplace

Each appointment to the faculty and each promotion within its ranks must be seen as both a significant decision and an important opportunity. In theory, at least, these decisions must be made with the quality of the university always foremost in mind. Policies, procedures, and practices characterizing the appointment, role, reward, and responsibilities of the faculty should be consistent with the overall goals of the institution and the changing environment in which it finds itself. In practice these decisions tend to be made at the level of individual disciplinary departments with relatively little consideration given to broader institutional concerns or long-range implications.

During the next decade, many universities will experience significant faculty turnover through retirement.[2] They face the challenge and opportunity to use these appointments to sustain and enhance the quality of their academic programs and their institutions more broadly. It is within this context of the challenge of building the next generation of faculty that we must address a number of challenges.

Although many colleges and universities operate much like K–12 education with unionized faculties and negotiated compensation systems, the very best institutions function as meritocracies. The academy is usually both rigorous and demanding in its evaluation of the abilities of its members, not only in promotion and tenure decisions, but also in determining compensation. The promotion ladder is relatively short, consisting primarily of the three levels of assistant professor, associate professor, and professor. Hence the faculty reward culture is unusually one-dimensional, based primarily upon salary. Although faculty honors and awards are common in higher education, including endowed professorial chairs, faculty members tend to measure their relative worth in terms of salary. Most public universities are required by freedom-of-information laws to publish faculty salaries. In private universities, one's salary can usually be compared to with those of others either through the informal grapevine or by testing the marketplace by exploring offers from other institutions. Hence the faculty reward structure creates a highly competitive environment that extends beyond a single institution as a national or even global marketplace for the very best faculty talent.

Academic leaders such as deans, provosts, and presidents spend much of their time either attempting to recruit outstanding faculty members to their institution or fending off raids on their faculty by other institutions. Although there have been attempts in the past to impose certain rules of behavior on faculty recruiting, for example, through informal agreements that institutions will refrain from recruiting faculty just prior to the start of a new academic year or avoid using the promise of reduced teaching load to lure a research star—in reality it is a no-holds-barred and ruthless competition. And the richer and more prestigious the institution, the more aggressively it plays the game. To be sure, there is a certain pecking order in higher education, determined in part by the reputation of the particular academic program (not that concocted by *US News and World Report* but rather as determined by peers) and in part by wealth. Sometimes weather also helps, as the recruiting success of California universities clearly demonstrates.

But there is an insidious nature to this intensely competitive market for faculty talent. First, such recruiting efforts are a major factor in driving up the costs of a college education. Whether it is the size of an offer put together to lure a star faculty member away, or the counteroffer the home university puts on the table to retain the individual, both can seriously distort the broader faculty compensation patterns. Furthermore, such offers usually go far beyond simply salary and can involve a considerable "dowry" including laboratory space, research support, graduate and research assistant support, and sometimes even a reduced teaching load.

But beyond this, several of the wealthiest and most elite universities, Harvard University being most prominent, play a particularly damaging role within higher education by preferring to build their faculties through raids on other institutions rather than developing them through the ranks from within. At these institutions, very few junior faculty members have an opportunity for tenure, since most senior faculty positions are filled by scholars recruited away from other universities, where they have been nurtured and developed by these institutions at rather considerable expense. These elite predators attempt to rationalize the process by arguing that by seeking only the very best faculty from the broader marketplace rather than developing them from within, they create competitive forces that improve the quality throughout all of higher education. In reality they instead decimate the quality of programs in other universities by raiding their best faculty members. Even unsuccessful attempts to raid faculty can result in a serious distortion of resource allocation in target institutions as they desperately attempt to retain their best faculty stars.

Tenure and the Faculty Contract

Certainly the most controversial, complex, and misunderstood issue related to the faculty in higher education, at least in the minds of the public, is tenure. In theory, tenure is the key mechanism for protecting academic freedom and for defending faculty members against political attack both within and outside the university. In practice, it has become something quite different: job security, protecting both outstanding and incompetent faculty alike not only from political intrusion but also from a host of performance issues that could lead to dismissal in many other walks of life. And, of course, it is this presumed guarantee of job security that so infuriates many members of the public, some of whom have felt the sting of corporate downsizing or job competition.

Because tenure represents such a major commitment by a university, it is only awarded to a faculty member following a rigorous process of evaluation. Faculty members must first navigate successfully a difficult six- or seven-year probation period, usually holding the title of assistant professor, during which their performance as both teachers and scholars is assessed. In most cases, universities seek evaluation of the credentials of the candidate by external referees, typically including several of the leading experts in the faculty member's field. Furthermore, other factors enter the decision such as the centrality of the candidate's teaching and research expertise to university priorities and the availability of sufficient funds for a tenured appointment. The tenure review process occurs in stages, first at the department level, then at the level of the school, and finally at the university level. At each stage a negative decision will stop the process, so that only if the review proceeds successfully through all levels will tenure be granted. Although there is considerable variability among universities and academic programs, in most of the leading research universities, less than half of new faculty survive the tenure review gauntlet.

Of course, tenure is a practice that arises in other professions. In contrast to professors, who must successfully navigate a difficult six- or seven-year probation period and then face rigorous reviews by the leading scholars in their fields before being granted tenure, most teachers in K–12 education are granted tenure after only two years of service—and protected by union contracts as well. Both employment regulations and collective bargaining agreements provide many other employees in our society with effective tenure, in the sense that it becomes very difficult to dismiss them, regardless of cause. Furthermore, as we will discuss later in this chapter, a significant fraction of the new faculty hired by universities are in temporary, part-time, or adjunct faculty positions that are not eligible for tenure.[3]

Higher education has long accepted the fundamental principle of protecting scholars so that they can pursue their work without fear of losing their jobs for unpopular views. In the United States, the formation of the American Association for University Professors in 1915 coincided with early efforts to codify this principle of academic freedom. In 1940 the AAUP adopted a written policy on tenure, calling it a principle designed to ensure scholarly freedom as well as "a sufficient degree of economic security to make the profession attractive to men and women of ability."[4]

Most university faculty members believe that tenure is a valuable and important practice in the core academic disciplines of the university, where independent teaching and scholarship require some protection from criticism and controversy. This privilege should also enable tenured faculty members to accept greater responsibility for the interests of the university rather than focusing solely on personal objectives. But even within the academy, many are beginning to question the appropriateness of current tenure practices. The abolition of mandatory retirement policies is leading to an aging faculty cohort, insulated from rigorous performance accountability by tenure, and this is depriving young scholars of faculty opportunities.

Many faculty members question the value of tenure in professional fields where there is a need to use more practitioners as faculty, drawing professionals into the university for a brief period as teachers before they return to their professional careers. This close relationship between teaching and practice, between the university and the profession, is apparent in fields such as medicine and engineering as well as the visual and performing arts. After all, students would prefer to learn from experienced surgeons, successful artists, or accomplished performers, from those who do rather than those who simply study. For these fields, in which faculty are drawn from society for a brief time with the intent that they return, tenure does not appear to be as relevant.

Increasingly, the academy itself is acknowledging that both the concept and practice of tenure—particularly when interpreted as guaranteed lifetime employment—needs to be reevaluated. One approach under consideration—and occasionally even mandated by some state legislatures—is post-tenure review. Faculty members would continue to be reviewed at regular intervals even after receiving tenure. While this makes it possible, in theory at least, to revoke tenure for inadequate performance, these reviews usually take a more constructive approach by identifying problems early and then working with the faculty member to see that they are corrected. Another approach is to reinterpret tenure as only applying to a portion of an academic appointment. For example, in many fields such as medicine, faculty members draw only a small fraction (20 percent or less) of their salaries from university funds, with the majority of support coming from clinical fees or research grants. The awarding of tenure would obligate the university to support only that component of a faculty appointment supported by academic funds.

While there are many who remain firm in their support of the fundamental concept of tenure, basing their arguments on academic freedom, the tenure system is likely to become increasingly diverse with respect to how tenure is provided and interpreted not only among institutions but also within institutions and among various academic programs. It is important for the academy to explore new employment arrangements that respond more realistically to the differing needs of individual faculty members while addressing societal concerns.

Publish or Perish . . . or Hustle?

The long-standing argument about the negative impact of research on teaching highlights the pressures on faculty to "publish or perish." Yet in many fields, the real pressure is not to publish, but to be a successful entrepreneur capable of attracting the resources to support not only one's own activities, but also one's students and department. For science and engineering, this is "grantsmanship"—the ability to compete successfully for sponsored research grants and contracts. For clinical disciplines such as medicine or dentistry, the challenge is somewhat different: the pressure to generate sufficient revenue from clinical services.

The modern university places enormous weight on the entrepreneurial efforts of the faculty. And well it should, since without sponsored research support and clinical revenue, the university would not have the resources to conduct the bulk of its activities in graduate education and research. Yet it is also clear that both the pace and character of this competitive, entrepreneurial culture, so critical to the quality and the survival of the research university, may also be at odds with the responsibility of the faculty for undergraduate education. The need to generate resources to support research and graduate education inevitably pull many of our most active faculty members out of the classroom, limiting the time and attention they can devote to under-graduate instruction.

Productivity

There is a new "p-word" that has replaced parking as the dominant faculty concern on campuses these days: *productivity*. From state capitals to Washington, from corpo-rate executive suites to newspaper editorial offices, there is a strong belief that if only faculty would work harder, by spending more hours in the classroom, the quality of a college education would rise while its cost would decline. Critics point to the fact that many college professors spend only "a few hours a week" in the classroom, as measured by student contact hours. (Of course, one could also claim that legislators only spend a few hours a week in session or that news editors spend only a few hours writing their editorials.)

To be sure, there are sometimes flagrant examples of faculty irresponsibility, tol-erated by universities in the name of academic freedom. For example, some faculty members are allowed to conduct research without any appreciable teaching responsi-bilities. Others are rarely on campus and available to students or colleagues. As Henry Rosovsky put it in his final report at Harvard, "The faculty has become a society largely without rules, or to put it slightly differently, the tenured members of the faculty, frequently as individuals, make their own rules."

Yet the story is more complex that this. Few realize just how much time faculty members spend outside of the classroom, preparing lectures, meeting with students, serving on committees, conducting research, hustling grants, writing books, and all of the other activities essential to the academy. Today's faculty member works far longer hours than in the past, averaging over fifty-five hours a week in all of higher education, and considerably more in research-intensive universities. Furthermore, there is some evidence that faculty effort actually increases after they achieve tenure, prob-ably due in part to the fact that they are relieved of the stress of the tenure probation period.

While it is certainly the case that productivity is an issue, it is not due to any lack of faculty effort. It is rather due to the labor-intensive nature of the current teaching and research paradigms. To be sure these paradigms are shifting, but driven more by the changing nature of student needs and scholarship rather than demands for greater productivity. We have noted that the changing nature of students and pedagogy will demand significant changes in the role of the faculty. As students become active learners, as universities evolve from faculty-centered to student-centered institutions, and as the classroom experience transforms into a highly interactive learning com-munity, perhaps distributed far beyond the campus, faculty members will be called upon to adapt to new forms of learning. They will have to master skills that will be new to many—inspiring, motivating, and managing active learning communities—and yet in other ways will be more akin to the roles of faculty before mass education and high-intensity research.

Faculty members will play a variety of roles, as scholars, mentors, evaluators, and certifiers of learning. These roles will not be played uniformly by all of the faculty, nor will they be static through a faculty member's career. It is likely that future learning institutions will not only allow but will require far greater differentiation in faculty roles.

For example, it could well be that limits on research funding will require federal research sponsors to focus available resources on only those faculty members who are truly outstanding at discovery research. Only these scholars would spend a significant amount of their time in this role. Other faculty members may be skilled at synthesizing knowledge, at identifying curricular content and designing learning experiences. Still others may be best at working directly with students, managing learning communities, counseling, and inspiring.

Faculty roles will undoubtedly change over time. Younger faculty may be somewhat more heavily involved in research and graduate education. As they gain more experience, they may shift to the role of synthesizing knowledge, designing new curricula or learning experiences. It will be important for universities to acknowledge and adapt to these differing faculty functions.

Retirement and the Impacted Wisdom Group

As the faculty ages in the wake of the elimination of mandatory retirement caps in the 1990s, we face the challenge of providing adequate opportunities to young teachers and scholars and renewing the academy. Although it was initially believed that the elimination of mandatory retirement would not have an appreciable effect, recent surveys suggest that a significant fraction of faculty reaching age seventy decide to continue.[5] This is not surprising, since university cultures provide wonderful, supportive, and effective environments for teaching and scholarship.

There is an interesting financial wrinkle to this issue. Most universities provide faculty and staff with "defined-contribution" retirement plans, in which a certain amount each year is placed into a tax-deferred investment account for each employee. Upon retirement, the accumulation in these accounts is used to purchase an annuity or reinvested in other income-generating instruments. As one becomes older, usually earning a higher salary, the value of yet another year's university contribution to the retirement plan becomes considerable. In addition, increasing age can have a major actuarial impact of the value of retirement annuities. Both of these factors create very strong incentives to delay retirement as long as possible.

As a result, we have created a situation in which de facto age discrimination will be a feature of academic life for a generation—age discrimination not against the old but rather against the young as we deprive them of the opportunity for academic careers. When one couples this with the growing number of part-time faculty hired by universities in their efforts to retain some measure of flexibility, one can almost see a caste system developing in the American professorate: a large group of aging and relatively prosperous senior faculty who have got their rewards and are going to keep them as long as they can, and a growing number of talented, hungry, and frustrated young scholars, desperately seeking the opportunity to enter the academy.

One might appeal to senior professors that they have an obligation to step aside at some point late in their careers to make room for the next generation, particularly when there are no serious financial sacrifices to doing so. In fact, at a national meeting concerned with the future of research universities, one of my colleagues challenged the audience, most of whom were rather senior, by suggesting that the most significant thing they could do to help their institutions was to retire! Immediately! (There were no takers.)

But there are less draconian approaches. Institutions might consider a new type of retirement plan, in which the university stops making contributions when the projected annuity income of the faculty member exceeds their present salary. They could also make the status of retired but still active faculty much more attractive. One could even create a new faculty rank for those faculty willing to remain fully active but supported by their own retirement annuities rather than university funds. In fact, if the faculty member were to work for a sufficient length of time supported by annuities rather than university salary, say ten years, these faculty positions might even be converted into fully endowed chairs that would continue in the faculty member's name, since the avoided salary expense would be comparable to the private gift necessary for a chair (typically $1 to 2 million).

The Changing Nature of the Academy

Just as with other aspects of the university, the academy is evolving, changing in important ways.

The Increasing Diversity of the Faculty

We have noted the great diversity in the various roles and responsibilities of the faculty driven by the diversity of our academic programs. Examples include the contrasts among the roles of medical faculty responsible for clinical care, engineering faculty with technology transfer obligations, business faculty with strong consulting activities, biomedical faculty working primarily with postdoctoral scholars. But there is also an ever-increasing diversity of the faculty with respect to characteristics such as gender and family responsibilities suggesting that the relationship between the faculty and the university must become more flexible and capable of change. For example, the tenure probation period frequently falls during the period of life when many faculty members want to start families. Rather than adapt to this reality, many universities continue to insist on adhering to traditional models, often forcing faculty members to choose between professional advancement and family responsibilities.

Temporary or Part-Time Faculty Appointments

Increasingly, the entry-level academic positions in a university available to recent graduates are part-time in nature. New Ph.D.s serve in a variety of roles, such as postdoctoral fellows, clinical professors, lecturers, instructors, research scientists and technical staff. None of these roles are "tenure-track," in the sense that they lead to permanent faculty positions. There are also an increasing number of affiliated faculty positions such as adjunct professors or professors of practice, accommodating individuals whose full-time position is outside the university, for example, in industry or government, but who provide instructional or research services to the institution.

The cadre of part-time faculty is increasing rapidly as universities seek to become more flexible within the constraints of tenure and the elimination of mandatory retirement. For example, over 40 percent of college faculty today have part-time appointments, ranging from 30 percent in research universities to over 60 percent in community colleges.[6] In fact, in some of the newly emerging institutions such as the University of Phoenix, the instructional faculty is comprised totally of practitioners with part-time teaching assignments. As one UP instructor put it, "We're not in academia, you know. We're not professional teachers; we're professionals who teach."[7]

As the fraction of temporary or part-time appointments grows in higher education, a number of issues are raised. For example, can the traditional values of the academy such as academic freedom and collegial debate be sustained when a significant fraction of the faculty is temporary, without protections such as tenure? Can traditions such as shared governance or liberal education be maintained? Will the nature of the faculty change as the number of temporary appointments increases?

Faculty Roles

Perhaps part of the problem is that we tend to structure and evaluate faculty roles far too narrowly. We fail to acknowledge that faculty interests and skills evolve over time. As faculty members become more experienced, their greater breadth of knowledge gives them more capacity for integrative and applied scholarship.

Ernest Boyer suggested in his book *Reinventing Scholarship* that we should recognize this potential by developing what he called "creativity contracts," arrangements by which faculty members define their professional goals for a multiple-year period, possibly shifting from one scholarly focus to another.[8] For example, a faculty member might devote most of his or her early career to specialized research. Later the scholar might wish to examine integrative questions—taking time to read in other fields, write interpretive essays or a textbook, or spend time with a mentor on another campus to discuss the implications of his or her work. Still later, the creativity contract might focus on an applied project, one that would involve the professor in school consultations or as an advisor to a government body.

Furthermore, we should stress to senior faculty members our belief that these broader, occasionally high-risk activities are of great importance. Perhaps the sabbatical leave could be used for such purposes, since one of its fundamental objectives is intellectual renewal. Suppose we were actively to encourage faculty to take a sabbatical leave teaching and conducting research in a quite different academic unit, intellectually far removed from their base discipline. For example, a humanist might spend a sabbatical in a professional school such as medicine or business administration. An engineering professor might spend a sabbatical leave in history or social work. A medical faculty member could take a leave in law or philosophy. Not only would such leaves provide a radically different experience for the visiting faculty member, but these visitors might stir up things a bit in their sabbatical home.

Changing the Paradigm

There is a need to evaluate and perhaps reshape the current appointment, promotion, and tenure policies and procedures. These should be consistent with the university's needs for preserving academic freedom and increasing institutional flexibility, while at the same time maintaining a faculty of strong scholars who are teachers of distinction, who serve the institution in an effective and collegial manner, and who adhere to the highest ethical standards in all their activities.

In this regard, the following questions are particularly worthy of consideration: How should we define "the faculty" of the university with respect to teaching obligations, expectations for scholarship, and appointment pattern? How do we recognize and accommodate the diversity of the faculty, both among various academic units and during the careers of individual faculty? How do we develop faculty policies tolerant of high-risk intellectual activities, sensitive to the particular challenges of gender and race, and committed to achieving a balance between professional and personal faculty aspirations? How can we ensure that faculty appointments and promotions respond to university priorities, when such faculty issues are tightly controlled at the department or school level?

Education and Empowerment of Faculty

The modern university is so complex, so multifaceted, that it seems that the farther one is from an institution, the more clearly it can be perceived. Ironically, those on the campus sometimes have the most difficulty in understanding the university. Such is the case with most faculties, divided up into an almost feudal department structures, frequently with little interaction even with disciplinary neighbors, much less with students, faculty, and staff across the university. However, rather than being connected only by a common concern for parking, today's faculty members are also linked by the misinformation they receive about their university from the local newspaper.

Many faculty members view with alarm the increasing concern about measuring performance and productivity, particularly when couched within the language of business or government. They resent any reference to professors as "employees" of the university. The shift toward more part-time or non-tenure-track faculty poses a serious threat to faculty governance. They see a trend toward the increasing use of professional administrators to manage the complex affairs of the university as yet another threat to faculty governance. Yet, during a time of rapid change, if the faculty is to play a significant role in shaping the evolution of the university, it will need not only a deeper understanding of the forces driving change in our society and our institutions, but as well a willingness to consider significant departures from the status quo.

The Staff

We might think of a university much like a city. It has buildings and roads, parks and theatres, apartments and neighborhoods—and all require knowledgeable professionals capable of building and maintaining, operating and repairing the infrastructure for the academic programs of the institution. By way of example, the University of Michigan's Ann Arbor campus has a population of thirty-seven thousand students, three thousand faculty, and seventeen thousand staff. It has over twenty-six million square feet of facilities, three thousand acres of land, and a budget of $3 billion per year. Thousands of students, hundreds of thousands of patients, and millions of citizens depend on the quality and competence of its many activities. And these, in turn, depend on the quality and effort of the staff of the university.

In most large universities, staff members outnumber the faculty several fold. They are characterized by a great diversity of roles and activities, experiences, and qualifications. In many areas such as finance, health care, and facilities senior staff members have educations and credentials every bit as extensive as faculty members. In fact, some staff are accepted by the faculty as peers and invited to participate in teaching and research activities.

Although we generally think of universities competing for the very best students and faculty, it is clear that the quality of staff is also very important in determining the quality of an institution. The modern university requires highly competent staff, in managing the intricacies of financing a multi-billion-dollar-a-year operation, in seeking the private gifts and government support, in maintaining the most sophisticated technical equipment and facilities, in providing competent and courteous service to students and patients. Beyond these services, we look to staff to provide key leadership for the institution. And in many cases, this leadership has been absolutely essential to the fortunes of the institution.

For example, it was exceptional ability and leadership in business and finance that enabled the University of Michigan to expand enrollments by threefold during the decades of the 1950s and 1960s. Similarly wise management of land holdings was key to Stanford University's rapid progress during the same period. The professional management of Harvard's endowment, now over $14 billion in magnitude, is legendary. Yale's fund-raising prowess has been extraordinary throughout the past two decades. And the University of California not only manages nine major campuses, but three gigantic Department of Energy laboratories as well. The experience of higher education over the past several decades underscores the importance of recruiting and maintaining staff of the highest quality.

To be sure, there are important cultural differences between the faculty and staff communities. The faculty in a university enjoys great freedom—freedom of expression, academic freedom to teach and conduct research—albeit with certain expectations for accountability. In contrast, the staff is expected to perform at high levels of professional competence. They are not necessarily provided with the same degree of choice or the same discretion as their faculty colleagues, although at times these two cultures become somewhat blurred and confused.

Yet, ironically, many staff members are far more loyal to the university than students or faculty. In one sense this is because they are more permanent than students and faculty. Students are essentially tourists, spending only a few short years on the campus, and seeing relatively little of its myriad activities. Similarly, many faculty members view their appointments in the university as simply another step up the academic ladder. Their presence at and loyalty to the institution is limited, usually outweighed by their loyalty to their disciplines and their careers. In contrast, many staff members spend their entire career at the same university, although they may assume a variety of roles. As a result, they not only exhibit a greater institutional loyalty than faculty or students, but they also sustain the continuity, the corporate memory, and the momentum of the university. Ironically, they also sometimes develop a far broader view of the university, its array of activities, and even its history, than do the relative short-timers among the faculty and students.

The faculty generally asserts that it is the core of the university—although it is hopefully acknowledged as well that students are its primary clients. Yet, while this is certainly true for the core missions of teaching and scholarship, the contemporary university is involved in a host of other activities, from health care to economic development to public entertainment, in which staff members play the key roles. Universities with large physical plants employ architects and engineers with skills and competencies that rival those at the very best firms. Senior-level staff members are frequently the full equivalent of top-level executives in major corporations.

Yet, one of the dilemmas faced in attracting and retaining outstanding staff is the relatively low degree of recognition and reward they usually receive within higher education. To be sure, the university environment sometimes provides staff with more freedom and flexibility than they would find in business or industry. But the advancement channels that might be open to them in the private sector are frequently closed off by academic requirements. For example, no staff member could ever aspire to be the CEO of a university. That is generally reserved for academic administrators. Furthermore, the human resource development function in most universities lags far behind its corporate counterparts, with relatively little attention given to career advancement. This may be one of the most compelling reasons for outsourcing an increasing amount of the staff work required by universities, since firms specializing in services such as accounting, investment management, and facilities management can provide far more attractive compensation and career paths for talented staff.

The Academic Administration

The perspective of academic administration reveals a good deal of ambivalence on the part of the faculty. On one hand, faculty members resist—indeed, deplore—the command/control style of leadership characterizing the traditional pyramid organizations of business and government. In fact, many faculty members sought careers in academe in part because they knew that there they would have no supervisor giving direct orders or holding them accountable. Faculty members can usually do as they wish. They enjoy exceptional freedom, as long as they are capable of strong teaching and scholarship in their field, and, at least at some universities, generating the resources necessary to support these activities.

Most among the faculty are offended by any suggestion that the university can be compared to other institutional forms such as corporations and governments. Pity the poor administrator who mistakenly refers to the university as a corporation, or to its students or the public at large as customers, or to its faculty as staff. The academy takes great pride in functioning as a creative anarchy. Indeed, the faculty generally looks down upon those who get mired in the swamp of academic administration. Even their own colleagues tapped for leadership roles become somehow tainted, unfit, no longer a part of the true academy, no matter how distinguished their earlier academic accomplishments, once they become academic administrators.

Yet the faculty also seeks leadership, not in details of its teaching and scholarship, but in the abstract, in providing a vision for their university, in articulating and defending fundamental values, stimulating a sense of optimism and excitement. Faculty members seek protection from the forces of darkness that rage outside the university's ivy-covered walls: the forces of politics, greed, anti-intellectualism, and mediocrity that would threaten the academic values of the university.

In many if not most universities, the concept of management is held in very low regard, particularly by the faculty. Yet all large, complex organizations require not only leadership at the helm, but also effective management at each level where important decisions occur. All presidents, provosts, and deans have heard the suggestion that any one on the faculty, chosen at random, could be an adequate administrator. After all, if you can be a strong teacher and scholar, these skills should be easily transferable to other areas such as administration. Yet, in reality, talent in management is probably as rare a human attribute as the ability to contribute original scholarship. And there is little reason to suspect that talent in one characteristic implies the presence of talent in the other.

To be sure, organizations in business, industry, and government are finding it important to flatten administrative structures by removing layers of management. Despite what the faculty, the press, many politicians, and even a few trustees think, most universities have rather thin management organizations compared to corporations, inherited from earlier times when academic life was far simpler and institutions were far smaller. In truth, universities, like other institutions, depend increasingly on strong leadership and effective management if they are to face the challenges and opportunities posed by a changing world.

Yet there remain many signs of a widening gap between faculty and administration on many campuses. The rank and file faculty sees the world quite differently from campus administrators.[9] There are significant differences in perceptions and understandings of the challenges and opportunities before higher education. It is clear that such a gap, and the corresponding absence of a spirit of trust and confidence by the faculty in their university leadership, can seriously undermine the ability of universities to make difficult yet important decisions and move ahead. Those universities that emerge as leaders in the twenty-first century may well be those institutions whose faculty develops the capacity to tolerate and sustain strong presidential leadership.[10]

The growing epidemic of presidential turnover—with the average tenure of public university presidents now below five years—is due in part to this absence of faculty understanding of the nature of the modern university and support for its leadership.

It is due as well to the stresses on universities and the deterioration in the quality of their governing boards. The faculty-administration gap has been exploited by external groups to attack universities. Such divisions have also been exploited by an array of special interest groups pushing one political agenda or another—not to mention an array of personal agendas.

In part, the widening gap between faculty and administration has to do with the changing nature of the university itself. The modern university is a large, complex, and multidimensional organization, engaged not only in the traditional roles of teaching and research, but in a host of other activities such as health care, economic development, and social change. At the same time, the intellectual demands of scholarship have focused faculty increasingly within their particular disciplines, with little opportunity for involvement in the far broader array of activities characterizing their university. While they are—and should always remain—the cornerstone of the university's academic activities, they rarely have deep understanding or responsibility for the many other missions of the university in modern society.

The increased complexity, financial pressures, and accountability of universities demanded by government, the media, and the public at large have required far stronger management than in the past. Recent furors over indirect cost reimbursement, unrelated business income taxation, financial aid and tuition agreements all involve complex accounting, financial management, and oversight. While perhaps long ago universities were treated by our society—and its various government bodies—as largely well-intentioned and benign stewards of education and learning, today we find the university facing the same pressures, standards, and demands for accountability of any other billion-dollar corporation.

The increasing specialization of faculty, the pressure of the marketplace for their skills, and the degree to which the university has become simply a way station for faculty careers have destroyed institutional loyalty and stimulated more of a "what's in it for me" attitude on the part of many faculty members. The university reward structure—salary, promotion, and tenure—is clearly a meritocracy in which there are clear "haves" and "have-nots." The former generally are too busy to become heavily involved in institutional issues. The latter are increasingly frustrated and vocal in their complaints. Yet they are also all too often the squeaky wheels that drown out others and capture attention.

Finally, many large campuses have allowed the deterioration in the authority and attractiveness of mid-level leadership positions such as department chairs or project directors. This has arisen in part due to the increasing accountability demands on the management structure of the university, and in part in deference to concerns of formal faculty governance bodies that generally harbor deep suspicions of all administrative posts. As a result, many universities are characterized by a structure that can best be characterized as a creative anarchy, in which faculty leaders in posts such as department chair simply do not have the authority to manage, much less lead their units. So too, the lack of career paths and mechanisms for leadership development for junior faculty and staff has decimated much of the midlevel management.

To be sure, the university remains very much a bottom-up organization, a voluntary enterprise. Nevertheless, leadership plays a critical role even in the university, just as it does in other social institutions. If we examine carefully any major accomplishment of the institution—the excellence of a program, its impact on society—invariably we will find a committed, forceful, visionary, and effective leader. Perhaps it is a principal investigator, or a department chair, or even a dean. Indeed, in some cases—as astounding as it may sound, the leadership may even be provided by a member of that most sinister of all academic organizations, the dreaded "central administration."

CHAPTER 8

Resources

We find a time bomb ticking under the nation's social and economic founda-
tions. At a time when the level of education needed for productive employment is
increasing, the opportunity to go to college will be denied to millions of Ameri-
cans unless sweeping changes are made to control costs, halt sharp increases in
tuition, and increase other sources of revenue (for higher education).
—Report of the Commission on National
Investment in Higher Education (1997)[1]

In the decades following World War II, the growth of higher education in America was sustained by growing public commitments. During this period, public institutions treated state and local governments as their primary revenue source, with tuition playing a relatively modest role. Even at private universities, the strong growth in federal research expenditures and student financial aid programs led to very significant increases in public support. This led not only to growth, both in the size of individual institutions and the higher education enterprise more generally, but it also led to a significant expansion of activities and missions. It was always easier to respond to the initiatives proposed by faculty or new needs of broader society when they could be funded from a growing resource base.

This situation began to change in the late 1970s as the growth of public support first began to slow and then actually began to decline. At all levels of government public resistance led to limitations on tax revenues and the reallocation of limited public resources to other priorities such as health care and corrections. Whether stated or not, it was the clear intent of public leaders at both the state and national level to shift more of the burden for the support of higher education from the shoulders of the taxpayer to those who benefited most from a college education, to students and parents. This was reflected, for example, in a series of policy decisions in the early 1970s that created federal student financial aid programs capable of supporting high-tuition/high-student-financial-aid approaches by both public and private universities.

Even in the face of declining public support, there was a continued expansion in the demand for higher education and a consequent expansion of the higher education enterprise.[2] Strong local interests drove both growth in the number of regional institutions and the addition of more advanced and expensive programs in established institutions, in spite of the fact that this further diluted limited public support and threatened quality.

Colleges and universities first responded to eroding public support in the early 1980s with short-term actions such as curtailing nonessential expenditures such as facilities maintenance and support services. As their financial situation became more serious, many institutions began to reduce academic programs, particularly in areas felt to be of marginal centrality or lower quality. Institutions attempted to compensate for the loss of public support by increasing tuition revenues, that is, by raising prices. In a sense, students, parents, and loyal alumni were asked to assume a larger share of the support of higher education as the public subsidy provided from tax dollars weakened.

Increasing tuition charges was only a near-term option for most institutions. Tuition at private colleges and universities had already reached levels where few families could afford them without substantial financial aid. While the tuition charged by public institutions was at far lower levels, even modest increases triggered strong public reaction and political efforts to limit further tuition increases.[3]

Many colleges and universities turned to private fund-raising as a more attractive and acceptable approach to revenue enhancement. Although the level of private support is increasing, the number of institutions seeking such support is also growing rapidly. Both public and private institutions are making major investments in private fund-raising efforts. But they are also increasingly competing for private gifts from the same sources. They have also explored whether their many self-supporting auxiliary activities, from health care to housing to services, might be used to generate profits, although for most institutions, these activities have limited revenue potential since they are heavily constrained and taxed by state and federal authorities.

Most institutions now realize that they need to focus instead on the other side of the ledger, on costs. Not only do they need to reduce costs and increase productivity, but they also need to consider reducing the number of activities so that they can better focus their limited resources. All universities have some capacity to become more efficient or productive. Such actions may allow some institutions to retain their existing portfolio of programs and activities, while achieving desired levels of quality. For most, the dominant strategy will still need to be the painful process of focusing resources to achieve quality by shedding missions and activities.

It is fair to suggest that, for the most part, our colleges and universities have yet to accept the need to change the basic paradigm for conducting and financing their education, research, and service missions. To be sure, higher education has met the challenge of making a transition from the growth era of the 1950s and 1960s, characterized by increasing public and private support and prestige, to the no-growth era of the 1980s and 1990s, largely by fine-tuning the traditional models. Yet our current mechanisms for financing and delivering higher education could well prove inadequate to meet changing societal demand with the available resources. Furthermore, the costs of quality in education and scholarship could well exceed the resources available to most colleges and universities, at least within the current paradigms.[4]

Despite the present euphoria generated by a prosperous economy, many believe that hard times are just over the horizon as other social priorities such as the needs of the elderly increasingly compete for limited public resources. Without a change in how we finance higher education, the combination of a growing demand for educational services, the increasing costs associated with such services, and stagnant or declining public support could lead to a financial crisis for the higher education enterprise in this nation.[5]

In this chapter we will examine the changing resource base of the university and the array of options available for universities to cope with these changes. We will also examine the implications for tuition, the price for a college education charged to students.

A Future of Limits

Like other enterprises in our society, the operation of a university requires the acquisition of sufficient resources to cover the costs of its activities. This is a complex task for academic institutions, because of both the wide array of their activities and the great diversity of the constituencies they serve. The not-for-profit culture of the university, whether public or private, requires a different approach to the development of a business plan than one would find in business or commerce.

Universities usually begin with the assumption that all of their current activities are both worthwhile and necessary. They then seek to identify the resources that can fund these activities. Beyond that, since there are always an array of worthwhile proposals for expanding ongoing activities or launching new activities, the university always seeks additional resources. The possibility of reallocating resources away from ongoing activities to fund new endeavors has only recently been seriously considered. Strategies from the business world aimed at cutting costs and increasing productivity are relatively new to our campuses.

Most universities depend upon the following as revenue sources:

- Tuition and fees paid by students
- State appropriations
- Federal research grants and contracts
- Gifts and endowment income
- Auxiliary activities (such as hospitals, residence halls, and athletics)

Strategies for the expenditure side of the ledger include:

- Cost containment
- Strategic resource management
- Innovation through substitution
- Total quality management
- Re-engineering administrative systems
- Selective growth strategies
- Restructuring the organization

The availability and attractiveness of each of these options varies greatly and depends upon the nature of the institution and its political environment. For many public institutions heavily dependent upon state appropriations, an appropriate strategy might be to build the political influence necessary to protect or enhance state support. Small private institutions with modest endowments depend heavily upon tuition and fees, and issues such as enrollments and tuition pricing play a key role in financial strategies. Highly focused research universities such as MIT and Caltech are heavily dependent upon federal research support and seek to influence federal research policies.

Although all dollars may be green, their utility for supporting the operations of the university varies greatly. Most funds have strings attached that restrict their use. For example, the funds provided by research grants and contracts are usually restricted to quite specific research activities. Most private support is given for particular purposes, such as supporting student financial aid or a specific building project. Tuition income and state appropriations generally have more flexibility, but here too there may be many constraints, for example, restrictions to the support of particular academic programs or the support of students who are state residents.

To understand better some of the issues involved in financing higher education, it is useful to comment briefly on each of these revenue and expenditure elements.

Federal Support

As we have noted, the federal government provides a significant share of the resources for student financial aid, campus-based research, graduate education, and health care. Although a robust economy allowed some growth in this federal support during the late 1990s, this followed a two-decade-long period of stagnant or declining funding. Furthermore, much of the federal support for purposes such as student financial aid or health care flows either directly or indirectly (via tax benefits) to individuals rather than institutions. Even those federal dollars flowing directly to universities for purposes such as research and graduate education are generally accompanied by tight restrictions on expenditures and associated federal regulations that require costly compliance (e.g., regulations imposed by the Occupational Safety and Health

Administration, Environmental Protection Agency, Nuclear Regulatory Commission, and Americans with Disabilities Act).

While the federal government will continue to be an important source of support for higher education in the years ahead, particularly for research- and graduate-intensive universities, there is growing concern. Without a major restructuring in federal entitlement programs or a dramatic increase in national productivity, the imbalance between federal commitments and revenues is likely to become even more serious over the next two decades as the baby boomers move into retirement. It is also likely that the trend toward increasing federal regulation will continue (health, safety, conflict of interest, scientific misconduct, foreign involvement), and the costs associated with compliance will continue to rise.

State Support

State support of higher education, on an inflation-adjusted, per student basis, has been declining in relative terms since the late 1970s.[6] As late as 1980, the states contributed 45 percent of all higher education revenues. By 1993 that share had fallen to 35 percent and continues to fall today. For public institutions, the contribution of state and local government spending has reached its lowest level since World War II, comprising roughly 53 percent of the support base. Cost shifting from the federal government through unfunded mandates, such as Medicare, Medicaid, ADA, and OSHA, has destabilized state budgets. Many states have made massive investments in corrections and commitments to funding K–12 education through earmarks off the top of the state budget. These have undermined their capacity to support higher education. In fact, in many states today the appropriations for prisons have now surpassed the funding for higher education and show no signs of slowing.[7] There is a growing consensus that, unlike the need for retrenchment experienced in the 1980s, the current erosion in state support for higher education is part of a more permanent shift in funding priorities. Generous public support of higher education is unlikely to be sustained in most states over the longer term.

Tuition

Whether public or private, most colleges and universities draw the majority of their revenues from operations—tuition from instruction, rentals from housing, clinical income from health care, and so on. In many states, even appropriations are indexed to instructional activity. The most significant and controllable revenue source for most universities is tuition, the price charged to students for their college education. In both public and private colleges and universities the true costs of a college education are heavily subsidized with public and private funds. Often tuition is discounted still further through financial aid programs. This is certainly an important consideration from the point of view of the student, but it is also important from the perspective of financial operations, since financial aid is a direct write-off against tuition revenue in many institutions, particularly at the margin. In fact, some institutions have found that the incremental cost of financial aid programs necessary to protect their student applicant pool actually exceeds the additional revenue from tuition increases. For most institutions, either market forces or political pressures strongly constrain tuition increases and revenues.

Private Fund-Raising

For some universities, private fund-raising provides the greatest opportunity for enhancing support.[8] For private colleges and universities, private fund-raising, particularly that aimed at building endowments, has long been a critical priority. Even for public universities, fund-raising may represent a more realistic option in the face of strong political opposition to tuition increases. While there are major costs with launching new fund-raising efforts, the more mature programs find these administrative costs level off at 15 percent to 20 percent of contributions. However the costs associated with private fund-raising may still be considerable, e.g., Harvard's investment of $35 million and 250 development staff to raise $427 million in 1998.

People give to universities for many reasons. Some contribute to say thanks, to pay institutions back for the educational opportunities they enjoyed. Others support higher education as a way to have impact on the future. Still others want monuments, perhaps through buildings. Some wish to achieve immortality through contribution to an endowment fund. Endowments are contributed funds, held and invested by the university in perpetuity, whose proceeds are dedicated for a particular purpose such as supporting a distinguished faculty member (an endowed professorial chair), a student (an endowed scholarship or fellowship), or perhaps an academic program. Generally the benefactor's name is associated with the endowed activity.

Since the management of endowments is intended to honor the original intent of the donor in perpetuity, only a fraction of the income derived from investing the fund is distributed for the designated purpose of the fund. The rest is reinvested to maintain the purchasing power of the fund in the face of inflation. For example, although an endowment fund might earn a 10 percent return, only 4 percent would be distributed while 6 percent would be reinvested, thereby allowing the endowment to appreciate.

However, even during the 1990s when endowment investment returns frequently have been in the 15 percent to 20 percent range, many of the wealthier institutions have set distributions at 3 percent or less, thereby allowing the funds to appreciate to enormous magnitudes (e.g., Harvard currently has an endowment of $14 billion; Yale, $5.6 billion; Texas, $4.6 billion; and Michigan $2.5 billion).[9] The soaring magnitude of some endowment funds has raised concerns about the appropriateness of such a low payout, which invests in future opportunity rather than meeting current needs. In fact, it has been suggested that some universities, from a financial perspective, look more like banks than educational institutions, since their most significant economic activity involves managing their endowment investments.

Yet it must also be stressed that in 1998, only 31 universities in America had endowments over $1 billion. In fact, only 10 percent of the nation's 3,600 colleges and universities had endowments above $50 million, with the vast majority having endowments well under $10 million. Hence, while endowment income is important to a small number of elite institutions, it is inconsequential to most of higher education in America.[10]

Auxiliary Funds

Universities engage in a host of other activities with resource implications. Technology transfer activities, through royalty licenses and equity interest in business start-ups, have provided modest revenue streams for some research universities. Others engage in auxiliary activities such as health-care delivery, extension services, and campus-based activities such as residential housing, food services, and book stores.

The revenue generated by auxiliary units of the universities—particularly, their academic health centers—has been the fastest growing component of their resource base through the past decade. Yet these are also the most uncertain elements of a university's resource base since they depend upon rapidly changing markets. With the rapid evolution of managed care and capitation and the entry of new for-profit health-care providers, the academic health center has become an endangered species. Most other auxiliary units such as intercollegiate athletics barely generate revenue sufficient to cover their own operating expenses. However, there are occasional opportunities for funding from these sources. For example, continuing education presents an excellent opportunity to generate additional revenue. The executive education programs conducted by many business schools provide examples of the degree to which high-quality programs, aggressively marketed, can generate resources that directly benefit academic units, while aligning well with the teaching mission of the institution.

The Entrepreneurial University Revisited

As we noted in Chapter 3, the diverse and ever-changing nature of the portfolio of resources available to finance higher education has stimulated and been tapped by marketlike or entrepreneurial behavior of universities and their faculties. For major private and public universities alike, most of the resources necessary to support academic activities are generated through the entrepreneurial activities of the institutions, for example, by attracting sufficient enrollment to generate the necessary tuition revenue, by competing for federal research grants, or by seeking private gifts. As a result, faculty members became quite skillful at generating the resources necessary to support their activities.[11]

While creating highly resilient institutions capable of weathering financial storms, such a market-driven, entrepreneurial culture has also had less beneficial consequences. Many contemporary universities resemble a shopping mall, with programs and activities determined largely by available resources rather than strategic intent. Those programs such as science and engineering with strong resource opportunities are usually winners; others such as the arts and the humanities, with fewer opportunities for external support, can become impoverished backwaters. Furthermore, with the ebb and flow of various elements of the university's resource portfolio, both its missions and programs would shift to adapt. Put another way, our shifting revenue streams and obsolete cost structures suggest that the very nature of our business is changing. For the longer term, we cannot depend upon simply substituting one revenue stream for another or cutting costs at the margin. We must consider changing our entire mix of activities to respond to the changing needs of those whom we serve.

The Costs of Higher Education

Today's university is like a conglomerate corporation, with many different business lines: education (undergraduate, graduate, professional), basic and applied research, health care, economic development, entertainment (intercollegiate athletics), international development, and so on. Each of these activities is supported by an array of resources: tuition and fees, state appropriation, federal grants and contracts, federal financial aid, private giving, and auxiliary revenues. Part of the challenge is to understand the cross-flows, that is, the cross-subsidies, among these various activities.

General Aspects of University Costs

A number of factors drive the costs of a college education: salaries paid to faculty and staff; costs of building and maintaining instructional facilities; infrastructure costs, such as libraries, computer centers, and laboratories; and costs of various support and administrative services.[12] As one attempts to understand the nature of cost increases in higher education, it is tempting to place the blame for the increasing costs of a college education on external forces—for example, the need to compete for high-quality faculty, staff, and students; the external imposition of federal rules and regulations; or the increasing litigiousness of our society. While these forces clearly influence a university's costs, they are only part of the picture. Just as important are those costs universities impose on themselves by operating in less than the most efficient manner by systems and processes that allow or even encourage waste and duplication.

For many years university expenditures have been growing more rapidly than the Consumer Price Index. In part this reflects the fact that the prices of the types of goods and services purchased by universities have been rising faster than the infla- tion rate. Colleges are both labor- and knowledge-intensive operations. These are the costs that have increased most rapidly over the past two decades. In addition, colleges must compete in a professional labor market, which always experiences some- what more rapid increases in personnel costs. But it is also important to note that universities have not only been paying more for the goods and services that they buy, but they have also been buying more of them. At most research universities this expansion is highly concentrated in facilities, state-of-the-art equipment, and other nonsalary areas.

What about the costs of administration? One of the great myths concerning higher education, particularly appealing to faculty members and trustees alike, is that universities spend too much money on administration. Actually, nothing could be further from the truth. The costs of the management of even the leanest of corpora- tion are many times greater relative to the total expenditure budget than any college or university. By almost any measure used by corporations or government, the Ameri- can university has a very thin administration–actually, precariously thin, in view of the increasing complexity and accountability of these institutions.

The major costs of higher education will always be in teaching and research programs. While many cost increases are due to external market factors, beyond the control of any single institution, some possibilities do exist to increase quality and reduce costs through more effective management while recognizing the essential collegial nature of academic decision-making processes.

Cost Drivers

Market-driven external forces that influence university costs are in large part the result of institutional objectives, for example, comprehensiveness or quality. Such objectives require that institutions of the same caliber compete with one another for both faculty and students. They must meet market rates for faculty salaries, workloads, and other resources and must compete effectively for the best undergraduate and graduate students. Faculty needs for computing services, library resources, labora- tory facilities, support staff, and associated expenses such as travel are also competi- tively driven. Different choices related to comprehensiveness or excellence lead to different markets and potentially lower cost resources.

Many costly external forces, however, are not market driven but rather result from rules, regulations, and social forces. The compliance with federal and state regulations is costly, now estimated to contribute over 10 percent of every tuition dollar charged.[13] Universities are asked to provide public service as well as time and talent to local, state, national, and international organizations for a wide variety of important activities and concerns.

From another perspective, the organizational structure of the university itself may be a primary cost driver. There is substantial cost and general overhead associated with centralized bureaucratic policies and procedures of any large, complex organization like the modern university. Activities such as financial operations, purchasing, plant operations, and information technology in most universities are simply not perceived as lean, efficient, customer-focused operations.

Another important cost driver is the cost related to space, which constitutes a large component of the total budget of all universities. This includes the costs of new construction and remodeling, together with those of utilities, maintenance, custodial services, and safety. Space growth is clearly limited by a university's total resource base and central allocation decisions. The fact that the allocation decisions are made at one level, while the needs are assessed at another, creates the strong possibility of misallocation, inefficiencies, and a greater-than-optimal supply of space.

Finally, it is important to understand the impact of the growth of knowledge itself on costs. As the knowledge associated with academic and professional disciplines continues to increase, so too do the costs of teaching and scholarship. The faculty of a university, at the project, department, or college level, can exhibit an inexhaustible appetite for expansion in funding, personnel, students, and space, justified by an ever-expanding knowledge base.

Cultural Factors

We should also acknowledge that certain cultural factors sustain the current cost structures of higher education.[14] Most institutions tend to focus on inputs rather than outputs. We tend to recruit those faculty members with the best reputations and those students with the highest scores on standardized tests. We measure the success of leaders of higher education by their success in increasing state appropriations or private giving. Rarely do we focus on more traditional measures of productivity or value-added, for example, the learning of students or the impact of scholarship.

Higher education has long had a monumental function. Wealthy donors prefer to give to wealthy universities, to see their names associated with buildings or endowed chairs at elite institutions. In fact, several of our campuses have become architectural parks, endowed far beyond the educational needs of their students or the scholarly needs of their faculty. The old maxim continues to apply to private giving in higher education: the rich get richer, the poor continue to fall further behind.

It is also the case that while society, through its media and its elected public officials, is both concerned and critical about the rising costs of a college education, it continues to convey its belief that the quality and reputation of an institution are directly correlated with expenditures. A case in point: Each year *U. S. News and World Report* devotes an issue to ranking the quality of the undergraduate education offered by various universities.[15] These rankings, based on a complex weighting of quantitative comparisons of universities, are taken very seriously by students and parents. They also represent a lucrative source of revenue for *USN&WR*. Yet, when one analyzes the ranking scheme in detail, it becomes evident that those institutions with the highest rankings are inevitably those institutions with the highest costs and highest tuition levels. The *USN&WR* rankings are so strongly correlated with measures of university expenditures on a per-student or per-faculty basis that public universities have essentially dropped entirely out of their rankings of leading institutions. Ironically, this same magazine has been one of the most strident critics of the increasing costs of higher education. Even as it voices such criticism, it sends the message through its rankings that the more a university spends—and charges—the more highly it will be ranked. In a perverse sense, the magazine itself has become one of the more significant cost drivers in higher education!

Cost Containment and Productivity

Higher education has been slow to focus creative attention on a careful understanding of quality and how quality relates to costs. As we face an era in which incremental resources become scarcer for the university, learning how to achieve higher quality while containing costs will be absolutely vital.

The 1980s were a period of extraordinary learning, change, and improvement in the area of quality, productivity, and cost containment in business and industry. While it is very important to be sensitive to the institutional differences between higher education and the private sector, there are valuable insights to be gained by reflecting on industry experience with quality improvement and considering what it means to higher education.[16] People in many organizations, in business, government, and health care, have learned that to improve quality and overall institutional performance, they need to carefully identify their customers, to learn more about their needs and expectations, and then to strive to improve their own performance based upon what they have learned.

In truth, the university does have customers. Those most obvious are external to the institution, such as prospective students or faculty. But customers may also be internal, that is, one university unit may be the customer of another. Attention to defining the customers of a unit and understanding their needs and expectations is key to quality improvement and a step toward understanding and eliminating unnecessary costs.

A second major insight from industry experience with quality in the 1980s is that the pursuit of certain dimensions of quality clearly increases costs (e.g., hiring "star" faculty members, increasing the specialized programs available to undergraduates, adding staff to improve the quality of support for any activity). But the pursuit of some dimensions of quality can actually lead to cost reductions. This is a major change from the traditional thinking that quality always costs more. Obviously, an institution dedicated to containing costs while improving quality needs to understand as much as possible about the cost-quality relationship. To be more specific, how can improving quality reduce costs? There are several ways that are relevant to the university.

First, resources and activities that do not meet real customer needs or help meet and exceed customer expectations are certainly candidates for close review and elimination.

Second, central to the pursuit of quality is elimination of waste in all work processes. Quality improvement always requires identification and analysis of key work processes and elimination of any steps or activities that add little or no value.

Third, quality can often be improved with a cost-reduction effect by requiring internally provided services to compete with those available in the open market. This requires the sometimes difficult step of allowing units to treat central services as simply another vendor candidate, as opposed to the sole or preferred vendor of services, in an effort to bring the quality and cost discipline of market competition into the institution.

Fourth, to achieve institutional excellence, it is important to identify, for every critical activity, what institutions in the world perform best and make that the target standard of performance for the university. This vital process is commonly called "benchmarking" in the business world, and it underpins continuous improvement.

Fifth, to make rapid and substantial progress in simultaneously improving quality and containing costs, the leaders of the university and its units must make quality the centerpiece of their institutional strategy. This is commonly called "strategic quality management." In addition, quality must undergo a transformation of meaning in the minds of these leaders and the members of the university community. It must go from meaning "more and better of everything" (with all the resource requirements that implies) to "being the best in that which we choose to do" (not everything) and "searching relentlessly for means of improving quality that reduce cost or are cost neutral or low cost in character."

The equivalent transformation in industry thinking about quality has been to shift from viewing it as an inspection problem, to an assurance problem, to a management problem, to a strategic opportunity. This series of changes has occurred over approximately sixty years. In the university, it is imperative we follow a less circuitous path and travel it more rapidly. A thoughtful approach that recognizes our differences from industry yet uses quality as a strategic opportunity has many potential benefits for the university. There are many sources to guide our efforts but no road map for instituting a total quality approach in higher education. However, there is good reason to believe that this approach could lead to similar successes in our environment similar to those in industry and in health services.

But here one must take care to recognize where corporate models can be usefully applied within the university, and where they could cause great harm to the academic mission. For example, best corporate practices in areas such as human resources development and staff benefits are long overdue in higher education. On the other hand, corporate methods that rely on characteristics such as teamwork, loyalty, discipline, and hierarchy could well be incompatible with the traditions of the academy which strongly favor individuality, creativity, and innovation.

Resource Allocation

Over the past decade, it has become increasingly clear that universities must develop more effective budgeting systems, capable of sustaining their core missions—teaching, research, and service—in the face of the rapid changes occurring in their resource base.[17] Good managers will make good, cost-effective decisions when they are provided with the necessary information and proper incentives. The first challenge for a university is to select good managers and to provide adequate training for them. The second challenge is to identify the appropriate level at which decision-making authority should lie with respect to each type of decision. If it is at too high a level there may not be an understanding of the primary impact on the unit or individuals (e.g., if the president were to assign individual faculty members to courses). If it is at too low a level there may not be an understanding of the secondary impact on related units or individuals (e.g., if each faculty member chose his or her own courses).

Many universities—particularly public universities—have relied for decades on a system of resource allocation best described as "incremental budgeting" based on a fund-accounting system.[18] In this system, a unit begins each fiscal year with the same base level of support it had received the previous year, incremented by some amount reflecting inflation, a unit's additional needs and aspirations, and the university's capacity to provide additional funds. These resources are partitioned into specific funds, more determined by historic traditions than strategic management, e.g., the general and education fund, restricted fund, restricted expendable fund, auxiliary fund, and capital fund. Beyond simply serving as an accounting tool, firewalls are constructed between these funds to limit transfers.

This system worked well enough during the three decades following World War ll when the increases in public support outpaced inflation. Universities had the additional dollars each year to launch many new initiatives, to do many important new things, without disturbing the resource stream to ongoing activities. But, with the erosion in public support—particularly state support—that began to occur in the late 1970s and has continued through today, it has become apparent that such incremental budgeting/fund-accounting approaches are increasingly incapable of meeting new challenges and opportunities. Indeed, in the face of a more limited resource base, they eventually lead to the starvation of all university activities.

The more constrained resource base facing higher education in the years ahead will force many institutions to abandon incremental budgeting if they are to preserve their core values, mission, and character. Universities must develop the capacity to set priorities and allocate resources to these priorities. There are many ways to do this. One could continue to implement targeted resource reallocation based upon decisions made by the central administration, assisted by faculty advisory groups. But in most universities today, not only are most costs incurred at the unit level, but this is also where most of the institution's revenues are generated. Hence centralized resource-management schemes are incompatible with the realities of highly decentralized resource generation and expenditure.

An alternative is to decentralize totally resource management, for example, an "every tub on its own bottom" budget strategy, like that used at Harvard and several other private institutions. In this system, each unit has full authority and responsibility for its financial operations. Yet this approach also suffers from its inability to address university-wide values or objectives with such a highly decentralized approach.

Many private universities and a few public universities, including the University of Michigan, have chosen an intermediate route to decentralize resource management through a system known as "responsibility center management."[19] This is a process that shares the resource allocation decisions through a partnership between academic units, administrative units, and the central administration. In its simplest form, this system allows units to keep the resources they generate, makes them responsible for meeting the costs they incur, and then levies a tax on all expenditures, to provide a central pool of resources necessary to support central operations (such as the university library) while providing the additional support needed by academic units unable to generate sufficient resources to support their activities.

More specifically, responsibility center management is aimed at three objectives. First, it enables resource allocation decisions to be driven by the values, core mission, and priorities of the university rather than dictated by external forces. Second, it provides a framework for such decisions, consisting of knowledge of the true resource flows throughout the university. Finally, responsibility center management allows both academic and administrative units to participate, as full partners with the central administration, in making these resource allocation decisions

It is clear that the highly centralized, incremental budgeting accompanied by fund-accounting systems may no longer suffice in the rapidly changing resource environment of the contemporary university. Moving from crisis to crisis or subjecting institutions to gradual starvation through across-the-board cuts simply are not adequate long-term strategies.

Innovation through Substitution

The fiscal pressures resulting from reduced revenue streams and uncontrolled cost drivers can be substantial. These pressures could lead to negative results within the normal university environment with a long tradition of incremental budgeting. How can such pressures be made positive, and how can the funds that will be needed for new ideas and continuing improvement be found?

The most dramatic change will have to be in the way universities plan. It will be necessary to start all planning exercises with significantly tightened and restrictive revenue assumptions. No longer will it be feasible—or even acceptable—to develop expenditure budgets first and then to close the gap between expenditure plans and revenue projections by a price increase (e.g., tuition). There will have to be much more care in setting priorities, along with a painful acknowledgment that in order to do something new we generally will have to eliminate something old. Innovation by substitution, not growth by incremental resources, will have to become the operative management philosophy. For instance, an academic unit that wishes to embrace a new subfield of its basic discipline may be required to phase out some other activity in order to make room for the new endeavor.

The necessity for cost containment need not be viewed negatively. It is an opportunity to restore credibility with the various clients and stakeholders of the university. It is also an opportunity to demonstrate to potential public and private supporters of the university that it is serious about cost effectiveness and institutional efficiency. They need to know that their future support will be used wisely in the delivery of instructional, research, and public service programs.

Underlying nearly all of these comments is the fundamental premise that higher education cannot continue to use "cost-plus" planning. We cannot always start with where we are in a given unit and allocate existing resources to ongoing activities, and then depend on additional resources to undertake a new or innovative activity. We must instead consider eliminating, reducing, or otherwise changing a current activity to make budgetary room for the new activity that we believe to be important.

To reduce costs, to improve productivity, to enhance quality in order to generate flexible operating funds does not sound easy. It will not be easy. But it has been done in other environments, and it can be done in the university.

Restructuring and Reengineering

Beyond the continual efforts to contain costs, increase productivity, and innovate through substitution rather than growth, universities need to follow industry's lead by asking more fundamental questions. They need to shift from asking, "Are we doing things right?" to "Are we doing the right things?" They need to grapple with the difficult challenge of restructuring and reengineering the most fundamental activities of the institution.

Most institutions have considered the redesign of administrative processes, such as managing financial operations, student services, and research administration. But since the core activity of the university involves academic processes, this too will eventually need fundamental reexamination. Here institutions face more serious challenges. First among these is the faculty culture that strongly resists business methods. But there are other fundamental obstacles as well.

For decades universities have defined academic quality in terms of inputs—student and faculty quality, resources, facilities—rather than outputs such as student performance. Rethinking the core academic functions of the university requires a shift in perspective from resources to results. This turns the institutional focus from faculty productivity to student productivity; from faculty disciplinary interests to what students need to learn; from faculty teaching styles to student learning styles. It reconceptualizes the university as learner-centered rather than faculty-centered. It grapples with the most fundamental processes, such as the way decisions are made, how information is shared, how students are taught, how students learn, how faculty work, how research is conducted, and how auxiliary enterprises are managed.

There are constraints on the internal actions an institution can take to control costs. The impact of tenure or collective bargaining agreements limits the institution's capacity to reduce faculty size. Political pressures can influence enrollment levels and program breadth. And, as a matter of fact, many institutions are already operating at the margin in terms of cost reduction—at least within the current higher education paradigms. Ironically, the only unconstrained variable that many institutions can adjust is quality. Efforts to reduce costs to stay within a given budget can sometimes only be achieved by accepting lower quality standards. In sharp contrast to the business sector, revenue-driven models of higher education could well lead to significant erosion in program quality.

Even those universities that accept the challenge of restructuring academic processes can be disappointed.[20] The pattern of retrenchment, reorganization, restructuring, and reengineering may not yield substantial productivity gains. Something more may be needed: fundamental transformation of both the university and the higher education enterprise, a topic for the later chapters of this book.

The Cost of a College Education

We have discussed the implications of resource limitations for the university. But it is important that we also examine their implications for those we serve, particularly for our students. Beyond the impact on the quality of education, the changing financial realities of the university have a direct bearing on the prices charged for their educational services, that is, for the cost of a college education to students and parents.

Certainly the cost of a college education is the most contentious issue in higher education today. Students and parents, taxpayers and politicians, and the media and public at large, all have raised concerns about the cost of a college education. They question the need for spiraling tuition levels. Some have even begun to wonder whether a college education is worth the investment. While the cost of a college education is a subject of great importance, it is also a subject surrounded by as much myth as reality.[21]

Among the concerns—and the myths—are the following:

- Tuition levels at most universities are out of control.
- Increasing tuition levels are pricing higher education out of reach of all but the wealthy.
- The fact that tuition rates are increasing faster than the Consumer Price Index provides evidence that universities are inefficient and exploiting the marketplace.
- The taxes paid by families should be sufficient to offset tuition charges in public colleges and universities.
- The price of a college education is no longer worth it.

Yet the facts suggest a more complex situation.[22] In 1999, while tuition at four-year private institutions averaged $14,508 (up 5 percent from the previous year), in four-year public institutions, tuition averaged only $3,243 (up 4 percent) because of strong public subsidy.[23] In addition financial aid programs provided over $60 billion of grants and loans to students (up 6 percent) which amounts to roughly $4,000 per student enrolled in higher education. This balance among public subsidy of higher education, tuition costs, and student financial aid determines the real cost of a college education to students.

During the decades following World War II, public support of higher education significantly increased through appropriations to public universities from state and local governments and from major federal programs aimed at supporting campus-based research, student financial aid, and specific disciplines such as the health professions. As a result, the fraction of the costs of a college education paid by families through tuition declined steadily into the 1970s.

However, as we noted earlier, there was a major policy shift in the 1970s toward high tuition/high-student-financial-aid policies in which government shifted its support of higher education from institutions to students through financial aid programs. However this occurred at a time when other social priorities such as health care and corrections began to compete for state and federal appropriations. This has shifted more of the burden of the support of higher education from the taxpayer to the student (or parent). More specifically, the average tuition per student, adjusted for inflation, has roughly doubled over the past twenty years.[24] Interestingly enough, however, the share of the costs of a college education borne by students and parents today has only returned to levels more typical of the 1950s than the 1970s and furthermore has receded once again during the past decade, from 69 percent in 1986–87 to 55 percent in 1997–98. Nevertheless, the increase in tuition associated with declining public support of higher education has stimulated strong public concerns about the affordability of higher education.

To separate myth from reality, we need to examine carefully two issues relating to the cost of a college education. First, we must understand the relationship between what it costs a university to operate, the price a student actually pays, and the value received by students through this education. Second, we need to consider the issue of just who should pay for a college education: parents, students, state taxpayers, federal taxpayers, private philanthropy, or the ultimate consumer (business, industry, and government). It is important to realize that quality in higher education does not come cheap; someone must pay for it. The real debate in our society is less about cost than about *who* should pay for higher education.

Tuition, the Price Paid by Students

Many factors determine the cost of a college education to students and their parents: the tuition charged for instruction, room and board, the cost of books, travel, and other incidental expenses. The most immediate concern here is tuition, since this represents the price that the institution charges for the education it provides.

At the outset, it must be recognized that no student pays the full cost of a college education. *All* students at *all* universities are subsidized to some extent in meeting the costs of their education through the use of public and private funds. Through the use of private gifts and income on endowment, many private institutions are able to set tuition levels (prices) at one-half to one-third of the true cost of the education. Public institutions manage to discount tuition "prices" even further to truly nominal levels—to as low as 10 percent of the real cost—through public tax support and financial aid programs.

For example, in 1998–99, the undergraduate tuition at the University of Michigan for a Michigan resident was about $6,000 per year. This represents 30 percent of the roughly $18,000 per year it costs to educate an undergraduate student for one year, with most of the subsidy coming from state taxpayers and private giving. If we were to discount this still further by the average financial aid available to instate students, the true average tuition is only about $3,000 per year.

This is a very important point. Even though tuition levels have increased at all institutions, public and private, they remain moderate and affordable for most colleges and universities. It is true that tuition levels at some universities such as Harvard, Stanford, and MIT have soared to $20,000 per year or more. But less than 1 percent of all college students attend such elite institutions.[25] In fact, over 80 percent of all college students today attend public colleges and universities, where the tuition averages less than $2,000 per year. To place this in perspective, it currently costs roughly $150 per week or $7,500 per year to provide a child with day care.

There is another reason for the current concerns about the rising costs of a college education. As we have noted, the costs of higher education have generally increased somewhat more rapidly than inflation for almost a century. Fortunately, however, average family income also increased substantially over this period. As long as family income increased at about the same rate as tuition, the costs of a college education were tolerated since they remained at roughly the same fraction of family expenses. In the 1980s, however, at about the same time that the public subsidy of higher education began to slow, driving up college tuition levels, the rate of increase of family income began to decline as well. Since 1980, the cost of sending a student to a public university has risen from 9 percent to 20 percent of the average family income, and from 20 percent to 40 percent of annual family income to send a student to a private university.[26] Little wonder there has been an outcry about the costs of a college education. The shift of the burden for meeting the costs of a college education from the taxpayer to the family occurred at a most inopportune time when the family budget was coming under increasing stress.

Financial Aid

While many families can still afford the costs of a college education for their children at public or even private universities, many others are not so fortunate. Yet, despite increasing tuition levels, today a college education is more affordable to more Americans than at any period in our history, as evidenced by the fact that enrollments have never been higher with two-thirds of high school graduates continuing on for some level of college education.. This is due in part to the availability of effective need-based financial aid programs. In truth, the real key to providing access to a college education for high school graduates has not been through low tuition, that is, prices, but rather through need-based financial aid programs. For low-income students attending a public university, the average contribution of federal, state, and institutional financial aid typically exceeds the level of tuition so that they, in effect, pay no tuition at all.

As we have noted, all students at all universities, public and private, are heavily subsidized by both public and private funds. As state and federal subsidies of the costs of education have declined, whether through declining appropriations to institutions or financial aid programs, tuition charges have understandably increased. Much of this new tuition revenue has been used to protect the financial aid programs critical to low-income families. Put another way, public universities, just as private universities, have asked more affluent families to pay a bit more of the true cost of education for their students—although not the full costs, of course—so that they can protect the financial aid programs that enable less fortunate students to attend.

Students and parents have also been caught by a significant shift in the nature of federal financial aid programs at the same time as tax support of public higher education has declined. In 1980 two-thirds of federal assistance to students came in the form of grants and work-study jobs, with the remaining one-third in the form of subsidized loans. Today, the reverse is true; grants typically comprise only one-third of a student's federal aid award, and the remaining two-thirds is extended in the form of loans. Although federal financial aid remains important, most of the growth over the past decade has been in the form of loans rather than grants. The nature of the federal loan program shifted again during the early 1990s when Congress extended the eligibility for loan subsidies to middle- and upper-middle-income students.[27] At the same time, the real funding declined for federal grant programs aimed at low-income students such as the Pell Grants.

Most recently, as part of the agreement reached between Congress and the Clinton administration on balancing the federal budget in 1997, major new tax credits and deductions have been introduced to help middle-class students and families meet the costs of a college education.[28] Furthermore, the Higher Education Act of 1998 provided for the increases in federal financial aid grants. While these are encouraging actions, there is also a worry that they will neither directly impact either the resource needs of colleges and universities nor improve access to higher education. In fact, some portray the $40 billion of tax benefits included in the Budget Balancing Act of 1997 as a massive middle-class entitlement program, politically very popular but not strategically aligned with the needs of the nation. There is concern that the major impact of the tax benefits will flow into middle-class consumption and not into expanding the opportunity for a college education.

Setting Tuition Levels

Determining tuition rates involves a complex set of considerations including the actual costs of instruction at the institution, the availability of other revenue sources that can be used to subsidize instructional costs (tax support, private giving, and income from endowment), competition with other institutions for students, and an array of political factors. These factors can be woven together in the determination of tuition levels in several ways.

Traditionally in many public institutions, tuition levels have been determined by first estimating the operating costs for the academic programs of the institution. Then, the available revenue from all other sources such as state appropriations, federal support, and endowment income is estimated. Finally, the level of tuition is set to make up the difference between projected operating costs and available income from other sources. Using this model, tuition is related to the costs of conducting the activities of the university and the resources available. Revenue from tuition fits together with other revenues in a carefully balanced structure. When any one source of income falls behind, other sources must take up the slack. More specifically, the erosion of support from other sources, especially falling state appropriations and reductions in financial aid, has driven increases in tuition rates.

Private universities rely instead on high-tuition/high-financial-aid strategies. In contrast to the "cost-driven" approach of public universities, private universities tend to be "market-driven." They first set their tuition based on both market sensitivity and the prices of competing institutions (although taking care to avoid federal constraints on price-fixing). This tuition revenue along with other projected revenue (endowment income, research support, etc.) then establishes the constraints on expenditure budgets. Because of the intense market competition, private institutions of comparable reputation generally have comparable tuition levels.

Despite these differences, the tuition levels at both public and private universities are heavily influenced by political considerations. Rising tuition levels trigger strong public reaction from students and parents, in turn triggering media attention and political action at the state and federal level. Political pressures also play a role in constraining the tuition levels of private institutions, since there would clearly continue to be demand for admission to the most selective institutions even if the tuition levels were to increase substantially.

Changing the Paradigm

Traditionally, we have depended upon a "pay as you go" approach to higher education. That is, most students—or their parents—have paid tuition on a term-by-term basis as they receive their education. A college education has been viewed as a temporary additional expense for a family (or a student), to be paid for by tightening the family budget and perhaps relying on additional resources through part-time student employment. As the cost, value, and price of education have risen, this traditional approach has become more and more of a burden to students and their families. The total cost—tuition, room and board, and so on—of a college education at a private institution, typically ranging from $15,000 to $30,000 per year, cannot be accommodated within most family budgets. Even at public universities, where total costs (dominated by room and board rather than tuition) range from $8,000 to $12,000 per year, financing a college education becomes a significant burden.

"Working one's way through college" has been a very important and very American tradition. Today, however, this has become difficult since wages for most student employment have not kept pace with the rising costs of education. "Work-study" programs, in which the work experience also has educational benefit, are still important. However, the minimum-wage type of employment available to most students is no longer an effective way to pay for college. Instead, many students seek cooperative education programs that alternate between full-time study and full-time work. Unfortunately, such programs are generally only available in high-demand areas such as engineering where students develop technical competence early in their studies and are of significant value to employers.

"Saving for a college education" has been another traditional approach to financing a college education, but very few parents manage to save more than token amounts toward this end. In fact, this inability to save may be one of the big factors driving public concerns about the rising costs of a college education. For that reason, there has been great interest in the development of more formal programs to assist families in adopting a more systematic and disciplined approach to setting aside the resources necessary to educate their children.

For some time many universities have provided families with mechanisms to prepay tuition costs at the time of enrollment, thereby avoiding concerns about rising tuition levels during the actual time spent in college. While these are occasionally financed by the institutions themselves, more frequently arrangements are made with commercial organizations. The general idea is that one pays either a lump sum or a set of installments at a fixed rate throughout the period of education. The interest earned on the payments then covers any increase in tuition costs.

More recently, a number of states have developed similar prepaid tuition plans in which a family can purchase "tuition futures," tuition credits at today's prices redeemable at any future date. For example, a family would use either lump sum or installment payments to purchase a contract for a four-year college education at present prices. This contract then would allow the child to attend at any time in the future, regardless of tuition levels at that time. Again, the premise behind such programs is that the rate of increase in tuition is roughly comparable to the interest earned on the prepayments.

Traditionally we have looked at a college education as a consumer good, requiring payment of the costs of tuition, room, board, and other expenses upon enrollment. Since these costs frequently exceed the resources that most students or families can generate during the actual period of enrollment, either savings or loan plans will play an increasingly important role in the future.

Peter Drucker has suggested that we really should think about financing a college education in a much different way: "The basic problem of American higher education is that traditionally it has been priced no differently from the way food, soap, or shoes are priced. Customers pay in full when they take delivery of the merchandise. But a college education is not a consumer good that will be used up and gone within a short time. It is a long-term investment in the lifetime earning power of the graduate."[29]

To the degree that a college education is in reality a long-term investment in the future, perhaps we should look at it as we would other major investments we make in our life. For example, we borrow money to buy an automobile and a house, and we pay off these loans over long periods of time, even as we enjoy the purchase. A college education seems to fit this model, since not only does it improve one's quality of life, but it enhances their earning capacity, thereby enabling the borrower to better pay off the loan.

Drucker proposes shifting the payment for a college education from the "front end," when most students have no money and next to no earning power, to a later period when their incomes are sizable and rapidly rising. In particular, those students choosing to pay later rather than at the time of enrollment would agree to have the installments paid through payroll deduction. They also would be required to take out twenty-year term life insurance for the amount of the outstanding liability; premiums for such insurance at the age of young college students are minimal.

With these steps, the repayment claim for the investment made by the college in the future earning power of the student becomes a marketable security, bearing little risk and a fair rate of return. The former student, now a wage earner, could carry the annual payment. The graduate's family would have little or no financial burden at all. The college could be certain of being paid, and it could charge what it needs to build faculty and curriculum and still not price itself out of the market.

To carry this one step further, perhaps as a society we should look upon a college education as we do our Social Security system. Perhaps we should restructure federal student loan programs to facilitate payment through payroll deduction, just as we do payment for Social Security programs. An alternative would be to use tax assessment strategies, using the Internal Revenue Service as the collection agency. The basic idea is to shift the burden for the support of higher education from the previous generation to the generation of students that benefit most directly, but at a time in their lives when they can afford these costs.

In a sense, the Higher Education Act of 1992 did just this with the Ford Direct Lending Program. This program allows students to receive their education load funds directly from the federal government via their colleges and universities, thereby eliminating much of the cost and bureaucracy of the commercial loan industry. But equally significant is the fact that the direct lending program provided an opportunity to base repayment rates on future income and repayments collected through income tax withholding, thereby reducing much of the risk associated with financing a college education. Like the national service initiative launched by the Clinton administration in 1996, income-contingent loan repayment is designed to ease the debt burden on college graduates, perhaps encouraging them to seek employment in fields of urgent national need such as teaching, public health, and community development.

Of course such approaches require a major change in public attitudes toward the value of a college education. The direct lending program, although supported by students and parents, was strongly opposed both by the banking industry and some in higher education. Yet in the end it has survived, in part because of the recognition that the increasing value of a college education, both to an individual and society more broadly, requires the exploration of new financing mechanisms.

A Broader Perspective

The current debate about the cost, price, and value of a college education suggests three quite different approaches to restructuring the financing of higher education in America. All three approaches begin with the premise that the university must get its house in order by better controlling costs, eliminating unnecessary or redundant programs, and transforming itself to serve society better.

Approach 1: Higher Education as a Public Good. The first approach would reestablish the principle of higher education as a public good, with strong public support to provide sufficient access to low cost, high-quality higher education to meet the growing needs of a knowledge-driven society. This approach would abandon the high-tuition/high-financial-aid policies that have dominated American higher education for the past several decades for several reasons: Such a high-tuition/high-aid model portrays higher education primarily as an individual benefit and contributes to public concerns and misunderstanding concerning the affordability of a college education. The high-tuition model does not contain sufficient incentives for cost controls. It furthermore drives a wedge between public and private higher education, since although both public and private institutions are heavily subsidized by federal financial aid programs and tax policy, private colleges and universities are constrained only by market concerns in setting their very high tuition levels, while public tuition levels are kept at low levels by political constraints.

This approach would argue that as a nation we should reaffirm that higher education represents one of the most important investments a society can make in its future, since it is an investment in our people. We are fortunate today to have one of the finest systems of higher education in the world, but we also remember this has resulted from the willingness of past generations to look beyond the needs and desires of the present and to invest in the future by building and sustaining educational institutions of exceptional quality—institutions that have provided many of us with unsurpassed educational opportunities.

We have inherited these institutions because of the commitments and sacrifices of previous generations. It is our obligation as responsible stewards—and as responsible parents—to sustain these institutions to serve our children and our grandchildren. It seems clear that if we are to honor this responsibility to future generations, we must reestablish the priority of both our personal and our public investments in education, in the future of our children, and in the future of our nation.

It is in our national interest to provide educational opportunity to all with the desire and the ability to learn. If we are to achieve this object, we must halt the erosion in public support of higher education and once again reaffirm the commitment from one generation to the next that has characterized our nation. Yet there is a formidable challenge to this approach. The fiscal constraints faced by local, state, and federal governments are likely to intensify in the years ahead, since there continues to be strong public resistance against further taxation.

Approach 2: Raising Prices to Reflect True Costs. A sharply contrasting approach would be to depend more heavily on market forces by removing hidden subsidies in higher education and raising prices to levels more accurately reflecting true costs. This approach would depend even more heavily on financial aid to provide access to those unable to pay. Such an approach would be motivated, in part, by the evidence that raising prices for middle- and upper-income students in higher education does not discourage enrollments. In a similar sense, using federal dollars to subsidize the lending costs of middle- and upper-income students does little to create new opportunities for college enrollment for those in most need of assistance. Hence, if the intent is to utilize increasingly limited public dollars for higher education, there is some justification for raising the price of a college education so that it more accurately reflects its true costs, particularly in public colleges and universities.

Some would go still further and suggest that the very principle of low tuition levels at public universities is, in reality, a highly regressive social policy that subsidizes the rich at the expense of the poor. Few families will ever pay sufficient state taxes to cover the educational costs of their children at a public university. Low tuition levels subsidize many middle- and upper-income families who could afford to send their students to far more expensive institutions. This subsidy is being provided through the tax dollars paid by many lower-income families whose children may never have the opportunity to benefit from a college education at four-year institutions, public or private, because of inadequate availability of financial aid.

This issue becomes even more serious when it is recognized that public higher education has increasingly become the choice of higher-income students. In 1994, 38 percent of students from families earning more than two hundred thousand dollars were enrolled in public institutions, compared to 31 percent in 1980.[30] Parents and students from wealthy backgrounds are increasingly asking why they should choose the elite private colleges when they can get an education almost as good for one-third the price. In fact, in several states, the average income of students enrolling in public universities is now higher than that of private colleges. Clearly this raises a public policy issue, since these wealthier students, who could afford to attend more expensive private institutions, are displacing students from less fortunate economic circumstances in public higher education. While holding tuition to nominal levels in public higher education may be good politics, it is questionable social policy. In effect we ask those who cannot afford a college education to pay taxes to subsidize those who can—welfare for the rich at the expense of the poor.

Approach 3: Shifting the Burden from One Generation to the Next. The third approach would change radically the very assumptions and values underlying the support of higher education in America. Rather than viewing the support of higher education as an obligation of one generation to the next, an investment in the future, instead we would take steps to allow this burden to be born directly by those who benefit most directly, the students. This approach would acknowledge the increasing value of a college education in a knowledge-intensive world, as well as the increasing resistance of parents and taxpayers to support this activity in the face of limited resources and other social priorities. As we have noted, this approach would shift the perspective of a college education from that of a duty or obligation of parents to that of a personal investment on the part of the student. Such an approach would require a quite different financing scheme such as the direct lending/income-contingent payback program developed by the Department of Education during the 1990s. Recasting the financing of higher education as an investment opportunity rather than a social obligation might be more consistent with the realities of the market-driven politics of our times.

While these are dramatic departures from the current paradigms for financing higher education, it is clear if we stay on our present course, we are likely to encounter disaster in the years ahead. The dilemma has been described earlier: if colleges and universities continue to use tuition alone to compensate for the imbalance between societal demand for higher education and rising costs on one hand, and stagnant public support on the other, millions of Americans will find a college education priced beyond their means.

While cost containment and renewed public investment are clearly needed, it seems increasingly clear that entirely new paradigms for providing and financing higher education are required for the longer term.

CHAPTER 9   # Diversity

I am now aiming merely to remind you that at an expenditure which it is simply ridiculous to call burdensome, this prosperous State of Michigan has, through the wisdom of her founders, succeeded in furnishing the higher education to all her sons and daughters, without distinction of birth, race, color, or wealth.
—James Burrill Angell, President,
The University of Michigan (1879) [1]

A distinguishing characteristic and great strength of American higher education is its growing commitment over time to serve all segments of our pluralistic society. Higher education's broadening inclusion of talented students and faculty of diverse ethnic, racial, economic, social, political, national, or religious background, has allowed our academic institutions to draw on a broader and deeper pool of talent, experience, and ideas than more exclusive counterparts in other places and times. This diversity invigorates and renews teaching and scholarship in American universities, helping to challenge long-held assumptions, asking new questions, creating new areas and methods of inquiry, and generating new ideas for testing in scholarly discourse.

We have never needed such inclusiveness and diversity more than today when differential growth patterns and very different flows of immigration from Asia, Africa, Latin America, the Caribbean, and Mexico are transforming our population. By the year 2030 current projections indicate that approximately 40 percent of all Americans will be members of minority groups, many—even most—of color. By mid-century we may cease to have any one majority ethnic group. By any measure, we are evolving rapidly into a truly multicultural society with a remarkable cultural, racial, and ethnic diversity. This demographic revolution is taking place within the context of the continuing globalization of the world's economy and society that requires Americans to interact with people from every country of the world. These far reaching changes in the nature of the people we serve and the requirements of global responsibility demand far-reaching changes in the nature and structure of higher education in America.

Our rapidly diversifying population generates a remarkable vitality and energy in American life and in our educational institutions. At the same time, it gives rise to conflict, challenging our nation and our institutions to overcome at last our long history of prejudice and discrimination against those groups who are different, particularly and most devastatingly, those groups identified by the color of their skin. Tragically, race remains a significant factor in our social relations that profoundly affects the opportunities, experiences, and perspectives of those discriminated against as well as those who discriminate. To change this racial and cultural dynamic, we need to understand better how others think and feel and to learn to function across racial and cultural divisions. We must replace stereotypes with knowledge and understanding. Slowly, we Americans are learning but there remains a great distance to go.

This final century of the second millennium, for all its advances in learning and technology, is likely to be most remembered for the horrors unleashed by racial, religious, and ethnic prejudice and discrimination. If anyone should doubt the urgency of our task in seeking to overcome this evil heritage, they have only to recall the Holocaust or to look around the world today at the religious, racial, and ethnic conflicts that have killed millions of innocents, made millions of others refugees, ripped nations asunder, set neighbor against neighbor, and poisoned the minds and hearts of generations. From Rwanda to Timor, from Kosovo to the Middle East, the endless toll of violence and suffering rises unabated. Some see this as evidence that the ideal of tolerance and understanding is impossible to achieve. We cannot accept such defeatism. We must meet this challenge to overcome prejudice and discrimination here and now. America's colleges and universities have a critical part to play in this struggle.

This means we must not falter in our national commitment to ending discrimination and achieving the promise of equal opportunity. In recent years academia has made a dedicated effort to make progress towards diversity. It can point to significant gains as a result of these efforts. Unfortunately, but perhaps not surprisingly, this progress has given rise to a growing backlash. An increasing number of Americans oppose our traditional approaches to achieving diversity such as affirmative action.[2] Federal courts are pondering cases that challenge racial preference. In state after state, voters are taking aim through referenda at an earlier generation's commitment to civil rights. At such a time, it seems particularly important that we in academe talk openly, with boldness, about the need for more, not less, diversity. There is plenty of room to debate the merits of various methods of achieving our ends, but as our nation and our world become ever more diverse, ever more interdependent and interconnected, it is vital that we stand firm in our fundamental commitment to our diversity.[3]

The Case for Diversity

When one discusses the topic of diversity in higher education, it is customary to focus on issues of race and ethnicity, and we shall do so in much of this chapter. But it is also important to recognize that human diversity is far broader, encompassing characteristics such as gender, class, national origin, and sexual orientation. These, too, contribute to the nature of an academic community. In both the narrow and broader sense, it is important to set out a compelling rationale for seeking diversity in American higher education. First and foremost, the case rests on moral responsibility and democratic ideals, based on our social contract with society. I would also contend that diversity is a critical element in sustaining the quality and relevance of our education and scholarship. Our nation's campuses have a unique opportunity to offer positive social models and provide leadership in addressing one of the most persistent and seemingly intractable problems of human experience—overcoming the impulse to fear, reject, or harm the "other." In addition, there are persuasive pragmatic reasons for academia to pursue diversity.

Social and Moral Responsibility

American colleges and universities are founded on the principle that they exist to serve their society through advancing knowledge and educating students who will, in turn, apply their knowledge for their own advancement but also to serve others. Hence, higher education, indeed all educational institutions, are responsible for modeling and transmitting essential civic and democratic values and helping to develop the experience and skills necessary to put them into practice. In this sense, then, higher education's commitment to reflect the increasing diversity of our society in terms of both our academic activities and the inclusiveness of our campus communities is based in part on the American university's fundamental social, institutional, and scholarly commitment to freedom, democracy, and social justice.

To further these lofty goals, our colleges and universities must overcome inequities deeply embedded in our society by offering opportunity to those who historically have been prevented from participating fully in the life of our nation. Over the years our universities have broadened their commitment to providing equal opportunity for every individual regardless of race, nationality, class, gender, or belief. They have done so as part of their basic obligations to serve those who founded and support us, to serve as models of social interaction, and to serve as a major source of leaders throughout society. This is a fundamental issue of equity and social justice that must be addressed if we are to keep faith with our values, responsibilities, and purposes.

Educational Quality

Nevertheless, universities are social institutions of the mind, not of the heart. While there are compelling moral and civic reasons to seek diversity and social equity on our campuses, the most effective arguments in favor of diversity to a university community tend to be those related to academic quality.

Perhaps most important in this regard is the role diversity plays in the education of our students. We have an obligation to create the best possible educational environment for the young adults whose lives are likely to be significantly changed during their years on our campuses. Their learning environment depends on the characteristics of the entire group of students who share a common educational experience. Students constantly learn from each other in the classroom and in extracurricular life. The more diverse the student cohort, the more opportunities for exposure to different ideas, perspectives and experiences and the more chances to interact, develop interpersonal skills, and form bonds that transcend difference.

There is ample research to suggest that diversity is a critical factor in creating the richly varied educational experience that helps students learn. Since students in late adolescence and early adulthood are at a crucial stage in their development, diversity (racial, demographic, economic, and cultural) enables them to become conscious learners and critical thinkers, and prepares them to become active participants in a democratic society.[4] Students educated in diverse settings are more motivated and better able to participate in an increasingly heterogeneous and complex democracy.[5]

We must accept as a fact of life in contemporary America that the persistence of separation by race and ethnicity, past and present, has shaped the life experiences and attitudes of whites and minorities in fundamental ways.[6] Americans of different races and ethnicities live in worlds that have a long history of separation and are still, to a great extent, separate. Indeed, in many regions, we are more sharply segregated than ever. Too few Americans of different racial and ethnic backgrounds interact in a meaningful way on a daily basis. A racially and ethnically diverse university student body has far-ranging and significant benefits for all students, non-minorities, and minorities alike. Students learn more and think in deeper, more complex ways in a diverse educational environment. Racial diversity in a college student body provides the very features that research has determined are central to producing the conscious mode of thought educators demand from their students.

Intellectual Vitality

Diversity is similarly fundamental for the vigor and breadth of scholarship. Unless we draw upon a greater diversity of people as scholars and students, we cannot hope to generate the intellectual vitality we need to respond to a world characterized by profound change. The burgeoning complexity and rapidly increasing rate of change forces us to draw upon a broader breadth and depth of human knowledge and understanding. Perhaps our society could tolerate singular answers in the past, when we could still imagine that tomorrow would look much like today. But this assumption of stasis is no longer plausible. As knowledge advances, we uncover new questions we could not have imagined a few years ago. As society evolves, the issues we grapple with shift in unpredictable ways. A solution for one area of the world often turns out to be ineffectual or even harmful in another. The dangers of unanticipated consequences of our actions multiply as we take on ever more complex social problems. Many academic and professional disciplines have found their very foundations radically transformed as they grapple with the impact of new perspectives, revolutionary technologies, and the exponential growth of knowledge.

For universities to thrive in this age of complexity and change, it is vital that we resist any tendency to eliminate options. Only with a multiplicity of approaches, opinions, and ways of seeing can we hope to solve the problems we face. Universities, more than any other institution in American society, have upheld the ideal of intellectual freedom, open to diverse ideas that are debated on their merits. We must continually struggle to sustain this heritage and to become places open to a myriad of experiences, cultures, and approaches.

In addition to these intellectual benefits, the inclusion of underrepresented groups allows our institutions to tap reservoirs of human talents and experiences from which they have not yet fully drawn. Indeed, it seems apparent that our universities could not sustain such high distinctions in a pluralistic world society without diversity and openness to new perspectives, experiences, and talents. In the years ahead we will need to draw on the insights of many diverse perspectives to understand and function effectively in our own as well as in the national and world community.

Serving a Changing Society

Our nation's ability to face the challenge of diversity in the years ahead will determine our strength and vitality. As I mentioned at the beginning of this chapter, our culture needs to come to grips with the fact that those groups we refer to today as minorities will become the majority population of our nation in the century ahead, just as they are today throughout the world. For instance, as we enter the next century, one of three college-age Americans today is a person of color, and roughly 50 percent of our school children (K–12) are African American or Hispanic American. By 2020, the American population, which now includes 26.5 million African Americans and 14.6 million Hispanic Americans, will include 44 million African Americans and 47 million Hispanic Americans. By the late twenty-first century, some demographers predict that Hispanic Americans will become the largest ethnic group in America.

The truth, too, is that most of us retain proud ties to our ethnic roots, and this strong and fruitful identification must coexist with—indeed enable—our ability to become full participants in the economic and civic life of our country. Pluralism poses a continuing challenge to our nation and its institutions as we seek to build and maintain a fundamental common ground of civic values that will inspire mutually beneficial cohesion and purpose during this period of radical transformation of so many aspects of our world.

Human Resources

The demographic trends we see in our future hold some other significant implications for national economic and political life and especially for education. Our clearly demonstrated need for an educated workforce in the years ahead means that America can no longer afford to waste the human potential, cultural richness, and leadership represented by minorities and women. Our traditional industrial economy is shifting to a new knowledge-based economy, just as our industrial economy had evolved from an agrarian society in an earlier era. Now, since people and knowledge are the source of new wealth, we will rely increasingly on a well-educated and trained workforce to maintain our competitive position in the world and our quality of life at home.

Higher education will play a particularly important role in this regard. For example, in the 1960s barely one percent of law students and two percent of medical students in America were black.[7] Through the use of affirmative action, financial aid programs, and aggressive recruiting, universities were able to attract more minorities into their professional programs, and by 1995, 7.5 percent of law school students and 8.1 percent of medical school students were black. Hence, it is clear that higher education can open the doors of opportunity to under-served components of our society. Our universities must make special efforts to expand educational achievement and workforce participation by minorities and women not just because that is good social policy, but because we cannot afford to waste their talents. America will need to call on the full contribution of all of its citizens in the years ahead.

The Challenges of Diversity

Although American higher education has long sought to build and sustain diverse campuses, this is a goal that has faced many challenges. Our nation continues to be burdened by prejudice and bigotry that plague our neighborhoods, our cities, and our social institutions. Although we think of America as a melting pot in which diverse cultures come together in common purpose, in reality, most among us seek communities of like rather than diverse colleagues. All too frequently we define ourselves in terms of our differences from others, and we have great difficulty in imagining the world as others see it. And, although change is always a difficult task for tradition-bound institutions such as universities, it has proven particularly so in the areas of diversity.

The Challenge of Racism

Prejudice and ignorance persist on our nation's campuses as they do throughout our society. American society today still faces high levels of racial segregation in housing and education in spite of decades of legislative efforts to reduce it. Furthermore, most students complete their elementary and secondary education without ever having attended a school that enrolled significant numbers of students of other races and without living in a neighborhood where the other races were well represented.

Yet, because of the distinctly different historical experiences of white and non-white Americans, race continues to affect outlook, perception, and experience. For example, most white Americans tend to think that race has only a minor impact on the daily experiences and future expectations of Americans whatever their background and that blacks receive the same treatment as they do both personally and institutionally. Most non-whites, in contrast, feel that race still matters a great deal, and considerable numbers report having experienced discriminatory treatment in shops and restaurants or in encounters with the public.[8] Whether explicitly or more subtlety, our society continues to perpetuate stereotypes which reinforce the idea that one race is superior to another.

Not surprisingly, new students arrive on our campuses bringing with them the full spectrum of these experiences and opinions. It is here that many students for the first time have the opportunity to live and work with students from very different backgrounds. In many ways our campuses act as lenses that focus the social challenges before our country. It is not easy to overcome this legacy of prejudice and fear that divides us. Not surprisingly, our campuses experience racial incidents, conflict, and separatism. When these occur, we must demonstrate clearly and unequivocally that racism on our campuses will not be tolerated. Programs are also needed to promote reflection on social values and to encourage greater civility in social relations. It is also critical to develop new networks and forums to promote interaction and open discussion among campus groups.

The Challenge of Community

In an increasingly diverse country, deep divisions persist between whites, blacks, Hispanics, Native Americans, and other ethnic groups. There is nothing natural about these divisions. They are not immutable facts of life. Rather they are a consequence of a troubled and still unresolved past. Racial and ethnic groups remain separated by residence and education. There are unfortunately few places in American society where people of different backgrounds interact, learn from each other, and struggle to understand their differences and discover their commonality. The fundamental issue that we face at the end of the twentieth century is to work to overcome our divisions in the spirit of the venerable American motto, *E Pluribus Unum*. To build unity from pluralism, to recognize diversity and learn from it, to fashion a democracy of many voices, is still an unfinished project. Its success is vital to our nation's future.

As a social institution, the university can find direction in its history and tradition of openness. We must set forth a vision of a more varied and tolerant environment—a more pluralistic, cosmopolitan community. We have to become a community in which all barriers to full participation of all people in the life of our institution are removed; a place where we can all draw strength from the richness of our human variety; but also a place where we can work constructively together as a community of scholars and as citizens of a democratic society. This is the challenge before us. As citizens we have to reaffirm our commitment to justice and equality. As scholars we have to support unwaveringly our shared commitment to academic freedom and the pursuit of excellence.

Seeing Difference Differently

We need to work diligently to transform our campuses, encouraging respect for diversity in all of the characteristics that can be used to describe our human species: age, race, gender, disability, ethnicity, nationality, religious belief, sexual orientation, political beliefs, economic background, and geographical origin. Yet, in doing so, we will have to move in two directions at once. We have to set aside the assumption that people from groups different from ours necessarily have the same needs, experiences, and points of view that we do. At the same time, we cannot succumb to the equally pernicious assumption that "they" are all the same. Real barriers, experiences, and culture may be shared by many in a group, but that does not give us permission to treat people as though they conform to some stereotyped image of "white," "gay," or "Latino." We seek a community where various cultures and ethnicity are valued and acknowledged, but where each individual has the opportunity to find her or his own path.

At the same time, we should recognize that not everyone faces the same consequences for their differences. The experience of an Asian American student on our campus is not the same as that of an African American student or a white woman or a person with a disability. We should not forget that issues of difference are inextricably intertwined with issues of power, opportunity, and the specific histories of groups and of each individual. As we pursue a pluralistic campus, we should realize that equality will require effort, resources, and commitment to both structural change and education. We must learn to see difference differently. The multicolored skein that would be a multicultural university has to be woven together, becoming a tapestry, with each thread retaining its unique character while remaining part of a larger design.

The Challenge of Change

It is important not to delude ourselves. Institutions do not change quickly and easily any more than do the societies of which they are a part. Achieving our democratic goals of equity and justice for all often requires intense struggle, and we remain far from our goals as a nation. In confronting the issues of racial and ethnic inequality in America we are probing one of the most painful wounds of American history.

Throughout the latter half of the twentieth century, progress towards greater racial equity in our society and our social institutions has been made, in part, through policies and programs that recognize race as an explicit characteristic. For some time, universities with highly selective admissions have used race as one of several factors (e.g., special athletic, artistic, scientific or leadership talent; or geographic origin; status as children of alumni; or unique qualities of character or experience) in determining which students to admit to their institutions. Special financial aid programs have been developed to address the economic disadvantages faced by underrepresented minority groups. Minority faculty and staff have been identified and recruited through targeted programs.

Yet, despite its utility, the use of race as an explicit factor in efforts to achieve diversity or address inequities is being challenged with great force through popular referenda, legislation, and by the courts. For example, actions taken in several states now prohibit the consideration of race in college admissions. In such instances, it is sometimes suggested that other approaches such as admitting a certain fraction of high school graduates or using family income could be used to achieve the same diversity objectives. Yet, the available evidence suggests such alternatives may not suffice. [9] Income-based strategies are unlikely to be good substitutes for race-sensitive admissions policies because there are simply too few blacks and Latinos from poor families who have strong enough academic preparation to qualify for admission to highly selective institutions. Furthermore, standardized admissions tests such as the SAT, ACT and LSAT are of limited value in evaluating "merit" or determining admissions qualifications of all students, but particularly for underrepresented minorities for whom systematic influences make these tests even less diagnostic of their scholastic potential. There is extensive empirical data indicating that experiences tied to one's racial and ethnic identify can artificially depress standardized test performance. [10]

Hence, progress toward diversity will likely require some significant changes in strategy in the years ahead. Unfortunately, the road we have to travel is neither frequently walked nor well marked. We can look to very few truly diverse institutions in American society for guidance. We will have to blaze new trails, and create new social models.

At the University of Michigan we saw that we needed both a commitment and a plan to achieve diversity. We took the long view, one that required patient and persistent leadership, as well as the commitment and hard work of people throughout our community and beyond.

The Michigan Mandate

It may be useful to consider the University of Michigan's experience in its effort to achieve diversity because it led to measurable progress and because, since it happened on my watch, I can describe some of the victories and pitfalls that occurred along the way. Like most of higher education, the history of diversity at Michigan has been complex and often contradictory. There have been too many times when the institution seems to take a step forward, only to be followed by two steps backward. Nonetheless, access and equality have always been a central goal of our institution. We are proud that the University has consistently been at the forefront of the struggle for inclusiveness in higher education.

From our earliest beginnings in 1817, the University of Michigan focused on making a university education available to all economic classes. This ideal was stated clearly by an early Michigan president, James Angell, when he said the goal of the University was "to provide an uncommon education for the common man."[11] At our founding, we attracted students from a broad range of European ethnic backgrounds. In the early 1800s, the population of the state swelled with new immigrants from the rest of the country and across the European continent. By 1860, the Regents referred "with partiality," to the "list of foreign students drawn thither from every section of our country." Forty-six percent of our students then came from other states and foreign countries. Today more than one hundred nations are represented at Michigan.

The first African American students arrived on our campus in 1868. In the years after Reconstruction, however, discrimination increased. Black students joined together to support each other early in the century and staged restaurant protests in the 1920s. It was not until the 1960s that racial unrest finally exploded into campuswide concerted action. Although the University had made efforts to become a more diverse institution, both black and white students, frustrated by the slow movement, organized into the first Black Action Movement (BAM) in 1970. The central administration building was occupied, and students boycotted classes. Many positive advances came from this outpouring of student solidarity. The number of African American faculty and students on campus increased; new goals and programs were established and old programs were funded. Yet only a few years later, enrollments began to fall again and funding waned. By the early 1980's, black enrollment began to increase but still fell short of the goals set a decade before.

It would take two more student uprisings (BAM II and III), several disturbing racial incidents, negative national media attention, mediation with Jesse Jackson, and powerful legislative political pressure before the University again took a systematic look at the difficult problems of race on campus. To put it mildly, it was a time of ferment built on the Michigan tradition of activism. In this instance, our students recalled us to our commitment and held us to our promises.

Demands for change came not only from black students. These protests were joined by Latino students, who had been involved in the BAM struggles from the beginning, but now raised their voices as a separate group to demand greater visibility and attention to their agenda.

The University had a disappointing record with respect to Native Americans, and they also began to protest as well. Ironically, in 1817 local tribes ceded 1,920 acres of land to the Northwest Territory to establish the "University of Michigania." Yet the Native American enrollments remained quite low, less than 0.5 percent, throughout most of the University's history.

Michigan's record is somewhat better with respect to inclusion of Asian and Asian Americans. Historically, the University played a major role in expanding the opportunities for students from Asia. In the late 1800s, Michigan became one of the first universities to admit foreign Asian students. It was the first university in the United States to award a doctoral degree to a Japanese citizen. Michigan eventually became a major center for Asian education. In recent years, the number of Asian American students has grown more quickly than any other group, and during the protests of the 1980s Asian Americans also made their voices heard.

By the late 1980s it had become obvious that the University had made inadequate progress in its goal to reflect the rich diversity of our nation and our world among its faculty, students and staff. As we learned from our minority and female constituencies, simply providing access to our institution was not sufficient to provide full opportunity for those groups that continued to suffer from social, cultural, and economic discrimination in our society. People from underrepresented groups who did manage to find their way here faced serious barriers to their success and advancement in a University (and national) culture still largely dominated by a white, male majority.

We also faced a particular challenge because of our geographic location. As a state university, we draw roughly two-thirds of our undergraduates from Michigan, with almost one-half of these from the metropolitan Detroit area. Unfortunately, Michigan ranks among the top four states in the nation in the degree of black/white school segregation: 82 percent of black students attend schools in all black school districts, while more than 90 percent of white students attend schools with a black enrollment of less than 10 percent. [12] Furthermore, Detroit is the second most segregated metropolitan area in the country (following only Gary, Indiana), and the rates of residential segregation in Detroit were higher in 1990 than in 1960. Many suburban communities on the borders of Detroit have remained almost completely white despite their proximity to adjoining minority-dominated city neighborhoods. Drawing a significant fraction of our undergraduate enrollment from such a racially segregated environment presented a particularly serious challenge and responsibility for the University.

To address these challenges we knew that the University would have to change dramatically to achieve diversity. Our first step was to convene a group of faculty with direct experience in organizational change and multicultural environments. We drew upon the expertise of faculty from the social sciences, management, law, and social work along with selected administrators. We wanted a free-wheeling, sky's-the-limit planning group. It took more than a year of intense discussion and study to arrive at the first outline of goals and a plan for increasing diversity, which was announced in 1987. Based on the experience of other strategic planning efforts, we knew that the plan would need to be strategic and long term, leaving operational details to be developed through extensive consultations. The plan was really only a road map. It set out a direction and pointed to a destination. It offered incentives for achieving goals but disbursed responsibility, authority and accountability for many of the specific steps to be taken by individual academic and administrative units. As the plan evolved, we took care to retain the difficult but essential requirements of community building and pluralism.

It was also essential to engage as many of our constituents as possible in a dialogue about the plan's goals and strategies with the hope of gradually building widespread understanding and support inside and beyond our campus. Early drafts of the plan, in outline form and expressed in general terms, were circulated to ever widening circles of administration and faculty, and their useful comments were incorporated. The plan was designed to be organic and evolving in such a way as to facilitate open exchange of views. The challenge was to construct a process that would engage the various constituencies of the institution, reflecting in the plan's text their ideas and experiences. The plan would provide the framework for a continuing dialogue about the very nature of the institution. In this sense, we wanted to engage in a dynamic process rather than delivering commandments from on high.

Over the first two years, hundreds of discussions with groups both on and off campus were held. We reached out to alumni, donors, and civic and political leaders and groups and met with countless student, faculty and staff groups. Great care was taken to convey the same message to everyone as a means of establishing credibility and building trust among all constituencies. Meetings were sometimes contentious, often enlightening, but rarely acrimonious. Gradually understanding increased and support grew. Although the plan itself came from the administration, it would be individuals and units that would devise most of the detailed actions for carrying it forward. University publications, administrators' speeches and meetings, Faculty Senate deliberations, all carried the message: Diversity would become the cornerstone in the University's efforts to achieve excellence in teaching, research, and service in the multicultural nation and world in which it would exist.

The initial planning process and early promulgation of the diversity initiative began when I served as University Provost with the full support of then President Harold Shapiro. When I was named to succeed him in 1987, I seized every opportunity to reiterate my three strategic goals: Making Michigan a national leader in achieving diversity, internationalizing education and research, and building a knowledge infrastructure for a twenty-first century learning institution. I wanted to leave no doubt about what our priorities should be in the years ahead.

It was the long-term strategic focus of our planning that proved to be critical. Institutions do not change quickly and easily any more than do the societies of which they are a part. It is easy to falter, to become discouraged or distracted. The University would have to leave behind many reactive and uncoordinated efforts that had characterized its past and move toward a more strategic approach designed to achieve long-term systemic change. Sacrifices would be necessary as traditional roles and privileges were challenged. In particular, we foresaw the limitations of focussing only on affirmative action; that is, on access, retention, and representation. We believed that without deeper, more fundamental institutional change these efforts by themselves would inevitably fail—as they had throughout the 1970s and 1980s.

The plan would have to build on the best that we already had. The challenge was to persuade the community that there was a real stake for everyone in seizing this moment to chart a more diverse future. More people needed to believe that the gains to be achieved through diversity would more than compensate for the necessary sacrifices. The first and vital step was to link diversity and excellence as the two most compelling goals before the institution, recognizing that these goals were not only complementary but would be tightly linked in the multicultural society characterizing our nation and the world in the future. As we moved ahead, we began to refer to the plan as *The Michigan Mandate: A Strategic Linking of Academic Excellence and Social Diversity*. But it continued to be modified as discussions broadened and experience was gained. It was to be several years before it was presented as a final product.

The early steps in developing the Michigan Mandate were to: 1) develop a carefully designed strategic process for achieving, using, and valuing diversity; 2) achieve a community strongly committed in philosophy to our goals and objectives; and 3) allocate the necessary resources to accomplish this task. Based on strategic models from other spheres, the plan featured clear, concise, and simple goals; proposed specific actions and evaluation mechanisms; and reflected extensive interaction with and direct comment from a variety of constituencies and individuals to assure responsiveness of the plan.

The mission and goals of the Michigan Mandate were stated quite simply:

Philosophy: To recognize that diversity and excellence are complementary and compelling goals for the University and to make a firm commitment to their achievement.

Representation: To commit to the recruitment, support, and success of members of historically underrepresented groups among our students, faculty, staff, and leadership.

Environment: To build on our campus an environment that seeks, nourishes, and sustains diversity and pluralism and that values and respects the dignity and worth of every individual.

Associated with these general goals were more specific objectives:

Faculty recruitment and development: To substantially increase the number of tenure-track faculty in each underrepresented minority group; to increase the success of minority faculty in the achievement of professional fulfillment, promotion, and tenure; to increase the number of underrepresented minority faculty in leadership positions.

Student recruitment, achievement, and outreach: To achieve increases in the number of entering underrepresented minority students as well as in total underrepresented minority enrollment; to establish and achieve a strong minority student presence in all schools and colleges; to increase minority graduation rates; to develop new programs to attract back to campus minority students who had withdrawn from our academic programs; to design new and strengthen existing outreach programs that had demonstrable impact on the pool of minority applicants to undergraduate, graduate, and professional programs.

Staff recruitment and development: To focus on the achievement of affirmative action goals in all job categories; to increase the number of underrepresented minorities in key University leadership positions; to strengthen support systems and services for minority staff.

Improving the environment for diversity: To foster a culturally diverse environment; to significantly reduce the number of incidents of racism and prejudice on campus; to increase community-wide commitment to diversity and involvement in diversity initiatives among students, faculty, and staff; to broaden the base of diversity initiatives; to assure the compatibility of University policies, procedures, and practice with the goal of a multicultural community; to improve communications and interactions with and among all groups; and to provide more opportunities for minorities to communicate their needs and experiences and to contribute directly to the change process.

A series of carefully focused strategic actions was developed to move the University toward these objectives. These strategic actions were framed by the values and traditions of the University, an understanding of our unique culture characterized by a high degree of faculty and unit freedom and autonomy, and animated by a highly competitive and entrepreneurial spirit.

The first phase of the Michigan Mandate from 1987 to 1990 was focused on the issue of increasing the representation of minority groups within the University community. Primarily our approach was based on providing incentives to reward success, encouragement of research and evaluation of new initiatives, and support for wide-ranging experiments. The plan very emphatically did not specify numerical targets, quotas, or specific rates of increase to be attained.

To cite just one highly successful example, we established what we called the Target of Opportunity Program aimed at increasing the number of minority faculty at all ranks. Traditionally, university faculties have been driven by a concern for academic specialization within their respective disciplines. This is fundamentally laudable and certainly has fostered the exceptional strength and disciplinary character that we see in universities across the country; however, it also can be constraining. Too often in recent years the University had seen faculty searches that were literally "replacement" searches rather than "enhancement" searches. To achieve the goals of the Michigan Mandate, the University had to free itself from the constraints of this traditional perspective. Therefore, the central administration sent out the following message to the academic units: be vigorous and creative in identifying minority teachers/scholars who can enrich the activities of your unit. Do not be limited by concerns relating to narrow specialization; do not be concerned about the availability of a faculty slot within the unit. The principal criterion for the recruitment of a minority faculty member is whether the individual can enhance the department. If so, resources will be made available to recruit that person to the University of Michigan.

From the outset, we anticipated that there would be many mistakes in the early stages. There would be setbacks and disappointments. The important point was to make a commitment for the long range and not be distracted from this vision. This long-range viewpoint was especially important in facing up to many ongoing pressures, demands, and demonstrations presented by one special interest group or another or to take a particular stance on a narrow issue or agenda. This was very difficult at times as one issue or another each became a litmus test of university commitment for internal and external interest groups. While these pressures were understandable and probably inevitable, the plan would succeed only if the University leadership insisted on operating at a long-term strategic rather than on a short-term reactive level. It was essential to keep our eyes firmly focused on the prize ahead resisting the temptation to react to every issue that arose. Commitment and support within and outside the University community were necessary ingredients for success, but as the University had learned over the past two decades, it would take more than this to succeed. It was essential to have a strategy, a plan designed to guide institutional change.

Over the next several years, through this and many other programs, the diversity of the campus improved dramatically. But increasing the numbers was the relatively easy part of the plan. Institutions can have a great many different people living in the same locale, working side-by-side, going to the same classes, but that will not mean that one has a community. Just increasing the numbers and mix of people will not provide one with a sense of mutual respect and a cohesive community. To achieve this, the University faced the challenge of creating a new kind of community—a community that drew on the unique strengths and talents and experiences of all of its members. And this was felt to be the important challenge of the second phase of the Michigan Mandate. More specifically, it was recognized that the traditional institutions of our society—our cities and neighborhoods, our churches and public schools, our business and commerce—all had failed to create a sense of community or to provide the models for creative interaction that were needed to build a new kind of society based on a general mutual dependence, trust, and respect. It was recognized that in America today it is on our college campuses that many students come together for the first time with students of other races nationalities, and cultures in an environment in which they are expected to live, work, and learn together. It was therefore not surprising that in our existing university structure there was a good deal of tension and frequent separatism among groups. It would take more than one generation to ease this situation.

By 1995 Michigan could point to significant progress in achieving diversity. By every measure, the Michigan Mandate was a remarkable success, moving the University far beyond our original goals of a more diverse campus. The representation of underrepresented students, faculty, and staff more than doubled over the decade of the effort. But, perhaps even more significantly, the success of underrepresented minorities at the University improved even more remarkably, with graduation rates rising to the highest among public universities, promotion and tenure success of minority faculty members becoming comparable to their majority colleagues, and a growing number of appointments of minorities to leadership positions in the University. The campus climate not only became far more accepting and supportive of diversity, but students and faculty began to come to Michigan because of its growing reputation for a diverse campus. And, perhaps most significantly, as the campus became more racially and ethnically diverse, the quality of the students, faculty, and academic programs of the University increased to their highest level in history. This latter fact seemed to reinforce our contention that the aspirations of diversity and excellence were not only compatible but, in fact, highly correlated.

In conclusion, while the Michigan Mandate has been a success, it should be made clear that no plan, no commitment, no goal, and no action could have brought us to this point, without the help and support of literally thousands of faculty, students, staff, alumni, and supporters. They are the ones who made change possible, and they continue to work for it today.

The University of Michigan as a diverse learning community is still very much a work in progress.

The Michigan Agenda for Women

While we pursued the goals of the Michigan Mandate, we could not ignore another glaring inequity in campus life. If we meant to embrace diversity in its full meaning, we had to attend to the long-standing concerns of women faculty, students, and staff. We had not succeeded in including and empowering women as full and equal partners in all aspects of the life and leadership of the University despite many promises and continuing struggle.

Michigan takes pride in the fact that it was one of the first large universities in America to admit women. At the time, the rest of the nation looked on with a critical eye. Many were certain that the "dangerous experiment" would fail. The first women who arrived in 1869 were true pioneers, the objects of intense scrutiny and resentment. For many years, women had separate and unequal access to facilities and organizations. Yet, in the remaining years of the nineteenth century, the University of Michigan provided strong leadership for the nation. By 1898 the enrollment of women had increased to the point where they received 53 percent of Michigan's undergraduate degrees.

These impressive gains were lost during the early part of the twentieth century and even more with the returning veterans after World War II. The representation of women in the student body declined precipitously. It only began to climb again during the 1970s and 1980s and, for the first time in almost a century, once again exceeded that of men in 1996. During the past several decades, the University took a number of steps to recruit, promote, and support women staff and faculty, modifying University policies to reflect their needs. Yet true equality came slowly and great challenges remained.

The Challenges

In faculty hiring and retention, despite the increasing pools of women in many fields, the number of new hires of women had changed only slowly during the late twentieth century in most research universities. In some disciplines such as the physical sciences and engineering, the shortages were particularly acute. We also continued to suffer from the "glass ceiling" phenomenon, that is, because of hidden prejudice women were unable to break through to the ranks of senior faculty and administrators though no formal constraints prohibited their advancement. The proportion of women decreased steadily as one moved up the academic ladder. Additionally, there appeared to be an increasing tendency to hire women off the tenure track as postdoctoral scholars, lecturers, clinicians, or research scientists. The rigid division among various faculty tracks offered little or no opportunity for these women to move onto tenure tracks.

Retention of women faculty was also a serious concern. Studies suggested that women were less likely than men either to be reviewed for promotion or recommended for promotion at the critical step between assistant professors and associate professors. Women faculty, like men, came to the University to be scholars and teachers. Yet because of their inadequate representation in our institutions, our women faculty were clearly stretched far too thinly by committee responsibilities and mentoring roles. While this was true for women faculty at all ranks, it took the greatest toll on junior faculty.

The period of greatest vulnerability in promotion and retention of women is in the early stage in their academic careers, when they are assistant professors attempting to achieve tenure. Women faculty experienced greater demands for committee service and mentoring of women students; inadequate recognition of and support for dependent care responsibilities; and limited support in the form of mentors, collaborators, and role models. The small number of women at senior levels was due in part to early attrition in the junior ranks. Women faculty at all ranks described their difficulties in juggling teaching, research, formal and informal advising, departmental and University-wide committee service, and family responsibilities. Many female faculty did not feel that these difficulties arose from overt or systematic discrimination, but rather from the interaction between a system that was becoming increasingly demanding and competitive and their personal lives, which were often more complex than those of their male colleagues because of dependent care responsibilities.

While the low participation of women in senior faculty ranks and among the University leadership was due in part to the pipeline effect of inadequate numbers of women at lower ranks, this absence of senior women was also due to the degree to which senior men faculty and administrators set the rules and performed the evaluations in a way—whether overt or unintended—that was biased against women. Old-boy networks, customs, and habits abounded. Women felt that in order to succeed, they had to play by the rules previously set up by the men in their fields. As one of our women faculty members put it, "My profession is male-oriented and very egalitarian. The men are willing to treat everyone the same as long as you act like a man."

At the same time, we faced serious challenges in the staff area. There was a concern that in higher education, we simply did not do an adequate job of placing women in the key staff positions to get them ready for senior assignments. Women were not provided with adequate stepping stones to senior management, and many believed they were all too frequently used as stepping stones for others. We also needed to rethink our philosophy of staff benefits. There was a need to move to more flexible benefits plans that could be tailored to the employee's particular situation (e.g., childcare in addition to dependent health care). Furthermore, we needed to aim at providing equal benefits for equal work that were independent of gender.

Many of our concerns derived from the extreme concentration of women in positions of lower status and power—as students, lower-level staff, and junior faculty. The most effective lever for change might well be a rapid increase in the number of women holding positions of high status, visibility, and power. This would not only change the balance of power in decision-making, but it would also change the perception of who and what matters in the university. Finally we needed to bring university policies and practices into better alignment with the needs and concerns of women students in a number of areas including campus safety, student housing, student life, financial aid, and childcare.

Over the longer term it was essential that we draw more women into senior faculty and leadership roles if we were to be able to attract top women students. We also needed to do more to encourage and support women in fields of study where they had been discouraged from entering for decades. Our colleges and universities were far from where they should be—from where they must be—in becoming institutions that provided the full array of opportunities and support for women faculty, students, and staff. Despite the efforts of many committed women and men over the past several decades, progress had been slow and frustrating. Women deserved to be full members and equal partners in the life of our universities. While most women faculty, students, and staff succeeded admirably in a variety of roles within higher education, they nonetheless struggled against subtle pressures, discrimination, and a still-common feeling of invisibility. Removing barriers and encouraging women's participation in the full array of university activities would transform the University, creating a community in which women and men shared equal freedom, partnership, and responsibility.

The Plan

It was clear in the 1990s that our university had simply not made sufficient progress in providing women with access to the full range of opportunities and activities in the institution. Not that we ignored these issues. Hundreds of dedicated members of the University community, women and men, had worked long and hard for women's equity. But our actions, while motivated by the best of intentions, had been ad hoc, lacking in coherence and precise goals and strategy, too independent of one another, and providing no assurance of progress or accountability for falling short. Here again we knew Michigan needed a bold strategic plan with firm goals for recruiting and advancing women at every level and in every arena. Programs could be tested against these goals, and our progress could be accurately measured and shared with the broader University community.

To this end, the University developed and executed a strategic effort known as the *Michigan Agenda for Women*. While the actions proposed were intended to address the concerns of women students, faculty, and staff, many of them benefited men as well. Just as the Michigan Agenda required a commitment from the entire University community, so too did its success benefit us all, regardless of gender.

In developing the Michigan Agenda we knew that different strategies were necessary for different parts of the University. Academic units varied enormously in the degree to which women participated as faculty, staff, and students. What might work in one area could fail miserably in another. Some fields, such as the physical sciences, had few women represented among their students and faculty. For them, it was necessary to design and implement a strategy which spanned the entire pipeline, from K-12 outreach to undergraduate and graduate education, to faculty recruiting and development. For others such as the social sciences or law, there already was a strong pool of women students, and the challenge became one of attracting women from this pool into graduate and professional studies and eventually into academe. Still other units such as Education and many departments in the humanities and sciences had strong participation of women among students and junior faculty, but suffered from low participation in the senior ranks.

There also was considerable variation among non-academic administrative areas of the University, with many having little or no tradition of women in key management positions. To accommodate this variation, each unit was asked to develop and submit a specific plan for addressing the inclusion of women. These plans were reviewed centrally, and the progress of each unit was then measured against their plan each year, as part of the normal interaction associated with budget discussions. The challenge here was to create a process that both permitted central initiative and preserved the potential for local development of unit-specific action plans. The Michigan Agenda for Women aimed at building a working and learning environment in which women could participate to their fullest. This plan represented a beginning, the sketch of a vision and a plan that would evolve over time as it was shaped through the interaction with broader elements of the University community.

Considerable progress has been made in the years since the Agenda for Women was proposed. More than half of the students in professional schools are now women. Women now serve in key administrative, executive, and management roles. These advances are the foundation for continued progress until full equity is achieved.

The Distraction of Political Correctness

As colleges and universities struggle to become more inclusive of people, they can never lose sight of the importance of preserving diverse views in academic discourse. We have a fundamental obligation to protect the expression of diverse ideas and opinions in classrooms, research, and public forums. Our academic freedoms are always at risk. While our campuses struggled to become more inclusive of people, there were those within and without our walls determined to limit or exclude ideas and discourse with which they disagreed.

Today as in earlier times, various forms of extremism on and beyond our campuses threaten academic freedom and our capacity to meet our responsibility as teachers and scholars. Recently, universities have been criticized for tolerating on our campuses a particular form of extremism known by the popular but misleading term "political correctness," defined as an effort to impose a new brand of orthodoxy on our teaching, our scholarship, and even our speech. Those who attack the university on the political correctness issue portray it as threatening not only the quality of our educational programs but the very values which undergird the academy itself: freedom of expression and academic freedom. In reality, extremist threats to our fundamental values come from all points along the political spectrum.

Assaults on the Academy

Threats to academic freedom and institutional autonomy are hardly new, nor are conflicts within our ranks about our direction and purpose. Over the centuries, there have been persistent struggles for the heart of the academy. There have been attacks from religious and political forces bent on capturing learning for their own purposes. The American university is no stranger to periodic ravages from all sorts of zealots and opportunists who would impose a particular belief or orthodoxy on scholarship and teaching. These historical experiences caution us that when academic freedom is threatened, the stakes are high for individuals as well as for the intellectual life and integrity of our institutions. [13]

Threats to academic inquiry unfortunately are alive and well in our world today. Indeed, in some societies, universities have been closed, faculty and students have been jailed or killed, and libraries have been burned. In others, rigid political or religious orthodoxy governs education and research. Why? The answer seems obvious. Free and open inquiry simply cannot be tolerated by tyrants, ideological zealots, inflamed mobs, or narrow interest groups seeking advantage. Not all threats to the academy are so obviously destructive or malicious. Many of the threats we experience today are motivated by the best of intentions. Often they are no more ominous than a new regulation to achieve a laudable goal or even an incentive to stimulate the right behavior promulgated by federal or state bureaucrats. But these efforts are sometimes myopically focused on a short-term goal and mindless of the longer-term erosion of intellectual and institutional autonomy that may result.

By and large, academic freedom has survived and prospered over hundreds of years. This is due to the inherent value of our contribution to society. It has also called upon the courage of scholars the world over who guard their autonomy and freedom; who resist tyrants; and who uphold free, scholarly inquiry. Eventually they win society's understanding, however grudging, because society has long ago learned that if it wishes to educate its young to be civilized citizens of the world and to advance learning to serve its interests, then it must grant freedoms to scholars and their institutions.[14] Still, we can never be complacent about our autonomy and our freedoms. Our compact with society is a delicate one. Like all liberties, freedom of inquiry requires eternal vigilance. Excesses and violations invite intervention from external authorities. We must not abuse academic freedoms or take them for granted. What is at stake here is not just the loss of our particular institutional freedoms and values but the erosion of one of humanity's finest and most enduring institutional achievements.

The Political Correctness Debate

Critics who assail us for imposing a new orthodoxy, a single standard of "political correctness" aim at many disparate targets. Some decry efforts to incorporate the study of other civilizations as an added part of the traditional curriculum. Others object to affirmative action efforts to build a more inclusive institution. Still others criticize new modes of disciplinary inquiry or what they see as an undermining of traditional values and received tradition or they single out more philosophical issues such as what they describe as the dominance of relativism over absolute moral values.

Of course, many of those who criticize political correctness are themselves extremists and polemicists with their own opportunistic political agenda. Much of what is being written on this issue is often depressingly superficial, factually incorrect, and wildly overstated. Some of it is pure ideological guerrilla warfare. A great deal of the criticism represents yet another chapter in the contemporary media debasement of public discourse about important social issues through hype, sound-bite simplification, and pandering to fads and base prejudices. Some of these folks are always on the lookout for a sensational new lightening rod for public dissatisfaction and frustration. During the past several years, the university has been taking the heat. Part of this anti-PC agenda is familiar, old-fashioned reactionary stuff. It resorts to polemic to try to stop the greater inclusiveness of people and ideas, to hold on to the status quo at whatever price, to protect unearned privilege.

At the same time, we have to face the painful truth that the critics of the politically correct do not lack examples of destructive, even ludicrous, extremism and zealotry on our campuses over the past decade or so. Political correctness is a real phenomenon. The left, like its rightward critics, exhibits its share of stridency, intolerance, and extremism. Proponents of politically correct views have taken strongly ideological stances and in some cases have attempted to constrain or eliminate entirely the expression of opposing viewpoints. While such foolish or destructive behavior is by no means rampant on our college campuses, those instances that have occurred have seriously undermined important academic values and served as a lightning rod for critics of academia. Thus, we should heed the basic message of those who criticize this new form of extremism on our campuses. What they are saying is that some in the academic community ideologically do not accept or have lost touch with our most fundamental missions and values. Their actions have struck a deep vein of public discontent with academia. Since the real issue concerns our commitment to our own values as teachers and scholars, it is on values that we must stand and debate with our academic colleagues and with our critics.

What Exactly Do the Critics Charge?

The term "political correctness" is just a code word for a range of concerns about the university:

The Insistence on "Correct" Language. Many on our campuses have argued that, as a supposedly civil and increasingly diverse community, we must strive to be aware of the preferences and sensitivities of those who have suffered from past exclusion and discrimination. Some urge that we regulate and enforce "speech codes." The fact remains that it is one thing to encourage people to be sensitive and considerate and quite another to require this behavior. The critics maintain that censoring speech, allowing or disallowing particular words or phrases, however well-intentioned, can have effects that range from truly damaging to merely embarrassing. There is a kind of sententious self-righteousness about much of the language policing that occurs on campuses, and this repulses people more than it persuades them.

Sensitivity Training. As a civil community, should we not try to be more sensitive to one another? Isn't it reasonable that as we become more inclusive, we should learn more about one another and learn skills that will help us to work and live together? But here again, it is one thing to educate and quite another to impose a single "orthodox" point of view upon our students, faculty, and staff. The critics argue that as teachers and employers we can require certain standards of civil behavior, but we cannot require "right" thinking without compromising our own values.

Harassment. In a similar vein, there are critics who assail codes or policies that prohibit racial and sexual harassment. This particular criticism raises very difficult and volatile issues about which there is strongly divided opinion. There is no denying the potential for abuse of such policies any more than we can deny the abuses that led to the codes in the first place. Such harassment and intimidation cannot be understood outside of the historical framework of violence and fear that has surrounded racial prejudice and discrimination. What is merely intimidating to one group can be experienced as a threat of violence by those who have been victimized by discrimination. Our best hope is to improve the campus climate to the point that the issue is moot.

Required Courses on Diversity. Many campuses have concluded that it is reasonable or even imperative that our students—and, of course, we ourselves—be educated about the culture and experience of other groups in our own pluralistic society and in an increasingly interdependent world. They believe it critical that all of us understand in some comparative perspective more about the nature of group relations and interactions in a world that is rampant with divisions of race, class, caste, belief, and nationality—divisions that affect all of us and threaten our very existence as a society. At the same time, there are many and various ways to provide education about diversity.

The critics rightly question whether academics can in good conscience require students to take any course that presents a single orthodox view of a subject, such as the value of diversity. Like many other important curriculum issues, these must be openly and widely debated. Fortunately, at Michigan we have a well-established framework and tradition of faculty autonomy for these faculty discussions. We have had many public debates that serve as models of the civility and intellectual seriousness that should surround such discussions and demonstrate that we can discuss these matters and make progress.

Censoring and Intimidating of Professors. Critics point to a dangerous form of intolerance in which professors who teach "incorrect" subjects, teach their subjects from an "incorrect point of view," or do research in "incorrect" areas are intimidated by extremist groups. Clearly, it is important to challenge ideas with which we disagree, but can we ever tolerate intimidating attacks on those with whom we differ? To our discredit, intimidation and reckless charges seem to have been accepted by many of us at times on our campuses, by students and faculty alike, as appropriate behavior. We cannot accept those who would shout down a person or an idea or who think that opinions should be imposed on others by intimidation or that ideas should be judged by the number of their adherents rather than on whether or not they are worthwhile.

Perhaps in a more subtle form this intimidation includes attempts, however well meaning, to impose a test of political orthodoxy in grading or hiring and professional advancement decisions. It is clear that we in academia have no business in silencing any view or any person. The test of an idea must be on its merits, not who propounds it or whether we like it or agree with it or not.

Censorship of Campus Speakers or Groups and Individuals. Some members of our community have argued that given all of the potential for conflict and sensitivity, certain people or views should be declared off-limits, that certain controversial speakers should not be invited at all or at least should be prevented from being heard. Apparently these people seem to feel that free speech is for them, but not for those with whom they disagree. There is a certain irony to this behavior, since the surest way to call attention to individuals is to attempt to disrupt or prevent their presence on a university campus.

Curriculum "Correctness." Universities are assailed from the right and the left by radical traditionalists and by radical radicals about curriculum reform. Some would confine our curriculum to a fixed and narrow set of "great books" that represent the great traditions of western civilization. Others would discount any work by "DWEMs"—dead white European males. Is it wrong to adapt our teaching to include a broader range of experience and expression from across time and around the world? Clearly, we must prepare our students to live in a world in which the majority of people come from very different backgrounds and beliefs. But does this have to mean that we abandon or denigrate the learning that is the foundation of our tradition? After all, many of our most profound concepts are derived from the heritage provided by western civilization: our faith in rationalism, in knowledge and science, and the notion of human progress itself. To abandon the study of the foundations of our culture is to abandon the understanding of what made us who and what we are.

Ethnic and Gender Studies. There are those who question the development of new academic programs such as ethnic and gender studies. Of course, a truly vigorous and rigorous scholarly institution will always give rise to new fields, new ideas and insights, and new paradigms along with the structures to accommodate them. That is one of the great virtues of the research university. Fortunately, if traditional and rigorous academic standards are used, excesses or deficiencies that develop in any new fields will be scrutinized and substantively debated. From this perspective new ideas or fields are no more of a threat than entrenched ones. Neither should be exempt from the time-honored test of whether they are intellectually worthwhile, whether they help us to understand our world and ourselves.

Affirmative Action. Much of the criticism aimed at political correctness is actually aimed at affirmative action programs in our institutions. Critics claim that affirmative action actually promotes increased segregation, balkanization, and separate and unequal educational services. These programs are seen as undemocratic, divisive, and ultimately a disservice to those whom they are meant to serve. The key here is the concern raised about "preferential treatment" of groups who have historically been subjected to discrimination. Throughout our long history, one of the most important distinguishing characteristics of higher education has been our attempt to serve all of our society and to treat human characteristics such as race, gender, or socio-economic background as irrelevant to academic ability. It is my belief that affirmative action programs are important tools in achieving this goal. Having said this, it is important to state as well the importance of allowing the debate over the merits of affirmative action programs to be heard. We in higher education have a strong case to make, but it can only be heard in an open dialogue that tolerates all viewpoints. If there is a better way to achieve our goals, a more effective or a more just way for us to proceed, then we need to hear about it.

Adhering to Academic Values

As we consider the arguments of our critics, it becomes apparent that an important part of the criticism and counter-criticism of higher education is about the pace, scope, and direction of social and institutional change. Much of it is about the struggle for greater inclusiveness, for more openness to ideas and people. Much of it is about the intellectual challenge of what we have called the new age of knowledge that characterizes our time. We must not become overly reactive to what is superficial or transitory or opportunistic in the criticism at the expense of the more important continuing debate concerning fundamental issues of our future and a renewal of our mission and a response to change.

Today, our universities are attempting to deal with some of the most painful, persistent, and intractable problems in human experience. In our efforts to deal with racism and sexism, we are combating centuries of prejudice and discrimination that have robbed the world of precious cultural wisdom, human talent, and leadership. At the same time, we are contending with an intellectual revolution, striving to incorporate interdisciplinary, comparative and international perspectives and experiences into our intellectual framework. We are scrambling to keep up with the breathtaking advances in knowledge that are transforming the academy and our society.

To address the intellectual and practical issues of our time we must be open to new paradigms, new theories, new combinations of knowledge. While many in society may prefer to ignore or deny that changes are taking place, as teachers and scholars we cannot responsibly do so. The university frequently will be in the uncomfortable position of being a vanguard of change. Possibly, the intensified criticism swirling about universities these days is in part a manifestation of the age-old practice of blaming the messenger for the message. Some may actually hold us responsible for social transformation now underway. In a sense, I suppose, they are right. After all, we are educating our students for a changing world, and we are producing much of the knowledge that drives the change.

Little wonder then that some are threatened and that many are unsure and concerned. Little wonder that with our growing influence on society, we have become an arena of special interest conflict. We are riding the tiger of a profound transformation of our society.

We have touched on a number of forces at work that threaten our ability to debate important questions and that undermine our teaching and research mission. These pose dangers, but we are by no means helpless in the face of them. Our best protection lies in the centuries-old traditions and values that preserved and extended the fundamental principles of free scholarly inquiry. Universities survive and they thrive because they represent the application of reason to human affairs and the free pursuit of truth through reasoned inquiry. These are the key principles upon which the university can confidently stand.

Over the centuries we have found that our objective of seeking truth and our means for seeking it have stood the test. We have not achieved perfection, but we do have a way of considering questions and problems that yields insight and lights the way to new and better questions. What binds us together then is the search for truth, the tested methods, the principles and values of scholarship. Society supports these values because universities over the centuries and around the globe have managed to teach successive generations a respect for the pursuit of truth and an ability to take up the quest themselves. Our methods and principles have succeeded in increasing our store of knowledge and our understanding. Society has granted us our academic freedoms in recognition, however reluctant at times, of our essential role in society.

The most effective protection for all of academia in the face of critics is to be steadfast in guarding the integrity of our teaching and research. Our fidelity to this primary mission is our best defense against the critics. It is what we do best to serve humanity. In this regard one thing is certain and unchanging: We cannot perform our primary mission of teaching and research properly, we cannot produce what society most needs from us, without the freedom to pursue truth wherever it takes us. This is fundamental.

In summary, through my experience at Michigan I have become convinced that excellence and diversity are not only mutually compatible but also mutually reinforcing objectives for the twenty-first century university. In an ever more diverse nation and world, the quality of a university's academic programs—its very relevance to our society—will be greatly determined by the diversity of our campus communities. After all, our social contract is with *all* of the society that sustains and supports us, not just with the privileged few. Beyond our social obligation, it is also clear that diversity contributes directly to the intellectual vitality of our teaching and our scholarship. Social diversity provides different ways of conceptualizing and addressing intellectual issues that give new vitality to our education, scholarship, and communal life.

Higher education in America is far more diverse today than it was fifty years ago or even ten years ago. Yet the university is not monolithic and neither is discrimination; both are shifting constantly. We move ahead, knowing we can never simply rest.

CHAPTER 10   Technology

The impact of information technology will be even more radical than the harnessing of steam and electricity in the 19th century. Rather it will be more akin to the discovery of fire by early ancestors, since it will prepare the way for a revolutionary leap into a new age that will profoundly transform human culture.

—Jacques Attali, Millennium: Winners and Losers in the Coming World Order (1992)[1]

If there was one sector that most strongly determined the progress of the twentieth century, it was transportation and its related industries—cars, planes, trains, oil, space. Transportation determined prosperity, national security, even our culture, with the growth of the suburbs and international commerce and culture—and, coincidentally, created the vast wealth to build America's great universities.

Things are very different today. We have entered a new era in which the engine of progress is not transportation but communication, enabled by the profound advances we are now seeing in computers, networks, satellites, fiber optics, and related technologies. We now face a world in which hundreds of millions of computers easily can plug into a global information infrastructure. These rapidly evolving technologies are dramatically changing the way we collect, manipulate, and transmit information. They change the relationship between people and knowledge.

From a broader perspective, today we find a convergence of several themes: the importance of the university in an age in which knowledge itself has become a key factor in determining security, prosperity, and quality of life; the global nature of our society; the ease with which information technology—computers, telecommunications, and multimedia—enables the rapid exchange of information; and networking—the degree to which informal cooperation and collaboration among individuals and institutions are replacing more formal social structures, such as governments and states. We are also seeing a convergence of technology as the television becomes a computer and hence a window into the Net. As a result, there is also a convergence in which computer, telecommunications, entertainment, and commerce are merging into a gigantic, $1 trillion "infotainment" marketplace. While technology has driven this convergence, the real beneficiaries will be those organizations capable of producing information content—whether they are entertainment companies like Disney, software companies like Microsoft, or educational organizations like the university.

Earlier we suggested that knowledge was both a medium and a product of the university as a social institution. Since information is the raw material for knowledge, it is reasonable to suspect that a technology that is expanding our ability to manipulate information by orders of magnitude every decade will have a profound impact on both the mission and the function of the university.

The University as a Knowledge Server

One frequently hears the primary missions of the university referred to in terms of teaching, research, and service. These missions can also be regarded as simply the twentieth century manifestations of the more fundamental roles of *creating, preserving, integrating, transmitting,* and *applying* knowledge. If we were to adopt the more contemporary language of computer networks, the university might be regarded as a "knowledge server," providing knowledge services (i.e., creating, preserving, transmitting, or applying knowledge) in whatever form needed by contemporary society.

From this more abstract viewpoint, it is clear that while the fundamental knowledge server roles of the university do not change over time, the particular manifestation of these roles do change—and change quite dramatically in fact. Consider the role of "teaching," that is, transmitting knowledge. Although we generally think of this role in terms of a classroom paradigm, that is, of a professor teaching a class of students, who in turn respond by reading assigned texts, writing papers, solving problems or performing experiments, and taking examinations, it is clear that today's generation of students may demand a quite different approach. We noted earlier that today's plug-and-play generation will likely demand that the university replace the classroom lecture with highly interactive and collaborative experiences.

It could well be that faculty members of the twenty-first century university will find it necessary to set aside their roles as teachers and, instead, become designers of learning experiences, processes, and environments. Tomorrow's faculty may have to discard the present style of solitary learning experiences, in which students tend to learn primarily on their own through reading, writing, and problem solving. Instead, they may be asked to develop collective learning experiences in which students work together and learn together, with the faculty member becoming more of a consultant or a coach than a teacher. Faculty members will be less concerned with identifying and then transmitting intellectual content and more focused on inspiring, motivating, and managing an active learning process by students. Of course this will require a major change in graduate education, since few of today's faculty members are taught these skills.

One can easily identify similarly profound changes occurring in the other roles of the university. The process of creating new knowledge is evolving rapidly away from the solitary scholar to teams of scholars, often spread over a number of disciplines. The use of information technology to simulate natural phenomena has created a third modality of research, on par with theory and experimentation. Entirely new methods of investigation are emerging that enable scholars to address previously unsolvable problems, e.g., proving the four-color conjecture in mathematics, analyzing molecules that have yet to be synthesized, simulating the birth of the universe, and analyzing a vast archive of literature for hidden themes and comparisons. Even the nature of knowledge creation is shifting somewhat away from the *analysis of what has been* to the *creation of what has never been*—drawing more on the experience of the artist than upon analytical skills of the scholar.

The preservation of knowledge is one of the most rapidly changing functions of the university. The computer—or more precisely, the "digital convergence" of various media from print-to-graphics-to-sound-to-sensory experiences through virtual reality—will likely move beyond the printing press in its impact on knowledge. Throughout the centuries, the intellectual focal point of the university has been its library, its collection of written works preserving the knowledge of civilization. Today such knowledge exists in many forms—as text, graphics, sound, algorithms, and virtual reality simulations—and it exists almost literally in the ether, distributed in digital representations over worldwide networks, accessible by anyone, and certainly not the prerogative of the privileged few in academe. The library is becoming less a collection house and more a center for knowledge navigation, a facilitator of information retrieval and dissemination.[2] In a sense, the library and the book are merging. One of the most profound changes will involve the evolution of software agents, collecting, organizing, relating, and summarizing knowledge on behalf of their human masters. Our capacity to reproduce and distribute digital information with perfect accuracy and with essentially zero cost has shaken the very foundations of copyright and patent law and threatens to redefine the nature of the ownership of intellectual property.[3] The legal and economic management of university intellectual property is rapidly becoming one of the most critical and complex issues facing higher education.

It is also clear that societal needs will continue to dictate great changes in the applications of knowledge society expects from universities. Over the past several decades, universities have been asked to lead in applying knowledge across a wide array of activities, from providing health care to protecting the environment, from rebuilding our cities to entertaining the public at large (although it is sometimes hard to understand how intercollegiate athletics represents knowledge application). In the years ahead higher education will be challenged to address our ever-changing social priorities, for example, economic competitiveness, K–12 education, and global change.

These abstract knowledge-centered roles of the university have existed throughout the long history of the university and will certainly continue to exist as long as these remarkable social institutions survive. But the particular realization of the fundamental roles of knowledge creation, preservation, integration, transmission, and application will continue to change in profound ways, as they have so often in the past. In this sense, the challenge of change, of transformation, is necessary simply to sustain our traditional roles in society.

Since the business of the university is knowledge, the extraordinary advances in information technology will have profound implications for universities. Rapidly evolving technologies are dramatically changing the way we collect, manipulate, and transmit information. This directly challenges the traditional paradigms of the university, where processes of knowledge creation, preservation, transmission, and application are still largely based on books, chalk boards, oral lectures, and static images.

Over the past several decades, computers have evolved into powerful information systems with high-speed connectivity to other systems throughout the world. Public and private networks permit voice, image, and data to be made instantaneously available across the world to wide audiences at low costs. The creation of virtual environments where human senses are exposed to artificially created sights, sounds, and feelings liberate us from restrictions set by the physical nature of the world in which we live. Close, empathic, multi-party relationships mediated by visual and aural digital communications systems are becoming common. They lead to the formation of closely bonded, widely dispersed communities of people interested in sharing new experiences and intellectual pursuits created within the human mind via sensory stimuli. Computer-based learning systems are also being developed, opening the way to new modes of instruction and learning. New models of libraries are being explored to exploit the ability to access vast amounts of digital data in physically dispersed computer systems, which can be remotely accessed by users over information networks.

New forms of knowledge accumulation are evolving; written text, dynamic images, voices, and instructions on how to create new sensory environments can be packaged in dynamic modes of communication never before possible. The applications of such new knowledge forms challenge the creativity and intent of authors, teachers, and students. Technology such as computers, networks, high-definition television, ubiquitous computing, knowbots, and other technologies may well invalidate most of the current assumptions and thinking about the future nature of the university.

Although the digital age will provide a wealth of opportunities for the future, we must take great care not simply to extrapolate the past but instead examine the full range of possibilities for the future.[4] It could well be that our present institutions such as universities and government agencies, which have been the traditional structures for intellectual pursuits, may turn out to be as obsolete and irrelevant to our future as the American corporation of the 1950s. There is clearly a need to explore new social structures that are capable of sensing and understanding the change and of engaging in the strategic processes necessary to adapt or control it.

The Digital Age

The Evolution of Information Technology

It is difficult to understand and appreciate just how rapidly information technology is evolving. Four decades ago, one of the earliest computers, ENIAC, stood 10 feet tall, stretched 80 feet wide, included more than 17,000 vacuum tubes, and weighed about 30 tons. (We have 10% of ENIAC on display as an artifact in the lobby of the computer science department at Michigan.) Today you can buy a musical greeting card with a silicon chip more powerful than ENIAC. Already a modern $1,000 notebook computer has more computing horsepower than a $20 million supercomputer of the early 1990s. For the first several decades of the information age, the evolution of hardware technology followed the trajectory predicted by "Moore's Law"—that the chip density and hence computing power for a given price doubles every eighteen months.[5] This corresponds to a hundredfold increase in computing speed, storage capacity, and network transmission rates every decade. At such rates, by the year 2020, the thousand-dollar notebook computer will have a computing speed of 1 million gigahertz, a memory of thousands of terabits, and linkages to networks at data transmission speeds of gigabits per second. Put another way, it will have a data processing and memory capacity roughly comparable to the human brain.[6]

Software is also evolving rapidly, with new genetic algorithms that improve themselves with experience. As networks threaten to overwhelm us with a knowledge-rich environment, we are beginning to use intelligent software "agents" as our personal interface with the digital world, with the capacity to roam the electronic globe, hunting down answers to any question or responding to any request we may have.

The Nature of Human Interaction

The most dramatic impact on our world today from information technology is not in the continuing increase in computing power. It is in a dramatic increase in bandwidth, the rate at which we can transmit digital information. From the 300 bits-per-second modems of just a few years ago, we now routinely use 10 megabit-per-second local area networks in our offices and houses. Gigabit-per-second networks now provide the backbone communications to link local networks together, and with the rapid deployment of fiber optics cables and optical switching, terabit-per-second networks are just around the corner.

As a consequence, the nature of human interaction with the digital world—and with other humans through computer-mediated interactions—is evolving rapidly.

We have moved beyond the simple text interactions of electronic mail and electronic conferencing to graphical-user interfaces (e.g., the Mac or Windows world) to voice to video. With the rapid development of sensors and robotic actuators, touch and action at a distance will soon be available. The world of the user is also increasing in sophistication, from the single dimension of text to the two-dimensional world of graphics to the three-dimensional world of simulation and role-playing. With virtual reality, it is likely that we will soon communicate with one another through simulated environments, through "telepresence," perhaps guiding our own software representations, our digital agents, to interact in a virtual world with those of our colleagues.

This is a very important point. When we think of digitally mediated human interactions, we generally think of the awkwardness of e-mail or perhaps videophones. But as William Wulf puts it, "Don't think about today's teleconference technology, but one whose fidelity is photographic and 3-D. Don't think about the awkward way in which we access information on the network, but about a system in which the entire world's library is as accessible as a laptop computer. Don't think about the clumsy interface with computers, but one that is both high fidelity and intelligent."[7] It is only a matter of time before information technology will allow human interaction with essentially any degree of fidelity we wish—3-D, multimedia, telepresence. Eventually, we will reach a threshold of fidelity sufficient to allow distance education (and most other human activities) that will be comparable to face-to-face interaction.

Virtual Environments

Virtual reality—the use of visual, audio, and tactile sensations to create a simulated total sensory experience—has become common both in training and simulation and in gaming. But higher education is more likely first to make use of distributed virtual environments,[8] in which computers create sophisticated three-dimensional graphical worlds distributed over networks and populated by the representations of people interacting together in real time. Such software representations of people in virtual worlds are known as avatars. Here the goal is not so much to simulate the physical world, but to create a digital world more supportive of human interaction. The software required for such distributed virtual environments is social in nature. It is not so much designed to simulate reality as to enable conversation and other forms of human collaboration.

These shared virtual worlds could radically alter the way we work, learn, and play. For example, one might imagine teaching a course in French language and culture through a distributed virtual environment representing a street in Paris. The virtual street could be lined with buildings, shops, restaurants, museums, and apartments. Language students and teachers would be represented by avatars in this world, along with native speakers or even software agents. Students entering this virtual world could practice a foreign language and experience its culture by speaking with other people in a nonthreatening environment.

One can imagine a host of other virtual environments that could support the human interactions necessary in learning communities. Even today we already have environments that simulate university campuses, complete with registration offices, classrooms, coffeehouses, and recreation facilities.

Ubiquitous Computing

Here is an interesting exercise. Think through your day's activities, from the moment you wake until you return to bed at the end of the day. Try to identify the various ways that you encounter computers. While most of us first think of the trusty old computer workstation on our desk top, it doesn't take much further reflection to realize that we are surrounded by computers. Our radio-alarm clock contains a computer. Our watch is really a computer with a timing circuit. Our house is chock full of computers—they control the temperature, make our coffee and toast, tune our television. The modern car is more computer and electronics these days—at least by cost—than it is metal and plastic. Our pager and cellular phone are computers. Our workplace is filled with computers. Even our credit card has become a tiny computer, capable of tracking our expenditures.

Information technology—computers, networks, and such—is rapidly becoming ubiquitous, disappearing into the woodwork just as electricity did a century earlier.[9] Today we don't look for the wires to hook a lightbulb up to a power source. Rather we just throw a switch (or perhaps just enter a room that senses our presence), and the light goes on. Now that chips with supercomputer power and high bandwidth networks are becoming cheap commodities, information technology also is becoming so pervasive in our everyday life that it is becoming invisible, taken for granted even as we become more dependent upon it.

Perhaps the ultimate example of ubiquitous computing will be the myriad of computers and networks that attach themselves to us to extend our personal capabilities. Imagine a "bodynet" of computers and other devices distributed throughout our clothing—perhaps even embedded in our body—seamlessly linked in a wireless bodynet that allows them to function as an integrated system and connected to the worldwide digital network.[10] At some point our very nervous system may plug into the Net. This fusion of the carbon and silicon worlds may or may not evolve into a *Neuromancer*[11] blend of physical space and cyberspace such that electronic existence masks the physical world. However, it is clear that these two personal "realities" will be superimposed and intertwined in very complex ways.

Changing Lifestyles

Information technology has already stimulated profound changes in our lifestyles.[12] We sense the loosening of the constraints of space and time. Many of us have already discarded the burden of the daily commute in favor of "telecommuting" via our computer, modem, and fax. Others are finding that they have become tethered to their workplace with the electronic umbilical cord of pager and cellular phone. Electronic mail, voice mail, and fax are rapidly replacing "snail mail." Whether it is a university department, a commercial enterprise, or an individual, all are increasingly identified not by phone number or address but rather by the URL of their website.

Other aspects of our daily activities have changed dramatically. In the digital age, economic activity is driven by the bit business, producing, transforming, distributing, and consuming digital information. The physical marketplace is rapidly disappearing, while "virtual" marketplaces based on networks and computers are emerging as the site of economic activity. Yet here there is an important difference; digital information is unlike any other type of economic good—natural resources, human labor, property—in the very interesting respect that it cannot be used up. Use actually multiplies rather than diminishes digital products. Digital products can be reproduced an infinite number of times with perfect accuracy at essentially zero cost.[13] The concepts of property, copyright, patents, and laws—all based on physical manifestations—may no longer apply.

The Need for Agents in a Knowledge-Rich World

This tendency of digital information to multiply and propagate rapidly through digital networks can also be a challenge. Already the vastness of the Internet and the access it provides to storehouses of information threaten to overwhelm us. As anyone who has "surfed the Net" can testify, it is easy to be amused but often difficult to find exactly what you need. Further, living and working in a knowledge-rich—indeed, knowledge-deluged—world will overload our limited human capacity to handle information.

The Net is already a complex and creative organism, something that has evolved far beyond the comprehension of any human. It is more than just a medium incorporating text, graphics, and sound. It incorporates ideas and mediates the interactions among millions of people. It can already do things no human can explain.

As a result, it will become necessary to depend on intelligent software agents to serve as our interface with the digital world. Many already use primitive constructs such as filters for electronic mail or web-crawlers to search through databases on the Net. But with the use of artificial intelligence and genetic algorithms, one can imagine intelligent agents dispatched by a user to search the digital networks for specific information. These agents could also represent their human user, serving as avatars, in mediating the interaction with the agents of other human users.

There are a couple of interesting possibilities here. Since software agents are easy to reproduce, one can imagine a cyberspace quickly flooded with billions of agents—similar to the software viruses that can propagate and cripple computer systems. There is already evidence of "wars" between software agents, where agents from one group of users seek out and destroy those from others. Perhaps the most significant evolutionary stage will occur when the distributed processing power of networks allows the appearance of "emergent behavior," wherein agents begin to exhibit self-organization, learning capability, and intelligent behavior. The predictions of science fiction of Clarke's HAL 9600 in *2001: A Space Odyssey* or Gibson's *Neuromancer* and the possibility that we may be unable to distinguish which of our colleagues in cyberspace are flesh-and-bones and which are silicon, may be only a few decades away.

Some Implications for Higher Education

Imagine the reactions of a nineteenth century physician, suddenly transported forward in time to a modern surgery suite, complete with all of the technological advances of modern medicine. Yesteryear's physician would recognize very little—perhaps not even the patient—and certainly would not be able to function in any meaningful way. Contrast this with a nineteenth century college professor, transported into a contemporary university classroom. Here everything would be familiar—the same lecture podium, blackboards, and students ready to take notes. Even the subjects— literature, history, languages—would be familiar and taught in precisely the same way.

Universities are supposed to be at the cutting edge of both knowledge generation and transmission. Yet their primary activity, teaching, is conducted today much as it was a century ago. Technologies that were supposed to drive radical change— television, computer-assisted instruction, wireless communications—have bounced off the classroom without a dent. To be sure, information technology has had great impact on the efficiency of administrative operations. It has revolutionized the conduct of research and the storage and synthesis of knowledge. But it has only had a modest impact on instruction and learning, primarily being used only at the margins to extend the current classroom-centered paradigm.

Today there are good reasons to believe that digital technology will indeed transform the university, perhaps beyond recognition. Why? What is different? Is it the ability of the new technology to cut the bonds of space and time? Is it its ubiquitous nature? No, it is the ability of the rapidly evolving digital technology to enable new forms of human interaction, to mediate communication, to stimulate the formation of new types of human communities. It will drive the focus of higher education from teaching to learning, and it will transform universities from faculty-centered to learner-centered institutions.

So what are possible paradigms for the "cyberspace university"? How can we create digitally mediated environments for learning?

Virtual Universities

Perhaps the most popular new approach is the so-called virtual university, most commonly conceived as the Internet extension of conventional distance learning. In cybertalk, "virtual" is an adjective that means existing in function but not in form. A virtual university exists only in cyberspace, without campus or perhaps even a faculty. Sophisticated networks and software environments are used to break the classroom loose from the constraints of space and time and make learning available to anyone, anyplace, at any time.

For many years universities have utilized passive telecommunications technology such as television to extend teaching to people unable or unwilling to attend campus-based classes. In its simplest form, such distance learning is really a "talking heads" paradigm, in which faculty lectures are simply delivered at a distance, either through live transmission or videotape. There have been efforts to broadcast such instruction on public television ("sunrise semesters"), augmented by written correspondence. A more effective approach utilizes onsite teaching assistants to work directly with the students. Recently, technology has allowed the use of feedback via electronic mail, chatrooms, or two-way video interaction.

The simplest conception of the virtual university uses multimedia technology via the Internet to enable distance learning. Such instruction could be delivered either into the workplace or the home. In one form, this Internet-mediated instruction would be synchronous—in real time with the instructor and the students interacting together. The more interesting teaching paradigms of the virtual university involve asynchronous interactions, in which students and faculty interact at different times. In a sense, this latter form of instruction would resemble a correspondence course, with multimedia computers and networks replacing the mailing of written materials. There is already sufficient experience with such asynchronous learning to conclude that, at least for many subjects, the learning process is just as effective as the classroom experience. Furthermore, because one need not invest in the physical infrastructure of the campus, there is opportunity for significant cost reductions in the long term. By using an inexpensive delivery mechanism such as the Internet to reach a potentially vast audience, many hope that a virtual university can provide instruction at costs far lower than campus-based instruction. There are presently for-profit entities[14] competing directly with traditional colleges and universities in the higher education marketplace through virtual university structures.

The attractiveness of virtual universities is obvious for adult learners whose work or family obligations prevent attendance at conventional campuses.[15] But perhaps more surprising is the degree to which many on-campus students are now using virtual university communities to augment their traditional education. Broadband digital networks can be used to enhance the multimedia capacity of hundreds of classrooms across campus and link them with campus residence halls and libraries. Electronic mail, teleconferencing, and collaboration technology is transforming our institutions from hierarchical, static organizations to networks of more dynamic and egalitarian communities.

Distance-Independent Learning Communities

Many believe that effective computer-network-mediated learning will not be simply an Internet extension of correspondence or broadcast courses. John Seely Brown and Paul Duguid of Xerox PARC believe that this model of the virtual university overlooks the nature of how university-based learning actually occurs.[16] They suggest that it is a mistake to think of learning as information transfer, the act of delivering knowledge to passive student receivers. Brown and Duguid see the learning process as rooted both in experience and social interaction. Learning requires the presence of communities.

This is the value of the university—to create learning communities and to introduce students into these communities. Undergraduates are introduced to communities associated with academic disciplines and professions. Graduate students and professional students are involved in more specialized communities of experience and expertise. From this perspective, one of the important roles of the university is to certify through the awarding of degrees that students have had sufficient learning experience with a variety of communities.

Once we have realized that the core competency of the university is not simply transferring knowledge, but developing it within intricate and robust networks and communities, we realize that the simple distance-learning paradigm of the virtual university is inadequate. The key is to develop computer-mediated communications and communities that are released from the constraints of space and time.

Distance learning based on computer-network-mediated paradigms allows universities to push their campus boundaries outward to serve learners anywhere, anytime. Those institutions willing and capable of building such learning networks will see their learning communities expand by an order of magnitude. In this sense, the traditional paradigm of "time-out-for-education" can be more easily replaced by the "just in time" learning paradigms, more appropriate for a knowledge-driven society in which work and learning fuse together.

Here we should recognize the importance of asynchronous learning.[17] Face-to-face conversation is both geographically local and temporally synchronous. In asynchronous communications, words are not heard as they are spoken but repeated at some point later. This delay allows thought and consideration to mediate the asynchronous communication. Such asynchronous interactions are ideally suited to the Net, since it allows low-cost ways to hold many-to-many conversations among people who are distributed in both space and time. Beyond simple interactions through e-mail and bulletin boards, role-playing games seem ideal for learning. These software constructions not only provide a virtual environment where interactions occur, but also provide common objects for participants to observe, manipulate, and discuss, making the Net both a medium for conversation and for circulating digital objects. Such Net-mediated communities allow open learning in which the student decides when, where, and how to interact with the learning community.[18]

Competition from Cyberspace

Of course, the use of information technology is already quite pervasive in higher education. Courses are increasingly being offered, both on campus and off, via the Internet. Students in geographically dispersed virtual communities meet together electronically. It is also clear that in most cases information technology is underutilized, serving as extensions rather than transformations of the way we learn and teach.[19]

To be sure, the current concept of distance learning, even if implemented via the Internet through virtual universities, is still bound to traditional ideas and approaches.[20] But as true learning communities are constructed in cyberspace, traditional educational institutions will feel increasing competition and pressure to change. The university will continue to be the primary source of "content" for educational programs, but other organizations more experienced in "packaging" content, for example, entertainment companies, may compete with universities to provide educational services to the mass market. In a similar sense, it could well be that the role of the faculty member will shift rapidly from that of organizing and teaching individual courses. As higher education shifts from a cottage industry to mass production, faculty may become members of design teams developing content for broader markets.

These changes could well force a structural reorganization of the university, perhaps breaking it up into its component functions such as credentialing, guidance, research, and instruction. The traditional lecture system, intrinsically inefficient in knowledge transmission, could decline in importance as robust electronically mediated technology becomes available. This technology may enable an expansion of other activities requiring direct human contact, such as guidance, tutorials, and hands-on mentoring.

It is ironic that the cyberspace paradigm of learning communities is a mechanism that may return higher learning to the older tradition of the scholar surrounded by disciples in an intense interrelationship. In a sense, it recognizes that the true advantages of universities are in the educational process, in the array of social interactions, counseling, tutorial, and hands-on mentoring activities that require human interaction. In this sense, information technology will not so much transform higher education—at least in the early phases—as enrich the educational opportunities available to learners.

Liberal arts colleges that continue to stress such mentoring, hands-on, tutorial-based education will be least challenged by the emerging knowledge media. It is the large, comprehensive universities that rely heavily on impersonal mass education that are at great risk. A significant share of this conventional mass education can be offered commercially and electronically. After all, a large part of the function of large universities is mass information transfer, which can be performed quite effectively and efficiently via information technology. Virtual universities, even when constructed along the conventional distance-learning paradigm, may well provide formidable competition to large universities in terms of both quality and price.

Perhaps we should pay more attention to developing new learning structures more appropriate for the evolving information technology. One example would be the "collaboratory" concept,[21] an advanced, distributed infrastructure that would use multimedia information technology to relax the constraints on distance, time, and even reality. It would support and enhance intellectual teamwork. There is a growing consensus that the next major paradigm shift in computing is in the direction of the collaboratory. Not only research but also a vast array of human team activities in commerce, education, and the arts would be supported by variants of this vision. Perhaps some form of the collaboratory is the appropriate infrastructure ("tooling") for the "learning organization" becoming popular in the business world; perhaps it is the basis for the world universities in the next century. It could well become the generic infrastructure on which to build the workplace of the emerging information age.

There is an important implication here. Information technology may allow—perhaps even require—new paradigms for learning organizations that go beyond traditional structures such as research universities, federal research laboratories, research projects, centers, and institutes. If this is the case, we should place a far higher priority on building the networks to link together our students and educators among themselves and with the rest of the world. This would be a modest investment compared with the massive investments we have made in the institutions of the past—university campuses, transportation, and urban infrastructure. It is none too early to consider an overarching agenda to develop deeper understanding of the interplay between advanced information technology and social systems. In some future time we may have the knowledge to synthesize both in an integrated way as a total system.

Some Operational Issues for Universities

All universities face major challenges in keeping pace with the profound evolution of information and its implication for their activities. Not the least of these challenges is financial, since as a rule of thumb most organizations have found that staying abreast of this technology requires an annual investment of roughly 10 percent of their operating budget. For a very large campus such as the University of Michigan, this can amount to hundreds of millions of dollars per year!

But there are other challenges. Many universities are simply unprepared for the new plug-and-play generation, already experienced in using computers and net-savvy, who will expect—indeed, demand—sophisticated computing environments at college. More broadly, information technology is rapidly becoming a strategic asset for universities, critical to their academic mission and their administrative services, that must be provided on a robust basis to the entire faculty, staff, and student body.

In positioning themselves for this technology, universities should recognize several facts of contemporary life. First, robust, high-speed networks are becoming not only available but also absolutely essential for knowledge-driven enterprises such as universities. Powerful computers are available at reasonable prices to students, but these will require a supporting network infrastructure. There will continue to be diversity in the technology needs of faculty, with the most intensive needs likely to arise in parts of the university such as the arts and humanities where strong external support may not be available.

Historically, technology has been seen as a capital expenditure for universities or as an experimental tool to be made available to only a few. In the future, higher education should conceive of information technology both as an investment and a strategic asset that will be used by the entire faculty, staff, and student body to sustain and enhance the mission of the university. The following are some possible guidelines for such investments, gleaned from many years of experience at Michigan and other universities:

Invest in "Big Pipes"

While the processing power of computers continues to increase, of far more importance to universities is the increasing bandwidth of communications technology. Both Internet access to off-campus resources and "intranet" capability to link students, faculty, and staff together are the highest priority. The key theme will be connectivity, essential to the formation and support of digitally mediated communities.

Universities are straining to keep up with the connectivity demands of students. Today's undergraduates are already spending hours every day interacting with faculty, students, and home while accessing knowledge distributed about the world. Simply keeping pace with an adequate number of modem ports to meet the demands of off-campus students for access to campus-based resources and the Internet is overloading many universities. Installing a modern on-campus network—a "wire plant"—has become one of the most critical capital investments faced by the university.

The Internet itself is evolving rapidly as a result of various efforts. University research initiatives such as the Internet2 project and broader federal efforts such as the Next Generation Internet or the National Information Infrastructure projects are contributing to this growth. This will compel universities to move rapidly to keep pace with the bandwidth of available backbone networks.[22]

Strive for Multi-Vendor, Open Systems Environments

Universities should avoid hitching their wagons to a small set of vendors. As information technology becomes more of a commodity marketplace, new companies and equipment will continue to appear. The great diversity in needs of various parts of the university community also will demand a highly diverse technology infrastructure. Humanists will seek robust network access to digital libraries and graphics processing. Scientists and engineers will seek massively parallel processing. Social scientists will likely seek the capacity to manage massive databases, for example, data warehouses and data mining technology. Artists, architects, and musicians will require multimedia technology. Business and financial operations will seek fast data processing, robust communications, and exceptionally high security.

Linking these complex multi-vendor environments together will be a challenge, since they use different equipment, diverse software and operating systems for varying purposes. For this reason, it is important to insist on open-systems technology rather than relying on proprietary systems. Fortunately, most information technology is moving rapidly away from proprietary mainframes ("big iron") to client-server systems based on standard operating systems such as Unix, Linux, or Windows-NT. There is a vast array of commercial off-the-shelf software available for such open systems.

As digital technology becomes increasingly ubiquitous, universities will have to make intelligent decisions as to just what components they will provide and which should be the personal responsibility of members of the community. While networks and specialized computing resources will continue to be the responsibility of the university, the purchase of other digital devices such as personal communicators will almost certainly be left to the student, faculty, or staff member.

Universities will need to strive for synergies in the integration of various technologies. Beyond the merging of voice, data, and video networks, there will be possibilities as well to merge applications across areas such as instruction, administration, and research. The issue of financing will become significant as institutions seek a balance between institution-supported central services and point-of-access payments through technologies such as smart cards.

Student Participation

There continues to be a debate about whether students should be required to purchase their own computers. Student experience with and their access to information technology is evolving rapidly. In 1997 surveys, the University of Michigan found that over 90 percent of its first-year students arrived on campus with at least three years of computer experience, and essentially all graduating seniors indicated they made extensive use of computers during their education. Over 60 percent owned computers when they first arrived on campus, and a far higher percentage owned personal computers by the time of graduation. Our students currently spend about twelve to fourteen hours a week on a computer, with roughly half of this on the Net. By way of comparison, faculty members indicated that they spend about twenty hours a week working on computers; a significant fraction of this work was done at home. Over 90 percent of the faculty have personal computers.[23]

Universities should be prepared to support the personal computing needs of students by providing robust network linkages both in residence halls and student commons areas. They should negotiate with community telecommunications companies—both telephone and cable television companies—to facilitate off-campus communications, while at the same time providing sufficient network communication ports to facilitate off-campus students.

The role that universities can play in negotiating discounts with hardware manufacturers for student personal computers is more controversial. Local retailers complain that this represents unfair competition (although, in reality, most will benefit significantly from consequent software and peripheral sales). It is my belief that universities have an obligation to assist students in acquiring the hardware and software that have become essential for their education.

As personal computer technology saturates the student body, universities should continue to build and maintain public computer sites where students can have access to more powerful technology. In a very real sense, these computer cluster sites are becoming analogous to the role that libraries played in the past. They provide students with the access to knowledge necessary for their studies, as well as places to study, gather, and collaborate.

Cultural Issues

Although making the necessary investment in the technology infrastructure and support services will strain university budgets, the most critical challenges may involve the culture of the university. We have already noted that there will be great diversity in the technology needs of various disciplines and programs, and these needs will likely not be aligned with financial resources. There is an important strategic issue facing most universities: Should the evolution of information technology be carefully coordinated and centralized or allowed to flourish in a relatively unconstrained manner in various units? Perhaps because of our size and highly decentralized culture, at Michigan we have long preferred a "let every flower bloom" approach. We have encouraged islands of innovation, in which certain units are strongly encouraged to move out ahead to explore new technologies. This has allowed some programs to move into leadership roles and serve as pathfinders for the rest of the university.

Another cultural issue involves just who within the university community will drive change. Many of our entering students—and soon, possibly most—have computing skills far beyond those of our faculty. Our experience tells us that it will not be the faculty or staff but rather the students themselves that will lead in the adoption of new technology. As members of the digital generation, they are far more comfortable with this emerging technology. They are a fault-tolerant population, willing to work with the inevitable bugs in "Version 1.0" of new hardware and software.

Although information technology today is used primarily to augment and enrich traditional instructional offerings, over the longer term it will likely change the learning paradigm. It will likely change the methods of scholarship. And it will certainly change the relationship between faculty and staff and the university. For example, as the university is viewed increasingly as a "content provider," with the evolution of the commodity classroom, learning ware, and the like, we will need to rethink issues such as ownership of faculty course materials.

As one example of this phenomenon, many students are already moving rapidly to embrace Net-based learning and take increasing control over their own education. They are still enrolling in traditional academic programs and participating in time-tested pedagogy such as lecture courses, homework assignments, and laboratory experiments. But many students approach learning in very different ways when they work on their own. They use the Net to become "open learners," accessing worldwide resources and Net-based communities of utility to their own learning objectives.

What about productivity? Information technology can certainly enhance the quality of academic programs. But extensive experience in the private sector has suggested that this technology is able to improve productivity and lower costs only if the fundamental process of work itself is re-engineered. In order words, before we can achieve an economic benefit from this technology, we must first reexamine our current paradigms for teaching and learning.

Here, it is important to recognize that effective use of the emerging knowledge media will require—indeed, drive—a major transformation in the teaching, learning, and administrative processes of higher education. While the traditional faculty culture and organization may at first resist the use of these technologies as they have in the past, the learner-centered, open-learning environments information technology makes possible seem inevitable.

No one knows what this profound alteration in the fabric of our world will mean, both for academic work and for our entire society. As William Mitchell, dean of architecture at MIT, stresses, "The information ecosystem is a ferociously Darwinian place that produces endless mutations and quickly weeds out those no longer able to adapt and compete. The real challenge is not the technology, but rather imagining and creating digitally mediated environments for the kinds of lives that we will want to lead and the sorts of communities that we will want to have."[24] It is vital that we begin to experiment with the new paradigms that this technology enables. Otherwise, we may find ourselves deciding how the technology will be used without really understanding the consequences of our decisions.

Concluding Remarks

Clearly, the digital age poses many challenges and opportunities for the contemporary university. For most of the history of higher education in America, we have expected students to travel to a physical place, a campus, to participate in a pedagogical process involving tightly integrated studies based mostly on lectures and seminars by recognized experts. As the constraints of time and space—and perhaps even reality itself—are relieved by information technology, will the university as a physical place continue to hold its relevance?

In the near term it seems likely that the university as a physical place, a community of scholars and a center of culture, will remain. Information technology will be used to augment and enrich the traditional activities of the university in much its traditional forms. To be sure, the current arrangements of higher education may shift. For example, students may choose to distribute their college education among residential campuses, commuter colleges, and online or virtual universities. They may also assume more responsibility for and control over their education. In this sense, information technology is rapidly becoming a liberating force in our society, not only freeing us from the mental drudgery of routine tasks, but also linking us together in ways we never dreamed possible, overcoming the constraints of space and time. Furthermore, the new knowledge media enables us to build and sustain new types of learning communities, free from the constraints of space and time.

But it also poses certain risks to the university. It will create strong incentives to standardize higher education, perhaps reducing it to its lowest common denominator of quality. It could dilute our intellectual resources and distribute them through unregulated agreements between faculty and electronic publishers. It will almost certainly open up the university to competition, both from other educational institutions as well as from the commercial sector.

It is our collective challenge as scholars, educators, and leaders to develop a strategic framework capable of understanding and shaping the impact that this extraordinary technology will have on our institutions. We are on the threshold of a revolution that is making the world's accumulated information and knowledge accessible to individuals everywhere, a technology that will link us together into new communities never before possible or even imaginable. This has breathtaking implications for education, research, and learning that cannot be ignored by the university.

CHAPTER 11

Governance and Leadership

There is no more delicate matter to take in hand, nor more dangerous to conduct, nor more doubtful of success, than to step up as a leader in the introduction of change. For he who innovates will have for his enemies all those who are well off under the existing order of things, and only lukewarm support in those who might be better off under the new.

—Niccolo Machiavelli, The Prince[1]

The contemporary university is one of the most complex social institutions of our times. The importance of this institution to our society, its myriad activities and constituencies, and the changing nature of the society it serves, all suggest the importance of experienced, responsible, and enlightened university governance and leadership. Yet many university leaders, particularly those associated with public universities, believe that one of the greatest challenges to their institutions lies not with financial constraints nor with the availability of strong students and faculty nor even with the need to change. Rather the greatest challenge lies in reforming the manner in which their universities are governed, both from within and from without.

American universities have long embraced the concept of shared governance involving public oversight and trusteeship, collegial faculty governance, and experienced but generally short-term administrative leadership. While shared governance engages a variety of stakeholders in the direction of the university, it does so with an awkwardness that tends to inhibit change and responsiveness.

The politics swirling about governing boards, particularly in public universities, not only distracts them from their important responsibilities and stewardship, but also discourages many of our most experienced, talented, and dedicated citizens from serving on these bodies. The increasing intrusion of state and federal government in the affairs of the university, in the name of performance and public accountability, can trample on academic values and micromanage many institutions into mediocrity. Furthermore, while the public expects its institutions to be managed effectively and efficiently, it weaves a web of constraints through public laws that make this difficult indeed. Sunshine laws prevent substantive discussions between governing boards and administrators. Even the most sensitive business of the university, such as its search for a president, must be conducted in the public arena.

Efforts to include the faculty in shared governance also encounter obstacles. To be sure, faculty governance continues to be both effective and essential for academic matters such as faculty hiring and tenure evaluation. But it is increasingly difficult to achieve effective faculty participation in broader university matters such as finance, capital facilities, or external relations. The faculty traditions of debate and consensus building, along with the highly compartmentalized organization of academic departments and disciplines, seem increasingly incompatible with the breadth and rapid pace required of the university-wide decision process.

Like other social institutions, the university requires strong leadership, particularly during at time of great change, challenge, and opportunity. Yet, as Machiavelli suggests, this may be in limited supply during just such times. The current environment for leadership on most university campuses today neither supports nor even tolerates strong leadership, and turnover rates among university presidents and senior administrators are high. At a time when universities require decisive, courageous, and visionary leadership, the shrinking tenure and deteriorating attractiveness of the modern university presidency pose a significant threat to the future of our institutions.[2]

In this chapter we will explore both of these important issues: the governance and the leadership of the university.

Governance

Throughout the long history of the university, it has been granted special governance status because of the unique character of the academic process. The university has been able to sustain an understanding that its activities of teaching and scholarship could best be judged and guided by the academy itself rather than by the external bodies such as governments or the public opinion that govern other social institutions. Key in this effort was the evolution of a tradition of shared governance involving several key constituencies: a governing board of lay trustees or regents as both stewards for the institution and protectors of broader public interest, the faculty as those most knowledgeable about teaching and scholarship, and the university administration as leaders and managers of the institution.

In the past most concerns about the governance of higher education in America have focused on two issues. First, there has been a continuing concern about whether universities can retain the independence, the autonomy, necessary for them to fulfill their academic mission in the intensely political environment characterizing such prominent social institutions. Second, there have long been concerns about the concept of "shared governance," in which governing boards of lay or nonresident trustees must share authority with the faculty in academic matters.

Today, however, a third critical issue has arisen: whether the current shared governance characterizing universities can achieve the capacity, the flexibility, to respond and adapt to a rapidly changing world. Public universities face a particularly great challenge in this regard because of the intensely political nature of their governance. For this reason, much of our discussion in this chapter will focus on governance issues associated with public higher education. To be sure, many of these issues are of more general interest, to public and private universities alike. But the complexity and political volatility characterizing the environment for public university governance seems to require particular attention.

Institutional Autonomy

The relationship between the university and the broader society it serves is a particularly delicate one, because the university has a role not only as a servant to society but as a critic as well. It serves not merely to create and disseminate knowledge, but to assume an independent questioning stance toward accepted judgments and values. To facilitate this role as critic, universities have been allowed a certain autonomy as a part of a social contract between the university and society. It is based on the value of independent teaching and scholarship that must accept controversy and a lack of consensus not only as tolerable but also as a normal state.

To this end, universities have enjoyed three important traditions: academic freedom, tenure, and institutional autonomy.[3] Although there is a considerable degree of diversity among American colleges and universities in practice, there is a general agreement about the importance of these traditions. *Academic freedom* is generally defined as that aspect of intellectual liberty that relates to the teaching and scholarly activity of the academic community. It is based on the premise that the role of critic can only be accomplished in an atmosphere entirely free from administrative, political, or religious constraints on thought or expression.

The concept of faculty *tenure* is closely related. After a certain probationary period, faculty members are provided with protection against removal on the basis of what they teach or study. Although actual practice has extended the definition of tenure to provide a broader form of job security, sometimes even protecting faculty members against poor performance and incompetence, in theory it was intended to secure academic freedom.

Universities have endeavored to equate academic freedom and its attendant focus upon the classroom with *institutional autonomy*, which effectively insulates virtually all decisions even remotely bearing upon the university's educational mission. Here the intent is that the government—and that includes lay boards, in the minds of most faculty members—may concern itself with education policy, but not academic policy. For example, the government may prescribe the broad character of the curriculum for a particular institution, but it may not prescribe the more immediate details of course content, methods of presentation, research, and similar matters that involve questions of academic competence.

Institutional autonomy is intended to insulate all decisions bearing upon the university's academic mission from political interference. While private institutions are generally distant enough from interference, public institutions rely on a more fragile autonomy from the society and the government that supports them. In many cases, explicit provisions in the state constitution vests exclusive management and control of the institution in its governing board, presumably to the exclusion of state executive and legislative authority. In other cases, institutional autonomy is provided in a far less effective form through statute.

No matter how formal the autonomy of a public university, whether constitutional or statutory, many factors can lead to the erosion of its independence.[4] In practice, government, through its legislative, executive, and judicial activities, can easily intrude on university matters. For example, in many states, sunshine laws relating to open meetings of public bodies or freedom of information laws have been extended to the point where they can paralyze the operation of public institutions. Public attitudes, as expressed through populist issues such as control of tuition levels or admission standards, also hinder public institutions from time to time.

The autonomy of the university also depends both on the attitudes of the public and the degree to which it serves a civic purpose. If the public or its voices in the media lose confidence in the university, in its accountability, its costs, or its quality, it will ask "autonomy for what and for whom." In the long run, institutional autonomy depends primarily on the amount of trust that exists between government and institutions of higher education.

The Influence of Governments

Although the direct funding of colleges and universities comes primarily from state appropriations, student fees, and private gifts, the federal government has played an important role in defining the nature of the contemporary university. Despite early resistance by the states to federal involvement in higher education, a sequence of federal policies and legislation have expanded dramatically the educational opportunities and services provided by our universities. From the Federal Ordinance of 1785 to the land-grant acts and the G.I. Bill, from the government-university research partnership of the post-World War II years to the Equal Opportunity Act, from federal support of student financial aid programs to beneficial tax treatment of charitable giving, it is clear that the federal government has had great impact on higher education in America.

State governments have historically been assigned the primary role for supporting and governing public higher education in the United States. At the most basic level, the principles embodied in the Constitution make matters of education an explicit state assignment. Public colleges and universities are largely creatures of the state. Certainly the federal government plays a significant role in shaping the directions of higher education. But federal influence is exercised indirectly through the clients of higher education rather than through direct action on the providers.

Through both constitution and statute, the states have distributed the responsibility and authority for the governance of public universities through a hierarchy of governing bodies: the legislature, state executive branch agencies or coordinating boards, institutional governing boards, and institutional executive administrations. Few outside of this hierarchy are brought into the formal decision process, although they may have strong interests at stake, for example, students, patients of university hospitals, and corporate clients.

As state entities, public universities must usually comply with the rules and regulations governing other state agencies. The fact that governments have tended to rely extensively on regulatory approaches (as opposed to incentive systems and other less directive mechanisms) to provide guidance to the entities under their control means that most public universities must cope with multiple regulatory requirements on an everyday basis. These vary widely, from contracting to personnel requirements to purchasing to even limitations on out-of-state travel. Policymakers are loath to eliminate regulation absent an alternative that assures them equivalent leverage. Regulation is the tool with which they are most familiar and comfortable, and no proven alternative exists for ensuring that the institutions will attend to priorities set outside academe.

Although regulation is probably the most ubiquitous of the policy tools employed by state government to influence university behavior, policies governing the allocation and use of state funds are probably ultimately the most powerful. First, the budget is the only available tool that involves both the use of incentives and explicit prohibitions on particular kinds of institutional action. Second, budget issues are revisited regularly—usually annually. Third, budget decisions affect all operations of the institution.

Beyond the detailed nature of the operating relationship between public universities and state government, there are a number of fundamental issues that relate directly to public policy. Just who is "the public" served by public universities? In the good old days when state appropriations were the primary source of support for public institutions, this was a straightforward issue. The state university was owned by the people of the state, supported by its taxpayers, and responsible to its citizens. Today, state appropriations have become a smaller and smaller component of the public university's operating budget, and an increasing fraction of its physical infrastructure is funded through private gifts or student fees. There are now other important constituencies to be considered that may not be adequately represented through the normal political structures characterizing state government. Who represents patients treated in academic medical centers? Who represents the interests of students attending the university from other states or nations? Who represents the interests of other important sponsors such as the federal government, industry, and foundations?

Governing Boards

The lay board has been the distinctive American device for "public" authority in connection with universities.[5] Most other nations impose government control through powerful government ministries. In the United States, we have long made use of lay boards of trustees or regents to govern universities in large measure to protect the university from such political interference.[6]

The function of the lay board in American higher education is simple, at least in theory. The governing board has final authority for key policy decisions and accepts both fiduciary and legal responsibility for the welfare of the institution. It also selects the president of the university. Because of its very limited expertise, the board is expected to delegate the responsibility for policy development, academic programs, and administration to professionals with the necessary training and experience. For example, essentially all governing boards share their authority over academic matters with the faculty, generally acceding to the academy the control of academic programs. Furthermore, the day-to-day management of the university is delegated to the president and the administration of the university, since these provide the necessary experience in academic, financial, and legal matters.

While governing board members are not expected to become personally involved in the detailed management of the institutions, they are expected to serve as trustees, always acting to protect and preserve the institution for current and future generations. While they may not always agree with the university—its faculty, students, and administration—they are expected to be "loving critics," always acting in the institution's interests and never on their own agenda or for their own constituencies.

While most governing boards of private institutions do approach their roles in this spirit, governing boards of public institutions frequently fall victim to politics, focusing instead on narrow forms of accountability to the particular political constituencies represented by their various members. Political considerations are frequently a major factor in appointing board members and often an important element in their actions and decisions.[7] Many public board members view themselves as "governors" rather than as "trustees" of their institutions, more concerned with their personal agendas or accountability to a particularly political constituency than with the welfare of their university. They are further constrained by many states in meeting their responsibilities by sunshine laws that require that their meetings, their deliberations, and their written materials all be open and available to the public, a situation that makes candid discussion and considered deliberation all but impossible.

A recent study commissioned by the Association of Governing Boards highlighted many of the weaknesses of public boards.[8] As Tom Ingram, Executive Director of AGB, put it, "The trusteeship of American public higher education requires sweeping reform it if is to serve its public purpose. Successful reform depends on state lawmakers, trustees, and public higher education leaders developing a mutual understanding of the appropriate roles, responsibilities, and authority of the modern university's governing board. Central to this new understanding is a heightened awareness among elected political leaders of the unique position the modern, complex university holds between government and the citizens who support it."

Too many trustees of public university boards lack a basic understanding of higher education or a significant commitment to it, understanding neither the concept of service on a board as a public trust nor their responsibilities to the entire institution. Public boards tend to spend far too much of their time concentrating on administrative rather than policy issues. Inexperienced boards all too often become captivated by the illusion of the quick fix or by the intoxication with power. They believe that if only the right strategic plan is developed, the right personnel change is made, then everything will be fine, their responsibilities will be met, and their personal influence over the university will be visible.

Most public university governing boards are quite small (eight to twelve) compared to private university governing boards (thirty to fifty). This makes it difficult for them to span the broad range of institutional interests and needs of the contemporary university. Furthermore, a small board can be held hostage by the special interests, narrow perspectives, or the personality of a single member.

The political process that selects public governing boards rarely yields individuals with sufficient experience or ability to understand the complex nature of the modern university. In fact, many of our most able citizens, by virtue of their experience, skills, personal philanthropy, and deep commitment to higher education, reject public trusteeship because they do not like what they see.[9] They refuse to be a part of politicized boards that function in all ways and at all times in the public fishbowl and operate under the heavy regulatory hand of state bureaucracies. As a result of their relatively inexperienced and highly political composition, many public governing boards receive limited respect on the campus. This can create a large gap between the board and the faculty—and occasionally even between the board and the administration.

One of the great challenges to public higher education today is assuring lay boards of the experience, quality, and distinction necessary to govern these complex and important institutions. As the AGB report noted, the fragmentation and contentiousness of modern politics undermines both board selection and conduct. The use of partisan political elections to select university governing board members long ago ceased to make sense. But even the alternative process of gubernatorial appointment is not yielding the quality of trustees necessary to govern the contemporary university. For many inexperienced board members, the importance of their board appointment to their own personal lives leads them to believe that their governing board is more important that the institution it serves. There used to be an old saying that "no institution can be better than its governing board." Today, however, the counterpoint seems to apply to public universities: "A governing board is rarely as good as the institution it serves."

To address these concerns, the Association of Governing Boards has made a number of important recommendations. First, it strongly recommends that the states reform trustee selection practices and board performance by explicitly incorporating merit criteria into trustee selection and developing a process to ensure that this occurs. The AGB urges states to enlarge public boards to accommodate a broader range of citizen views and experience and mitigate the impact of aberrant personalities. It believes that trustees should be selected for single terms of limited duration, overlapping to assure board continuity. It is particularly critical of those few remaining states that use popular election to determine university governing boards (i.e., Michigan, Colorado, Nebraska, and Nevada), since this encourages trustees to conduct themselves as political rather than deliberative bodies.

The modern university is one of the most complex and consequential institutions in modern society, and it requires a governing board of great experience and distinction. To allow political patronage or party politics to determine board membership is to court disaster. While such a political process may reflect the public character of the university, it should be tempered by a thorough review process that publicly assesses the credentials of all candidates considered for governing boards to ascertain if they have the requisite experience for these important roles. Furthermore, all boards should be subject to regular, public review and held accountable for their performance.

Faculty Governance

There are actually two levels of faculty governance in the contemporary university. The heart of the governance of the academic mission of the university is actually not at the level of the governing board or the president but rather at the level of the academic unit, typically at the department or school level. There has long been an acceptance of the premise that faculty members should govern themselves in academic matters, making key decisions about what should be taught, whom should be hired, and other key academic issues. At the level of the individual academic unit, a department or school, the faculty generally has a very significant role in most of the key decisions concerning who gets hired, who gets promoted, what gets taught, how funds are allocated and spent, and so on. The mechanism for faculty governance at this level usually involves committee structures, for example, promotion committees, curriculum committees, and executive committees. Although the administrative leader, a department chair or dean, may have considerable authority, it is generally tolerated and sustained only with the support of the faculty leaders within the unit.

The second level of faculty governance occurs at the university level and usually involves an elected body of faculty representatives, such as an academic senate, that serves to debate institution-wide issues and advise the university administration. Faculties have long cherished and defended the tradition of being consulted in institutional matters, of sharing governance with the governing board and university officers. In sharp contrast to faculty governance at the unit level that has considerable power and influence, the university-wide faculty governance bodies are generally advisory on most issues, without true power. Although they may be consulted on important university matters, they rarely have any executive role. Most key decisions are made by the university administration or governing board.

The history of higher education in America suggests that, in reality, the faculty has had relatively little influence over the evolution of the university. Indeed, one might well make the case that higher education has been more influenced and transformed by the pressures from the society it serves, by government policy, and by market forces than by any actions taken on our campuses.

There are several reasons for this. While faculties have been quite influential and effective within the narrow domain of their academic programs, the very complexity of their institutions has made substantive involvement in the broader governance of the university problematic. The current disciplinary-driven governance structure makes it very difficult to deal with broader, strategic issues.[10] Since universities are highly fragmented and decentralized, one frequently finds a chimney organization structure, with little coordination or even concern about university-wide needs or priorities. The broader concerns of the university are always someone else's problem.

Beyond the fact that it is frequently difficult to get faculty commitment to—or even interest in—broad institutional goals that are not necessarily congruent with personal goals, there is an even more important characteristic that prevents true faculty governance at the institution level. Authority is always accompanied by responsibility and accountability. Deans and presidents can be fired. Trustees can be sued or forced off governing boards. Yet the faculty, through important academic traditions such as academic freedom and tenure, are largely insulated from the consequences of their debates and recommendations. It would be difficult if not impossible, either legally or operationally, to ascribe to faculty bodies the necessary level of account-ability that would have to accompany executive authority.

Many universities follow the spirit of shared governance by selecting their senior leadership, their deans, directors, and executive officers, from the faculty ranks. These academic administrators can be held accountable for their decisions and their ac-tions, although, of course, even if they should be removed from their administrative assignments, their positions on the faculty are still protected. However, even for the most distinguished faculty members, the moment they are selected for administra-tive roles, they immediately become suspect to their faculty colleagues, contami-nated by these new assignments.

There is yet another factor that mitigates against faculty governance. As we have seen, the fragmentation of the faculty into academic disciplines and profes-sional schools, coupled with the strong market pressures on faculty in many areas, has created an academic culture in which faculty loyalties are generally first to their scholarly discipline, then to their academic unit, and only last to their institution. Many faculty move from institution to institution, swept along by market pressures and opportunities. In sharp contrast, most nonacademic staff remain with a single university throughout their careers, developing not only a strong institutional loy-alty but in many cases a somewhat broader view and understanding of the nature of the institution. Although faculty decry the increased influence of administrative staff, it is their own academic culture, their abdication of institution loyalty, coupled with the complexity of the contemporary university, that has led to this situation.

There are other forces undermining the effectiveness of shared governance. As broader society and its representatives in government challenge all social institutions to accept greater accountability for both quality and productivity, the faculty culture that prizes individual freedom and consensual decision making becomes more suspect. Furthermore, as the time scales for decisions and actions compress, during an era of ever more rapid change, authority tends to concentrate so that the institution can become more flexible and responsive. Perhaps because of the critical nature of aca-demic disciplines, universities suffer from an inability to allocate decisions to the most appropriate level of the organization and then to lodge trust in the individuals with this responsibility. If higher education is to keep pace with the extraordinary changes and challenges in our society, someone in academe must eventually be given the authority to make certain that the good ideas that rise up from the faculty and staff are actually put into practice. We need to devise a system that releases the creativity of individual members while strengthening the authority of responsible leaders.

The academic tradition of extensive consultation, debate, and consensus build-ing before any substantive decision is made or action taken will be one of our greatest challenges, since this process is simply incapable of keeping pace with the profound changes swirling about higher education. A quick look at the remarkable pace of change required in the private sector—usually measured in months, not years—suggests that universities must develop more capacity to move rapidly. This will require a willingness by leaders throughout the university to occasionally make difficult decisions and take strong action without the traditional consensus-building process.

Leadership

Leadership plays a critical role in the university, just as it does in other social institutions. If we examine carefully any major accomplishment of a university—the quality of its faculty and students, the excellence of a program, its impact on society—invariably we will find a committed, forceful, visionary, and effective leader. Leadership is dispersed throughout academic institutions, through department chairs and program directors, deans and executive officers, and influential leaders of the faculty and the student body. However, in most institutions, both the responsibility and authority of leadership flow from the top of the organizational pyramid, from the president and the governing board of the university.

The American university presidency is both distinctive and complex. In Europe and Asia the role of institutional leadership—a rector, vice-chancellor, or president—is a temporary assignment to a faculty member, sometimes elected, and generally without true executive authority, serving instead as a representative of collegial faculty views. In contrast, the American presidency has more of the character of a chief executive officer. Although today's university presidents are less visible and authoritative than in earlier times, they are clearly of great importance to higher education in America. Their leadership can be essential, particularly during times of change.[11]

Responsibility and Authority

The presidency of a major university is an unusual leadership position. Although the responsibility for everything involving the university usually floats up to the president's desk—the buck stops there—the direct authority for university activities almost invariably rests elsewhere. There is a mismatch between responsibility and authority that is unparalleled in other social institutions.

The academic organization of a university is best characterized as a creative anarchy. Consider it for a moment. A faculty member has two perquisites that are extraordinary in contemporary society: academic freedom, which means that faculty members can say, teach, or study essentially anything they wish; and tenure, which implies lifetime employment and security. Faculty members do what they want to do. And there is precious little one can do to steer them in directions where they do not wish to go. There is an old expression that leading the faculty is a bit like herding cats. But I like better the analog of pushing a wheelbarrow filled with live frogs. They can—and will—hop out to another institution if they are not happy!

The corporate side of the university—the professional staff responsible for its financial operations, plant maintenance, public relations, and so forth—might be expected to behave according to the command-communication-control hierarchy of a business. After all, major universities are in reality very complex multi-billion-dollar enterprises, with all of the accountability and demands of a modern business. Yet here too one occasionally finds an erosion of the normal lines of authority, almost as if the "I'll do it only if I choose to" culture of the faculty has also infected professional staff. Indeed, this blurring of academic and corporate cultures has been one of the great challenges in putting into place the programs to enhance productivity so successful in the business world.

The Presidential Search

Despite the stress and rigor of the position, many people view a university presidency as the top rung in the academic ladder (although most faculty would tend to rank it almost at the bottom, suggesting that anyone aspiring to such a position is surely lacking in intellectual ability, good judgment, and perhaps even moral character). Yet the university presidency can be—or at least, should be—an important position, if only because of the importance of this remarkable social institution. It is therefore logical to expect that the selection of a university president would be a careful, thoughtful, and rational process. In reality, however, the search for a university president is a complex, time-consuming task conducted by the governing board of the university using a Byzantine process more akin to the selection of a pope than a corporate CEO. In fact, in public universities, presidential searches are more similar to a political campaign and election than a careful search for an academic leader.

The search process usually begins rationally enough. Typically a group of distinguished faculty is asked to serve as a screening committee, with the assignment of sifting through the hundreds of nominations of candidates to determine a small group for consideration of the governing board. This task seems straightforward enough, yet it can be difficult in public universities because of the impact of sunshine laws—notably those laws requiring public meetings of governing bodies and allowing press access to written materials such as nomination letters via freedom of information laws. So too, faculty members on the search committee are lobbied hard by their colleagues, by neighbors, and even occasionally by trustees to make certain that the right people appear on the short list of candidates they finally submit to the governing board.

In an effort both to expedite and protect the faculty search process, there is an increasing trend among major universities to use executive search firms to assist in the presidential search process. These search consultants are useful in helping the faculty search committees to keep the search process on track, in gathering background information, developing realistic timetables, and even in identifying key candidates. Furthermore, particularly for public institutions subject to sunshine laws, search consultants can provide a secure, confidential mechanism to communicate with potential candidates without public exposure—at least during the early stages of the search.

Of course, there are sometimes downsides to the use of search consultants. Some consultants tend to take on too many assignments at one time. There have been many instances of failure to check background references thoroughly. There have even been instances in which search consultants have actually attempted to influence the search process by pushing a preferred candidate. Yet most consultants act in a highly professional way and view their role as one of facilitating rather than influencing the search.

While the early stage of a presidential search is generally steered in a thoughtful way by the faculty screening committee, the final selection phase more frequently than not involves a bizarre interplay of politics and personalities. Trustees are lobbied hard both by internal constituencies (e.g., faculty, students, and administrators) and by external constituencies (e.g., alumni, key donors, politicians, and the press). Since the governing board making the selection is usually rather small, strong personalities among governing board members can have a powerful influence over the outcome.

The politics of presidential selection becomes particularly intense for public universities, since their governing boards are themselves selected by a partisan political process. Many states have sunshine laws that not only require the final slate of candidates to be made public, but moreover require these candidates to be interviewed and even compared and selected in public by the governing board. The open nature of these searches allow the media to have unusual influence in not only evaluating candidates but actually putting political pressure on governing board members to select particular individuals.

These public beauty pageants can be extremely disruptive both to integrity of the search process as well as to the candidates. In fact, many attractive candidates will simply not participate in such a public circus because of the high risk such public exposure presents to their current jobs. Universities subject to such sunshine laws generally find their candidate pools restricted to those who really have nothing to lose by public exposure, for example, those in lower positions such as provosts or deans or perhaps leaders of lower-ranked institutions or perhaps even politicians. For these candidates public exposure poses little risk with the potential for significant gain.

Presidential Leadership

There are many, including many university presidents, who have become quite convinced that the contemporary public university is basically unmanageable and unleadable. It is true that the modern university is almost incomprehensible, with a scope and complexity far beyond the capacity of most within or without to fathom its myriad interacting missions and roles—much less to adequately communicate them to others. Many are convinced that, at most, a president can hope to deflect the course of a university slightly in one or two particular areas.

To be sure, there are many examples from the dim past of higher education in which presidents of unusual vision and ability have had great impact, both on their institutions and on higher education more generally: Angell of Michigan, Eliot of Harvard, and Hutchins of Chicago, to name only a few.

But as the modern university has become more complex, with responsibilities not only for the classical triad of teaching, research, and service, but also for health care, economic development, social change, and even big-time show biz (i.e., intercollegiate athletics), the modern presidency has truly taken on a management character more like that of the CEO of a Fortune 500 corporation. In many universities, it has taken on a more entrepreneurial role, with the president carrying the primary responsibility for generating the massive resources—from the state, from the federal government, from private donors—necessary for the teaching and scholarly pursuits of the faculty.

But there are still other roles. The president has become a defender of the university and its fundamental qualities of knowledge and wisdom, truth and freedom, academic excellence and public service against the forces of darkness that rage outside its ivy-covered walls.

So, just what are the leadership functions of the university president? First there is substantive leadership. A president is expected to develop, articulate, and implement visions of the university that sustain and enhance the quality of the institution. This includes bold and creative long-range thinking about a broad array of intellectual, social, financial, human, and physical resources, and political issues that envelope the university. Here it is essential to keep the institution's focus on the future, but with a firm understanding of the present and appreciation of the tradition and values of the past.

So too, there are significant management responsibilities, since in the end the buck does indeed stop on the president's desk. However, these generally require the expertise and experience of talented specialists. Hence, a second major role of the president is recruiting—the ability to recognize talented people, recruit them into key university positions, and support and sustain their activities.

There is a broad range of important responsibilities that might best be termed symbolic leadership. In the role as head of the university, the president has a responsibility for the complex array of relationships with both internal and external constituencies. These include students, faculty, and staff on the campus. The myriad of external constituencies include alumni and parents, local, state, and federal government, business and labor, foundations, the higher education community, the media, and the public at large. Needless to say, the diverse perspectives and often-conflicting needs and expectations of these various groups make the management of relationships an extremely complex and time-consuming task.

A final leadership role of the president might best be termed pastoral care. In a very real sense, the president frequently becomes a key source of guidance, energy, and emotional support for the institution. Not only must this critical role be kept in mind when working directly with university colleagues, but it must also always be kept in mind when working in broader university venues such as ceremonial events or communications.

Here there is an important and obvious fact of life. No president can possibly fulfill all the dimensions of this role. One must first determine which aspects of the role best utilize his or her talents. Then a team of executive officers and senior staff must be assembled that can extend and complement the activities of the president to deal with the full spectrum of the university leadership role.

There are numerous approaches to university leadership.[12] Some presidents adopt a fatalistic approach, believing that since the university is basically unmanageable, it is best to focus their attention on a small set of issues, usually tactical in nature, and let the institution essentially evolve in a nondirected fashion in other areas. For example, they might pick a few things to fix every few years or so—state relations or private fundraising or student life. This laissez-faire approach assumes that the university will do fine on its own. And most institutions can drift along for a time without strategic direction, although they will eventually find themselves mired in a swamp of past commitments that are largely reactive rather than strategic.

Others view themselves as change agents, setting bold visions for their institution, and launching efforts to move toward these visions. Like generals who lead their troops into battle rather than sending orders from far behind the front lines, these leaders recognize that winning the war sometimes requires personal sacrifice. The risks associated with proposing bold visions and leading change are high, and the tenure of such leaders is short—at least in public universities. Higher education is fortunate that from time to time such venturesome presidents burst on the scene, if only to disappear in a few short years. The impact of these presidential supernovas is generally far beyond that of more passive, conservative, and longer-tenured presidencies.

Far more common are those individuals who view their presidency as simply another step in a career path, from one academic institution to another, or perhaps between public and private life. While some itinerant presidents can occasionally accomplish a good deal in the short time they remain at a particular institution, more frequently they simply take the easy course, appeasing trustees, faculty, and alumni, and avoiding anything that might rock the boat. The short tenure of most university presidents (now averaging less than five years) and the tendency of most boards to go off campus for a new president accommodate such a transient career.

In the good old days, selection as a university president usually occurred late in one's career, typically at age 50 to 60. It was common to serve in this role for five to ten years and then retire from academe. However, the challenges of today's university require great energy and stamina. It is a job for the young. We find the itinerant president model has become more the norm—individuals who serve in executive roles at several universities, jumping from institution to institution every five years or so, leaving just before the honeymoon ends (or the axe falls).

The Environment for Leadership

The concept of leadership encounters a good deal of ambivalence on the part of faculty. On one hand, faculty members resist—indeed, deplore—the command/control style of leadership characterizing the traditional pyramid organizations of business and government. In fact, many faculty members sought careers in academe in part because they knew that in a university they would have no "supervisor" giving direct orders or holding them accountable. Faculty members can usually do as they wish. They enjoy exceptional freedom, as long as they are capable of strong teaching and scholarship in their field.

Yet the faculty also seeks leadership, not in details of its teaching and scholarship, but in the abstract, in providing a vision for the university, in articulating and defending fundamental values, and stimulating a sense of optimism and excitement. It also seeks protection from the forces of politics, greed, anti-intellectualism, and mediocrity that would threaten the important values of the university—knowledge, wisdom, excellence, service—truth, justice, and the American way.

There are many signs of a widening gap between faculty and administration on many campuses. The rank-and-file faculty sees the world quite differently from campus administrators.[13] There are significant differences in perceptions and understandings of the challenges and opportunities before higher education. It is clear that such a gap, and the corresponding absence of a spirit of trust and confidence by the faculty in their university leadership, could seriously undercut the ability of universities to make difficult yet important decisions and move ahead. Indeed, those universities that emerge as leaders in the years ahead may well be those where the faculty develops the capacity to tolerate and sustain strong presidential leadership.[14]

The growing epidemic of presidential turnover is due in part to this absence of faculty understanding of the nature of the modern university and support for its leadership. Of course it is due as well to the stresses on universities and the deterioration in the quality of their governing boards. The faculty-administration gap has been exploited by external groups to attack universities, for example, Congress's attack on indirect costs, the media attacks on political correctness, and a variety of whistle-blower incidents. Such divisions have also been exploited by an array of special interest groups pushing one political agenda or another—not to mention an array of personal agendas.

In part, the widening gap between faculty and administration has to do with the changing nature of the university itself. The modern university is a large, complex, and multidimensional organization, engaged not only in the traditional roles of teaching and research, but in a host of other activities such as health care, economic development, and social change. At the same time, the intellectual demands of scholarship have focused faculty increasingly within their particular disciplines, with little opportunity for involvement in the far broader array of activities characterizing their university. While they are—and should always remain—the cornerstone of the university's academic activities, they rarely have deep understanding or responsibility for the many other missions of the university in modern society.

The increased complexity, financial pressures, and accountability of universities demanded by government, the media, and the public at large has required far stronger management than in the past.[15] Recent furors over federal research policy, labor relations, financial aid and tuition agreements, and state funding models, all involve complex policy, financial, and political issues.

The increasing specialization of faculty, the pressure of the marketplace for their skills, and the degree to which the university has become simply a way station for faculty careers have destroyed institutional loyalty and stimulated more of a "what's in it for me" attitude on the part of many faculty members. The university reward structure—salary, promotion, and tenure is clearly a meritocracy—in which there are clear "haves" and "have-nots." The former generally are too busy to become heavily involved in institutional issues. The latter are increasingly frustrated and vocal in their complaints. Yet they are also all too often the squeaky wheels that drown out others and capture attention.

Finally, many large campuses have allowed the deterioration in the authority and attractiveness of midlevel leadership positions such as department chairs or project directors. This has arisen in part due to the increasing accountability demands on the management structure of the university, and in part in deference to concerns of formal faculty governance bodies that generally harbor deep suspicions of all administrative posts. Faculty members who step into leadership roles in positions such as department chair simply do not have the authority to manage, much less lead their units. The lack of career paths and mechanisms for leadership development for junior faculty and staff also has decimated much of the mid-level management.

The report of the AGB-sponsored National Commission on the Academic Presidency[16] reinforced these views about the limited capacity of the modern university presidency to provide leadership. The commission stressed its belief that the governance structure at most colleges and universities is inadequate. At a time when higher education should be alert and nimble, they believed that most institutions were slow and cautious instead, hindered by traditions and mechanisms of governing that did not allow the responsiveness and decisiveness the times required. At the heart of this situation was the weakness of the academic presidency. The commission found that the authority of university presidents was being undercut by all of its partners—trustees, faculty members, and political leaders—and, at times, by the presidents' own lack of assertiveness and willingness to take risks for change.

As a result, the commission concluded that most university presidents were currently unable to lead their institutions effectively. They operated from one of the most anemic power bases in any of the major institutions in American society. They often lacked the clear lines of authority they needed to act effectively, and were compelled to discuss, negotiate, and seek consensus. And all too often, when controversy developed, presidents found that their major partner—their governing board—did not back them up.

With trustees and faculty immersed in a broad range of everyday decision-making processes, presidents were bogged down by demands for excessive consultation, a burdensome requirement for consensus, and a fear of change. In practice, either of the two groups—governing boards or faculty—could effectively veto proposals for action, through either endless consultation or public opposition.

Yet, governance in higher education is far more complex, particularly in a world in which various constituencies, including both faculty bodies and governing boards, may occasionally drift away from the best interests of the university. As the commission put it, "The current practice of shared governance leads to gridlock. Whether the problem is with presidents who lack the courage to lead an agenda for change, trustees who ignore institutional goals in favor of the football team, or faculty members who are loath to surrender the status quo, the fact is that each is an obstacle to progress."

Public universities seem to face a particular challenge in this regard, since there are strong pressures to seek leaders who will preserve the status quo, who will not rock the boat. Stated simply, the current environment for leadership on most public campuses today neither tolerates nor supports strong, visionary leadership. The governing boards of public institutions are far too political, far too focused on personal agendas or chained to special interest groups, and far too threatened by anyone who would challenge the status quo. The faculty is highly fragmented, comfortable in its own narrow worlds, and resistant to any changes that might threaten the status quo, even if it would benefit the university. Scattered throughout our institutions is a large herd of sacred cows—obsolete programs, outdated practices, archaic policies— grazing on the seed corn of the future, and defended by those determined to hang onto power and control, even at the expense of the institution's future. Public opinion is largely reactionary, and when manipulated by the media, can block even the most urgently needed change.

Some have even suggested that the president of a university should be simply an employee of its governing board, arguing that in the case of public universities, the president and other senior officers are essentially senior civil servants. As such, they are obligated to carry out with total dedication—and silence—all decisions and edicts of their boards, whether they agree with them or not. In this sense, presidents are seen as primarily administrators carrying out governing board policies rather than leaders of the institution.

Governance and Leadership for a Time of Change

It is simply unrealistic to expect that the governance mechanisms developed decades or even centuries ago can serve well either the contemporary university or our society more broadly. It seems clear that the university of the twenty-first century will require new models of governance and leadership capable of responding to the changing needs and emerging challenges of our society and its educational institutions. The contemporary university has many activities, many responsibilities, many stakeholders, and many overlapping lines of authority. From this perspective, shared governance models still have much to recommend them: a tradition of public oversight and trusteeship, shared collegial internal governance of academic matters, and, experienced administrative leadership.

Yet shared governance is, in reality, an ever-changing balance of forces involving faculty, trustees, staff, and administration. The increasing politicization of public governing boards, the ability of faculty councils to use their powers to promote special interests, delay action, and prevent reforms; and weak, ineffectual, and usually short-term administrative leadership all pose risks to the university. Clearly it is time to take a fresh look at the governance of our institutions.

Governing boards should focus on policy development rather than management issues. Their role is to provide the strategic, supportive, and critical stewardship for their institution. Faculty governance should become a true participant in the academic decision process rather than simply a watchdog of the administration or defender of the status quo. Faculty members also need to accept and acknowledge that strong leadership, whether from chairs, deans, or presidents, is important if their institution is to flourish during a time of significant change.

The contemporary American university presidency also merits a candid reappraisal and likely a thorough overhaul. The presidency of the university may indeed be one of the more anemic in our society, because of the imbalance between responsibility and authority. Yet it is nevertheless a position of great importance. While a particular style of leadership may be appropriate for a particular institution at a particular time, the general leadership attributes outlined in this chapter seem of universal importance.

Governing boards, faculty, students, alumni, and the press tend to judge a university president on the issue of the day. Yet the true impact of a president on the institution is usually not apparent for many years after his or her tenure ends. Decisions and actions must always be taken within the perspective of the long-standing history and traditions of the university and for the benefit of not only those currently served by the institution, but on behalf of future generations.

Yet, as the quote from Machiavelli at the beginning of this chapter suggests, leading in the introduction of change can be both a challenging and a risky proposition. The resistance can be intense, and the political backlash threatening. As one who has attempted to illuminate the handwriting on the wall and to lead an institution in transformation, I can attest to the lonely, hazardous, and frequently frustrating life of a change agent.

To be sure, it is sometimes difficult to act for the future when the demands of the present can be so powerful and the traditions of the past so difficult to challenge. Yet, perhaps this is the most important role of the university president.

PART 3   THE
          CHALLENGE
          OF CHANGE

CHAPTER 12   Transforming the
University

*The transition from a paradigm in crisis to a new one is, in effect, a reconstruc-
tion of the field from new fundamentals, a reconstruction that changes some of
the field's most elementary theoretical generalizations as well as many of its
paradigm methods.*
                              —Thomas Kuhn, The Structure of Scientific Revolutions[1]

The recurrent theme of this book involves the need for change in higher education if
our college and universities are to serve a rapidly changing world. We have recognized that the university as a social institution has always been quite remarkable in its
capacity to change and adapt to serve society. Higher education has changed quite
significantly over time and continues to do so today. Yet the forces of change upon
the contemporary university, driven by social change, economic imperatives, and
technology, may be far beyond the adaptive capacity of our current educational paradigms. We may have reached the point of crisis in higher education when it is necessary to reconstruct the paradigm of the university from its most fundamental elements, perhaps even to reinvent the university.

Part of the challenge is simply to recognize and address the great diversity in the
perspectives of change in high education held by its numerous constituencies. A
brief anecdote illustrates. Several years ago I conducted an informal survey by asking
a number of groups on our campus to quantify how much they thought the university
would change over the next decade, using a scale of zero to ten, where zero represented no change, and ten represented radical change, in a sense, a total reinvention
of the university. Faculty tended to be rather modest in their predictions of change,
typically in the range of three to four on the scale of ten. Academic administrators—
deans, provosts, and the like—suggested there would be more radical change, perhaps in the range of seven to eight.

A national meeting of university presidents provided an opportunity to pose the
same question to university leaders. Most of my colleagues estimated the magnitude
of the changes to be about twenty—on a scale of ten! Incidentally, that was also my
own estimate of the degree of change that would occur in the American university.
And perhaps this is not so surprising, since the roles of university presidents include
managing the complex relationships between their institution and the society it serves.
They have a better sense than most about just how the university will be challenged
by the rapid and profound changes in the world we serve.

Yet it is also clear that our institutions simply must acquire greater flexibility and capacity to change to serve a changing society. They must transform themselves if they are to preserve their most fundamental traditions and values. Our challenge, as institutions, as complex communities, will be to learn how to work together to provide environments in which such change is regarded not as threatening, but rather as an exhilarating opportunity to engage in the primary activity of the university which, of course, is learning. To succeed, we must develop a more flexible culture, one more accepting of occasional failure as the unavoidable corollary to any ambitious effort. We must learn to adapt quickly while retaining the values and goals that give us a sense of mission and community. We must ask ourselves: What will our students need in the twenty-first century? What will citizens of our new world require? How can we forge a new mission for a changing society as we hold firmly to the deep and common values that have guided us over two centuries of evolution?

This capacity for change, for renewal, is the key objective that we must strive to achieve in the years ahead—a capacity that will allow us to transform ourselves once again as the university has done so many times in the past, to become an institution capable of serving a changing society and a changing world. Such institutional transformation has become commonplace in other sectors of our society. We frequently hear about companies restructuring themselves to respond to rapidly changing markets. Government is also challenged to transform itself to be more responsive and accountable to the society that supports it. Yet transformation for the university is necessarily more challenging, since our various missions and our diverse array of stakeholders give us a complexity far beyond that encountered in business or government. It must be approached strategically rather than reactively, with a deep understanding of the role and character of our institutions, their important traditions and values from the past, and a clear and compelling vision for their future.

Planning

Strategic planning in higher education has had mixed success, particularly in institutions of the size, breadth, and complexity of the research university. Even the word "strategic" sends shivers up the spine of some faculty members and triggers vitriolic attacks against bureaucratic planners on the part of many others. Yet all too often universities tend to react to—or even resist—external pressures and opportunities rather than taking strong, decisive actions to determine and pursue their own goals. So too, they frequently become preoccupied with process rather than objectives, with "how" rather than "what."

As many leaders in higher education have come to realize, our changing environment requires a far more strategic approach to the evolution of our institutions.

It is critical for higher education to give thoughtful attention to the design of institutional processes for planning, management, and governance. The ability of universities to adapt successfully to the profound changes occurring in our society will depend a great deal on the institution's collective ability to develop and execute appropriate strategies. Key is the recognition that in a rapidly changing environment, it is important to develop a planning process that is not only capable of *adapting* to changing conditions, but to some degree capable of *modifying* the environment in which the university will find itself in the decades ahead. We must seek a progressive, flexible, and adaptive planning process, capable of responding to a dynamic environment and an uncertain—indeed, unknowable—future.

The Classical Approach to Planning

Strategic planning first became important to the university in the post–World War II years, as higher education attempted to respond to the growing educational needs of returning veterans and then to a rapidly expanding population of young adults. Although most institutions simply grew as rapidly as resources allowed, there were important planning efforts such as the California Master Plan for higher education.[2] Most universities had formal planning units, generally lodged in the office of the chief academic officer and staffed by professionals. Typically these efforts were more focused on the gathering of data for supporting the routine decision process than providing a context for longer-term issues. These university planning activities were decidedly tactical in nature and usually did not play a significant role in the key strategic decisions at the executive officer or governing board level.

The marginal role of institutional planning changed in the 1980s as universities began to grapple with a more constrained resource base and increasingly frequent financial crises. Planning was used to determine institutional priorities and identify candidate activities for possible downsizing or elimination. Planning units became active if sometimes reluctant participants in support of actions adapted from the business world such as downsizing, reengineering processes, and restructuring activities. As the pace of change in the environment of the university began to accelerate during the 1980s, these formal planning activities were largely ignored as university leaders sought more immediate strategies in response to one crisis after another. When formal planning was used at all, it was generally employed to support resource allocation decisions that had frequently already been made by more ad hoc or political mechanisms.

Today, although the financial crises of the 1980s and 1990s are behind us, there is a growing recognition of the importance of strategic planning at the highest leadership level of the university, particularly during a period of ever accelerating change. But there are many approaches to planning in higher education. As we noted in an earlier chapter, some universities leaders accept the premise that the university is basically unmanageable, constrained by traditions, a culture, a complexity, and a momentum that allow only a modest deflection in one direction or another. Hence they focus on a few specific issues, usually tactical in nature, and let the institution continue to evolve in a nondirected fashion. They might select several items to fix every few years, for example, capital facilities in one cycle, fund-raising in another, and so on. This small-wins approach essentially assumes that the university will do just fine on most fronts, moving ahead without an overarching strategy.[3] And perhaps for some institutions, during times of stability, this is an appropriate strategy. However, when the planning environment is changing significantly, such an approach can be dangerous. A series of decisions unrelated to a broader vision or goal for the institution can lead to a de facto strategy counter to the university's long-term interests.

Institutions all too frequently choose a timid course of incremental, reactive change because they view a more strategically driven transformation process as too risky. They are worried about making a mistake, about heading in the wrong direction or failing. While they are aware that this incremental approach can occasionally miss an opportunity, many mature organizations such as universities would prefer the risk of missed opportunity to the danger of heading into the unknown.

Another characteristic of small wins or incremental strategies is that they generally rely on extrapolation rather than interpolation to guide decisions.[4] That is, they develop a vision for the future by simply extrapolating the past. But in a world of dramatic change, the past may not be a useful guide. It may be more appropriate to first develop a bolder vision of the future of an institution, and then develop strategies that interpolate between the future vision and the present reality. Such approaches are sometimes called scenario planning, since there will frequently be a number of possible options considered for the future.[5] Although such scenario planning or interpolative approaches can sometimes miss the mark, in general during a time of change they are superior to incremental strategies that simply cannot cope with dramatic change.

A contrasting approach might be best characterized as opportunistic planning. Here the idea is to develop flexible strategies that take advantage of windows of opportunity, that avoid confining the institution to rigid paths, or deep ruts. In a sense, this corresponds to an informed dead-reckoning approach, in which one selects strategic objectives—where the institution wants to go—and then follows whichever course seems appropriate at the time, possibly shifting paths as opportunities arise and updating strategic plans with new information and experience, always with the ultimate goal in mind.

In such opportunistic planning, one assumes that the planning framework is never rigid. What first appear to be constraints may, in fact, be transformed into opportunities. The key is to begin with the challenging question of asking what one can do to modify the planning environment. We always have an opportunity to control constraints—and the future—if we take a proactive approach. We are rarely playing in a zero-sum game. Instead we may have the opportunity to increase (or decrease) resources with appropriate (or inappropriate) strategies. The university is not really a closed system.

In an institution characterized by the size and complexity of the contemporary university, it is usually not appropriate (or possible) to manage centrally many processes or activities. We can, however, establish institutional priorities and goals and establish a process that encourages local management to move toward these objectives. To achieve institutional goals, we can stimulate processes throughout the institution aimed at strategic planning consistent with institutional goals, but with management authority residing at the local level. What we seek is an approach with accurate central information support and strong strategic direction.

Here there is an important distinction to make. *Strategic planning* is deciding what should be done, that is, choosing objectives ("What do we want to do?"); *tactics* are operational procedures for accomplishing objectives ("How do we go about doing it?"). Note as well that long-range planning is not the same thing as strategic planning. Long-range planning establishes quantitative goals, a specific plan. Strategic planning establishes qualitative goals and a philosophy. Because strategic planning should always be linked to operational decisions, some prefer to use the phrase strategic management rather than strategic planning to denote it.

While there are many ways to organize strategic planning, most fit into the following framework of steps:

1. Mission, vision, and strategic intent
2. Environmental assessment
3. Goals
4. Strategic actions
5. Tactical implementation
6. Assessment and evaluation

Clearly an understanding of institutional mission is a prerequisite to effective planning. The development of a vision is also important to the strategic process. A successful strategic planning process is highly iterative in nature. While the vision remains fixed, the goals, objectives, actions, and tactics evolve with progress and experience. During a period of rapid, unpredictable change, the specific plan chosen at a given instant is of far less importance than the planning process itself. Put another way, one seeks an "adaptive" planning process appropriate for a rapidly changing environment.

Many organizations go beyond this to develop a *strategic intent*, a stretch vision that cannot be achieved with current capabilities and resources. The adoption of a strategic intent is intended to force an organization to change. The traditional view of strategy focuses on the fit between existing resources and current opportunities; strategic intent creates an extreme misfit between resources and ambitions. Through this, we are able to challenge the institution to close the gap by building new capabilities.[6]

At Michigan, we chose a particular refinement of opportunistic strategic planning known as logical incrementalism.[7] As with most strategic processes, one begins with a clear vision statement for the institution. Within the context of this vision, one then sets out intentionally broad and rather vague goals—for example, goals such as excellence, diversity, and community. The strategic approach is then to engage broad elements of the institution in efforts to refine and articulate these goals while developing strategic plans and operational objectives aimed at achieving them. Key to the success of logical incrementalism is the skill of separating the wheat from the chaff, that is, separating out only those plans (actions and objectives) that move the institution toward the vision statement and deflecting those that do not.

Although logical incrementalism is a small-wins strategy, relying on a series of small steps to move toward ambitious goals, it also is a highly opportunistic strategy in the sense that it prepares the organization to take far more aggressive actions when the circumstances allow it. The planning process is evolutionary in other respects. It moves from broad goals and simple strategic actions to increasingly complex tactics.

The planning process works simultaneously on various institutional levels, ranging from the institution as a whole to various academic and administrative units. The ability to coordinate these multiple planning processes is, of course, one of the great challenges and keys to the success of the approach.

A Postmodernist Approach to Planning and Change

Since my background was in science and engineering, it was not surprising that my own leadership style tended to be compatible with strategic processes. Yet it should also be acknowledged that my particular style of planning and decision making was rather unorthodox, sometimes baffling both our formal university planning staff and my executive officer colleagues alike. Once I overheard a colleague describe my style as "fire, ready, aim," as I would launch yet another salvo of agendas and initiatives.

This was not entirely a consequence of my impatience or lack of discipline, however. Rather it grew from my increasing sense that traditional planning approaches were simply ineffective during times of great change. Far too many leaders, when confronted with uncertainty, tend to fall into a "ready, aim . . . ready, aim . . . ready, aim . . . " mode and never make a decision. By the time they are finally forced to pull the trigger, the target has moved out of their sights. Hence, there was logic to my "anticipatory, scattershot" approach to planning and decision making.[8]

Traditional planning processes are frequently found to be inadequate during times of rapid or even discontinuous change.[9] Tactical efforts such as total quality management, process reengineering, and planning techniques such as preparing mission and vision statements, while important for refining status quo operations, may actually distract an institution from more substantive issues during volatile periods. Furthermore, incremental change based on traditional, well-understood paradigms may be the most dangerous course of all, because those paradigms may simply not be adequate to adapt to a future of change. If the status quo is no longer an option, if the existing paradigms are no longer viable, then more radical transformation becomes the wisest course. Furthermore, during times of very rapid change and uncertainty, it is sometimes necessary to launch the actions associated with a preliminary strategy long before it is carefully thought through and completely developed.

Complex systems, whether natural systems, social institutions, or even academic disciplines, often appear stable but actually fluctuate constantly, sometimes existing in a precarious state of equilibrium. Chaos theory[10] has taught us that even very small changes can threaten this complex balance of forces. This phenomenon is sometimes known as the "butterfly effect," because it suggests that the minute disturbance of a butterfly's wings could effect major weather patterns halfway around the globe. Dramatic change is often triggered by a single new idea or exceptional individual.

This vision of disciplines as complex, chaotic systems echoes philosopher Thomas Kuhn's theory of scientific revolutions.[11] In essence, Kuhn argues that individual disciplines operate under what he calls paradigms. In a sense, a paradigm is what the members of a community of scholars share, their accepted practices or perspectives. Paradigms are not rules, but more like subjects for further study and elaboration, beliefs in certain metaphors or analogies about the world and shared values. For Kuhn, most research consists not of major breakthroughs, but of mopping up, or sweating out the details of existing paradigms. Major progress is achieved and new paradigms are created, not through gradual evolution, but through revolutionary, unpredictable transformations after the intellectual field reaches saturation.

Translated into more human terms, what these conceptions tell us is that transformations, whether in nature, knowledge, or social organizations, are frequently launched by a few remarkable people with unusual ability. Those who invent new paradigms, who destabilize the structure of a field, are often very young or very new to their field. Uncommitted to current disciplinary rules, they are, as Kuhn says, "particularly likely to see that [these] rules no longer define a playable game and to conceive another set that can replace them." They must also, however, be willing to take risks, to participate in the early, flatter, and less productive portion of the S-shaped learning curve where the broad outlines of new fields are hammered out. These intellectual renegades lend rich new vitality to our scholarship while challenging the status quo.

Note that this view suggests that one of the greatest challenges for universities is to learn to encourage more people to participate in the high-risk, unpredictable, but ultimately very productive confrontations of stagnant paradigms. We must jar as many people as possible out of their comfortable ruts of conventional wisdom, fostering experiments, recruiting restive faculty, turning people loose to "cause trouble," and simply making conventionality more trouble than unconventionality.

There is one final aspect of change in complex, dynamic systems worthy of mention here. Such systems are most adaptable or responsive at just that point before the onset of chaos. Put another way, while evolutionary, incremental change may suffice during normal times, more dramatic transformations may be necessary when the environment is changing very rapidly. It may be necessary to drive an organization toward instability, toward chaos, in order to shift it from one paradigm to the next. Sometimes this happens naturally as external forces drive an organization into crisis; sometimes it results from the actions of a few revolutionaries; and sometimes it even happens through leadership, although as Machiavelli observed, it is rarely well received by those within the organization.

Transformation

How does an institution as large, complex, and tradition-bound as the modern university transform itself to fulfill its mission, achieve its vision, and move toward its strategic intent during a time of great change? Historically, universities have accomplished change using a variety of mechanisms:

- buying change with additional resources
- building the consensus necessary for grassroots support of change
- changing key people
- finesse, stealth of night
- a "Just do it!" approach—that is, top-down decisions followed by rapid execution (following the old adage that "it is better to seek forgiveness than to ask permission")

The major paradigm shifts that will likely characterize higher education in the years ahead will require a more strategic approach to transformation, capable of staying the course until the desired changes have occurred. Many institutions already have embarked on transformation agendas similar to those characterizing the private sector.[12] Some even use similar language as they refer to their efforts to "transform," "restructure," or even "reinvent" their institutions. But herein lies one of the great challenges to universities, since our various missions and our diverse array of constituencies give us a complexity far beyond that encountered in business or government. For universities, the process of institutional transformation is necessarily more complex and possibly more hazardous.

Some believe that major change in higher education can occur only when driven by forces from outside the academy. Certainly, earlier examples of change, such as the evolution of the land-grant university, the growth of higher education following World War II, and the evolution of the research university all represented responses to powerful external forces and major policies at the national level. The examples of major institutional transformation driven by strategic decisions and plans from within are relatively rare. Yet, the fact that reactive change has been far more common than strategic change in higher education should not lead us to conclude that the university is incapable of controlling its own destiny. Self-driven strategic transformation is possible and probably necessary to cope with the challenges of our times.

At Michigan, we have grappled with such transformation efforts for a number of years. During the early 1980s, it was necessary to restructure the financing of the university. Later in that decade, we launched a series of transformations in key units, such as the university medical center. Finally, in the mid-1990s, we began a more dramatic transformation process to position the institution to face the challenges and opportunities of a rapidly changing world.

Through these efforts, and from the experience of other organizations in both the private and public sector, we can identify several features of the transformation processes that should be recognized at the outset:

- It is critical to define the real challenges of the transformation process properly. The challenge, as is so often the case, is neither financial nor organizational; it is the degree of cultural change required. We must transform a set of rigid habits of thought and organization that are incapable of responding to change rapidly or radically enough.[13]
- True faculty participation in the design and implementation of the transformation process is necessary, because the transformation of faculty culture is the biggest challenge of all. Both the creativity and the commitment of the faculty are essential to success. Policies come and go without perturbing the institution; change happens in the trenches where faculty and students are engaged in the primary activities of the university, teaching and research.
- The involvement of external groups is not only very helpful, but also probably necessary to provide credibility to the process and assist in putting controversial issues on the table (e.g., tenure reform).

- Unfortunately, universities, like most organizations in business and government, are rarely able to achieve major change through the motivation of opportunity and excitement alone. It often takes a crisis to get the community to take the transformation effort seriously, and sometimes even this is not sufficient.
- The president must play a critical role as leader, educator, and evangelist in designing, implementing, and selling the transformation process to the university community, particularly to the faculty.

Institutional transformation is not a linear process. It consists instead of a number of simultaneous and interacting elements such as developing a strategic vision, redesigning or perhaps even reinventing the core processes of an institution, and reassigning roles and responsibilities. It is also highly iterative, since as an institution proceeds, experience leads to learning that can modify the transformation process. To make headway in a complex institution such as a university, the transformation effort must spread among many participants and align with other institutional and personal goals.

Universities need to consider a broad array of transformation areas that go far beyond simply restructuring finances in order to respond to a future of change.[14] The transformation process must encompass every aspect of our institutions, including:

- the mission of the university
- financial restructuring
- organization and governance
- general characteristics of the university
- intellectual transformation
- relations with external constituencies
- cultural change

While such a broad, almost scattershot approach is complex to design and challenging to lead, it has the advantage of engaging a large number of participants at the grassroots level.

The most important objective of any broad effort at institutional transformation is not so much to achieve a specific set of goals, but rather to build the capacity, the energy, the excitement, and the commitment to move toward bold visions of the university's future. The real aims include removing the constraints that prevent the institution from responding to the needs of a rapidly changing society; removing unnecessary processes and administrative structures; questioning existing premises and arrangements; and challenging, exciting, and emboldening the members of the university community to view institutional transformation as a great adventure.

In summary, the first and most important objective of any such effort is to simply build the capacity for strategic change, change necessary to enable our universities to respond to a changing society and a changing world.

Steps in the Transformation Process

Experience demonstrates that the process of transforming an organization is not only possible, but also understandable and even predictable, to a certain degree. The process starts with an analysis of the external environment and a recognition that radical change is the organization's best response to the challenges it faces. The early stages are sometimes turbulent, marked by conflict, denial, and resistance. But, gradually, leaders and members of the organization begin to develop a shared vision of what their institution should become and turn their attention to the transformation process. In the final stages, grassroots incentives and disincentives are put into place to create the market forces required to drive institutional change, and evaluation methods are developed to measure the success of the transformation process. A possible approach would include the following steps:

Step 1: Commitment at the Top. It is critical that the senior leadership of the university buy into the transformation process and fully support it. The leadership for the transformation effort should be provided by a team of executive officers, deans, and directors, possibly augmented by an advisory group of faculty experts on organizational change.

It is essential that the governing board of the university be supportive—or at least not resist—the transformation effort. Key elements could include informal discussions with trustees, both one-on-one and in public sessions; joint retreats with the executive officers on key strategic issues; joint meetings with key university visiting groups; and the preparation of position papers to provide the necessary background for key decisions that the trustees make as the transformation effort moves forward. External advisory bodies are useful to provide alternative perspectives and credibility to the effort.

Step 2: Seeking Community Involvement. It is important to provide mechanisms for active debate concerning the transformation objectives and process by the campus community. At Michigan, we launched a series of presidential commissions on key issues such as the organization of the university, recruiting outstanding faculty and students, and streamlining administrative processes. Each of our schools and colleges was also encouraged to identify key issues of concern and interest.

Effective communication throughout the campus community is absolutely critical for the success of the transformation process. Since there is extensive experience in the design and implementation of such communications programs in the private sector, it may sometimes be advisable to hire private consultants to help design and execute this effort.

Step 3: Igniting the Sparks of Transformation. There are two general approaches to changing organizations: in "command and control" approaches, one attempts to initiate and sustain the process through top-down directives and regulations. However, since power declines rapidly with the distance from the leadership, this approach has limited effectiveness in large organizations. The alternative approach, more appropriate for large, complex organizations such as universities, is to create self-sustaining market dynamics, for example, incentives and disincentives that will drive the transformation process. For each of our goals, we need to identify highly targeted actions—leverage points—that create the incentives and disincentives and ignite the sparks necessary for grassroots change. This process requires the real creativity in the design of the transformation.

It is important to identify individuals at all levels, and in various units of the university, who will buy into the transformation process and become active agents on its behalf. In some cases, these will be the institution's most influential faculty and staff. In others, it will be a group of junior faculty or perhaps key administrators. We need to design a process to identify and recruit these individuals. Every opportunity should be used to select leaders at all levels of the university—executive officers, deans and directors, chairs and managers—who not only understand the profound nature of the transformations that must occur in higher education in the years ahead, but who are effective in leading such transformation efforts.

One of the objectives of a university transformation process is to empower the best faculty and enable them to exert their influence on the intellectual directions of the university. This can be a particular challenge since the faculties of many universities have become so encumbered with rules and regulations, committees and academic units, and ineffective faculty governance that the best teachers and scholars are frequently disenfranchised, outshouted by their less productive colleagues who have the time and inclination to play the game of campus politics. It requires determination and resourcefulness to break this stranglehold of process and free our very best minds.

Step 4: Controlling and Focusing the Transformation Agenda. Since the transformation of a complex institution such as a university is broad and multifaceted, part of the challenge is focusing members of the university community and its multiple constituencies on those aspects of the agenda that are most appropriate for their attention. For example, it is clear that the faculty should focus primarily on the issues of educational and intellectual transformation. The governing board, because of its unusual responsibility for policy and fiscal matters, should play a key role in the financial and organizational restructuring of the university. Faculty and staff with strong entrepreneurial interests and skills should be asked to guide the development of new markets for the knowledge-based services of the university.

Universities, like most large, complex, and hierarchical organizations, tend over time to grow more bureaucratic, conservative, and resistant to change. They become encrusted with policies, procedures, committees, and organizational layers that discourage risk taking and creativity. It is important to take decisive action to streamline processes, procedures, and organizational structures to enable the university to adapt effectively to a rapidly changing world.

Experience has revealed the great difficulty in persuading existing programs of an organization to change in order to meet changing circumstances. This is particularly the case in a university, where top-down hierarchical management has limited impact in the face of the creative anarchy of the academic culture. One approach is to identify, and then support, "islands of entrepreneurism"—those activities within the university that are already adapting to a rapidly changing environment. Another approach is to launch new or "green field" initiatives that are designed from the beginning with the necessary elements for change. If we provide these initiatives with the necessary resources and incentives, faculty, staff, and students can be attracted into the new activities. Those initiatives that prove successful will grow rapidly, and, if designed properly, they will draw resources away from existing activities resistant to change. In a sense, a green-field approach may create a Darwinian process in which the successful new initiatives devour older, obsolete efforts, while unsuccessful initiatives are unable to compete with ongoing activities capable of sustaining their relevance during a period of rapid change.

Clearly, significant resources are required to fuel the transformation process, probably at the level of 5 percent to 10 percent of the academic budget. During a period of limited new funding, it takes considerable creativity (and courage) to generate these resources. As we noted earlier in our consideration of financial issues, usually the only sources of funding at the levels required for such major transformation are tuition, private support, and auxiliary activity revenues, so that reallocation must play an important role.

Step 5: Staying the Course. Large organizations will resist change. They will try to wear leaders down, or wait them out ("This, too, shall pass."). We must give leaders throughout the institution every opportunity to consider carefully the issues compelling change, and encourage them to climb on board the transformation train.

For change to occur, we need to strike a delicate balance between the forces that make change inevitable (whether threats or opportunities) and a certain sense of stability and confidence that allows people to take risks. For example, how do we establish sufficient confidence in the long-term support and vitality of the institution, even as we make a compelling case for the importance of the transformation process?

As noted earlier, from a more abstract viewpoint, major change involves taking a system from one stable state to another. The transition itself, however, involves first forcing the system to the brink of instability, which will present certain risks. It is important to minimize the duration of such instability, since the longer it lasts, the more likely the system will move off in an unintended direction, or sustain permanent damage.

The Michigan Experience

During the late 1980s and 1990s, we led just such a transformation process at the University of Michigan. Like many large organizations, strategic planning exercises at the University of Michigan had proceeded through a variety of mechanisms, formal and informal, centralized and distributed among various units. We began with a classical approach to planning, by developing a campuswide process to arrive at a mission statement and a vision statement. This was challenging since the university's mission was so complex, varied, and evolving. The university produced not only educated people but also knowledge and knowledge-intensive services such as research, professional consultation, health care, and economic development. Yet all of these activities are based upon the core activity of learning. Hence we converged on a particularly simple mission statement: "The mission of the University is learning, in the service of the state, the nation, and the world."

The visioning process involved a great many groups, including faculty members, staff, students, and alumni. Despite the great diversity of planning groups, visioning efforts generally converged on two important themes: leadership and excellence, as captured in a simple vision statement: "The University of Michigan should position itself for leadership in the twenty-first century, through the quality and leadership of its academic programs and through the achievements of its students, faculty, and staff."

We recognized that this strategic plan, given the name Vision 2000 because of our intent to achieve its goals by the end of the 1990s, was essentially a positioning strategy. It was designed to move the institution toward a series of ambitious goals in areas such as quality, funding, and diversity, but largely within the traditional university paradigms. We implemented the plan through a series of strategic thrusts or initiatives, each targeting a major goal. Each strategic thrust was designed as a self-contained effort, with a clearly defined rationale and specific objectives. Care was taken to monitor and coordinate carefully these strategic thrusts at the level of the central administration, since we recognized they would interact quite strongly with one another.

During this period some of the most important strategic directions of the university were established: for example, the Michigan Mandate to achieve greater diversity, rebuilding the University, financial restructuring, the Campaign for Michigan, state and federal relations strategies, the research environment, the undergraduate experience, and student life. Associated with these initiatives were the recruitment and appointment of key leaders capable of leading the effort at various levels of the University, from executive officers and deans, to chairs and directors. A brief list of some of the more significant initiatives of Vision 2000 are listed below:

The Michigan Mandate and the Michigan Agenda for Women (diversity)
Initiatives to improve the undergraduate experience
Initiatives to improve the research climate on campus
Initiatives to stimulate and support interdisciplinary scholarship
Living-learning communities in residential halls
Campus climate (campus safety, student conduct code)
New academic initiatives (e.g., molecular medicine, global change,
    humanities institute, new music laboratory)
Rebuilding the campuses of the university
M-Quality (total quality management)
M-Pathways (systems reengineering)
The Campaign for Michigan ($1.4 billion)
Restructuring endowment management
Financial restructuring (e.g., increasing tuition revenue and private
    support to compensate for the erosion of state support)

The positioning strategy associated with the Vision 2000 plan was successful by any measure. One by one the various goals of the strategy were achieved. Largely as a consequence of this decade-long effort, by the mid-1990s the University of Michigan had become a better, stronger, more diverse, and more exciting institution. Some .of the more important indicators include:

- National rankings of the quality of the university's academic programs by the mid-1990s were the highest since these evaluations began several decades ago.
- Detailed surveys throughout the university indicated that Michigan had been able to hold its own in competing with the best universities throughout the world for top faculty. In support of this effort to attract and retain the best, the University was able to increase average faculty salaries over the decade to the point where they ranked first among public universities and fifth to eighth among all universities, public and private.

- Through the remarkable efforts of our faculty, the university became the nation's leader in research expenditures, attracting more federal, state, and corporate support for our research efforts than any other university in America (in 1996 exceeding $450 million).[15]
- Despite the precipitous drop in state support over the past two decades, the university emerged financially as one of the strongest universities in America. It became the first public university to receive an Aa1 credit rating by Wall Street, with its bonds trading at AAA ratings. Our endowment increased sixfold to over $2 billion. And thanks to the generosity of our alumni and friends, the university became the first public university to raise over $1 billion in its Campaign for Michigan—with $1.4 billion raised by the campaign's end in 1996.
- We made very substantial progress in our efforts to restructure the financial and administrative operations of the university, including award-winning efforts in total quality management, cost containment, and decentralized financial operations.
- The university was able to launch and execute a massive $2 billion facilities improvement plan that rebuilt, renovated, or updated essentially all of the buildings on our campuses, including the completion of the university's master plan for landscaping.
- The University Medical Center underwent a profound transformation, placing it in a clear leadership position in health care, research, and teaching, while accumulating over $800 million in financial reserves.
- We launched a number of initiatives destined to have great impact on the future of the university and higher education more generally, such as the Institute of Humanities, the Media Union, the Institute of Molecular Medicine, the Davidson Institute for Emerging Economies, and the Tauber Manufacturing Institute.
- Through efforts such as the Michigan Mandate and the Michigan Agenda for Women, we had achieved the highest representation of people of color and women among our students, faculty, staff, and leadership in our history, doubling the number of underrepresented minority students and faculty. Michigan had become known as a national leader in building the kind of diverse learning community necessary to serve an increasingly diverse society.

This progress achieved through the Vision 2000 plan was not serendipitous. Rather it resulted from the efforts of a great many people following a carefully designed and executed strategy. Working together, we had managed to strengthen Michigan's position as one of the leading universities in the world. But we also recognized that we had strengthened the university within a twentieth century paradigm, and that century was rapidly coming to an end. As the pace of change in the world accelerated, we sensed the need to develop a bolder vision—in the language of strategic planning, a *strategic intent*[16]—aimed at achieving excellence and leadership during a period of great change.

Hence, even as our Vision 2000 strategy moved through its execution phase, we were already engaged in a far more ambitious plan with the code name "Vision 2017" in reference to the year of the two hundredth anniversary of the university's founding. It was aimed at providing Michigan with the capacity to reinvent the very nature of the university, to transform itself into an institution better capable of serving a new world in a new century. More specifically, our strategic intent was "To provide the University with the capacity to transform itself into an institution better capable of serving a changing state, nation, and world."

We created a campus culture in which both excellence and innovation were our highest priorities. We restructured our finances so that we became, in effect, a privately supported public university. We dramatically increased the diversity of our campus community. We launched major efforts to build a modern environment for teaching and research using the powerful tools of information technology. Yet with each transformation step we took, with every project we launched, we became increasingly uneasy.

Experimenting with New Paradigms

As we came to understand better the forces driving change in our society and its institutions, we realized that these were stronger and more profound than we had first thought. Change was occurring far more rapidly that we had anticipated. The future was becoming less certain as the range of possibilities expanded to include more radical options.

We came to the conclusion that in a world of such rapid and profound change, as we faced a future of such uncertainty, the most realistic near-term approach was to explore possible futures of the university through experimentation and discovery. That is, rather than continue to contemplate possibilities for the future through abstract study and debate, it seemed a more productive course to build several prototypes of future learning institutions as working experiments. In this way we could actively explore possible paths to the future. We came to realize that change in the university should flow from our basic character as an inquiring institution. We should approach transformation as a learning process, preserving our most valuable traditions, understanding our immediate challenges, and launching experiments to help us better anticipate possible futures. In a sense, this exploratory approach to the future became our theory of institutional change.[17]

But how could we organize these experiments so that they could help us better understand the alternatives for a twenty-first century university? We chose to organize the effort in terms of a series of hypothetical paradigms, each in sharp contrast to the contemporary university. As a baseline we defined the traditional paradigm of the university as the following:

- Classroom-based pedagogy in a residential campus environment.
- Undergraduate education in a four-year, 120-credit-hour curriculum involving lecture, seminar, and laboratory courses in specific majors.
- Student experience augmented by an array of extracurricular activities, ranging from athletics to performing arts to social organizations to politics, designed to broaden their educational, social, and cultural experiences and perspectives.
- Graduate education in academic disciplines and professional schools.
- Faculty members active in research and scholarship.
- Traditional service activities such as health care and economic development.

As we have noted in earlier chapters, this traditional model is already inadequate to describe much of higher education in America today. But it can serve as a useful baseline to frame a discussion of possible paradigm shifts for the future.

We face a particular dilemma in developing more revolutionary models for the American university of the future. The pace and nature of the changes occurring in our world today have become so rapid and so profound that social institutions such as the university have great difficulty in sensing and understanding the true nature of the changes buffeting them about, much less in responding and adapting adequately. Any process aimed at articulating and analyzing new models for the university must do so with the recognition that these models must themselves adapt to an environment of continual change.[18]

With this caveat in mind, let us consider several of the more provocative themes that illustrate the broad range of possibilities for the university of the twenty-first century. What follows are some "possible futures," educational visions of the university beyond the year 2000. They suggest the extraordinary transformations that universities may undergo in the years ahead. These include:

- the world university
- the diverse university
- the creative university
- the divisionless university
- the cyberspace university
- the adult university
- the university college
- the lifelong university
- the ubiquitous university
- the laboratory university

At the outset, let us acknowledge that it is unlikely that any university will assume the form of any one of these models. But each paradigm has features that will almost certainly be a part of the character of higher education in America in the century ahead. Furthermore, each represents a path that should be explored as we seek to determine the nature of the university capable of serving a rapidly changing world.

The World University

Many of our leading universities have evolved over time from regional or state universities into, in effect, national universities. Because of their service role in areas such as agriculture and economic development, some universities have gone even beyond this to develop a decidedly international character. Furthermore, the American research university dominates much of the world's scholarship and research, currently enrolling over 450,000 international students and attracting faculty from throughout the world.[19] In view of this global character, some of our institutions may evolve into a new paradigm, the world university.

The evolution of a world culture over the next century could lead to the establishment of several world universities (Europe, Asia, Africa, and Latin America) as the focal point for certain sorts of study of international order—political, cultural, economic, and technological. Since the genius of higher education in America during the latter half of the twentieth century was the research university, perhaps these are the institutions destined to play this role for North America.

The Diverse University

Today our institutions serve a society of growing diversity—ethnic, racial, cultural, economic, and geographical—and this new reality will only intensify in the future. Although our colleges and universities have taken steps to reflect better this diversity on our campuses, we might imagine a bolder paradigm, the diverse university, which would draw its intellectual strength and its character from the rich diversity of humankind. It would provide a model for our society of a pluralistic learning community in which people respect and tolerate diversity as they live, work, and learn together as a community of scholars. Diversity is essential to any university as we approach the new century. Unless we draw upon a vast range of people and ideas, we cannot hope to generate the intellectual and social vitality we need to respond to a world characterized by great change. For universities to thrive in this age of complexity and change, it is vital that we resist any tendency to eliminate options. Only with a multiplicity of approaches, opinions, and ways of seeing can we hope to solve the problems we face.

Universities, more than other institutions in American society, have pursued a vision of tolerance and intellectual freedom. We must continually struggle to advance this heritage and to become places where myriad experiences, cultures, and approaches are valued, preserved, discussed, and embraced. Critical to this model is a recognition that these social institutions are first and foremost a "uni"-versity, not a "di"-versity. Our challenge is to weave together the dual objectives of diversity and unity in a way that strengthens our fundamental goal of academic excellence and serves our academic mission and our society.

The Creative University

The professions that have dominated the late twentieth century—and to some degree, the late-twentieth-century university—have been those that manage knowledge and wealth, professions such as law, business, and politics. Yet today there are signs that our society is increasingly valuing those activities that actually create new knowledge and wealth, professions such as art, music, architecture, and engineering. Perhaps the university of the twenty-first century will also shift its intellectual focus and priority from the preservation or transmission of knowledge to the process of creation itself. After all, the tools of creation are expanding rapidly in both scope and power. Today, we have the capacity literally to create objects atom by atom. We are developing the capacity to create new life-forms through the tools of molecular biology and genetic engineering. And we are now creating new intellectual life-forms through artificial intelligence and virtual reality.

The university may need to reorganize itself quite differently, stressing forms of pedagogy and extracurricular experiences to teach and nurture the art and skill of creation. This would probably imply a shift away from highly specialized disciplines and degree programs to programs placing more emphasis on integrating knowledge. Universities might form strategic alliances with other groups, organizations, or institutions in our society whose activities are characterized by great creativity, for example, the art world, the entertainment industry, or even Madison Avenue.

But herein lies a great challenge. While we are experienced in teaching the skills of analysis, we have far less understanding of the intellectual activities associated with creativity. In fact, the current disciplinary culture of our campuses sometimes discriminates against those who are truly creative, those who do not fit well into our stereotypes of students and faculty.

The Divisionless University

Academic disciplines tend to dominate the modern university, controlling curricula, faculty hiring and promotion, and resources. As we have built stronger and stronger disciplinary programs, however, we have also created powerful intellectual forces that push apart our scholarly community. Understandably, faculty members increasingly focus their loyalty on their disciplines instead of their home institutions.

Yet, from a broader perspective, disciplinary configurations are changing so rapidly that departments have difficulty coping with new ways of seeing. Today, those who are at the cutting edge of their fields are often those who travel across them. New ideas are often birthed in the collision between disciplines. Responding to these fundamental changes in the nature of knowledge is critical to the continued relevance of institutions like research universities.

There are many signs, however, that the university of the future will be far less specialized and far more integrated through a web of structures, some real and some virtual, that provide both horizontal and vertical integration among the disciplines. We have witnessed the blurring of the distinction between basic and applied research, between science and engineering, and between the various scientific disciplines. So, too, we are seeing a far more intimate relationship between basic academic disciplines and the professions. For example, much of the most important basic biological research is now conducted by clinical departments in medicine, for example, human gene therapy. The professional schools of business, law, public health, and social work are deeply engaged in fundamental scholarship as well as teaching in the social sciences. And, the performing arts are continually energized and nourished by the humanities—and vice versa.

The Cyberspace University

Some universities of the twenty-first century may evolve into invisible, worldwide networks—"cyberspace" or "virtual" universities—linking students, faculty, and society. Some of our campuses might become "knowledge servers" linked into a vast information network, providing their services (teaching, research, and public service) to whomever might request and need them. As distributed virtual environments become more common, one might even conceive of a time when the classroom experience itself becomes a "commodity," provided to anyone, anywhere, at any time—for a price.

To be sure, there are significant forces driving such a paradigm shift. Many people cannot put their lives on "pause," moving perhaps hundreds of miles from home to attend a degree program on campus. They have families, jobs, and other commitments—barriers that prevent many qualified students, often women and people from low-income areas—from pursuing their dreams.

The idea of a cyberspace university has its limitations. For many purposes a strong residential component is critical, especially for our undergraduates. Yet the new possibilities opened up by computer-mediated distance learning and distance collaboration promise to enhance the intellectual environment of all, while opening up our community to the vast potential of a world-spanning dialogue.

The Adult University

To achieve excellence in advanced education and scholarship, research universities are required to make extensive investments in attracting world-class scholars, maintaining extensive libraries, and constructing state-of-the-art laboratory facilities. Some of these institutions may well decide that it is simply no longer cost-effective to use their campuses for general education programs for young high school graduates, and, instead, may admit only advanced, academically and emotionally mature students directly into disciplinary concentrations or professional schools, similar to the practice of some universities in Europe and Asia.

The need to examine such a paradigm is also driven by demographics. Clearly an aging society will have different educational needs and priorities. Furthermore, the increasing educational requirements of a knowledge-driven society have created a growing need for advanced education and training of our national workforce. When one adds to this the increasing desire of senior citizens for more formal learning opportunities to enrich their lives, the magnitude of this additional educational need among adult learners becomes truly staggering.

It is not surprising that some institutions, such as the University of Phoenix, have decided to focus entirely on adult education. But beyond market opportunity, there may be other reasons to consider such a focus, even for the research university. This would allow the universities to focus their extensive—and expensive—resources where they are most effective: on intellectually mature students who are ready to seek advanced education and training in a specific discipline or profession. It would relieve them of the responsibility of general education and parenting, roles for which many large universities are not very well suited in any event. It might also allow them to shed their activities in remedial education, a rather inappropriate use of the costly resources of the research university. Focusing universities only on advanced education and training for academically mature students could actually enhance the intellectual atmosphere of the campus, thereby improving the quality of both teaching and scholarship considerably. Adult learners would be far more mature and able to benefit from the resources of these institutions.

And, ironically, such a focusing of efforts might even reduce public criticism of higher education. Most students—and parents—appear quite happy with the quality of both upper-class academic majors and of professional education. Furthermore, they seem quite willing to pay the necessary tuition levels, both because they accept the higher costs of advanced education and training, and because they see more clearly the benefits of the degree to their careers, "the light at the end at the tunnel." In contrast, most of the concern and frustration expressed by students and parents with respect to quality and cost are focused on the early years of a college education, on the general education phase, since they perceive this style of pedagogy much as they would a high school experience.

The University College

There is a contrasting paradigm to the adult university. In recent years there have been calls for research universities to make a new commitment to quality undergraduate education, particularly at the lower-division level.[20] Here, we must acknowledge the difficulties that large research universities have had in providing general education and in supporting the intellectual and emotional development of younger students. It seems increasingly clear that we need to develop a new paradigm of the "university college," the undergraduate programs surrounded by the graduate and professional programs of the comprehensive university.

Universities have always been good at teaching students the facts and methods of specific fields like biology, history, or psychology. We have been much less successful, however, at helping students decide who to "be" or how to make effective and ethical choices in a complex world. In an environment where specific details become quickly obsolete, our students increasingly need a facility for inquiry and an ability to adapt and respond to new situations. Instead of quickly channeling young students into very narrow disciplinary tracks, we should think of at least the first two years of an undergraduate degree as an opportunity for students to try on different lives as they explore the richness of our diverse cultural and academic heritage.

Some universities have chosen to focus undergraduate education in a single unit, a university college, drawing upon the resources of the broader campus. As a focal point for the undergraduate mission of the academic community, the university college may be better able to tap the intellectual resources and experiences of the modern research university: its scholars, libraries, museums, laboratories; its graduate and professional programs; its remarkable diversity of people, ideas, and endeavors.

As learning becomes an increasingly lifetime responsibility, the community experience of a residential undergraduate degree could become even more crucial. The learning communities that students build while undergraduates, the decisions they make, their activities outside of class—all build a foundation for future inquiry. The university college would emphasize this sense of a learning community, bringing professors and students into close proximity, perhaps in a single multi-purpose facility, blurring the boundaries between classroom academics, extracurricular activities, and social life. The university college would also emphasize a broad range of service activities, making the needs of our communities an integral part of this rich intellectual environment.

The Lifelong University

In a world in which education becomes a lifetime need, perhaps we should redesign the university as an education continuum, in which we interact with our students throughout their lifetimes. In this case, we need to consider an evolutionary path through which the university becomes a lifelong educational institution, with an involvement across the entire spectrum of educational needs.

In this model, the university would commit itself to a lifetime of interaction with its students—once a university student/graduate, always a member of the university family—providing them throughout their lives with the education necessary to respond to changing goals and needs. Further, we could design our programs to bring together students with alumni who have established themselves in a particular career, thereby blurring the distinction between student and graduate, between the university and the external world.

The concept of a lifelong university might also allow us to develop a different vision of what kinds of education we provide. Many feel that traditional self-contained, time-limited "degree" programs may have increasingly limited use in a world where information and skills become quickly obsolete. Education has already become a lifetime process, and with the advent of a lifelong university, coupled with other paradigms such as the cyberspace university, comes the possibility of providing the learning people need, when they need it, wherever they happen to be.

With this new vision of ourselves and our mission, "alumni" will soon cease to refer to those who have graduated and moved on. Instead, joining a university as an undergraduate may begin a potentially lifelong educational relationship. Ultimately, this connection will be very empowering, freeing people to follow the unique life-paths that make the most sense for them, unrestricted by limitations in knowledge or skills.

The Ubiquitous University

We have entered an age in which knowledge—and hence education—is not only critical for prosperity and social well being, but also key to one's personal quality of life. The need for education can no longer be confined to a particular level or a time in one's life. Instead, we are challenged to develop new learning paradigms, capable of providing educational opportunities at the college level throughout one's life, whenever, wherever, and however they desire it, at high quality, and at a cost they can afford. In other words, education may well become a universal need, and the university may be challenged to become a ubiquitous provider of learning opportunities.

To be sure, there are other social institutions committed to universal learning: libraries, museums, the performing arts, the media. Today, as knowledge becomes an even more significant factor in determining both personal and societal well-being, and as rapidly emerging information technology provides the capacity to build new types of communities, one might anticipate the appearance of a new social structure, the ubiquitous university. This might be conceived as a nexus of our public culture, a structure capable of linking and connecting social institutions such as schools, librar-ies, museums, hospitals, parks, media, computer networks, and the growing universe of information providers on the Internet.[21] Perhaps the ubiquitous university will be a new social "life-form" capable of providing community learning and knowledge networks that are open and available to all. These might evolve from existing institu-tions such as libraries or schools or universities. They might be a physically located hub or distributed in cyberspace. However, they also might appear as entirely new constructs, quite different from anything we have experienced to date.

There are some interesting trends in technology suggesting that new types of "community knowledge structures" may, in fact, appear that will not be derivative of traditional institutions such as schools or libraries. One such trend is the evolu-tion of global computer networks such as the Internet. In addition to their ability to link people together into electronic communities, they also link us to increasingly diverse and rich sources of knowledge. In a sense, they have become "knowledge and learning networks," giving us the capacity to build communities with access to vast intellectual resources. We now have the capacity to create a new paradigm for learn-ing, a new infrastructure, comprised of not only technological but also organiza-tional and social components, which will link together people and their social insti-tutions with knowledge and learning resources.

The Laboratory University

Experience has revealed the difficulty of approaching change in higher education by modifying existing programs and activities. While such a direct approach may suf-fice for incremental changes at the margin, an effort to achieve more dramatic change usually creates so much resistance that little progress is possible. It is far more effec-tive to take a "green-field" approach, by building separately a model of the new para-digm, developing the necessary experience with it, and, then, propagating successful elements of the model to modify or, perhaps, replace existing programs.

One possible approach to major university transformation, taken in earlier and more affluent times, was to build an entirely new campus. The efforts of the Univer-sity of California in the 1960s to explore academic colleges, built around research themes at UC–San Diego and residential learning at UC–Santa Cruz, are examples of this approach. However, the resource-limited 1990s are a much different time than the population-boom-driven 1960s, and it is difficult to justify such separate new campuses to explore new educational paradigms, not to mention finding sites comparable to the redwood groves overlooking the Pacific (although the new Cali-fornia State University campus at Monterey Bay is an interesting exception). But there is a more important reason to consider an alternative approach: it may be far more effective to develop and explore such new paradigms of the university directly within an existing university community in order to rapidly propagate successful efforts.

To this end, we might consider a paradigm known simply as the laboratory university, aimed at providing an environment in which creative students and faculty could join with colleagues from beyond the campus to develop and test new paradigms of the university. The laboratory university would be a testing site where new paradigms concerning the fundamental missions of the university—teaching, research, service, extension—could be developed and tested. But it would also be aimed at developing a new culture, a new spirit, of excitement and adventure that would propagate to the university at large. In such an academic enterprise, we would hope to build a risk-tolerant culture in which students and faculty are strongly encouraged to "go for it," in which failure is accepted as part of the learning process associated with ambitious goals rather than poor performance.

In terms of structure, we see the laboratory university organized not along conventional disciplinary lines, but, rather, stressing integrative themes. While it would offer academic degrees, the laboratory university would stress far stronger linkages among undergraduate, graduate, professional, and lifetime education programs than those offered by the traditional university. We also see the laboratory university more effectively integrating the various activities of the university by engaging its students in an array of teaching, research, service, and extension activities. Further, the laboratory university would almost certainly involve an array of outreach activities, e.g., linking alumni to the on-campus activities of the university or providing richer and more meaningful international experiences for students.

The laboratory university would address a second important issue in higher education, the need to invest in efforts to improve their activities in fundamental areas such as teaching and learning. As a rule of thumb, most major corporations invest an amount comparable to several percent of their gross revenues in research and development. Ironically, however, although the contemporary university stresses disciplinary research and scholarship as a part of its mission, it actually invests very little in research aimed at exploring possible future forms of education, scholarship, and service. For example, if the University of Michigan were to follow the trend in business and government, it would be investing roughly $30 to $40 million per year in such research. In reality, it, like most universities, spends only a fraction of this, perhaps $1 to $2 million per year.

This under-investment in research on issues related to the core activities of the university has become a serious issue as the future of higher education becomes increasingly uncertain. The laboratory university could be one way to address this need. It could be a prototype of what the university of the twenty-first century might be, a corporate R&D laboratory or proving ground for various possibilities. It could also be a more permanent part of the university that would always try to keep a decade or more ahead of the rest of the institution.

Paths to the Future

Each of our paradigms, our scenarios for possible futures of the university, was chosen to provoke, to jar our thinking. Yet each also not only contains elements that represent future possibilities but also links to needs and concerns of today. They provide a useful framework for discussion, for futuring, and for brainstorming.

The university paradigms outlined in the previous section could be regarded merely as abstract planning scenarios, a useful framework for discussion, for futuring, and for brainstorming. However, they were something far more for the University of Michigan. They framed not only our thinking but also our actions and our experiments.

For example, through the major strategic effort known as the Michigan Mandate discussed in Chapter 8, we altered very significantly the racial diversity of our students and faculty, thereby providing a laboratory for exploring the themes of the diverse university. We established campuses in Europe, Asia, and Latin America, linking them with robust information technology, to understand better the implications of becoming a world university. We launched major initiatives such as the Media Union (a sophisticated multimedia environment), and a virtual university (the Michigan Virtual University), and we played a key role in the management of the Internet to explore the cyberspace university theme. We launched new cross-disciplinary programs and built new community spaces that would draw students and faculty together as a model of the divisionless university. We placed a high priority on the visual and performing arts, integrating them with disciplines such as engineering and architecture, to better understand the challenges of the creative university. And we launched an array of other initiatives, programs, and ventures, all designed to explore the future.

All of these efforts were driven by the grass-roots interests, abilities, and enthusiasm of faculty and students. Our approach as leaders of the institution was to encourage strongly a "let every flower bloom" philosophy, to respond to faculty and student proposals with "Wow! That sounds great! Let's see if we can work together to make it happen! And don't worry about the risk. If you don't fail from time to time, it is because you aren't aiming high enough!"

To be sure, some of these experiments were costly. Some were poorly understood and harshly criticized by those preferring the status quo. All ran a very high risk of failure, and some crashed in flames—albeit spectacularly. Yet, while such an exploratory approach was disconcerting to some and frustrating to others, fortunately there were many on our campus and beyond who viewed this phase as an exciting adventure. And all of these initiatives were important in understanding better the possible futures facing our university. All have had influence on the evolution of our university.

There is an old saying in engineering that the best way to predict the future is to invent it. By seeking to build experiments to understand better the possible paradigms of the university of the twenty-first century, we were, in fact, taking steps to invent it.

Concluding Remarks

The remarkable resilience of institutions of higher education, their capacity to adapt to change in the past, has occurred because in many ways they are characterized by intensely entrepreneurial, transactional cultures. We have provided our faculties the freedom, the encouragement, and the incentives to move toward their personal goals in highly flexible ways, and they have done so through good times and bad. Our challenge is to tap this energy and creativity in our efforts to transform our institutions to better serve a changing world.

Yet we must do so within the context of an exciting and compelling vision for the future of our institutions. Rather than allowing the university to continue to evolve as an unconstrained, transactional, entrepreneurial culture, we need to guide this process in such a way as to preserve our core missions, characteristics, and values. We must work hard to develop university communities where uncertainty is an exhilarating opportunity for learning. The future belongs to those who face it squarely, to those who have the courage to transform themselves to serve a new society.

A key element will be efforts to provide universities with the capacity to transform themselves into entirely new paradigms that are better able to serve a rapidly changing society and a profoundly changed world. We must seek to remove the constraints which prevent our institutions from responding to the needs of their numerous and diverse stakeholders, to remove unnecessary processes and administrative structures, to question existing premises and arrangements, and to challenge, excite, and embolden the members of our university communities to embark on this great adventure. Our challenge is to work together to provide an environment in which such change is regarded not as threatening but rather as an exhilarating opportunity to engage in the primary activity of a university, *learning*, in all its many forms, to serve our world as best we can.

Those institutions that can step up to this process of change will thrive. Those that bury their heads in the sand, that rigidly defend the status quo or, even worse, some idyllic vision of a past which never existed, are at very great risk. Those institutions that are micromanaged, either from within by faculty politics or governing boards or from without by government or public opinion, stand little chance of flourishing during a time of great change.

It is often scary and difficult to let go of old and comfortable roles, to be open to new possibilities and ways of being. Yet change brings with it the possibility of deeper connections to our students and the potential for serving a much broader range of our society. Growth, both for an institution and for the individuals that comprise it, can come only with a step into the unknown. We move forward together, not recklessly, but thoughtfully—with care and a deep sense of commitment to the lives and dreams of our students.

Though we can never actually predict the future, we are not relieved of the responsibility of vision. Society is changing. We can either respond to these changes as active participants, constructing our own future, or we will find ourselves driven into the future by social forces beyond our control.

The future is not yet written, but we should not wish it any other way. The excitement that comes with uncertainty and discovery draws us inexorably into tomorrow.

CHAPTER 13

The Future of the
Higher Education
Enterprise

As a result, we believe education represents the most fertile new market for inves-
tors in many years. It has a combination of large size (approximately the same
size as health care), disgruntled users, lower utilization of technology, and the
highest strategic importance of any activity in which this country engages. . .
Finally, existing managements are sleepy after years of monopoly.
—From an investment report by
Nations Bank Montgomery Securities (1996)

Most of this book has examined the challenges facing higher education from the
perspective of a single college or university. Yet higher education in America is a vast
and diverse enterprise, consisting of thousands of institutions that have evolved to
serve the diverse needs of a growing nation. Hence it is important to examine changes
in higher education from this broader perspective.

Of course, here one can adopt several different approaches. We might view
higher education in America much as we would an industry, responding to the needs
of society with educational services, while competing in an array of marketplaces for
students, faculty, and funding from public and private sources. Although most higher
education institutions are nonprofit, the market is just as competitive for them as for
any other industry. And, like other industries, market forces play a very significant
role in shaping the nature of the higher education enterprise. In fact, the current
concerns about the changes facing the contemporary university could be the first
waves of competition lapping onto the beach of higher education. Over the horizon
there may be a tsunami of market forces, sweeping toward higher education, capable
of driving a massive restructuring of the higher education enterprise.

But higher education also has higher purposes, which cannot adequately be characterized by an industrial model. Our colleges and universities are expected to produce the educated citizens necessary for a democratic society, transmit our cultural
heritage from one generation to the next, and serve as responsible critics of society.
These roles could be at some risk if market forces alone determine the future of the
university. One need only consider the evolution of other education-like enterprises
such as television and journalism to understand that the commercial marketplace can
also drive institutions toward mediocrity. Yet if we are to preserve the most important values and traditions of the university, it is of paramount importance that we

understand the potential of powerful market forces to reshape dramatically the higher education enterprise in America.

The Higher Education Enterprise

We have noted that the higher education enterprise in America consists of some 3,600 institutions of postsecondary education, ranging from small colleges to gigantic state university systems, from religious to secular institutions, from single-sex to coeducational colleges, from vocational schools to liberal arts colleges, from land-grant to urban to national research universities. One might also include in this enterprise a number of other organizations and institutions in this enterprise, including textbook publishers, accreditation agencies, coordination bodies, and an increasing array of technology companies.

Traditionally, the higher education enterprise has been pictured as a learning pyramid, with the community colleges at the base, the accredited public and private four-year colleges at the next level, the institutions offering graduate degrees next in the pyramid, and the research universities at the pinnacle. In some states these roles are dictated by a master plan. In others, the role and mission of educational institutions are not constrained by public policy but rather determined by available resources or political influence.

In reality, however, institutional roles are far more mixed. It is true that community colleges serve primarily local communities, but they provide quite a broad range of educational services, ranging from two-year associate degrees to highly specialized training. They also provide an increasing amount of postgraduate education to individuals currently holding baccalaureate degrees who wish to return to a college in their community for later specialized education in areas such as computers or foreign languages.

Many small liberal arts colleges strongly encourage—in some case, even pressure—their faculty members to be active scholars, seeking research grants and publishing research papers in addition to teaching. Certainly too, many four-year colleges have added graduate programs and adopted the title "university" in an effort both to serve regional interests and to acquire visibility and prestige. At the other end of the spectrum, many research universities have been forced to take on significant responsibilities in remedial education at the entry level, particularly in areas such as language skills and mathematics, as a result of the deterioration of K–12 education. Many have even moved directly into the K–12 education arena, creating and managing charter schools or even entire school systems. These trends will only increase an already significant blurring of roles among various types of institutions.

Some suggest that we need to think of higher education in the twenty-first century as a mature industry.[1] After all, most states are already providing postsecondary education to 60 percent or more of high school graduates. Public support of higher education for traditional purposes, whether from state or from federal governments, is unlikely to increase. And as is happening with other mature industries such as health care, both the public and private sector are asking hard questions about the cost, efficiency, productivity, and effectiveness of our colleges and universities.

To view higher education only from the perspective of its traditional constituencies, however, is to miss the point of the transformation that must occur as we enter an age of knowledge. For example, if lifetime education becomes a necessity for job security—as it has in many careers already—the needs for college-level education and training will grow enormously. So too American higher education could well be one of this nation's most significant export commodities, particularly if we can take advantage of emerging technologies to deliver high-quality educational services on a global scale. Higher education could be—should be—one of the most exciting growth industries of our times, but this will depend on the development of new models of higher education that utilize far more effective systems for financing and delivering learning services.

The Growing Demand for Higher Education

There are powerful forces driving an increasing societal demand for higher education services in the United States. We have noted that population growth in the years ahead will cause a significant expansion of demand for educational services in the years ahead, estimated as a growth of roughly 4.4 million additional students by the year 2010. Beyond the additional needs of a growing population, there are even more fundamental forces at work that will almost certainly drive a major expansion of the higher education enterprise.

As we move further into an age of knowledge, the workforce will require more sophisticated education and training to sustain its competitiveness. We have entered an era when the need for, and the demand for, advanced education and learning opportunities will grow rapidly. Increasingly, the education and skills of individuals are seen as the key to both their personal quality of life and the broader strengths of their society. Furthermore, the need for ongoing education of the existing workforce has created a rapidly growing market for adult education at the college level.

People have always looked to education as the key to prosperity and social mobility. But now more than ever, people see education as their hope for leading meaningful and fulfilling lives. The level of one's education has become a primary determinant of one's economic well-being. Just as a high school diploma became the

passport for participation in the industrial age, today, a century later, a college education has become the requirement for economic security in the age of knowledge.

We have noted that today's typical college graduates will change careers several
times during their lives, requiring additional education at each stage. Furthermore,
with the ever-expanding knowledge base of many fields, along with the longer life
span and working careers of our aging population, the need for intellectual retooling
will become even more significant. Even those without college degrees will soon find
that their continued employability requires advanced education. Dolence and Norris
estimate that just to keep an individual on pace with evolving workplace skills and
knowledge will require a time commitment of roughly one day of education per
week.[2] This translates to one-fifth of the workforce in college level educational
programs at any time, or roughly 28 million full-time-student equivalents—compared to the 12.1 million full-time-equivalent students currently enrolled in our colleges and universities.[3]

Knowledge workers are likely to make less and less distinction between work
and learning. In fact, continuous learning will be a necessity for continued work
relevance and security. Employers will seek individuals who can consistently learn
and master new skills to respond to new needs. They will place less emphasis on the
particular knowledge of new employees than on their capacity to continue to learn
and grow intellectually throughout their careers. From the employee's perspective,
there will be less emphasis placed on job security with a particular company and
more on the provision of learning opportunities for acquiring the knowledge and
skills that are marketable more broadly.

As we have noted, there will be a shift from "just in case" learning, in which
formal education is confined to specific degree programs early in one's life in the
hope that the skills learned will be useful later, to "just in time" lifelong learning, in
which both informal and formal learning will be expected to occur throughout one's
life. This suggests that most of one's learning will occur after their undergraduate
education, either in the workplace or other learning environments.

Clearly higher education should flourish in this growing market for advanced
education and learning.[4] But just as clearly, our current campus-based, high-cost,
ivory tower approach to higher education simply cannot respond to this staggering
demand.[5] Fresh vision will be needed to create the new learning paradigms, the institutions and enterprises for serving this great demand, and the mechanisms for financing this effort.

The Restructuring of the Higher Education Enterprise

During the past century, there has been a noticeable concentration of control over
disciplines, faculty, students, and credentials by the university. Universities serve as

the gatekeepers not only for the definition of the academic disciplines and member-ship in the academy, but as well controlling entry to the professions that so domi-nate contemporary society. While there is competition among institutions for stu-dents, faculty, and resources—at least in the United States—the extent to which institutions control the awarding of degrees has led to a tightly controlled competi-tive market. Furthermore, most colleges and universities serve primarily local or re-gional areas, where they have particularly strong market positions. As with most monopoly organizations, today's university is provider-centered, essentially function-ing to serve the needs and desires of the faculty rather than the students they teach or the broader society that supports them.

Today this monopoly character is being strongly challenged, however. No uni-versity can control the growth of knowledge nor the educational needs of a society. Information technology is rapidly eliminating the barriers of space and time that have largely shielded the campus. New competitive forces are entering the market-place to challenge credentialing.

Competitive Forces

As the need for advanced education becomes more intense, there are already signs that some institutions are responding to market forces and moving far beyond their traditional geographical areas to compete for students and resources. There are hun-dreds of colleges and universities that increasingly view themselves as competing in a national or even international marketplace. Even within regions such as local com-munities, colleges and universities that used to enjoy a geographical monopoly now find that other institutions are establishing beachheads through extension services, distance learning, or even branch campuses. With advances in communication, trans-portation, and global commerce, several universities in the United States and abroad increasingly view themselves as international institutions, competing in the global marketplace.

Beyond competition among colleges and universities, there are new educational providers entering the marketplace.[6] Sophisticated for-profit entities such as the University of Phoenix and Sylvan Learning are moving into markets throughout the United States, Europe, and Asia. Already more than seven hundred virtual universi-ties are listed in college directories with over one million students enrolled in their programs, including major efforts such as the Western Governors University and the Michigan Virtual University. It has been estimated that today there are over one thousand corporate training schools in the United States providing both education and training to employees at the college level. Industry currently spends over $60 billion per year on corporate training. It is only a matter of time before some corpo-rate efforts enter the marketplace to provide educational services more broadly.

Although traditional colleges and universities enjoy competitive advantages based upon long-standing reputation and control of accreditation and credentialing, these could be eroded quite rapidly by the vast resources that the industrial sector is capable of focusing on these efforts. Furthermore, the higher comfort level of industry with technology, strategic alliances, and rapid decision making could prove to be decisive advantages in intensely competitive marketplaces. Finally, with access to the vast resources of capital markets and unhindered by other social commitments or public governance, for-profit providers could cherry pick the best faculty and most attractive products (learning software, courses, or programs) from traditional educational institutions. The competitive threat is very real.

From Teaching to Learning

The faculty has long been accustomed to dictating what it wishes to teach, how it will teach it, and where and when the learning will occur. Students must travel to the campus to learn. They must work their way through the bureaucracy of university admissions, counseling, scheduling, and residential living. And they must pay for the privilege, with little of the power of traditional consumers. If they navigate through the maze of requirements, they are finally awarded a certificate to recognize their experience—a college diploma. This process is sustained by accrediting associations, professional societies, and state and federal governments.

This carefully regulated and controlled enterprise could be eroded by several factors. First, the great demand for advanced education and training cannot be met by such a carefully rationed and controlled enterprise. Second, the expanding marketplace will attract new competitors exploiting new learning paradigms and increasingly threatening traditional providers. And perhaps most important of all, newly emerging information technology will not only eliminate the constraints of space and time, but it will also transform students into learners and consumers. Open learning environments will provide learners with choice in the marketplace—access to learning opportunities, knowledge-rich networks and digital libraries, collections of scholars and expert consultants, and other mechanisms for the delivery of learning.

The evolution from faculty-centered and controlled teaching and credentialing institutions to distributed, open learning environments is already happening. New learning services are increasingly available from many providers, learning agents, and intermediary organizations. Such an open, network-based learning enterprise certainly seems more capable of responding to the staggering demand for advanced education, learning, and knowledge. It also seems certain not only to provide learners with far more choices but also to create far more competition for the provision of knowledge and learning services.

A Global Knowledge and Learning Industry

As a result, higher education is likely to evolve from a loosely federated system of colleges and universities serving traditional students from local communities to, in effect, a *global knowledge and learning industry*. With the emergence of new competitive forces and the weakening influence of traditional regulations, education is evolving like other "deregulated" industries, for example, health care, communications, or energy. Yet, in contrast to these other industries that have been restructured as government regulation has disappeared, the global knowledge industry will be unleashed by emerging information technology as it releases education from the constraints of space, time, and the credentialing monopoly. Peterson and Dill suggest that as our society becomes ever more dependent upon new knowledge and educated people, upon knowledge workers, this global knowledge business will represent one of the most active growth industries of our times.[7]

Many in the academy undoubtedly view with derision or alarm the depiction of the higher education enterprise as an "industry" or "business." After all, higher education is a social institution with broader civic purpose and not traditionally driven by concerns about workforce training and economic development. Furthermore, the perspective of higher education as an industry raises concerns that short-term economic and political demands will dominate broader societal responsibilities and investment. Yet, in an age of knowledge, the ability of the university to respond to social, economic, and technological change will likely require a new paradigm for how we think about postsecondary education. No one, no government, is in control of the emerging knowledge and learning industry; instead it responds to forces of the marketplace. Universities will have to learn to cope with the competitive pressures of this marketplace while preserving the most important of their traditional values and character.

Who will drive the restructuring of higher education? State or federal governments? Not likely. Traditional institutions such as colleges and universities working through statewide systems or national alliances such as the Association of American Universities or the American Council on Education? Also unlikely. The marketplace itself, as it did in health care, spawning new players such as virtual universities and for-profit educational companies? Perhaps.

Today the higher education enterprise consists of a constellation of traditional institutions, research universities, four-year colleges and universities, two-year colleges, proprietary institutions, and professional and specialized institutions. However the postsecondary enterprise of tomorrow will contain as well computer hardware and software companies, telecommunications carriers, information services companies, entertainment companies, information resource organizations, and corporate and governmental educational organizations.

Regardless of who or what drives change, the higher education enterprise is likely to be dramatically transformed over the next decade.[8] It could happen from within, in an effort to respond to growing societal needs and limited resources. But it is more likely to be transformed by new markets, new technologies, and new competition. In this rapidly evolving knowledge business, the institutions most at risk will not be of any particular type or size but rather those most constrained by tradition, culture, or governance.

A Comparison: The Restructuring of the Health-Care Industry

Will this restructuring of the higher education enterprise really happen? Jack Gregg has developed an interesting comparison of the situation currently faced by higher education with that faced by health care a decade ago.[9] Both health care and higher education are not only very significant in size, $600 billion and $180 billion respectively, but they both represent activities of critical importance to the nation. Both enterprises are world-class in quality.

Beyond size and quality, there are other similarities between health care in the 1980s and higher education in the 1990s. Both enterprises were provider-centered and controlled by professional guilds, that is, physicians and professors. Both paid relatively little attention to the changing needs of the marketplace and had little respect for management issues such as productivity and cost-containment. Both relied heavily upon subsidies, both public and private, to support the high prices charged to customers. And both eventually encountered strong resistance to rapid cost increases from market pressures and political forces.

A decade ago, as health-care costs continued to escalate rapidly, many looked to government to provide the answers, to regulate the industry and either to subsidize or constrain costs. Yet, government intervention foundered on the shoals of the complexity of the matter and the intense political disagreements over the nature of the federal role. Instead, the marketplace took over and rapidly and profoundly changed the nature of the health-care industry. New organizations appeared, such as managed health-care organizations, massive for-profit health-care providers, and new consortia of employers and others, facilitated by brokers, all determined to drive down health-care costs.

As health care became a commodity in a highly competitive marketplace, health-care providers soon learned that they had to view the patient—or, more frequently the employer or broker negotiating health-care contracts for employees—as the center of their attention. While they took pride in highly skilled physicians and sophisticated medical facilities, they learned that in the end, these were only assets if they were capable of providing high-quality, cost-competitive health care. Health-care providers learned rapidly that they had to operate as businesses in an intensely competitive marketplace. Having one of the leading tertiary care medical centers in the nation was of little value if patients believed they could get better care at lower costs elsewhere. This attention to the needs and concerns of patients became critical to the financial viability of health-care providers. Patients wanted to see doctors, not allied health-care professionals. They were frustrated with bureaucracy. They wanted to deal with only a single bill for medical treatment, rather than the array of billings from various clinics for various services. They wanted convenient access to health care, near their homes or places of work.

As a result of these forces, over less than a decade the health-care industry has been dramatically restructured. While Washington debated federal programs to control health-care costs, the marketplace took over with new paradigms such as managed care and for-profit health centers. While some contend that the industry remains in chaos, there is little doubt it has been changed very significantly by market forces.

The comparisons with higher education are obvious. The university remains very much a "provider-centered" organization, organized around the needs and desires of faculty rather than students. Students seeking an education are required to conform to the faculty-driven characteristics of the university, living on its campus, dealing with its bureaucracy, learning from graduate teaching assistants rather than professors, and paying rapidly increasing prices for the privilege. The faculty resists efforts to contain costs or increase productivity. While the use of technology is extensive, it is rarely used to improve the quality or efficiency of learning.

In many ways the education industry represents the last of the economic sectors dominated by public control and yet at risk because of quality, cost-effectiveness, and changing demands. As information technology breaks apart monopolies and opens up the market by releasing students from the constraints of space and time, competition among both existing and newly emerging institutions is intensifying. Just as with health care, the higher education enterprise is entering a period in which market forces could well lead to massive restructuring.

Unbundling the University

The modern university has evolved into a monolithic institution controlling all aspects of learning. Universities provide courses at the undergraduate, graduate, and professional level, and they support residential colleges, professional schools, lifelong learning, athletics, libraries, museums, and entertainment. They have assumed responsibility for all manner of activities beyond classroom education: housing and feeding students, providing police and other security protection, counseling and financial services—we even operate power plants on many Midwestern campuses!

Today's comprehensive universities, at least as full-service organizations, are at considerable risk. These institutions have become highly vertically integrated over the past several decades. Yet today we are already beginning to see a growing number of differentiated competitors for many of these activities. Universities are under increasing pressure to spin off or sell off or close down parts of their traditional operations in the face of this new competition. They may well find it necessary to unbundle their many functions, ranging from admissions and counseling to instruction and certification.

An example might be useful here. We have discussed earlier the concept of a virtual university, a university without a campus or faculty that provides computer-mediated distance education. The virtual university develops and focuses on the core competencies of marketing and delivery. It works with the marketplace to understand needs, then it outsources courses, curriculum, and other educational services from established colleges and universities—or perhaps individual faculty—and delivers these through sophisticated information technology.

Capitalizing on one's strengths and outsourcing the rest is commonplace in many industries. Consider, for example, the computer industry, in which webs of alliances exist among hardware developers, manufacturers, software developers, and marketers of hardware and software. These are constantly being created and modified in response to competitive dynamics.

This idea can be applied to academia. While we are very good at producing intellectual content for education, there may be others who are far better at packaging and delivering that content. While in the past universities have had a monopoly on certifying learning, there may be others, whether they are accreditation agencies or other kinds of providers, more capable of assessing and certifying that learning has occurred. Many of our other activities, for example, financial management and facilities management, are activities that might be outsourced and better handled by specialists.

Some time ago, a leading information services company visited my institution to share with us their perspective on the higher education market. They believe the size of the higher education enterprise in the United States during the next decade could be as large as $300 billion per year ($635 billion if K-12 is included), with 30 million students, roughly half comprised of today's traditional students and the rest as adult learners in the workplace. (Incidentally, they also put the size of the world market at $3 trillion.) Their operational model of the brave, new world of market-driven higher education suggests that this emerging domestic market for educational services could be served by a radically restructured enterprise consisting of fifty thousand faculty "content providers," two hundred thousand faculty learning "facilitators," and one thousand faculty "celebrities" who would be the stars in commodity learning-ware products. The learner would be linked to these faculty resources by an array of for-profit services companies, handling the production and packaging of learning ware, the distribution and delivery of these services to learners, and the assessment and certification of learning outcomes. Quite a contrast with the current enterprise!

An even bolder arrangement of the elements of the future higher education enterprise was suggested by Brown and Duguid.[10] In their model, students would not be constrained to a particular college or university, but rather would become active learners with many options. They would first select a suitable "degree-granting body," which would determine degree requirements, develop appropriate assessment measures, and provide the appropriate credentials when evidence of learning has been achieved. Working with the degree-granting body, students would have the opportunity to design their education, drawing upon the services of various faculty and learning environments.

In this enterprise, faculty would behave as independent contractors, first becoming associated with various degree-granting bodies and perhaps campus environments. Although some learning environments would very much resemble today's college campuses, others would be virtual, distributed over powerful knowledge networks. This model would allow the student/learner's educational program to be assembled from a variety of learning providers and experiments, which might change as an individual's educational needs change throughout his or her life.

Higher education is an industry ripe for the unbundling of activities. Universities, like other institutions in our society, will have to come to terms with what their true strengths are and how those strengths support their strategies—and then be willing to outsource needed capabilities in areas where they do not have a unique advantage.

The Emergence of a Commodity Market

Throughout most of its history, higher education has been a cottage industry. Individual courses are handicraft, made-to-order products. Faculty members design from scratch the courses they teach, whether they are for a dozen or several hundred students. They may use standard textbooks from time to time—although many do not—but their organization, their lectures, their assignments, and their exams are developed for the particular course at the time it is taught. Clearly this handicraft model of instruction is very expensive, since each lecture is largely custom-designed for a particular class of student. In fact, the tuition price per hour of lecture at our more elite universities amounts to over fifty dollars, about that for an expensive night out on the town for most students.

In a very real sense, the industrial age bypassed the university. So too our social institutions for learning—schools, colleges, and universities—continue to favor programs and practices based more on past traditions than upon contemporary needs. Yet, it may be quite wrong to suggest that higher education needs to evolve into a mass production mode or broadcasting mode to keep pace with the needs of our society. In a sense, this was the evolutionary path taken by K–12 education, with disastrous consequences. Besides, even industry is rapidly discarding the mass production approach of the twentieth century and moving toward products more customized to particular markets.

Our ability to introduce new, more effective avenues for learning, not merely new media with which to convey information, will change the nature of higher education. This will bring with it new modes of organization, new relationships among universities and between universities and the private sector. The individual handicraft model for course development may give way to a much more complex method of creating instructional materials. Even the standard packaging of an undergraduate education into "courses," in the past required by the need to have all the students in the same place at the same time, may no longer be necessary with new forms of asynchronous learning. Of course, it will be a challenge to replace the handicraft model while still protecting the traditional independence of the faculty to determine curricular content. Beyond that, there is also a long-standing culture in which the faculty has come to believe they own the intellectual content of their courses and are free to market these to others for personal gain, for example, through textbooks or off-campus consulting services. But universities may have to restructure these paradigms and renegotiate ownership of the intellectual products represented by classroom courses if they are to constrain costs and respond to the needs of society.

Let us return to our earlier example of content preparation. As we have noted, universities—more correctly, faculty members—are skilled at creating the content for educational programs. Indeed, we might identify this as one of their core competencies. But they have not traditionally been particularly adept at "packaging" this content for mass audiences. To be sure, many faculty have written best-selling textbooks, but these have been produced and distributed by textbook publishers. In the future of multimedia, net-distributed educational services, perhaps the university will have to outsource both production and distribution to those most experienced in reaching mass audiences—the entertainment industry.

As distributed virtual environments become more common, there may come a time when the classroom experience itself becomes a "commodity," provided to anyone, anywhere, at any time—for a price. You want to take Vincent Scully's course in modern architecture? Just sign up here. How about Stephen Jay Gould's "Life on Earth" course? Available as well. If students could actually obtain the classroom experience of these talented teachers, why would they want to take classes from the local professor—or, in many cases, the local teaching assistant?

In such a commodity market, the role of the faculty member would change substantially. Rather than developing content and transmitting it in a classroom environment, a faculty member might instead have to manage a learning process in which students use an educational commodity (e.g., the Microsoft Virtual Modern Architecture Course). Clearly this would require a shift from the skills of intellectual analysis and classroom presentation to those of motivation, consultation, and inspiration. Welcome back, Mr. Chips!

Mergers, Acquisitions, and Hostile Takeovers

The perception of the higher education enterprise as a deregulated industry has several other implications. While the 3,600 colleges and universities in the United States are characterized by a great diversity in size, mission, constituencies, and funding sources, they also exhibit great duplication of services and inefficiencies in operations. Not only are we likely to see the appearance of new educational entities in the years ahead, but as in other deregulated industries, we may experience a period of fundamental restructuring of the enterprise itself. Some colleges and universities might disappear. Others might merge. Some might actually acquire other institutions.

A case in point: The Big Ten universities (actually there are twelve, including the University of Chicago and Penn State University) have already merged many of their activities, such as their libraries and their federal relations activities. They are exploring ways to allow students at one institution to take courses or even degree programs from another institution in the alliance in a transparent and convenient way. Could one imagine the Big Ten universities becoming a university system for "the heartland of America"?

One might also imagine affiliations between comprehensive research universities and liberal arts colleges. This might allow the students enrolling at large research universities to enjoy the intense, highly personal experience of a liberal arts education at a small college while allowing the faculty members at these colleges to participate in the type of research activities occurring only on a large research campus.

One might even imagine "hostile takeovers," as a Darwinian process emerges such that some institutions devour their competitors. Such events have occurred in deregulated industries in the past, and all are possible in the future we envision for higher education.

One of my colleagues made an interesting point about this evolution. He suggested that the past fifty years might be referred to as the "Harvardization" of higher education, in the sense that most American colleges and universities attempted to become more like Harvard as their ideal model. Yet the first half of the twenty-first century could be the "de-Harvardization" of American higher education, both because the high-cost elitist model is no longer an attractive model for most institutions, and because the competitive marketplace will demand more differentiation among institutions if they are to survive.

A recent report on the fiscal crisis in higher education recommended a more traditional taxonomy:[11]

- *Community colleges* would take a leadership role in workforce preparation, expending more effort on education and training targeted to workforce preparation, adult education, and remedial education.
- *State undergraduate institutions* would take the lead in teacher training and areas related to regional economic development, with faculty encouraged to assume a strong leadership role in research and technical assistance for regional enterprises.
- *Major research universities* would focus on the promotion of research and graduate education, with federal investment in research concentrated in the nation's top-ranked research universities and not distributed broadly across institutional types.

While such a proposal to define more clearly the missions of various institutional types is admirable, it falls far short of responding to the growing gap between societal need for educational services and its will and capacity to pay for these services within the traditional paradigm. Perhaps part of the problem is that we need a new taxonomy. For example, Zemsky and Massey propose that we allow the market to classify institutions:

- *Brand-name campuses*: Selective, high-status, high-cost institutions offering campus-based education to traditional age groups (e.g., Harvard, Berkeley)
- *Mass-provider institutions*: Enrolling most students in low-cost but relatively traditional programs (e.g., local regional universities and community colleges)
- *Convenience institutions*: Offering a broad range of educational services in cost-effective, customer-focused business models (e.g., University of Phoenix)

From a broader perspective, we can see the rapid evolution of a global knowledge and learning industry as a continuation of an ever-expanding role and presence of the university during the past century. From the commitment to universal access to higher education after World War II to the concern about cost and efficiency in the 1980s to the role of the university in a knowledge-driven society, there have been both a growth in the number and complexity of the missions of the university and the entry into postsecondary education of new players and competitors. Today we think of the postsecondary education industry as consisting of a core of educational institutions, research, doctoral, and comprehensive institutions; four-year colleges; two-year colleges; proprietary institutions, and professional and specialized institutions. This core is supported, sustained, and augmented by an array of external players, including state and federal government, business and industry, and foundations. The traditional postsecondary institutions will be joined at the core of the emerging knowledge and learning industry by new players: telecommunications companies, entertainment companies, information technology companies, information service providers, and corporate and governmental education providers.[12]

Emerging Learning Structures

We have already discussed several market-driven possibilities: the formation of a global knowledge industry, the shift from a teaching franchise to a learning franchise, unbundling the university, and the explosion of commodity markets. But we could be surprised by the growth of entirely new learning organizations.

The New University

With increasing differentiation, there will be many "new" universities as institutions attempt to define themselves in the marketplace both by core competencies and by differentiation. Some colleges and universities may continue to focus on the traditional educational paradigms discussed in earlier chapters. But many others will undergo or exploit significant transformations to explore an array of themes:

- From teaching to learning organizations
- From passive students to active learners
- From faculty-centered to learner-centered
- From solitary learning to interactive, collaborative learning
- From classroom learning to learning communities
- From linear, sequential curricula to hyperlearning experiences
- From credit-hour or seat-time credentialling to learning assessment
- From just-in-case learning to just-in-time learning to just-for-you learning
- From student or alumnus to lifelong member of a learning community
- From campus-based to asynchronous to ubiquitous learning opportunities

Here it is both useful and important to note that such "new" universities are not merely conjectures. They represent paradigms that are actually evolving today, in many guises, across the nation and around the world.

The New Competitors

In recent years we have seen an explosion in the number of new competitors in the higher education marketplace. It is estimated that in 1998 the revenues of for-profit and proprietary educational providers were in excess of $3.5 billion and growing rapidly. Many of these efforts target highly selective markets, such as the University of Phoenix, which already operates over one hundred learning centers in thirty-two states, serving over fifty thousand students. Phoenix targets the educational needs of adult learners whose career and family responsibilities make access to traditional colleges and universities difficult. By relying on highly structured courses, arranged in a form convenient to the student, and taught by practitioners as part-time instructors, Phoenix has developed a highly competitive paradigm.

Other for-profit industry-based educational institutions are evolving rapidly, such as Sylvan Learning Systems and its subsidiaries, Athena University, Computer Learning Centers, and the World Learning Network. These join an existing array of proprietary institutions such as the DeVry Institute of Technology and ITT Educational Services. Not far behind are an array of sophisticated industrial training programs, such as Motorola University and the Disney Institute, originally formed to meet internal corporate training needs, but now exploring offering educational services to broader markets. Of particular note here are the efforts of information services companies such as Anderson Consulting that are increasingly viewing education as just another information service.

It is important to recognize that while many of these new competitors are quite different than traditional academic institutions, they are also quite sophisticated both in their pedagogy, their instructional materials, and their production and marketing of educational services. For example, some such as Caliber Learning and the Open University invest heavily in the production of sophisticated learning materials and environments, utilizing state-of-the-art knowledge concerning learning methods from cognitive sciences and psychology. They develop alliances with well-known academic institutions to take advantage of their brand names (e.g., Wharton in business and MIT in technology). They approach the market in a highly sophisticated manner, first moving into areas characterized by limited competition, unmet needs, and relatively low production costs, but then moving rapidly up the value chain to more sophisticated programs.

In the face of such competition, the not-for-profit higher education enterprise is also responding with an array of new activities. Most university extension programs are moving rapidly to provide Internet-based instruction in their portfolios. University collaboratives such as the National Technological University and the Midwest University Consortium for International Activities have become quite formidable competitors. They are being joined by a number of new organizations such as the Western Governors' University, the California Virtual University, and the Michigan Virtual University that aim to exploit both new technology and new paradigms of learning.

By way of example, in 1997 the University of Michigan and Michigan State University launched a venture known as the Michigan Virtual Automotive College

(MVAC) as a private, not-for-profit, 501(c)3 corporation aimed at developing and delivering technology-enhanced courses and training programs to the automobile industry.[13] MVAC is a college without walls that serves as an interface between higher education institutions, training providers, and the automotive industry. Courses and programs can be offered from literally any site in the state to any other technologically connected site within the state, the United States, or the world. Although technologies are rapidly emerging, it is expected that MVAC will broker courses that utilize a wide array of technology platforms including satellite, interactive television, Internet, CD-ROM, videotape, and combinations of the above. It will seek to develop common technology standards between and among providers and customers for the ongoing delivery of courses. It currently offers over one hundred courses and twenty degree programs to several thousand students, ranging from the advanced postgraduate education in engineering, computer technology, and business administration to entry-level instruction in communications, mathematics, and computers.

The Open University

For many years, the educational needs of many nations have been addressed by open universities, institutions relying on both televised courses and correspondence education to enable students to study and earn degrees at home. Perhaps most notable has been the British Open University, but this is only one of many such institutions that now enroll over three million students worldwide.[14]

These institutions are based upon the principle of open learning, in which technology and distance education models are used to break down barriers and provide opportunities for learning to a very broad segment of society. In these models, the student becomes a more active participant in learning activities, taking charge of their own academic program as much as possible. Many of these open universities are now embracing information technology, particularly the Net, to provide educational opportunities to millions of students unable to attend or afford traditional residential campuses.

The motivation behind open universities involves cost, access, and flexibility. The open university paradigm is based not on the extension of the classroom but rather the one-to-one learning relationship between the tutor and the student. It relies on very high-quality learning materials, such as books, videotapes, and CD-ROM or Net-based software, augmented by facilitators at regional learning centers and by independent examiners. Using this paradigm, for example, the British Open University has been able to provide high-quality learning opportunities (currently ranked among the upper 15 percent of British universities) at only a fraction of the cost of residential education ($4,200 compared to $12,500 per student year in North America).

To date, most open universities rely heavily on self-learning in the home environment, although they do make use of interactive study materials and decentralized learning facilities where students can seek academic assistance when they need it. However, with the rapid evolution of virtual distributed environments and learning communities, these institutions will soon be able to offer a mix of educational experiences.

Clearly, the open university will become an increasingly important player in higher education at the global level. The interesting question is whether these institutions might also gain a foothold in the United States. After all, newly emerging institutions such as the Western Governors' University and the University of Phoenix are exploiting many of the concepts pioneered by the open university. In 1998, the British Open University launched a new venture known as the Open University of the United States. They have signed cooperative agreements with Florida State University, the California State University, and the Western Governor's University as they prepare to enter the North American marketplace.[15]

EMOs: Education Maintenance Organizations

One of the great themes of higher education in America has been access. Each evolutionary wave of higher education has aimed at educating a broader segment of society—the public universities, the land-grant universities, the normal and technical colleges, and the community colleges.[16] Today we find that higher education is more important than ever. But we need a new paradigm for delivering it to even broader segments of our society. Fortunately, today's technology is rapidly breaking the constraints of space and time. It has become clear that most people, in most areas, can learn and learn well using asynchronous learning technology. The barriers are no longer cost or technology but rather perception and habit. Lifetime education will soon become a reality, making learning available for anyone who wants to learn, at the time and place of choice, without great personal effort or cost. Perhaps this is an important part of the future for the American university in the digital age.

Returning again to our analogy between the restructuring of the health care industry in America and that faced by higher education, we might well see some similar organizations evolve. For example, in managed care paradigms, the health maintenance organization (HMO) contracts to provide the full range of health care needs for an individual. In return, it either provides health-care services from its own organization or outsources these from other health-care providers. In a similar sense, we might see the formation of educational maintenance organizations that agree to provide whatever learning opportunities individuals need throughout their lives. Some comprehensive universities might evolve into this role, essentially entering into lifetime agreements with their students, graduates, and alumni to meet their educational needs. However it is more likely that the EMO would be a broker of educational services, much like the virtual university, which would link learners with educational service providers whenever, wherever, and however they need new knowledge and skills.

Learning Networks

Driven by information technology, the network has become more than a web which links together learning resources. Dolence and Norris suggest it has become the architecture of advanced learning organizations.[17] Information, knowledge, and learning opportunities are now distributed across robust computer networks to hundreds of millions of people. The knowledge, the learning, the cultural resources that used to be the prerogative of a privileged few are rapidly becoming available anyplace, anytime, to anyone.

The impact on all social organizations has been profound. Business and industry are moving rapidly away from the hierarchy of the organizational pyramid to networked organizations of relatively autonomous components. The command-communication-control structure of General Motors and IBM has been replaced by the "chaordic" network[18] organization of Visa.

It is important for the academy to appreciate how profound this new network architecture is for learning organizations.[19] Today's learners can learn anywhere, anytime, acquiring learning and knowledge from sources in any location.[20] Today, learners are in command of what, how, where, and when they learn, and they will be increasingly in control of what they pay for the learning opportunity as well.

The implications of a networked learning architecture are manifold. First, it makes less and less sense for institutions to attempt to be comprehensive, to go it alone. Rather the key will be forming alliances, sharing resources, specializing in what they can be really good at, and relying on other focused institutions to provide the rest. The important lesson learned through painful experience in business and industry is that only world-class, competitively priced products will succeed in a global marketplace. This does not mean that the largest, most prestigious institutions, the Michigans and the Harvards, will necessarily be the most successful. Indeed, smaller, more focused, and more nimble institutions may be able to develop world-class learning services that could compete very effectively with traditional offerings.

Learning networks may also work to couple together different levels of education. For example, we are already seeing evidence that many high school students are entering college with degree credit in college-level courses taken over the Net. By the same token, many colleges must provide remedial education at the secondary school level. At the other end, adults are seeking further educational services from higher education to respond to changing career requirements. A network architecture works best for the delivery of educational services when and where they are needed—that is, for "just in time" rather than "just in case" education. Granted that this may not be the appropriate architecture for the general subjects associated with a liberal education. But it will in all likelihood increasingly dominate professional education and work-related learning.

One can imagine the learning networks evolving into a seamless continuum of educational opportunities and services, in which the degree becomes less and less relevant, and what a person has learned becomes far more significant. Learning communities will be more extended and diverse with a network architecture. Since they will evolve unconstrained by space and time, the number of off-campus learners will vastly outnumber on-campus students. Beyond that, the distinction between learner, teacher, and researcher may become blurred. All will be able to make contributions to learning, teaching, and scholarship.

The University as a Content Provider or Certifier of Knowledge

As we have noted, universities play many roles in the creation, preservation, transmission, and application of knowledge. As technology enables and the marketplace demands ever more sophisticated methods of producing, marketing, and delivery educational services, it is likely that the sector of American higher education associated with the research university may focus increasingly on its core competence in providing knowledge content. The research intensive nature of these institutions, the research character of their faculties, and their remarkable infrastructure of libraries, laboratories, and cultural resources position them well to provide the intellectual content needed by our society. Of course, this has long been an important role, as manifested both in the impact of these institutions on education through teaching materials and pedagogical models and in their research role in responding to the broader needs of our nation. But as the competition for educational services becomes more intense, with the possibility of a commodity marketplace, this content provider role may become more valuable.

The university may also play an increasingly important role in evaluating and certifying knowledge. Many fear that knowledge networks such as the Internet may be following the same path as other mass media—the radio and television—with the same fate of commercialization. There is a growing concern about both the amount and the validity of the information now deluging participants in these knowledge networks.

In the anarchy of the Internet (considered a good thing by some), there is currently no way to certify the accuracy of information. Traditional authorities such as the news media have become fringe elements of a global entertainment industry and have long since lost much of their credibility.[21] Perhaps it is time to create new organizations to play this role of certifying knowledge. This has been one role of the university throughout its history; other organizations such as the national academies of science and engineering, libraries, and museums have this credibility. Perhaps it is time to create a new type of institution on the information superhighway to act as an authenticator, to help others navigate through the chaff to find the wheat.

New Civic Lifeforms

Today, as knowledge becomes an ever more significant factor in determining both personal and societal well being, and as rapidly emerging information technology provides the capacity to build new types of communities, we might well see the appearance of new social structures.[22] A century ago, stimulated by the philanthropy of Andrew Carnegie, the public library became the focal point for community learning. Today, however, technology allows us to link together public and private resources such as schools, libraries, museums, hospitals, parks, media, and cultural resources. Further, communities can easily be linked with the knowledge resources of the world through the Internet.

There are some interesting trends in technology that suggest that new types of "community knowledge structures" may, in fact, appear, ones that will not be derivative of traditional institutions such as schools or libraries. The first trend involves the evolution of global computer networks such as the Internet. In addition to their ability to link people together into electronic communities, they link us as well to increasingly diverse and rich sources of knowledge. In a sense, they have become "knowledge networks," giving us the capacity to build communities with access to vast intellectual resources.

The second trend is our growing understanding of how learning and intelligent systems function. Modern computers are increasingly simulating natural cognitive processes, utilizing structures such as massively parallel computers, neural networks, and genetic algorithms. This convergence not only enables us to simulate and understand natural intelligence better, but it may also be the key to building artificial systems capable of learning and intelligent behavior.

The third trend is related to our developing understanding of the behavior of complex adaptive systems. We are learning that even the most primitive systems can frequently exhibit quite complex behavior. And many complex systems can exhibit self-organizing behavior, in which quite sophisticated and complex behavior evolves out of what appears first as chaotic, random processes.

These three themes—knowledge networks, learning and intelligent systems, and complex adaptive systems—may provide the key to understanding the evolution of a global structure, linking together billions of people, their knowledge resources, and their communities through robust communications technology.

Implications for the Twentieth Century University

The Public University

An important, perhaps even dominant, theme of American higher education in the twentieth century has been the evolution of the public university. With an expanding population, a prosperous economy, and compelling needs such as national security and industrial competitiveness, the public was willing to make massive investments in higher education. While elite private universities were important in setting the standards and character of higher education in America, it was the public university that provided the capacity and diversity to meet our nation's vast needs for postsecondary education.

Today, however, in the face of limited resources and more pressing social priorities, this expansion of public support of higher education has slowed. While the needs of our society for advanced education will only intensify as we evolve into a knowledge-driven world culture, it is not evident that these needs will be met by further expansion of our existing system of public universities. The terms of the social contract that led to these institutions are changing rapidly. The principle of general tax support for public higher education as a public good and the partnership between the federal government and the universities for the conduct of basic research are both at risk. These changes are being driven in part by increasingly limited tax resources and the declining priority given higher education in the face of other social needs.[23]

There is a paradox here. Both state governments and the public at large call on public universities to achieve greater access, quality, and cost savings. Yet they also encourage—indeed, expect—them to draw an increasing share of their resource base from non-state sources. Public universities are challenged to demonstrate that they are not solely dependent upon the state, that they can increase faculty productivity and lower costs, all the while improving educational quality. In a sense, higher education funding policy in many states has shifted from tax-support of the public university as a public good to a philosophy of procuring low-cost educational services.[24]

When I began my academic career at the University of Michigan some thirty years ago, over 60 percent of the financial support for the University's Ann Arbor campus came from state appropriations (with 10 percent from tuition, 10 percent from research grants, and 20 percent from hospital activities). In sharp contrast, today state appropriations contribute $300 million, only 10 percent of the University's roughly $3 billion operating budget. Tuition revenue and sponsored research grants and contracts each generate about $500 million or 15 percent, private support another $300 million or 10 percent, and auxiliary activities such as the hospitals about $1.3 billion or 45 percent.

We usually explained this by noting that over the past three decades the University of Michigan has evolved from a "state-supported" to a "state-assisted" to a "state-related" to a "state-located" university. In fact, with campuses in Europe and Asia, even "state-located" may no longer be accurate. Perhaps a better way to summarize this fact of life is to note that like several other leading public research universities, today the University of Michigan is a "privately supported but publicly committed" university. But a state-*supported* university we surely are not . . .

So how might one explain this evolution? Was it due to a bold plan, a "strategic intent"? To be sure, there was a conscious effort to take some actions to compensate for declining state support: We ramped up prices, namely tuition, as rapidly as the politics would allow. Although our instate tuition remains quite low ($6,000 per year), our tuition for nonresidents has risen to private levels (above $20,000 per year). We launched major private fund-raising efforts, culminating in a fund-raising campaign that raised $1.4 billion. Through both energetic fund-raising and aggressive management, we increased the university's endowment from next to nothing ($200 million) to over $2.0 billion. We adopted a far more businesslike approach to major university activities such as the UM Medical Center and (unfortunately) our entertainment company, the Michigan Wolverines, which now resembles a professional franchise.

But this was also an evolution both driven and, at least to some degree, demanded by the policies of our state government.[25] As the state moved toward more of a procurement relationship with its universities, seeking to focus its support on the undergraduate education of Michigan resident students and the delivery of specific services such as economic development, it became necessary to generate other revenue streams to cover the broader mission of the universities in areas such as research and graduate education. In fact, political leaders, both those in state government and those elected to governing boards, challenged public universities to generate income from nonstate sources and to become even less dependent on state appropriations.

This forced strategy was accommodated by the entrepreneurial character of the university, consisting as it was of thousands of highly enterprising faculty members. The university faculty adapted quite easily to the new world of limited state support, and rapidly extended its entrepreneurial skills into other areas such as private fund-raising and industrial spin-offs.

Here the University of Michigan was obviously not alone. Declining state support is driving many public research universities to become increasingly similar to their private counterparts in the development of an entrepreneurial faculty culture, in the manner in which priorities are set and assets are managed. Many of the nation's leading public universities are already far down the path taken by the University of Michigan as it has evolved into a privately financed public university. In such universities only a small fraction of operating or capital support comes from state appropriation. Like private universities, these hybrid institutions depend on tuition, federal grants and contracts, private gifts, and revenue from auxiliary services such as health care for most of their support.

There is already more than a decade of evidence that the states are simply not able—or willing—to provide the resources to sustain growth in public higher education, at least at the rate experienced in the decades following World War II. In many parts of the nation, states will be hard pressed to even sustain the present capacity and quality of their institutions. Little wonder that public university leaders are increasingly reluctant to cede control of their activities to state governments. Some institutions are even bargaining for more autonomy from state control as an alternative to growth in state support, arguing that if they are granted more control over their own destiny, they can better protect their capacity to serve the public.

Today, one might even conclude that America's great experiment of building world-class public universities supported primarily by tax dollars has come to an end. It could well be that the concept of a world-class, comprehensive state university might not be viable over the longer term. It may not be possible to justify the level of public support necessary to sustain the quality of these institutions in the face of other public priorities, such as health care, K–12 education, and public infrastructure needs—particularly during a time of slowly rising or stagnant economic activity.[26]

One obvious consequence of declining state support is that the leading public universities may increasingly resemble private universities in the way they are financed. Many will follow the path toward becoming increasingly privately financed, even as they strive to retain their public character. In such universities only a small fraction of operating or capital support will come from state appropriation. Like private universities, these hybrid institutions will depend primarily upon revenue they generate directly from their activities–tuition, federal grants and contracts, private gifts, and revenue from auxiliary services such as health care—rather than upon direct appropriations.

State universities forced to undergo this "privatization" transition in financing must appeal to a broad array of constituencies at the national—indeed, international—level, while continuing to exhibit a strong mission focused on state needs. In the same way as private universities, they must earn the majority of their support in the competitive marketplace, that is, via tuition, research grants, and gifts, and this will sometimes require actions that come into conflict from time to time with state priorities. Hence the autonomy of the public university will become one of its most critical assets, perhaps even more critical than state support for some institutions.

This is a particularly important challenge to the privately supported, publicly committed paradigm that now appears to be evolving in public higher education. It has become increasingly clear that few states are able or willing to commit the resources to build and sustain world-class research universities. To sustain the quality of their programs, these remarkable public institutions, built during earlier times when state support was more abundant, must now earn support from a far broader set of constituencies than the state alone. Yet the capacity to position state universities to attract these resources occasionally require actions that come into conflict with state priorities, for example, by admitting more out-of-state students.

How might we embark on this path to serve far broader public constituencies without alienating the people of our state—or risking our present (albeit low) level of state support? One constructive approach would be to attempt to persuade the public—and, particularly, the media—that our universities are vital to the state in a far more multidimensional way than simply education alone—through health care, economic development, pride (intercollegiate athletics), professionals (doctors, lawyers, engineers, and teachers), and so forth. We might shift the public perception of our universities from that of a consumer to that as a producer of state resources. We might argue that, for a relatively modest contribution toward our educational costs, the people of our states get access to the vast resources and benefit from the profound impact of some of the world's great universities.

The public university has always responded quite effectively to the perceived needs—and opportunities—of American society. Today these institutions are straining to balance public needs for greater access, high quality, and cost-effectiveness in a period of limited resources and political turmoil. The incompatibility of the demands placed upon the public university during a time of constrained resources could well erode the quality, the public character, and the civic purpose of these important institutions. It seems clear that we need a new dialogue concerning the future of public higher education in America, one that balances both its democratic purpose with economic imperatives.

The Research University

As a primary source of basic research and the next generation of scholars and professionals, the research university will remain an asset of great value. At a time when both industry and government are shifting more toward applied research and development, the research university has become ever more important as an intellectual force in our society. Today the research faculties in these institutions have become both the leaders and the arbiters of science and scholarship for the world. This group not only leads in knowledge production and distribution, but they have become the gatekeepers and standard-bearers, leading a complex knowledge system that both drives and sustains world education and learning. Furthermore, as highly educated scholars and professionals are increasingly sought as leaders in a knowledge-driven world, these institutions should continue to play a critical role.

Yet the broader higher education enterprise is changing rapidly, driven by market forces and social policies, to serve a changing world. While the unique roles, the prestige, and the prosperity of the research university may allow it to defend the status quo for a time, this, too, will pose certain dangers. Furthermore, the research university is no longer seen as the top level of academic pecking order but instead as just one player in a broader higher education enterprise, where the priority will be educational services for a knowledge-driven society rather than specialized scholarship. To be sure, it would be both unrealistic and inappropriate for our research universities to abandon their critical roles in elite education and scholarship to become heavily involved in the universal education, the ubiquitous education, needed by our society. Furthermore, the market for educational services will be broad and diverse, and the brand name for exceptional quality characterizing these institutions will still carry considerable value.

Throughout most of history of higher education in America, these same institutions have been the leaders for the broader enterprise. They have provided the faculty, the pedagogy, the textbooks and scholarly materials, and the standards for all of higher education. They have maintained a strong relationship and relevance to the rest of the enterprise, even though they were set apart in role and mission. Yet, as the rest of the enterprise changes, there is a risk that if the research university becomes too reactionary and tenacious in its defense of the status quo, it could well find itself increasingly withdrawn and perhaps even irrelevant to the rest of higher education in America and throughout the world.

There are already some early signs of this decoupling. Many colleges and universities no longer look to the graduates of the elite research universities for their faculty, since they seek candidates with broader educational backgrounds who are committed to teaching, rather than the narrowly focused scholars produced by our leading graduate schools. A quick survey of the textbooks used in higher education also suggests that the dominance of the elite institutions has come to an end. And many of the most exciting experiments in pedagogy are happening in small colleges and regional public universities, where there is more incentive to take risks when change is inevitable.

Of particular concern here is the fate of the public research university. As we have noted, public policy at the state level appears to be shifting to a procurement mentality, where issues of productivity, accountability, and cost-effectiveness in the delivery of educational services are increasingly dominating other priorities such as the quest for a world-class research university. There is likely to be greater differentiation among public research universities, with a number being downgraded to a status more like that of the comprehensive university, engaged in undergraduate education, graduate education at the M.S. level, but few doctorate programs or major sponsored research activities. If this scenario continues, those major public universities that are able to sustain their research and doctorate activities are likely to be concentrated in those states with high populations and economic strength. They are also likely to be public universities with sufficient reputation and determination to make the transition to "privately supported but publicly committed" status.

It is within this context of recognizing the unique mission and value of the research university even as we seek to preserve its relevance to the rest of higher education that we should examine several possibilities:

Isolation. Some of the most elite institutions may adopt a strategy of relying on their prestige and their prosperity to isolate themselves from change, to continue to do just what they have done in the past, and to be comfortable with their roles as niche players in the higher education enterprise. And this may be a very appropriate strategy for some unique institutions, places such as MIT, Caltech, Princeton, and Chicago. But for most of the larger and comprehensive institutions, the activities of elite education and basic research are simply too expensive to sustain without some attention to the marketplace.

Pathfinders. Perhaps a more constructive approach would be to apply the extraordinary intellectual resources of the research university to assist the broader higher education enterprise in its evolution to new learning forms. Although the research universities may not be appropriate for direct involvement in mass or universal education, they certainly are capable of providing the templates, the paradigms, that others could use. They have done this before in other areas such as health care, national defense, and the Internet. To play this role, the research university must be prepared to participate in experiments in creating possible futures for higher education.

Alliances. Extending this role somewhat, research universities might enter into alliances with other types of educational institutions, regional universities, liberal arts colleges, community colleges, or even newly emerging forms such as for-profit or cyberspace universities. This would allow them to respond to the changing needs of societies while remaining focused on their unique missions as research universities. One could also imagine forming alliances with organizations outside of higher education, for example, information technology, telecommunications, or entertainment companies, information services providers, or even government agencies.

Core-in-Cloud Models. Many research universities are already evolving into so-called "core in cloud" organizations,[27] in which academic departments or schools conducting elite education and basic research are surrounded by a constellation of quasi-university organizations—research institutes, think tanks, corporate R&D centers—that draw intellectual strength from the core university and provide important financial, human, and physical resources in return. Such a structure reflects the blurring of basic and applied research, education and training, the university and broader society.

More specifically, while the academic units at the core retain the traditional university culture of faculty appointments, such as tenure and intellectual traditions, such as disciplinary focus, those quasi-academic organizations evolving in the cloud can be far more flexible and adaptive. They can be multidisciplinary and project focused. They can be driven by entrepreneurial cultures and values. Unlike academic programs, they can come and go as the need and opportunity arise. And, although it is common to think of the cloud being situated quite close to the university core, in today's world of emerging electronic and virtual communities, there is no reason why the cloud might not be widely distributed, involving organizations located far from the campus. In fact, as virtual universities become more common, there is no reason that the core itself has to have a geographical focus.

To some degree, the core-in-cloud model could revitalize core academic programs by stimulating new ideas and interactions. It could provide a bridge that would allow the university to better serve society without compromising its core academic values. But, like the entrepreneurial university, it could also scatter and diffuse the activities of the university, creating a shopping-mall character with little coherence.

Conclusion

While some may continue to debate, to suggest that the status quo will remain intact, to others the choice has become clear. We can either accept the risks and the uncertainties of attempting to transform the higher education enterprise to serve a society with new needs and new imperatives, or we can wait for the market to reshape our institutions, perhaps even relegating them to a backwater role in the emerging global knowledge industry. Clearly, embracing the status quo, treading water, also has very real risks. After all, there are many commercial sharks swimming just below the surface.

Here it is important to stress once again that while America's colleges and universities may indeed evolve as a component of a global knowledge and learning industry, it would be both misleading and dangerous to view higher education simply as an industrial model. There are broader civic purposes to the university such as transmitting our cultural heritage and undergirding our democracy, essential to recognize and preserve, and yet highly vulnerable to market forces. Furthermore, most will acknowledge that the conventional university campus provides a unique and extraordinarily rich environment for learning and scholarship. But if market forces alone are allowed to determine the future of higher education, we could well find ourselves facing a future in which only the rich and privileged would have the opportunity for campus-based learning, while the majority of our population would be relegated to media-based, standardized educational experiences.

The learners of our future society will demand that their educational experiences prepare them for a lifetime of learning opportunities, fused both with work and with life. They will seek just-in-time and just-for-you learning through networked organizations. They will seek the integration of timeless and timely knowledge.

The system of higher education that emerges in the century ahead will almost certainly be far different from today's. Higher education will either transform itself or be transformed as financial imperatives, changing societal demands, emerging technologies, and new competitors reshape the knowledge enterprise, changing in the process how colleges and universities organize and deliver learning opportunities as well as how they structure and manage their institutions.

For most of our history, the growth of higher education in America has been sustained by tax dollars, either direct through state or federal appropriation, or indirectly through favorable tax policy. As a result, higher education has been strongly shaped by public policies and public agendas, from Jefferson's writings to the land-grant acts, from the GI Bill to Pell Grants, from the government-university research partnership to the Equal Opportunity Act. Public investment has both determined and protected the public purpose of higher education in America.

Today, however, there is an increasing sense that the growth of higher education in the twenty-first century will be fueled by private dollars. Public policy will be replaced increasingly by market pressures. Hence the key question: Will a privately funded, market-driven "global knowledge and learning industry" be able to preserve the important traditions, values, and broader purposes of the university? Or will a renewed public investment and an enlightened public interest be necessary to protect the important civic purposes of higher education in America?

Evolution or
Revolution

It was the best of times, it was the worst of times,
It was the age of wisdom, it was the age of foolishness,
It was the epoch of belief, it was the epoch of incredulity,
It was the season of Light, it was the season of Darkness,
It was the spring of hope, it was the winter of despair.
—Charles Dickens, *A Tale of Two Cities* [1]

The familiar opening lines from Charles Dickens' novel characterizing eighteenth century France also portray the situation of universities in America today. Revolution is in the air!

In many ways these do indeed seem like both the best of times and the worst of times for higher education. Universities are increasingly seen as key sources to the new knowledge and educated citizens so necessary for a knowledge-driven society. After two decades of eroding public support at the state and federal level, there is an increasing call for reinvestment in higher education.

Yet there is great unease on our campuses. Throughout society we see erosion in support of important university commitments such as academic freedom, tenure, broad access, and racial diversity. Even the concept of higher education as a public good is being challenged, as society increasingly sees a college education as an individual benefit determined by values of the marketplace rather than the broader needs of a democratic society. The faculty feels increasing stress, fearing an erosion in public support as unconstrained entitlements grow, sensing a loss of scholarly community with increasing disciplinary specialization, and being pulled out of the classroom and the laboratory by the demands of grantsmanship.

To continue with Dickensian themes, while we may be entering an age of wisdom—or at least knowledge—it is also an age of foolishness. In 1997 the noted futurist Peter Drucker shook up the academy when, during an interview in *Forbes*, he speculated: "Thirty years from now the big university campuses will be relics. Universities won't survive. It's as large a change as when we first got the printed book."[2] One can imagine the network of interactions that ricocheted across university campuses in the months following Drucker's conjecture. It was fascinating to track the conversations among the University of Michigan deans on electronic mail. Some, of course, responded by blasting Drucker, always a dangerous thing to do. Others were simply moot. A few even surmised that perhaps a former president of the University of Michigan might agree with Drucker. (He doesn't, incidentally.)

So what are we facing? A season of light or a season of darkness? A spring of hope or a winter of despair? More to the point, and again in a Dickensian spirit, is higher education facing yet another period of evolution? Or will the dramatic nature and compressed time scales characterizing the changes of our time trigger a process more akin to revolution?

To be sure, most colleges and universities are responding to the challenges and opportunities presented by a changing world. They are evolving to serve a new age. But most are evolving within the traditional paradigms, according to the time-honored processes of considered reflection and consensus that have long characterized the academy. Is such glacial change responsive enough to allow the university to control its own destiny? Or will the tidal wave of societal forces sweep over the academy, both transforming the university in unforeseen and unacceptable ways while creating new institutional forms to challenge both our experience and our concept of the university?

We have come to a fork in the road that might best be illustrated by imaging two sharply contrasting futures for higher education in America. The first is a rather dark future in which strong market forces drive a major restructuring of the higher education enterprise. Although traditional colleges and universities play a role in this future, they are both threatened and reshaped by shifting societal needs, rapidly evolving technology, and aggressive for-profit entities and commercial forces. Together these drive the higher education enterprise toward the mediocrity that has characterized other mass media markets such as television and journalism.

A contrasting and far brighter future is provided by a culture of learning, in which universal or ubiquitous educational opportunities are provided to meet the broad and growing learning needs of our society. Using a mix of old and new forms, learners are offered a rich array of high-quality and affordable learning opportunities. Our traditional institutional forms, including both the liberal arts college and the research university, continue to play key roles, albeit with some necessary evolution and adaptation.

Although market forces are far more powerful than most realize, we also believe that it is possible to determine which of these or other paths is taken by higher education in America. Key in this effort is our ability as a society to view higher education as, in part, a public good that merits support through public tax dollars. In this way, we may be able to protect the public purpose of the higher education enterprise and sustain its quality, important traditions, and essential values.

Yet, if we are to do this, we must also recognize the profound nature of the rapidly changing world faced by higher education. The status quo is no longer an option. We must accept that change is inevitable and use it as a strategic opportunity to control our destiny, while preserving the most important of our values and our traditions.

The Forces Driving Change

Throughout this book, we have discussed the various forces driving change in our society and the institutions that serve it. It is useful to summarize those forces of change of most direct concern to higher education once again as part of a closing argument about their implications for the future of the university. They can be grouped into four areas: 1) financial imperatives, 2) changing social needs, 3) technology drivers, and 4) market forces.

Financial Imperatives

Since the late 1970s, higher education in America has been caught in a financial vise.[3] On the one hand, the magnitude of the services demanded of our colleges and universities has increased considerably. Enrollments have increased steadily; the growing educational needs of adult learners have compensated for the temporary dip in the number of high school graduates associated with the postwar baby boom/bust cycle. University research, graduate education, and professional education have all grown in response to societal demand. Professional services provided by colleges and universities also continue to increase in areas such as health care, technology transfer, and extension—all in response to growing needs.

The costs of providing education, research, and service per unit of activity have increased at an even faster rate, since these university activities are dependent upon a highly skilled, professional workforce (faculty and staff); they require expensive new facilities and equipment; and they are driven by an ever-expanding knowledge base. Higher education has yet to take the bold steps to constrain cost increases that have been required in other sectors of our society such as business and industry. This is in part because of the way our colleges and universities are organized, managed, and governed. But, even if our universities should acquire both the capacity and the determination to restructure costs more radically, it is debatable whether those actions adopted from the experience of the business community in containing cost and enhancing productivity could have the same impact in education. The current paradigm of higher education is simply too people- and knowledge-intensive.

As the demand for educational services has grown and the operating costs to provide these services have risen, public support for higher education has flattened and then declined over the past two decades.[4] The growth in state support of public higher education peaked in the 1980s and now has fallen in many states in the face of limited tax resources and the competition of other priorities such as entitlement pro-grams and corrections. While the federal government has sustained its support of research, growth has been modest in recent years and could well decline as discre-tionary domestic spending comes under increasing pressure from growing entitle-ment commitments. There has been significant downsizing in federal financial aid programs over the past two decades, with a corresponding shift from grants to loans as the predominant form of aid. While the federal budget-balancing agreement of 1997 and the Higher Education Act of 1998 provided relief to middle-class parents, they are unlikely to bring major new resources to colleges and universities.

To meet growing societal demand for higher education at a time when costs are increasing and public support is declining, most institutions have been forced to increase tuition and fees sharply—substantially faster than the Consumer Price In-dex. While this has provided short-term relief, it has also triggered a strong public concern about the costs and availability of a college education, along with accelerat-ing forces to constrain or reduce tuition levels at both public and private universi-ties.[5] As a result, most colleges and universities are now looking for ways to control costs and increase productivity, but most are also finding that their current organiza-tion and governance makes this very difficult.

The higher education enterprise in America must change dramatically if it is to restore a balance between the costs and availability of educational services needed by our society and the resources available to support these services. Put another way, *The current paradigms for conducting, distributing, and financing higher education may not be able to adapt to the demands and realities of our times.*

Societal Needs

The needs of our society for the services provided by our colleges and universities will continue to grow. Significant expansion will be necessary just to respond to the needs of a growing population that will create a 30 percent growth in the number of college-age students over the next two decades. But these traditional students are only part of the picture; we must recognize the impact of the changing nature of the educational services sought by our society.

Today's undergraduate student body is no longer dominated by eighteen- to twenty-two-year-old high school graduates from affluent backgrounds. It is com-prised also of increasing numbers of adults from diverse socioeconomic backgrounds, already in the workplace, perhaps with families, seeking the education and skills necessary for their careers. When it is recognized that this demand for higher educa-tion may be significantly larger than that for traditional undergraduate education, it seems clear that either existing institutions will have to change significantly or new types of institutions will have to be formed. The transition from student to learner, from faculty-centered to learner-centered institutions, from teaching to the design and management of active learning experiences, and from student to a lifelong member of a learning community—all suggest great changes are ahead for our institutions.

We already see the early stages of a major transformation in the educational activities of the university, driven in part by the changing character of our students. Today's college students require a different form of education in which interactive and collaborative learning will increasingly replace the passive lecture and classroom experience. The student has become a more demanding consumer of educational services, although frequently this is directed at obtaining the skills needed for more immediate career goals. We are beginning to see a shift in demand from the current style of "just in case" education in which we expect students to complete degree programs at the undergraduate or professional level long before they actually need the knowledge, to "just in time" education in which education is sought when a person needs it through non-degree programs, to "just for you" education in which educational programs are carefully tailored to meet the specific lifelong learning requirements of particular students. So too the shift from synchronous, classroom-based instruction to asynchronous computer network–based learning, to the provision of ubiquitous/pervasive learning opportunities throughout our society will demand major change.

The needs for other higher education services are also changing dramatically. The relationship between the federal government and the research university is shifting from a partnership in which the government is primarily a patron of discovery-oriented research to a process of procurement of research aimed at addressing specific national priorities. The academic health center has come under great financial pressure as it has been forced to deal with a highly competitive health-care marketplace and the entry of new paradigms such as managed care. While the public appetite for the entertainment provided by intercollegiate athletics continues to grow, our colleges also feel increasing pressures to align these activities better with academic priorities and national imperatives (such as the Title IX requirements for gender equity).

Even as the nature of traditional activities in education, research, and service changes, society is seeking new services from higher education, for example, revitalizing K–12 education, securing economic competitiveness, providing models for multicultural societies, rebuilding our cities and national infrastructure. All of this is occurring at a time when public criticism of higher education is high, and trust and confidence in the university is relatively low.

The inability of our existing institutions to meet the growing need for higher education is magnified many times throughout the world. Today over half of the world's population is under twenty years of age, most seeking education as the key to their future quality of life. To meet this staggering demand, a major new university would need to be created every week. Yet in most of the world, higher education is mired in a crisis of access, cost, and flexibility. Unless we can address and solve this crisis, billions of people in coming generations will be denied the education so necessary to compete in—indeed, to survive in—an age of knowledge.

Sir John Daniels, chancellor of the British Open University, observes that although the United States has the world's strongest university system this seems ill suited to guiding us out of this global education crisis. Our colleges and universities continue to be focused on high-cost, residential education and on the outmoded idea that quality in education is linked to exclusivity of access and extravagance of resources. In fact, the American concept of the campus university would deny higher education to nearly all of the billions of young people who will require it in the decades ahead. *Again there are many signs that the current university paradigms are no longer adequate for meeting growing and changing societal needs.*

Technology Drivers

As knowledge-driven organizations, colleges and universities are greatly affected by the rapid advances in information technology—computers, telecommunications, networks. This technology has already had dramatic impact on campus research activities, enabling the computer simulation of complex phenomena, linking scholars together in networked communities such as collaboratories, and providing them access to the vast resources of digital libraries and knowledge networks. Many of our administrative processes have become heavily dependent upon information technology—as the concern with the date reset of Year 2000 made all too apparent. But this new technology will have an even more profound impact on the educational activities of the university and how we deliver our services. To be sure, there have been earlier technology changes such as television, but never before has there been such a rapid and sustained period of technological change with such broad social applications.

Most significant here is the way in which emerging information technology has obliterated the constraints of space and time. We can now use powerful computers and networks to deliver educational services to anyone at anyplace and anytime, confined no longer to the campus or the academic schedule. The market for university services is expanding rapidly, but so is competition, as new organizations such as virtual universities and "learning ware" providers enter this marketplace to compete with traditional institutions. *Again, we must face the possibility that the current paradigm of the university may not be capable of responding to the opportunities or the challenges of the new knowledge media or the needs of the digital generation.*

Market Forces

We generally think of public higher education as public enterprise, shaped by public policy and actions to serve a civic purpose. Yet market forces also act on our public colleges and universities. Society seeks services such as education and research. Academic institutions must compete for students, faculty, and resources. To be sure, the market is a strange one, heavily subsidized and shaped by public investment so that prices are always far less than true costs. Furthermore, if prices such as tuition are largely fictitious, even more so is much of the value of education services, based on myths and vague perceptions such as the importance of a college degree as a ticket to success or the prestige associated with certain institutions. Ironically, the public expects not only the range of choice that a market provides but also the subsidies that make the price of a public higher education less than the cost of its provision.

In the past, most colleges and universities served local or regional populations. While there was competition among institutions for students, faculty, and resources—at least in the United States—the extent to which institutions controlled the awarding of degrees, that is, credentialing, led to a tightly controlled competitive market. Universities enjoyed a monopoly over advanced education because of geographical location and their monopoly on the accreditation of academic programs necessary for awarding degrees. However, today all of these market constraints are being challenged. The growth in the size and complexity of the postsecondary enterprise is creating an expanding array of students and educational providers. Information technology eliminates the barriers of space and time as new competitive forces enter the marketplace to challenge credentialing.

The weakening influence of traditional regulations and the emergence of new competitive forces, driven by changing societal needs, economic realities, and technology, are likely to drive a massive restructuring of the higher education enterprise. From the experience with other restructured sectors of our economy such as health care, transportation, communications, and energy, we could expect to see a significant reorganization of higher education, complete with the mergers, acquisitions, new competitors, and new products and services that have characterized other economic transformations. More generally, we may well be seeing the early stages of the appearance of a global knowledge and learning industry, in which the activities of traditional academic institutions converge with other organizations such as telecommunications, entertainment, and information service companies.

This perspective of a market-driven restructuring of higher education as an industry, while perhaps both alien and distasteful to the academy, is nevertheless a useful framework for considering the future of the university. While the postsecondary education market may have complex cross-subsidies and numerous public misconceptions, it is nevertheless very real and demanding, with the capacity to reward those who can respond to demand and punish those who cannot. Universities will have to learn to cope with the competitive pressures of this marketplace while preserving the most important of their traditional values and character. Again we conclude, *The current faculty-centered, monopoly-sustained university paradigm is ill suited to the intensely competitive market of a global knowledge and learning industry.*

Evolution or Revolution?

In spite of the growing awareness of these social forces, many within the academy still believe that change will occur only at the margins of higher education. They see the waves of change lapping on the beach as just the tide coming in, as it has so often before. They stress the role of the university in stabilizing society during a period of change rather than leading those changes. This too shall pass, they suggest, and demand that the university hold fast to its traditional roles and character. And they will do everything within their power to prevent change from occurring.

Yet, history suggests that the university must change and adapt in part to preserve its ancient values and traditional roles. This reality is accepted by many, both within and outside the academy, who realize that significant change must occur not simply in the higher education enterprise but in each and every one of our institutions. Yet, even most of these people see change as an evolutionary, incremental, long-term process, compatible with the values, cultures, and structure of the contemporary university.

There are a few voices, however, primarily outside the academy, who believe that both the dramatic nature and compressed time scales characterizing the changes of our times will drive not evolution but revolution. They have serious doubts about whether the challenges of our times will allow such gradual change and adaptation. They point out that there are really no precedents to follow. Some even suggest that long before reform of the educational system comes to any conclusion, the system itself will collapse.[6]

The forces driving change in higher education, both from within and without, may be far more powerful than most people realize. It could well be that both the pace and nature of change characterizing the higher education enterprise both in America and worldwide will be considerably beyond that which can be accommodated by business-as-usual evolution. As one of my colleagues put it, while there is certainly a good deal of exaggeration and hype about the changes in higher education for the short term—meaning five years or less—it is difficult to overstress the profound nature of the changes likely to occur in most of our institutions and in our enterprise over the longer term—a decade and beyond.

While some colleges and universities may be able to maintain their current form and market niche, others will change beyond recognition. Still others will disappear entirely. New types of institutions—perhaps even entirely new social learning structures—will evolve to meet educational needs. In contrast to the last several decades, when colleges and universities have attempted to become more similar, the years ahead will demand greater differentiation. There will be many different paths to the future.

Brave, New World

The market forces unleashed by technology and driven by increasing demand for higher education are very powerful. If they are allowed to dominate and reshape the higher education enterprise, we could well find ourselves facing a brave, new world in which some of the most important values and traditions of the university fall by the wayside. While the commercial, convenience-store model of the University of Phoenix may be a very effective way to meet the workplace skill needs of some adults, it certainly is not a paradigm that would be suitable for many of the higher purposes of the university. As we assess these market-driven emerging learning structures, we must bear in mind the importance of preserving the ability of the university to serve a broader public purpose.

The experience with restructuring in other industries has not been altogether encouraging. While the dissolution of the AT&T monopolies has indeed stimulated competition in telecommunications, it also resulted in the weakening of one of this nation's greatest intellectual assets, the Bell Laboratories. Furthermore, anyone who has suffered through the cattle-car experience of hub-spoke air travel can question whether the deregulation of commercial aviation has been worth it. And although the rate of increase in the cost of health care has been slowed very significantly by the competition unleashed in a restructured marketplace, there are increasing concerns about the quality and convenience of health-care delivery in our intensely competitive—and many would maintain chaotic—deregulated health-care marketplace.

There is an important lesson here. Without a broader recognition of the growing learning needs of our society, an exploration of more radical learning paradigms, and an overarching national strategy that acknowledges the public purpose of higher education and the important values of the academy, higher education will be driven down roads that would indeed lead to a winter of despair. Many of the pressures on our public universities are similar to those that have contributed so heavily to the current plight of K–12 education. Education has been viewed as an industry, demanding higher productivity according to poorly designed performance measures. The political forces associated with mass education have intruded on school management in general and governing boards in particular. The faculty has no recourse but to circle the wagons, to accept a labor-management relationship, and to cease to regard their vocation as a calling rather than a job.

Furthermore, our experience with market-driven, media-based enterprises has not been positive. The broadcasting and publication industries suggest that commercial concerns can lead to mediocrity, an intellectual wasteland in which the lowest common denominator of quality dominates. For example, although the campus will not disappear, the escalating costs of residential education could price this form of education beyond the range of all but the affluent, relegating much if not most of the population to low-cost (and perhaps low-quality) education via shopping-mall learning centers or computer-mediated distance learning. In this dark future, the college campus could well become the gated community of the higher education enterprise, available only to the rich and privileged.

A Society of Learning

But there is also a spring of hope, stimulated by the recognition of the role that knowledge and learning will play in our future. Whether one refers to our times as the information age or the age of knowledge, it is clear that educated people and the knowledge they produce and utilize have become the keys to the economic prosperity and well-being of our society. One's education, knowledge, and skills have become primary determinants of one's personal standard of living, the quality of one's life. We are realizing that, just as our society has historically accepted the responsibility for providing needed services such as military security, health care, and transportation infrastructure in the past, today education has become a driving social need and societal responsibility. Today it has become the responsibility of democratic societies to provide their citizens with the education and training they need, throughout their lives, whenever, wherever, and however they desire it, at high quality and at an affordable cost.

Of course, this has been one of the great themes of higher education in America. Each evolutionary wave of higher education has aimed at educating a broader segment of society, at creating new educational forms to do that—the public universities, the land-grant universities, the normal and technical colleges, the community colleges. But today, we must do even more.

The dominant form of higher education in America today, the research university, was shaped by a social contract during the last fifty years in which national security was regarded as America's most compelling priority, as reflected in massive investments in campus-based research and technology. Today, in the wake of the Cold War and at the dawn of the age of knowledge, one could well make the argument that education itself will replace national defense as the priority for the twenty-first century. Indeed, one might suggest that this will be the new social contract that will determine the character of our educational institutions, just as the government-university research partnership did in the latter half of the twentieth century. We might even conjecture that a social contract based on developing and maintaining the abilities and talents of our people to their fullest extent could well transform our schools, colleges, and universities into new forms that would rival the research university in importance.

So what might we expect over the longer term for the future of the university? It would be impractical and foolhardy to suggest one particular model for the university of the twenty-first century. The great and ever-increasing diversity characterizing higher education in America makes it clear that there will be many forms, many types of institutions serving our society. But there are a number of themes that will almost certainly factor into at least some part of the higher education enterprise.

- *Learner-centered:* Just as other social institutions, our universities must become more focused on those we serve. We must transform ourselves from faculty-centered to learner-centered institutions.
- *Affordable:* Society will demand that we become far more affordable, providing educational opportunities within the resources of all citizens. Whether this occurs through greater public subsidy or dramatic restructuring of our institutions, it seems increasingly clear that our society—not to mention the world—will no longer tolerate the high-cost, low-productivity paradigm that characterizes much of higher education in America today.
- *Lifelong Learning:* In an age of knowledge, the need for advanced education and skills will require both a willingness to continue to learn throughout life and a commitment on the part of our institutions to provide opportunities for lifelong learning. The concept of student and alumnus will merge. Our highly partitioned system of education will blend increasingly into a seamless web, in which primary and secondary education; undergraduate, graduate, and professional education; on-the-job training and continuing education; and lifelong enrichment become a continuum.
- *Interactive and Collaborative:* Already we see new forms of pedagogy: asynchronous (anytime, anyplace) learning that utilizes emerging information technology to break the constraints of time and space, making learning opportunities more compatible with lifestyles and career needs; and interactive and collaborative learning appropriate for the digital age, the plug-and-play generation.
- *Diverse:* Finally, the great diversity characterizing higher education in America will continue, as it must to serve an increasingly diverse population with diverse needs and goals.

- *Intelligent and adaptive:* Knowledge and distributed intelligence technology will increasingly allow us to build learning environments that are not only highly customized but adapt to the changing needs of the learner.

Perhaps access to advanced educational opportunities will be the defining domestic policy issue for a knowledge-driven society. If so, however, we will need to develop new paradigms for delivering education to even broader segments of our society, perhaps to all of our society, in convenient, high-quality forms, at a cost all can afford. Fortunately, today's technology is rapidly breaking the constraints of space and time. It has become clear that most people, in most areas, can learn and learn well using asynchronous learning, that is, "anytime, anyplace, anyone" education. Lifetime education is rapidly becoming a reality, making learning available for anyone who wants to learn, at the time and place of their choice, without great personal effort or cost. With advances in modern information technology, the barriers in the educational system are no longer cost or technological capacity but rather perception and habit.

But even this may not be enough. Perhaps we should instead consider a future of "ubiquitous learning"—learning for everyone, every place, all the time. Indeed, in a world driven by an ever-expanding knowledge base, continuous learning, like continuous improvement, has become a necessity of life.

Rather than an "age of knowledge," we could instead aspire to a "society of learning," in which people are continually surrounded by, immersed in, and absorbed in learning experiences. Information technology has now provided us with a means to create learning environments throughout one's life. These environments are able not only to transcend the constraints of space and time, but they, like us, are capable as well of learning and evolving to serve our changing educational needs. Higher education must define its relationship with these emerging possibilities in order to create a compelling vision for its future as it enters the next millennium.

The Questions before Us

Yet many questions remain unanswered. Who will be the learners served by these institutions? Who will teach them? Who will administer and govern these institutions? Who will pay for them? What will be the character of our universities? How will they function? When will they appear?

Perhaps the most profound question of all concerns the survival of the university in the face of the changes brought on by the emergence of new competitors. That is the question raised by Drucker and other futurists. Could an institution such as the university, which has existed for a millennium, disappear in the face of such changes?

As William Wulf suggests, if you have doubts, check on the state of the family farm, a social institution existing for centuries that has largely disappeared over the past three decades in our country.[7]

Most of us, of course, believe quite strongly that the university as a social institution is simply too valuable to disappear. On the other hand, there may well be forms of the university that we would have great difficulty in recognizing from our present perspective.

Rather than debating the survival of the university, it seems more constructive to suggest a somewhat different set of questions in an effort to frame the key policy issues facing higher education:

1. How do we respond to the diverse educational needs of a knowledge driven society? Here we must realize that while the educational needs of the young will continue to be a priority, we will be challenged to also address the sophisticated learning needs of adults in the workplace while providing broader lifetime learning opportunities for all of our society.

2. Is higher education a public or a private good? To be sure, the benefits of the university clearly flow to society as a whole. But it is also the case that two decades of public policy have stressed instead the benefits of education to the individual student. The issues of access and diversity have largely disappeared from the broader debate about the purpose of the university.

3. How do we balance the roles of market forces and public purpose in determining the future of higher education in America? Can we control market forces through public policy and public investment so that the most valuable traditions and values of the university are preserved? Or will the competitive and commercial pressures of the marketplace sweep over our institutions, leaving behind a higher education enterprise characterized by mediocrity?

4. What should be the role of the research university within the broader context of the changes likely to occur in the higher education enterprise? Should it be a leader in change? Or should it simply strive to protect the important traditions and values of the academy during this time of change?

These are some of the issues that should frame the debate about the future of higher education in America. As social institutions, universities reflect the values, needs, and character of the society they serve. These issues of access and opportunity, equality and justice, private economic benefits and public purpose, freedom and accountability, all are part of a broader public debate about the future of our nation.

They provide the context for any consideration of the future of the university in America.

An Action Agenda

So where to next? How do we grapple with the many issues and concerns swirling about higher education? Let me suggest the following action agenda for consideration and debate, both for individual institutions and for the broader higher education enterprise:

1. **Determine those key roles and values** that must be protected and preserved during this period of transformation, for example:
   Roles: education of the young, preservation of culture, basic research and scholarship, and criticism of society.
   Values: academic freedom, a rational spirit of inquiry, a community of scholars, a commitment to excellence, and shared governance.

2. **Listen carefully to society** to learn and understand its changing needs, expectations, and perceptions of higher education, along with the forces driving change.

3. **Prepare the academy for change and competition**, e.g., by removing unnecessary constraints, linking accountability with privilege, and redefining tenure as the protection of academic freedom rather than lifetime employment security. Begin the task of transforming the academy by radically restructuring graduate education.

4. **Restructure university governance**—particularly lay boards and shared governance models—so that it responds to the changing needs of society rather than defending and perpetuating an obsolete past. Develop a tolerance for strong leadership. Shift from lay boards to corporate board models where members are selected based on expertise and commitment and held accountable for their performance and the welfare of their institutions.

5. **Develop a new paradigm for financing higher education** by first determining the appropriate mix of public support (i.e., higher education as a "public good") and private support (higher education as a personal benefit). This should include a full accounting of both direct public support (e.g., appropriations, research grants, and student financial aid) and indirect public subsidy (e.g., "tax expenditures" currently represented by favorable tax treatment of charitable gifts and endowment earnings and distributions). Furthermore, consider key policy issues such as:

- The appropriate burdens borne by each generation in the support of higher education as determined, for example, by the mix of grants versus loans in federal financial aid programs.
- The degree to which public investment should be used to help shape powerful emerging market forces to protect the public purpose of higher education.
- New methods for internal resource allocation and management that enhance productivity.

6. **Encourage experimentation** with new paradigms of learning, research, and service by harvesting the best ideas from within the academy (or elsewhere), implementing them on a sufficient scale to assess their impact, and disseminating their results.

7. **Place a far greater emphasis on building alliances** among institutions that will allow individual institutions to focus on core competencies while relying on alliances to address the broader and diverse needs of society. Here alliances should be encouraged not only among institutions of higher education (e.g., partnering research universities with liberal arts colleges and community colleges) but also between higher education and the private sector (e.g., information technology and entertainment companies). Differentiation among institutions should be encouraged, while relying upon market forces rather than regulations to discourage duplication.

Concluding Remarks

We have entered a period of significant change in higher education as our universities attempt to respond to the challenges, opportunities, and responsibilities before them.[8] This time of great change, of shifting paradigms, provides the context in which we must consider the changing nature of the university.

Much of this change will be driven by market forces—by a limited resource base, changing societal needs, new technologies, and new competitors. But we also must remember that higher education has a public purpose and a public obligation.[9] Those of us in higher education must always keep before us two questions: "Whom do we serve?" and "How can we serve better?" And society must work to shape and form the markets that will in turn reshape our institutions with appropriate civic purpose.

From this perspective, it is important to understand that the most critical challenge facing most institutions will be to develop the capacity for change. As we noted earlier, universities must seek to remove the constraints that prevent them from responding to the needs of a rapidly changing society. They should strive to challenge, excite, and embolden all members of their academic communities to embark on what should be a great adventure for higher education.

While many academics are reluctant to accept the necessity or the validity of formal planning activities, woe be it to the institutions that turn aside from strategic efforts to determine their futures. The successful adaptation of universities to the revolutionary challenges they face in the century ahead will depend a great deal on an institution's collective ability to learn and to continuously improve its core activities. It is critical that higher education give thoughtful attention to the design of institutional processes for planning, management, and governance. Only a concerted effort to understand the important traditions of the past, the challenges of the present, and the possibilities for the future can enable institutions to thrive during a time of such change.

Certainly the need for higher education will be of increasing importance in our knowledge-driven future. Certainly, too, it has become increasingly clear that our current paradigms for the university, its teaching and research, its service to society, its financing, all must change rapidly and perhaps radically. Hence the real question is not whether higher education will be transformed, but rather *how* . . . and by *whom*. If the university is capable of transforming itself to respond to the needs of a culture of learning, then what is currently perceived as the challenge of change may, in fact, become the opportunity for a renaissance, an age of enlightenment, in higher education in the years ahead.

For a thousand years the university has benefited our civilization as a learning community where both the young and the experienced could acquire not only knowledge and skills, but the values and discipline of the educated mind. It has defended and propagated our cultural and intellectual heritage, while challenging our norms and beliefs. It has produced the leaders of our governments, commerce, and professions. It has both created and applied new knowledge to serve our society. And it has done so while preserving those values and principles so essential to academic learning: the freedom of inquiry, an openness to new ideas, a commitment to rigorous study, and a love of learning.[10]

There seems little doubt that these roles will continue to be needed by our civilization. There is little doubt as well that the university, in some form, will be needed to provide them. The university of the twenty-first century may be as different from today's institutions as the research university is from the colonial college. But its form and its continued evolution will be a consequence of transformations necessary to provide its ancient values and ageless contributions to a changing world.

Chapter 1

1. Robert Zemsky and Gregory R. Wegner, eds., "A Very Public Agenda," *Policy Perspectives*, 8, 2 (1998).
2. Peter F. Drucker, interview, *Forbes*, 159 (1997): 122–128.
3. Frederick Rudolph, *The American College and University* (Athens: University of Georgia Press, 1962).
4. Eric Ashby, *The Rise of the Student Estate in Britain* (Cambridge: Harvard UniversityPress, 1970).

Chapter 2

1. Paul Valery, *The Art of Poetry: Collected Works* (Princeton: Princeton University Press, 1989) 345.
2. Frederick Rudolph, *The American College and University* (Athens: University of Georgia Press, 1962).
3. Peter F. Drucker, "The Age of Social Transformation," *Atlantic Monthly*, November 1994, 53–80; Peter F. Drucker, *Post–capitalist Society* (New York: Harper Collins, 1993).
4. Erich Bloch, National Science Foundation, testimony to Congress, 1988.
5. Derek Bok, *Universities and the Future of America* (Durham: Duke University Press, 1990).
6. Steve Lohr, "The Future Came Faster in the Old Days," *New York Times*, October 5 1998.
7. Harold L. Hodgkinson, *All One System: Demographics of Education—Kindergarten through Graduate School* (Washington, D.C.: Institute for Educational Leadership, 1985).
8. Peter Schwartz, *The Art of the Long View* (New York: Doubleday Currency, 1991), 124–40.
9. John S. Daniel, *Mega–Universities and Knowledge Media* (London: Kogan Page, 1996).
10. Diane J. Macunovich, "Will There Be a Boom in the Demand for U.S. Higher Education among 18– to 24–Year-Olds?" *Change*, 29 (May–June 1997): 34–44.
11. Walter B. Wriston, *The Twilight of Sovereignty: How the Information Revolution Is Transforming Our World* (New York: Scribner, 1992).
12. General Accounting Office, *Executive Guide: Effectively Implementing the Government Performance and Results Act*, GAO/GGD, 96–118 Washington, D.C. (June 1996), 56.

13. Vernon Ehlers, *Toward a New National Science Policy*, Report to Congress by the House Committee on Science, September 24, 1998.

14. Donald E. Osterbrock and Peter H. Raven, eds., *Origins and Extinctions* (New Haven: Yale University Press, 1992).

15. A sampler of the critics: Allan Bloom, *The Closing of the American Mind: How Higher Education Has Failed Democracy and Impoverished the Souls of Today's Students* (New York: Simon and Schuster, 1987); Charles J. Sykes, *Profscam: Professors and the Demise of Higher Education* (New York: Kampmann, 1988); Peter Shaw, *The War against the Intellect: Episodes in the Decline of Discourse* (Iowa City: University of Iowa Press, 1989); Roger Kimball, *Tenured Radicals: How Politics Has Corrupted Our Higher Education* (New York: Harper and Row, 1990); Page Smith, *Killing the Spirit: Higher Education in America* (New York: Viking, 1990); Charles J. Sykes, *The Hollow Men: Politics and Corruption in Higher Education* (Washington: Regnery Gateway, 1990); Dinesh D'Souza, *Illiberal Education: The Politics of Race and Sex on Campus* (New York: Free Press, 1991); William J. Bennett, *The De-valuing of America: The Fight for Our Culture and Our Children* (New York: Summit, 1992); Martin Anderson, *Imposters in the Temple: American Intellectuals Are Destroying Our Universities and Cheating Our Students of Their Future* (New York: Simon and Schuster, 1992).

16. Government-University-Industry Research Roundtable, National Academy of Sciences, *Stresses on Research and Education at Colleges and Universities: A Grass Roots Inquiry* (Washington, D.C.: National Research Council, National Academy Press, 1994); *Stresses on Research and Education at Colleges and Universities: Phase II*, <http://www4.nas.edu/pd/guirrcon.nsf>.

17. American Council on Education, *The American College President: A 1998 Edition* (Washington, D.C.: American Council on Education, 1998).

18. National Commission on the Academic Presidency, *Renewing the Academic Presidency: Stronger Leadership for Tougher Times* (Washington, D.C.: Association of Governing Boards of Universities and Colleges, 1996).

19. National Commission on the Cost of Higher Education, *Straight Talk about College Costs and Prices*, (Phoenix: American Council on Education and the Oryx Press, 1998).

20. Jamie Merisotis and Jane Wellman, *Reaping the Benefits: Defining the Public and Private Value of Going to College* (New York: Institute for Higher Education Policy, Ford Foundation, 1998).

21. Joseph L. Dionne and Thomas Kean, *Breaking the Social Contract: The Fiscal Crisis in Higher Education*, report of the Commission on National Investment in Higher Education (New York: Council for Aid to Education, 1997).

22. Harold T. Shapiro, *Tradition and Change: Perspectives on Education and Public Policy* (Ann Arbor: University of Michigan Press, 1987).

23. David W. Breneman, Joni E. Finney, and Brian M. Roherty, *Shaping the Future: Higher Education Finance in the 1990s* (San Jose: California Higher Education Policy Center, April 1997).

24. Tara-Jen Ambrosio and Vincent Schiraldi, *From Classrooms to Cellblocks: A National Perspective* (Washington, D.C.: Justice Policy Institute, February 1997) <http://www.cjcj.org/jpi/highernational.html>.

25. Dionne and Kean, *Breaking the Social Contract*. See note 21.

26. Patricia J. Gumport, *Academic Restructuring in Public Higher Education: A Framework and Reseach Agenda* (Stanford: National Center for Postsecondary Improvement, 1998), 111.

27. Howard R. Bowen, *The Costs of Higher Education* (San Francisco: Jossey-Bass, 1980).

28. Robert Zemsky, "Rumbling," *Policy Perspectives*, Pew Higher Education Roundtable, sponsored by the Pew Charitable Trusts (Philadelphia: Institute for Research on Higher Education, April 1997).

29. Institute for Higher Education Policy, *Taxing Matters: College Aid, Tax Policy, and Equal Opportunity* (Washington, D.C.: Institute for Higher Education Policy, February 1997).

30. Robert Zemsky, "Rumbling." See note 28.

Chapter 3

1. Benjamin Disraeli, Speech to the House of Commons (March 8, 1873).

2. John Henry Newman, *The Idea of a University (Rethinking the Western Tradition)*, ed. Frank Turner (New Haven: Yale University Press, 1996).

3. Harold T. Shapiro, "The New University? The 'New' Liberal Education?" in *Changing in a World of Change* (Ithaca: Cornell University Press, 1995).

4. Gerhard Casper, "Come the Millennium, Where the University?" paper presented to the Annual Meeting of the American Educational Research Association, San Francisco, April 18, 1995.

5. John Dewey, *Democracy and Education* (New York: Macmillan, 1916).

6. *A Survey of Student Views on the University* (Washington, D.C.: American Council of Education, 1998).

7. Derek Bok, *Universities and the Future of America* (Durham: Duke University Press, 1990).

8. Henry Rosovsky, *The University: An Owner's Manual* (New York: W. W. Norton, 1991).

9. Carnegie Foundation for the Advancement of Teaching, *A Classification of Institutions of Higher Education* (Princeton: Carnegie Foundation for the Advancement of Teaching, 1994), <http://www.carnegiefoundation.org> (1998).

10. Joseph L. Dionne and Thomas Kean, *Breaking the Social Contract: The Fiscal Crisis in Higher Education*, report of the Commission on National Investment in Higher Education (New York: Council for Aid to Education, 1997).

11. *Value Added—The Economic Impact of Public Universities* (Washington, D.C.: National Association of State Universities and Land–Grant Colleges, 1997).

12. *In Brief 1996: Facts about Public Universities* (Washington, D.C.: National Association of State Universities and Land–Grant Colleges, 1996).

13. K. E. Weick, "Educational Organizations as Loosely Coupled Systems," *Administrative Science Quarterly*, 21 (1976): 1–19.

14. R. S. Lowen, *Creating the Cold War University: The Transformation of Stanford* (Berkeley and Los Angeles: University of California Press, 1997).

15. Burton R. Clark, *Creating Entrepreneurial Universities: Organizational Pathways of Transformation* (Surrey: Pergamon Press, 1998).

16. Peter M. Senge, *The Fifth Discipline* (New York: Doubleday Currency, 1990).

17. Eric Ashby, *Any Person, Any Study; An Essay on Higher Education in the United States* (New York: McGraw–Hill, 1979).

18. Clark Kerr, *The Uses of the University* (Cambridge: Harvard University Press, 1982).

19. Donald Kennedy, "Making Choices in the Research University," the American Research University, *Daedelus*, 122, no. 4 (1993): 127–56; Donald Kennedy, *Academic Duty* (Cambridge: Harvard University Press, 1997).

20. National Commission on the Academic Presidency, *Renewing the Academic Presidency: Stronger Leadership for Tougher Times* (Washington, D.C.: Association of Governing Boards of Universities and Colleges, 1996).

21. Constance E. Cook, *Lobbying for Higher Education: How Colleges and Universities Influence Federal Policy* (Nashville: Vanderbilt University Press, 1997), 248.

22. John Immerwahr, *The Price of Admission: The Growing Importance of Higher Education* (Washington, D.C.: National Center for Public Policy and Higher Education, spring 1998).

23. John Immerwahr, *Taking Responsibility: Leaders' Expectations of Higher Education* (Washington, D.C.: The National Center for Public Policy and Higher Education, January, 1999).

24. John Immerwahr and Steve Farkas, *The Closing Gateway: Californians Consider Their Higher Education System* (San Jose: California Higher Education Policy Center, 1993).

25. Kennedy, "Making Choices." See note 19.

26. National Commission on the Acedemic Presidency, *Renewing Academic Presidency*. See note 20.

27. Dionne and Kean, *Breaking the Social Contract*. See note 10.

28. Patricia J. Gumport and Brian Pusser, "Academic Restructuring: Contemporary Adaptation in Higher Education," in *Planning and Management for a Changing Environment: A Handbook on Redesigning Post–Secondary Institutions*, ed. M. Petersen, D. Dill, and L. Mets (San Francisco: Jossey-Bass, 1997).

Chapter 4

1. Ralph Waldo Emerson, Phi Beta Kappa address delivered to the senior class, Harvard (1838).
2. Allan Bloom, *The Closing of the American Mind: How Higher Education Has Failed Democracy and Impoverished the Souls of Today's Students* (New York: Simon and Schuster, 1987).
3. Charles J. Sykes, *Profscam: Professors and the Demise of Higher Education* (New York: Kampmann, 1988).
4. Harold T. Shapiro, "The New University? The 'New' Liberal Education?" in *Changing in a World of Change* (Ithaca: Cornell University Press, 1995).
5. Bloom. *Closing of the American Mind*. See note 2.
6. Derek Bok, *Higher Learning* (Cambridge: Harvard University Press, 1986).
7. Shapiro, "The New University?" See note 4.
8. Business–Higher Education Forum, *Preparing for the High–Performance Workplace: A Survey of Corporate Leaders* (Washington, D.C.: American Council on Education, 1995)
9. Frank H. T. Rhodes, "The Advancement of Learning: Prospects in a Cynical Age," Proceedings of the American Philosophical Society, 142, 2, (1998): 218-243.
10. John Henry Newman, *The Idea of a University (Rethinking the Western Tradition)*, ed. Frank Turner (New Haven: Yale University Press, 1996).
11. Boyer Commission on Educating Undergraduates in the Research University, *Reinventing Undergraduate Education: A Blueprint for America's Research Universities* (Menlo Park: Carnegie Foundation for the Advancement of Teaching, 1998).
12. Harold T. Shapiro, "The Functions and Resources of the American University of the Twenty–First Century," paper presented to the University of Chicago Symposium on the Twenty–First Century, October 5, 1991.
13. Peter House and Roger D. Shull, *The Rush to Policy: Using Analytic Techniques in Public Sector Decision Making* (New Brunswick, N.J.: Transaction Books, 1988).
14. Kellogg Commission on the Future of State and Land–Grant Universities, *Returning to Our Roots: The Student Experience* (Washington, D.C.: National Association of State Universities and Land–Grant Colleges, 1997).

15. Richard Lanham, *The Electronic Word: Democracy, Technology, and the Arts* (Chicago: University of Chicago Press, 1993).

16. Lewis J. Perelman, *School's Out* (New York: Avon, 1993).

17. John Seely Brown and Paul Duguid, "Universities in the Digital Age," *Change* (July 1996): 11–19.

18. Brown and Duguid., "Universities in the Digital Age." See note 17.

19. Gregory C. Farrington, "The New Technology and the Future of Residential Undergraduate Education," in *Dancing with the Devil: Information Technology and the New Competition in Higher Education*, ed. Richard N. Katz (San Francisco: Educause and Jossey-Bass, 1998), 73–94.

20. Government-University-Industry Research Roundtable, National Academy of Sciences, *Stresses on Research and Education at Colleges and Universities: A Grass Roots Inquiry* (Washington, D.C.: National Research Council, National Academy Press, 1994); *Stresses on Research and Education at Colleges and Universities: Phase II*, <http://www4.nas.edu/pd/guirrcon.nsf>.

21. National Science Board, *The Federal Role in Science and Engineering Graduate and Postdoctoral Education*, NSF 97–235 (Washington, D.C.: National Science Foundation, 1998).

22. Shirley Tilghman, chair, *Trends in the Early Careers of Life Scientists*, National Research Council (Washington, D.C.: National Academy Press, 1998).

23. Robert Atwell, *Final Letter to the Membership* (Washington, D.C.: American Council on Education, August 30, 1996).

24. Tilghman, *Trends in Early Careers*. See note 22.

25. Committee on Postdoctoral Education, *Report and Recommendations* (Washington, D.C.: American Association of Universities, 1997).

26. National Science Board, *Federal Role in Science and Engineering*. See note 21.

27. Committee on Science, Engineering, and Public Policy, National Academy of Sciences, *Reshaping the Graduate Education of Scientists and Engineers* (Washington, D.C.: National Academy Press, 1995), 144.

28. M. R. C. Greenwood, chair, *Science in the National Interest*, Office of Science and Technology Policy (Washington, D.C.: U. S. Government Printing Office, 1996).

29. Terrance Sandalow, "The University and the Aims of Professional Education," in *Intellectual History and Academic Culture at the University of Michigan: Fresh Explorations*, ed. Margaret A. Lourie (Ann Arbor: University of Michigan Press, 1989).

Chapter 5

1. Vannevar Bush, *Science, the Endless Frontier*, report to the President on a Program for Postwar Scientific Research (Office of Scientific Research and Development, July 1945; Washington, D.C.: National Science Foundation, 1990), 192.

2. Derek Bok, *Universities and the Future of America* (Durham: Duke University Press, 1990).

3. Bush, *Science, the Endless Frontier*. See note 1.

4. "The Research University as the Jewel in the Crown," editorial, *New York Times*, February 9, 1994.

5. National Science Board, "Economic and Social Significance of Scientific and Engineering Research," in *Science and Engineering Indicators 1996* (Washington, DC: National Science Foundation, 1996), 8–3 to 8–6.

6. William J. Broad, Science Tuesday, *New York Times*, May 13, 1997; NSF Study, Research Policy, Sussex.

7. Jonathan R. Cole, "Balancing Acts: Dilemmas of Choice Facing Research Universities," American Research University, *Daedelus*, 122, no. 4 (1993).

8. Charles M. Vest, "Research Universities: Overextended, Underfocused, Overstressed, Underfunded," paper presented to Cornell Symposium on the American University, May 22, 1995, 11.

9. Donald Kennedy, "Making Choices in the Research University," the American Research University, *Daedelus*, 122, no. 4 (1993): 127–56.

10. Government–University–Industry Research Roundtable, "Convocation on Stresses on Research and Education at Colleges and Universities" (Government–University–Industry Research Roundtable and National Science Board (Washington, D.C.: National Academy of Sciences, 1997). <http://www2.nas.edu/guirrcon/>.

11. Jaroslav Peliken, *The Idea of the University: A Reexamination* (New Haven: Yale University Press, 1992), 238.

12. National Science Board, *Science and Engineering Indicators–1998* (Arlington, VA: National Science Foundation, 1998) preface.

13. Peter F. Drucker, interview, *Science*, July 18, 1997.

14. Richard A. Feynman, *The Feynman Lectures on Physics* (Reading, Mass: Addison-Wesley, 1963).

15. Edward O. Wilson, *Consilience: The University of Knowledge* (New York: Knopf, 1998).

16. Donald E. Stokes, *Pasteur's Quadrant: Basic Science and Technological Innovation* (Washington: Brookings Institute, 1997).

17. Vernon Ehlers, *Toward a New National Science Policy*, Report to Congress by the House Committee on Science, September 24, 1998.

18. John Armstrong, *The Bridge* (Washington, D.C.: National Academy of Engineering, 1996).

19. Daniel Alpert and William C. Harris, "Renewal of the University's Compact with the Society It Serves," draft (September 18, 1996), 18.

20. Frank Rhodes, "The New American University," in *Looking to the Twenty-First Century: Higher Education in Transition* (Urbana: University of Illinois Press, 1995); Walter E. Massey, "The Public University for the Twenty-First Century: Beyond the Land Grant," 16th David Dodds Henry Lecture, University of Illinois at Chicago, (1994); J. W. Peltason, "Reactionary Thoughts of a Revolutionary," 17th David Dodds Henry lecture, University of Illinois at Urbana-Champaign (October 18, 1995).

21. Alpert and Harris, "Renewal of the University's Compact." See note 19.

22. Michael E. Porter and Scott Stern, "Evaluating United States Innovation Capacity," National Innovation Summit, Council on Competitiveness, MIT, Cambridge (March 1998).

Chapter 6

1. James Angell, The Papers of James Angell (Ann Arbor: University of Michigan Press, 1964).

2. Derek C. Bok, *Beyond the Ivory Tower: Social Responsibilities of the Modern University* (Cambridge: Harvard University Press, 1982).

3. Bok, *Beyond the Ivory Tower*. See note 2.

4. Sheldon Hackney, "The University and Its Community: Past and Present," *Annals of the American Academy of Political and Social Science*, 488 (1986): 1351–67.

5. Barry Checkoway, "Reinventing the University for Public Service," *Journal of Planning Literature*, 11, no. 3 (1997): 307–319.

6. Donald E. Detmer, editorial, *Science*, March 28, 1997, 1859.

7. William N. Kelley, "The University of Pennsylvania Health System Model: The Academic Health Center as the Nucleus of an Integrated Health-Care Delivery System," in *New Models for Higher Education*, ed. William F. Massey and Joel W. Meyerson (New York: Peterson's Guides, 1997), 37–64.

8. Samuel Their and Nanerl Keohane, "How Can We Assure the Survival of Academic Health Centers?", *Chronicle of Higher Education* (March 13, 1998), A64.

9. David Korn, letter to the editor, *Science*, March 28, 1997.

10. Mary Lindenstern Walshok, *Knowledge without Boundaries: What America's Research Universities Can Do for the Economy, the Workplace, and the Community* (San Francisco: Jossey-Bass, 1995), 299.

11. National Science Board, *Science and Engineering Indicators 1998* (Arlington: National Science Foundation, 1998), 6–6

12. Bok, *Beyond the Ivory Tower*. See note 2.

Chapter 7

1. Burton R. Clark, "Small Worlds, Different Worlds: The Uniqueness and Troubles of the American Academic Professions," *Daedelus*, 126, no. 4 (1997): 21–42; Burton R. Clark, *The Academic Life: Small Worlds, Different Worlds* (Princeton: Carnegie Foundation for the Advancement of Teaching, Princeton University Press, 1987).

2. William G. Bowen and Neil Rudenstine, *In Pursuit of the Ph.D.* (Princeton: Princeton University Press, 1992), 446.

3. *Parttime Faculty, the New Majority* (New York: Alfred P. Sloan Foundation, 1998).

4. *1940 Statement of Principles on Academic Freedom and Tenure (With 1970 Interpretive Comments)* (Washington: American Association of University Professors, 1998).

5. *Parttime Faculty, the New Majority*. See note 3.

6. *Parttime Faculty, the New Majority*. See note 3.

7. Courtney Leatherman, "Providing a Different Education: The University of Phoenix," *Chronicle of Higher Education*, October 16, 1998.

8. Ernest L. Boyer, *Scholarship Reconsidered: Priorities of the Professorate* (Princeton: Carnegie Foundation for the Advancement of Teaching, Princeton University Press, 1991).

9. Government–University–Industry Research Roundtable, *Convocation on Stresses on Research and Education*.

10. Donald Kennedy, "Making Choices in the Research University," the American Research University, *Daedelus*, 122, no. 4 (1993): 127–56.

Chapter 8

1. Joseph L. Dionne and Thomas Kean, *Breaking the Social Contract: The Fiscal Crisis in Higher Education*, report of the Commission on National Investment in Higher Education (New York: Council for Aid to Education, 1997).

2. David W. Breneman, Joni E. Finney, and Brian M. Roherty, *Shaping the Future: Higher Education Finance in the 1990s* (San Jose: California Higher Education Policy Center, April 1997).

3. Arthur M. Hauptman, *The College Tuition Spiral* (Washington D.C.: American Council on Education and The College Board, 1990).

4. Harold T. Shapiro, "The Functions and Resources of the American University of the Twenty–First Century," paper presented to the University of Chicago Symposium on the Twenty–First Century, October 5, 1991.

5. Dionne and Kean, *Breaking the Social Contract*. See note 1.

6. Michael McPherson and Morton Shapiro, "Are We Keeping College Afford-able: The Most Recent Data on Student Aid, Access, and Choice." Stanford Forum for Higher Education Futures, The Aspen Institute (1996); P. M. Callen and J. E. Finney, eds., *Public and Private Financing of Higher Education: Shaping Public Policy for the Future* (Phoenix: Oryx Press, 1997).

7. *From Classrooms to Cellblocks: A National Perspective* (Washington, D.C.: Justice Policy Institute, 1997).

8. James L. Fisher and Gary H. Quehl, *The President and Fund-Raising* (New York: American Council on Education, Macmillan, 1989): 238.

9. Factfile on University Endowments, *Chronicle of Higher Education* (April 1999).

10. Terry W. Hartle, letter to the editor, *Wall Street Journal*, March 16, 1999.

11. Burton R. Clark, "The Entrepreneurial University: Demand and Response," *Tertiary Education and Management*, 4, no. 1 (1998): 5–16; S. Slaughter and L. L. Leslie, *Academic Capitalism: Politics, Policies, and the Entrepreneurial University* (Baltimore: Johns Hopkins University Press, 1997).

12. Gilbert R. Whitaker, *Enhancing Quality in an Era of Resource Constraints*, report of the Task Force on Costs in Higher Education, The University of Michigan, (March, 1990).

13. Terry W. Hartle, "Complex Government Rules Increase the Cost of Tuition," *Chronicle of Higher Education* (March 6, 1998), A60.

14. R. Zemsky and W. F. Massey, "Cost Containment: Committing to a New Economic Reality," *Change*, 22, no. 6 (1990), 16–22; R. Zemsky and W. F. Massey, "Expanding Perimeters, Melting Cores and Sticky Functions," *Change*, (Nov–Dec 1995), 41–51.

15. "America's Best Colleges: What School Is Right for You?", *U. S. News and World Report* (1997), Annual Guide.

16. Daniel T. Seymour, *Causing Quality in Higher Education*, (New York: American Council on Education, Macmillan, 1992).

17. W. F. Massey, ed., *Resource Allocation in Higher Education* (Ann Arbor: University of Michigan Press, 1996).

18. Frederick E. Balderston, *Managing Today's University: Strategies for Viability, Change, and Excellence* (San Francisco: Jossey-Bass, 1995), 398.

19. Edward L. Whalen, *Responsibility Center Management* (Bloomington: Indiana University Press, 1991), 204.

20. Patricia J. Gumport and Brian Pusser, "Academic Restructuring: Contemporary Adaptation in Higher Education," in *Planning and Management for a Changing Environment: A Handbook on Redesigning Post–Secondary Institutions*, ed. M. Petersen, D. Dill, and L. Mets (San Francisco: Jossey-Bass, 1997).

21. "Anxiety over Tuition: A Controversy in Context," *Chronicle of Higher Education* May 30, 1997, A10–A21.

22. McPherson and Shapiro, "Are We Keeping College Affordable." See note 6.

23. *Trends in College Pricing–1998* (New York: The College Board, 1999).

24. Dionne and Kean, *Breaking the Social Contract*. See note 1.

25. Donald M. Steward, *Annual Report on College Tuition and Fees* (New York: College Board, 1998).

26. John S. Daniel, "Why Universities Need Technology Strategies," *Change*, 29 July–August 1997, 10–17.

27. *Making College Affordable Again* (Washington, D.C.: National Commission for Financing Post-secondary Education, (1993).

28. Institute for Higher Education Policy, *Taxing Matters: College Aid, Tax Policy, and Equal Opportunity* (Washington, D.C.: Institute for Higher Education Policy, February 1997).

29. Peter Drucker, "A Better Way to Pay for College," Eastern Edition, *Wall Street Journal* May 9, 1991: A14.

30. Peter Passell, "Affluent Turning to Public Colleges Threatening a Squeeze for Others, *New York Times* August 13, 1997: A16.

Chapter 9

1. Alfred North Whitehead, *Essays in Science and Philosophy* (New York: Philosophical Library, 1947), 64–65.

2. Donald R. Kinder and Lynn M. Sanders, *Divided by Color: Racial Politics and Democratic Ideals* (Chicago: University of Chicago Press, 1996); Stanley Greenberg, *Middle Class Dreams: The Politics and Power of the New American Majority* (New Haven: Yale University Press, 1990).

3. William Bowen and Derek Bok, *The Shape of the River: Long-Term Consequences of Considering Race in College and University Admissions* (Princeton: Mellon Foundation, Princeton University Press, 1998).

4. P. Gurin, G. Lopez, and B. R. Nosda, "Context, Identity, and Intergroup Relations, in *Cultural Divides: The Social Psychology of Integroup Contact*, ed. D. Prentice and D. Miller (New York: Russell Sage, 1999).

5. Bowen and Bok, *The Shape of the River*. See note 3.

6. Eric Foner, *The Story of American Freedom* (New York: W. W. Norton and Company, 1998).

7. Bowen and Bok, *The Shape of the River*. See note 3.

8. Lee Sigelman and Susan Welch, *Black Americans' Views of Racial Inequality: The Dream Deferred* (New York: Cambridge University Press, 1991).

9. Bowen and Bok, *The Shape of the River*. See note 3.

10. Claude M. Steele, "A Threat in the Air: How Stereotypes Shape Intellectual Identify and Performance," *American Psychologist*, 52 (1997): 613–619.

11. James Angell, The Papers of James Angell (Ann Arbor: University of Michigan Press, 1964).

12. U.S. Bureau of the Census, *State and Metropolitan Area Data Book, 1997–98* (Washington, D.C.: U. S. Government Printing Office, 1998); Thomas J. Sugrue, *The Origins of the Urban Crisis: Race and Inequality in Postwar Detroit* (Princeton: Princeton University Press, 1996).

13. Lawrence W. Levine, *The Opening of the American Mind* (Boston: Beacon Press, 1996).

14. A. Bartlett Giamatti, *A Free and Ordered Space: The Real World of the University* (New York: W. W. Norton, 1988), 306.

Chapter 10

1. Jacques Attali, *Millennium: Winners and Losers in the Coming World Order* (New York: Times Books, 1992), 11.

2. "Books, Bricks, and Bytes," *Daedelus* 125, no. 4, (1996), v–vii.

3. John Perry Barlow, "The Economy of Ideas: A Framework for Rethinking Patents and Copyrights in the Digital Age," *Wired*, 2.03 (March 1994).

4. For an excellent introduction to scenario planning in this area, see the website <http://www.si.umich.edu/V2010> for the Vision 2010 project, directed by Daniel E. Atkins and sponsored by the Carnegie Foundation for the Advancement of Teaching.

5. Peter J. Deming and Robert M. Metcalf, *Beyond Calculation: The Next Fifty Years of Computing* (New York: Springer–Verlag, 1997).

6. Ray Kurzweil, *The Age of Spirtual Machines: When Computers Exceed Human Intelligence* (New York: Viking, 1999).

7. William A. Wulf, "Warning: Information Technology Will Transform the University," *Issues in Science and Technology*, (summer 1995), 46–52.

8. Martin R. Stytz, "Distributed Virtual Environments," *IEEE Computer Graphics and Applications*, 16 (May 1996), 19–31.

9. Mark Weiser and John Seely Brown, "Designing Calm Technology," *PowerGrid Journal*, 101 (July 1996), <http//powergrid.electriciti.com/1.01>.

10. William J. Mitchell, *City of Bits: Space, Place, and the Infobahn* (Cambridge: MIT Press, 1995).

11. William Gibson, *Neuromancer* (New York: Ace, 1984).

12. Mark Stefik, *Internet Dreams* (Cambridge: MIT Press, 1996), 412.

13. Barlow, "The Economy of Ideas." See note 3.

14. Ted Marchese, "Not-So-Distant Competitors: How New Providers Are Remaking the Postsecondary Marketplace," *AAHE Bulletin* May 1998, <http://www.aahe.org/bulletin/bull_1/May 98 html>.

15. For an excellent example of such virtual universities, see the website for the Michigan Virtual Automotive College at <http://www.mvac.org> and the article by Scott Bernato, "Big 3 U," *University Business*, September–October 1998, 20–27.

16. John Seely Brown and Paul Duguid, Universities in the Digital Age, *Change*, July, 1996, pp. 11–19.

17. Ralph Gomery, Asynchronous Learning Technology (October 1996).

18. Carol A. Twigg, "The Need for a National Learning Infrastructure," *Educom Review* (September–October 1994), 17–24; Carol Twigg, "Toward a National Learning Infrastructure: Navigating the Transition," National Learning Infrastructure, part 3, *Educom Review* November–December 1994, 3. Posted on the Internet to the Horizon List, courtesy of Dr. Twigg.

19. Richard N. Katz, ed., *Dancing with the Devil: Information Technology and the New Competition in Higher Education* (San Francisco: Educause and Jossey-Bass, 1998).

20. Myles Brand, "The Wise Use of Technology," *Educational Record*, fall 1995, 39–46.

21. "All the World's a Lab," *New Scientist*, 2077 April 12, 1997, 24–27; T. A. Finholt and G. M. Olson, "From Laboratories to Collaboratories: A New Social Organizational Form for Scientific Collaboration," *Psychological Science* 9, 1 (1997), 28–36.

22. For information concerning the Internet II project, see the website for the University Corporation for the Advancement of Internet Development at <http://www.internet2.edu;>.

23. Student–Faculty Computer Survey, Information Technology Division, University of Michigan, Ann Arbor, 1997.

24. Mitchell, *City of Bits*. See note 10.

Chapter 11

1. Niccolo Machiavelli, *The Prince* (New York: Random House, 1950).

2. National Commission on the Academic Presidency, *Renewing the Academic Presidency: Stronger Leadership for Tougher Times* (Washington, D.C.: Association of Governing Boards of Universities and Colleges, 1996).

3. Harold T. Shapiro, *Tradition and Change: Perspectives on Education and Public Policy* (Ann Arbor: University of Michigan Press, 1987).

4. Teresa J. MacTaggart, ed., *Seeking Excellence through Independence* (San Francisco: Jossey-Bass, 1997).

5. Cyril O. Houle, *Governing Boards* (San Francisco: Jossey-Bass, 1989) 223.

6. Clark Kerr, *The Guardians: Boards of Trustees of American Colleges and Universities: What They Do and How Well They Do It* (Washington, D.C.: Association of Governing Boards, 1989).

7. Martin Trow, "The Chiefs of Public Universities Should be Civil Servants, Not Political Actors," *Chronicle of Higher Education*, (May 16, 1997); Richard T. Ingram, "Transforming Public Trusteeship," *Public Policy Paper Series* (Washington, D.C.: Association of Governing Boards, 1998).

8. National Commission on the Academic Presidency, *Renewing Academic Presidency*. See note 2.

9. Ingram, "Transforming Public Trusteeship." See note 7.

10. Donald Kennedy, "Making Choices in the Research University," the American Research University, *Daedelus*, 122, no. 4 (1993): 127–56.

11. William G. Bowen and Harold T. Shapiro, eds., *Universities and Their Leadership* (Princeton: Princeton University Press, 1998).

12. Peter Flawn, *A Primer for University Presidents* (Austin: University of Texas Press, 1990).

13. Government–University–Industry Research Roundtable, *Convocation on Stresses on Research and Education*.

14. Kennedy, "Making Choices." See note 10; R. Birnbaum, *How Academic Leadership Works: Understanding Success and Failure in the College Presidency* (San Francisco: Jossey–Bass, 1992); Nannerl O. Keohane, "More Power to the President?", in *The Presidency*, (American Council on Education, 1998), 12–18.

15. Frederick E. Balderston, *Managing Today's University: Strategies for Viability, Change, and Excellence* (San Francisco: Jossey-Bass, 1995), 398.

16. National Commission on the Academic Presidency, *Renewing Academic Presidency*. See note 2.

Chapter 12

1. Thomas S. Kuhn, *The Structure of Scientific Revolutions*, 2nd edition (Chicago: The University of Chicago Press, 1970).

2. Michael A. Shires, *The Future of Public Undergraduate Education in California* (Santa Monica: RAND Institute on Education and Training, 1996).

3. Karl E. Weick, "Small Wins: Redefining the Scale of Social Problems," *American Psychologist* 39, no. 1 (1984): 40–49.

4. R. C. Heterick, Jr. and C. A. Twigg, "Interpolating the Future," *Educom Review* 32, no. 1 (1997): 60.

5. Peter Schwartz, *The Art of the Long View* (New York: Doubleday Currency, 1991), 124–40.

6. C. K. Prahalad and Gary Hamel, "The Core Competence of the Corporation," *Harvard Business Review*, 68 (1990): 79–91.

7. James Brian Quinn, *Intelligent Enterprise: A Knowledge and Service Based Paradigm for Industry* (New York: Free Press, 1992), 473.

8. Larry Downs and Chunka Mui, *Killer App* (Cambridge: Harvard Business School Press, 1998).

9. Michael E. Porter, *Competitive Strategy: Techniques for Analyzing Industries and Competitiveness* (Boston: Free Press, 1998).

10. James Gleick, *Chaos: Making a New Science* (New York: Penguin, 1988).

11. Kuhn, *Structure of Scientific Revolutions*. See note 1.

12. Patricia J. Gumport and Brian Pusser, "Academic Restructuring: Contemporary Adaptation in Higher Education," in *Planning and Management for a Changing Environment: A Handbook on Redesigning Post–Secondary Institutions*, ed. M. Petersen, D. Dill, and L. Mets (San Francisco: Jossey-Bass, 1997); Patricia J. Gumport, *Academic Restructuring in Public Higher Education: A Framework and Reseach Agenda* (Stanford: National Center for Postsecondary Improvement, 1998), 111.

13. Eamon Kelly, Remarks made to the presidents of the Association of American Universities, Indianapolis, 1994.

14. Michael G. Dolence and Donald M. Norris, *Transforming Higher Education: A Vision for Learning in the 21st Century* (Ann Arbor: Society for College and University Planning, 1995).

15. Here, it should be noted that many such lists put Johns Hopkins University as the nation's leader in research expenditures. However, it is most consistent to subtract from their expenditures the amounts contributed by the Johns Hopkins Applied Physics Laboratory, a Department of Defense laboratory, that operates quite apart from the university (much like the Jet Propulsion Laboratory at Caltech, Lincoln Laboratory at M.I.T., or Los Alamos Scientific Laboratory with the University of California).

16. C. K. Prahalad and Gary Hamel, *Competing for the Future* (Cambridge: Harvard Business School Press, 1994), 327.

17. Gumport, *Academic Restructuring*. See note 12.

18. For an excellent introduction to scenario planning in this area, see the website <http://www.si.umich.edu/V2010> for the Vision 2010 project, directed by Daniel E. Atkins and sponsored by the Carnegie Foundation for the Advancement of Teaching.

19. Philip G. Altbach, "An International Academic Crisis," *Daedalus* 126, no. 4 (1997): 315–38.

20. Boyer Commission on Educating Undergraduates in the Research University, *Reinventing Undergraduate Education: A Blueprint for America's Research Universities* (Menlo Park: Carnegie Foundation for the Advancement of Teaching, 1998).
21. *Buildings, Books, and Bytes: Libraries and Communities in the Digital Age*, (Washington D.C.: Benton Foundation, 1996).

Chapter 13

1. Arthur Levine, "Higher Education's New Status As a Mature Industry," *Chronicle of Higher Education* (January 31, 1997), A48.
2. Michael G. Dolence and Donald M. Norris, *Transforming Higher Education: A Vision for Learning in the 21st Century* (Ann Arbor: Society for College and University Planning, 1995).
3. Dolence and Norris, *Transforming Higher Education*. See note 2.
4. Peter J. Deming and Robert M. Metcalf, *Beyond Calculation: The Next Fifty Years of Computing* (New York: Springer–Verlag, 1997).
5. Levine, "Higher Education's New Status." See note 1.
6. William H. Graves, "Free Trade in Higher Education: The Meta University," *Journal on Asynchronous Learning Networks*, Vol 1, Issue 1 (1997).
7. Marvin W. Peterson, and David D. Dill, "Understanding the Competitive Environment of the Postsecondary Knowledge Industry," in *Planning and Management for A Changing Environment*, ed. Marvin W. Peterson, David D. Dill, Lisa Mets, and associates (San Francisco: Jossey-Bass Publishers, 1997), 3–29.
8. Donald N. Langenberg, "Taking Control of Change: Reinventing the Public University for the 21st Century," *Reinventing the Research University*, Kumar Patel, ed. (Los Angeles: University of California Press, 1994).
9. Jack Gregg, *Educom Review*, 32, no. 4 (June, 1997); Third Report of Pew Health Professionals Commission, *Critical Challenges: Revitalizing the Health Professions for the 21st Century* (San Francisco: University of California, December 1995); <http://www.pewtrusts.com/publications>.
10. John Seely Brown and Paul Duguid, "Universities in the Digital Age," *Change* (July, 1996), 11–19.
11. Joseph L. Dionne and Thomas Kean, *Breaking the Social Contract: The Fiscal Crisis in Higher Education*, report of the Commission on National Investment in Higher Education (New York: Council for Aid to Education, 1997).
12. Peterson and Dill, "Understanding the Competitive Environment." See note 7.
13. See the website for the Michigan Virtual Automotive College at <http:/www.mvac.org>, and also the article by Scott Bernato, "Big 3 U," *University Business* (September–October, 1998): 20–27.

14. John S. Daniel, "Why Universities Need Technology Strategies," *Change* (July, 1997), 10–17.

15. John Palattella, "The British Are Coming; the British Are Coming," *University Business*, (July–August, 1998), 25–30.

16. Frank Rhodes, "The New American University," in *Looking to the Twenty-First Century: Higher Education in Transition* (Urbana: University of Illinois Press, 1995).

17. Dolence and Norris, *Transforming Higher Education.* See note 2.

18. Dee Hock, "Chaordic Organizations"; see also the website for the Chaordic Alliance at <http://www.chaordic.org>.

19. Carol A. Twigg, "The Need for a National Learning Infrastructure," *Educom Review* (September–October 1994), 17–24.

20. Carol A. Twigg, "Toward a National Learning Infrastructure: Navigating the Transition," National Learning Infrastructure, part 3, *Educom Review* November–December 1994, 3. Posted on the Internet to the Horizon List, courtesy of Dr. Twigg.

21. Lawrence K. Grossman, *The Electronic Republic: Reshaping Democracy in the Information Age* (New York: Penguin, 1996).

22. *Buildings, Books, and Bytes: Libraries and Communities in the Digital Age*, (Washington D.C.: Benton Foundation, 1996).

23. Robert Zemsky, "Rumbling," *Policy Perspectives*, Pew Higher Education Roundtable, sponsored by the Pew Charitable Trusts (Philadelphia: Institute for Research on Higher Education, April 1997); Robert Zemsky and Gregory R. Wegner, eds., "A Very Public Agenda," *Policy Perspectives*, 8, 2 (1998).

24. S. Slaughter and L. L. Leslie, *Academic Capitalism: Politics, Policies, and the Entrepreneurial University* (Baltimore: Johns Hopkins University Press, 1997).

25. Mario C. Martinez and Thad Nodine, *Michigan: Fiscal Stability and Constitutional Autonomy* (San Jose: California Higher Education Policy Center, 1997), 36.

26. Dionne and Kean, *Breaking the Social Contract.* See note 11.

27. "Inside the Knowledge Factory," *The Economist*, October 4, 1997; See also Michael Gibbons, *The New Production of Knowledge* (London: Sage, 1994).

Chapter 14

1. Charles Dickens, A Tale of Two Cities (Philadelphia: T. B. Peterson & Brothers, 1859), 1.

2. Robert Lenzer and Stephen S. Johnson, "Seeing Things as They Really Are," Peter Drucker interview, *Forbes* 159 (1997), 122–28.

3. Joseph L. Dionne and Thomas Kean, *Breaking the Social Contract: The Fiscal Crisis in Higher Education*, report of the Commission on National Investment in Higher Education (New York: Council for Aid to Education, 1997).

4. David W. Breneman, Joni E. Finney, and Brian M. Roherty, *Shaping the Future: Higher Education Finance in the 1990s* (San Jose: California Higher Education Policy Center, April 1997).

5. Patricia J. Gumport and Brian Pusser, "Academic Restructuring: Contemporary Adaptation in Higher Education," in *Planning and Management for a Changing Environment: A Handbook on Redesigning Post–Secondary Institutions*, ed. M. Petersen, D. Dill, and L. Mets (San Francisco: Jossey-Bass, 1997).

6. Lewis Perelman, "Barnstorming with Lewis Perelman," *Educom Review*, 32, no.2 (1997): 18–36.

7. William A. Wulf, "Warning: Information Technology Will Transform the University," *Issues in Science and Technology*, (summer 1995), 46–52.

8. Werner Z. Hirsch and Luc E. Weber, "The Glion Declaration: The University at the Millennium," *The Presidency*, Washington, D.C.: American Council on Education, fall 1998): 27–31.

9. Robert Zemsky and Gregory R. Wegner, eds., "A Very Public Agenda," *Policy Perspectives*, 8, 2 (1998).

10. Hirsch and Weber, "The Glion Declaration." See note 8.

INDEX